Human Rights and America's War on Terror

This volume examines the success of the 9/11 attacks in undermining the cherished principles of Western democracy, free speech and tolerance, which were central to US values. It is argued that this has led to the USA fighting disastrous wars in Afghanistan and Iraq, and to sanctioning the use of torture and imprisonment without trial in Guantánamo Bay, extraordinary rendition, surveillance and drone attacks. At home, it has resulted in restrictions of civil liberties and the growth of an ill-affordable military and security apparatus. In this collection the authors note the irony that the shocking destruction of the World Trade Center on 9/11 should become the justification for the relentless expansion of security agencies. Yet, this is a salutary illustration of how the security agencies in the USA have adopted faulty preconceptions, which have become too embedded within the institution to be abandoned without loss of credibility and prestige.

The book presents a timely assessment of both the human rights costs of the 'war on terror' and the methods used to wage and relentlessly continue that war. It will be of interest to researchers, academics, practitioners and students in the fields of human rights law, criminal justice, criminology, politics and international studies.

Satvinder Singh Juss, PhD (Cantab), FRSA, is a Professor of Law at King's College London, a barrister-at-law practising from 3 Hare Court, Temple, London, and a Deputy Judge of the Upper Tribunal (IAC) in London and Birmingham. He is a former Human Rights Fellow at Harvard Law School, Boston.

Routledge Research in Human Rights Law

Available titles in this series include:

International Human Rights Law and Domestic Violence
The Effectiveness of International Human Rights Law
Ronagh McQuigg

The Right to Religious Freedom in International Law
Between Group Rights and Individual Rights
Anat Scolnicov

The Right to Development in International Law
The Case of Pakistan
Khurshid Iqbal

Global Health and Human Rights
Legal and Philosophical Perspectives
John Harrington and Maria Stuttaford

Human Rights, Constitutional law and Belonging
The Right to Equal Belonging in Democratic Society
Elena Drymiotou

Dignity, Degrading Treatment and Torture in Human Rights Law
The Ends of Article 3 of the European Convention on Human Rights
Elaine Webster

The Right to Housing in Law and Society
Nico Moons

Human Rights and America's War on Terror
Edited by Satvinder Juss

Beyond Human Rights and the War on Terror
Edited by Satvinder Juss

For more information about this series, please visit: www.routledge.com/Routledge-Research-in-Human-Rights-Law/book-series/HUMRIGHTSLAW

Human Rights and America's War on Terror

Edited by
Satvinder S. Juss

Routledge
Taylor & Francis Group
LONDON AND NEW YORK

First published 2019
by Routledge

2 Park Square, Milton Park, Abingdon, Oxfordshire OX14 4RN
52 Vanderbilt Avenue, New York, NY 10017

Routledge is an imprint of the Taylor & Francis Group, an informa business

First issued in paperback 2020

British Library Cataloguing in Publication Data
A catalogue record for this book is available from the British Library

Library of Congress Cataloging in Publication Data
Names: Juss, Satvinder S. (Satvinder Singh), editor.
Title: Human rights and America's war on terror / edited by Satvinder S. Juss.
Description: New York : Routledge, 2018. |
Series: Routledge research in human rights law | Includes bibliographical references and index.
Identifiers: LCCN 2018023960 | ISBN 9781138543867 (hardback)
Subjects: LCSH: Human rights--Government policy--United States. | Criminal justice, Administration of--Political aspects--United States. | Extraordinary rendition--United States. | War on Terrorism, 2001-2009. | Civil rights--United States. | United States--Foreign relations.
Classification: LCC KF9223 .H86 2018 | DDC 363.325/170973--dc23
LC record available at https://lccn.loc.gov/2018023960

ISBN: 978-1-138-54386-7 (hbk)
ISBN: 978-0-367-49903-7 (pbk)

Typeset in Galliard
by Taylor & Francis Books

Contents

Contributors

Stephen Ellmann is the Martin Professor of Law at New York Law School, and the former Director of its Office of Clinical and Experiential Learning. He is an award-winning author on legal ethics and an expert in clinical legal education, constitutional law and South African law.

Martin Ewi is a Regional Coordinator for Southern Africa/Coordonnateur régional pour l'Afrique austral, ENACT, Institute for Security Studies, Pretoria, having previously served as a Political Affairs Officer at the headquarters of the Organisation for the Prohibition of Chemical Weapons (OPCW) based in The Hague.

Jonathan Hafetz is a Professor of Law at Seton Hall Law School, who formerly worked as a senior attorney for the National Security Project of the American Civil Liberties Union

Satvinder S. Juss is a Professor of Law at King's College London and a former Human Rights Fellow at Harvard Law School, Boston.

Victor Kattan is a Senior Research Fellow at the Middle East Institute and an Associate Fellow at the Faculty of Law at the National University of Singapore.

Annique M. Lockhard is an Attorney at Law, Legal Services of North Dakota.

Joseph Margulies is a Professor of Law and Government at Cornell University, Ithaca, NY.

Steven R. Morrison is an Assistant Professor of Law, University of North Dakota School of Law.

Margaret L. Satterthwaite is the faculty director of the Robert L. Bernstein Institute for Human Rights and a co-chair and faculty director of the Center for Human Rights and Global Justice at NYU school of law.

Milena Sterio is a Professor of Law and Associate Dean for Academic Enrichment, Cleveland-Marshall College of Law.

Alexandra M. Zetes is Human Rights Fellow at Vance Center for International Justice, New York.

Foreword

There is no doubt that the substantive and symbolic damage done by the 9/11 attacks was traumatic in its impact well beyond what was initially imagined. To have so exposed American vulnerability to low-technology attacks made the huge American military machine seem almost obsolete overnight. To have struck hard at the World Trade Center and the Pentagon, the economic and military symbols of American global leadership, was to pose an unprecedented challenge for which the political leadership of the country was clearly unprepared, as well as unequipped. The US government was adept over the course of the country's history at winning major wars, and its policymakers were proud in recent years of what they identify as "full spectrum dominance," boasting of this claimed capacity to prevail on any battlefield at any scale anywhere on the planet. At the same time, 9/11 made a huge hole in the hubristic fabric of American grand strategy. Its leaders and their advisors had no experience, doctrine, or weaponry with which to fight this new formidable ideological enemy that possessed seemingly unstoppable tactics that could be directed at soft targets everywhere in the world by a suicidal band of trained followers seemingly impatient for martyrdom.

The disturbing elements of the situation surrounding 9/11 became evident to many close observers of the incident even before the smoke cleared at Ground Zero. The mood of concern was epitomized by the pithy abstraction "this changes everything," loosely attached to the momentous occurrences on that day. The contributors to this volume focus on a series of chosen counterterrorist responses that began to be formulated on the day after, that is, on 9/12. What sets this book apart is its comprehensive critical interrogation of these responses, illuminating the disturbing dialectic that has been evident in subsequent years between terrorism and counterterrorism. It raises the stressful question as to whether the real danger of terrorism is the entrapment of the targeted society in a behavioral logic that ends up establishing an unwanted moral symmetry between terrorism and counterterrorism. It seems crucial to distinguish the traumatic context of the attacks, labeled 9/11, from the less frenzied, if more consequential, selection of counterterrorist responses, here identified by the shorthand of 9/12.

Until this brilliant book of essays, few even discussed this provocative hypothesis that the American counterterrorist tactics and measures from 9/12 until today have caused more damage to the United States, its way of life, and essential political identity as a constitutional and humane democracy than did the horrific attacks themselves. This is a startling assertion difficult, at first, even to comprehend, and made even more frightening by the realization that the forces let loose by the 9/12 logic of "securitizing everything" (to borrow a phrase from Martin Ewi's excellent chapter) are virtually impossible to constrain even after their failure and depravity became manifest.

What compounds the seeming perversity of this situation is that even the counterterrorist mission that was supposed to vindicate what Dick Cheney described as "going to the dark side" has also actually gone awry, giving rise to as at least as much violent extremism as it eliminated. Donald Rumsfeld, of all unlikely people, confirmed this point years ago when he famously acknowledged that no "metrics" existed to help the government decide whether America was winning or losing the "War on Terror." He describes the puzzle as follows: "Are we capturing, killing or deterring and dissuading more terrorists every day than the *madrassas* and the radical clerics are recruiting, training and deploying against us?" Despite this candid acknowledgment, it seemed never to occur to Rumsfeld, then Secretary of Defense, whether in light of such radical uncertainty it was not time to reconsider existing counterterrorist policies since the current ones seemed not to be working, and were responsible for widespread death, destruction, massive suffering, and, yes, a worldwide chorus of allegations directed at the United States, essentially charging war crimes, violations of human rights, and, to top it all, "state terrorism." The names of Abu Ghraib and Guantanamo entered the political vocabulary of wrongdoing as places designating degenerate political behavior. As the 9/11 victim morphed into the 9/12 victimizer, the words of Kurt Vonnegut's celebrated refrain in *Slaughterhouse Five* have a new resonance: "and so it goes."

What this volume achieves better than any competitor is a comprehensive interpretative overview of the costly deficiencies of what has been known ever since 9/11 as the War on Terror, which Satvinder Juss, the editor of this undertaking, aptly describes as "the ill-crafted War on Terror." In a series of scholarly chapters such policies and practices as torture, extraordinary rendition, black sites, drone warfare, and indefinite detention are authoritatively and critically depicted as departures from centuries of humanitarian efforts to impose some limits on the behavior of states in wartime situations. Other chapters depict the homeland encroachments on civil liberties that have entailed totalizing surveillance in ways that badly erode the privacy of ordinary American citizens, arouse acute suspicions of immigrants, minorities, and foreigners, nurture a taste for autocratic and demagogic leadership, and adopt a good and evil simplistic calculus with which to castigate non-state adversaries. This black and white thinking by policymakers and leaders makes diplomacy irrelevant and virtually ensures the permanence of what has previously been acknowledged by the US Department of Defense as "the long war," or more popularly known as "the forever war."

Of course, the haunting question we are left with is whether the 9/12 pattern of response could and should have been handled differently to achieve better results in relation to national security with particular reference to the effectiveness of counterterrorist tactics. A reevaluation of the 9/12 approach would also consider whether it was necessary to encroach so flagrantly upon civil liberties and human rights, international humanitarian law, and the sovereign rights of foreign countries, in meeting a range of threats never previously encountered. It is always a temptation to be a retrospective wise man or woman, knowingly re-running history on the basis of armchair hindsight while being freed from the urgencies and anxieties of meeting challenging existential threats credibly associated with feared terrorist sequels to 9/11. Without ignoring this cautionary *caveat*, there still seems to be an immense learning opportunity present that could have been useful when confronting future crises or even now to correct some of the worst 9/12 missteps.

At the same time, while critical evaluation is clearly overdue, especially in the nerve centers of government, it is also the case that for reasons earlier mentioned, 9/11 produced a challenging menu of threats that could not be handled by either the available toolbox of weaponry and doctrine nor could be addressed effectively within the framework of existing international law. For one thing, that framework had evolved to regulate behavior among states, without taking account of non-state actors that were assumed to be manageable through the exercise of sovereign rights. For another, the non-territorial nature of the terrorist adversary meant that deterrence and defense had become almost irrelevant, and in their place an almost irresistible temptation created to strike preemptively whenever and wherever potential terrorists were found in the world. And as a corollary to such an assessment, the acquisition of information was deemed critical, and could only be reliably acquired from captured suspects or trusted informers. It is this logic that probably accounted for the kind of 9/12 response structure that was put together in a hurry, and arguably in far too great a hurry.

My view is that the challenging innovative dimensions of 9/11 could have been taken into account while also making a much more serious effort to minimize damage to the normative frameworks embodied in international law and constitutionally protected liberties. Precisely because of the pressures exerted on the rules previously governing international recourse to force, there should have been an extra effort made to avoid gratuitous displays of depraved behavior of the kind that occurred in Iraqi and Afghan prison complexes, verified by the shocking Abu Ghraib pictures of humiliating torture with no plausible rationale, which discredited the already unacceptable reliance on torture of detained suspects, which had violated one of the most respected prohibitions in international law. In my view, the core mistake was to declare this undifferentiated *war* on terrorism, without seeking a more nuanced counterterrorist security template, perhaps combining criminal law enforcement with a new kind of very limited war claim.

Was it, in other words, really necessary to opt for the war paradigm, without even offering supportive arguments, capriciously departing thereby from the crime paradigm that had been long relied upon by governments in the past to cope with even the most formidable non-state violent political movements? Until 9/11, it never occurred to counterterrorist specialists to declare war in response to a terrorist incident even if severe. Prior to 9/11, the main effort of governments at the UN and in other lawmaking contexts was to achieve the criminalization of terrorism, domestically and internationally. The biggest obstacle on this path was definitional, whether to confine terrorism to the violent initiatives of non-states, or to broaden the conception to refer to acts of political violence deliberately targeting civilian society, whether the actor was state or non-state. This issue was never authoritatively resolved, thus making "terrorism" a language of opprobrium that is used by states to demonize their non-state opponents, and hence functions as part of statist ideology.

Why, then, the immediate conceptual leap by the Bush presidency, framing the attack as an act of war, which made it reasonable to respond by adopting war modalities while at the same time denying enemy combatants the benefits of international humanitarian law as encapsulated in the Geneva Conventions? Was it the magnitude or trauma generated by the event? It could be argued, and seemed widely believed, that 9/11 was worse in terms of trauma and impact than the Pearl Harbor attack 60 years earlier, which was unquestionably an act of war, and this helps explain the disastrously inflated response. Or was it possibly a too literal reading of the fiery language of Osama bin Laden, leader of al-Qaeda, who insisted that the encounter between the West and Islam was one of warfare without mercy? A significant indicator of the post-9/11 frenzied mood was the almost total absence of any meaningful dissent from this rush to war even from the Democratic Party opposition and hardly a murmur of doubt voiced in the mainstream media.

Undoubtedly, these factors were influential, but were they the whole, or even the true, story? The political leadership at the time, including its entourage of neocon advisors definitely saw 9/11 as more than what it appeared to the public to be. They saw it as an opportunity to mobilize the citizenry to support a much expanded reliance on force in carrying out American foreign policy. Undoubtedly analytical clarity was thus diminished by strategic ambition, which saw a window of opportunity wide open on 9/12. In this interpretation, 9/12 was at least as much about Western grand strategy in the Middle East as it was about counterterrorism. This still doesn't explain the silence of the lambs, that is, the Democrats. This passivity was partly a patriotic reflex to the widespread collective trauma caused by 9/11, a national unity mood magnified by media frenzy, and partly a golden occasion for Democrats to support long held Israeli goals of regime change in several key Arab countries.

With the election of Donald Trump many observers expected policy discontinuity, especially given his strong criticisms of the Democratic Party's costly failures in its Middle Eastern interventions before he entered the White House. In fact, there has been far more continuity than discontinuity during the Trump presidency, who even more than Obama follows faithfully the precepts of neocon thinking in the region, being especially deferential to Israel's ill-advised confrontational approaches in Iran and Syria, and his affirmation of the worst side of the 9/12 counterterror tactics, including torture, CIA black sites, and Guatanamo.

From an international law point of view the issue has been dramatically joined by a pair of recent landmark decisions by the European Court of Human Rights, *Nashiri v. Romania* and *Abu Aubaydah v. Lithuania*, which condemned the whole gamut of 9/12 tactics from an authoritative legal perspective. These decisions also pose challenges to European governments as to whether or not to continue its cooperation with US-style counter-insurgency operations. As such, there is exhibited an almost 360-degree reversal of attitudes. Following 9/11 there was no normative gap between the United States and Europe, while currently the width of the gap confirms the view of this volume that it is increasingly difficult on moral or legal grounds to distinguish al-Qaeda or ISIS terrorism from US counterterrorism. At the very least the present policy atmosphere should provide the occasion for a profound and comprehensive review of the War on Terror, whether it is working and still necessary, and whether such distasteful departures from law and ethics can any longer be rationalized under the rubric of security given the persistence of terrorist threats.

Despite these considerations retaining the crime approach to counterterrorism had strong arguments on its side, especially in the 9/11 context. The rest of the world, almost without exception, condemned the attacks, and expressed solidarity with America's need to react effectively to these attacks. These governments seemed genuinely ready to lend unprecedented cooperation in facilitating effective law enforcement against al-Qaeda leaders and operatives for their apparent engagement in these gross crimes against humanity. It is instructive to recall that even the Taliban in Afghanistan offered to cooperate if Washington provided convincing evidence that al-Qaeda was responsible for 9/11. In addition to offering a show of sympathy and a readiness to cooperate in a robust law-enforcement campaign, there were important world order issues at stake. All sovereign states had a double interest in a prudent 9/12 approach: first of all, to achieve the effective suppression of transnational mega-terrorist attacks of this sort that potentially threatened the primacy of all states; and secondly, in the avoidance of war in all instances except self-defense in response to attacks by states on other states.

The US government seemed uninterested in pursuing this option of criminal law enforcement plus diplomacy, apparently more determined from the beginning to have a pretext for toppling the Taliban, which was accorded precedence over the stated objective of weakening the al- Qaeda threat. Similarly, in 2003 when it launched a regime-changing war of aggression against Iraq, the rather lame excuse was 9/11, and an accompanying belief that pre-emptive warfare was a necessary element of national security in an Age of Terrorism, but the principal motivation for the war policy was different. The rationale for such a military operation against the regime of Saddam Hussein was already present in the pre-9/11 outlook of the neoconservative foreign-policy advisors who were so influential during the presidency of George W. Bush. Leading neocons had actually expressed in a widely read report distributed by their ideological vehicle, Project for the New American Century, the need for "a new Pearl Harbor" a year before Bush was elected president, and two years prior to 9/11, so that they could initiate a series of regime-changing interventions in the Middle East. These neocon heavyweights acknowledged the prior need to create a political climate in the United States that would support military interventions in the region that was convincing enough to the American people to overcome their lingering opposition to overseas ventures that might produce American casualties. 9/11 created that desired atmosphere. It allowed previously dubious military undertakings to receive a green light from the political process, including the mainstream media, thereby overcoming the previously skeptical public opinion.

Both of these wars proved expensive and counterproductive in almost every respect, with little net positive results from the perspective of global security or even the national security of the United States. Indeed, the Iraq War unquestionably gave rise to ISIS, which has spread terror on a far broader scale than al-Qaeda, relying on barbaric tactics. The Iraq War was also notable for achieving a political outcome that was the direct opposite of what was sought. It actually expanded Iran's regional reach and influence rather than frustrating its ambitions by constructing an iron wall of containment with a Baghdad government beholden to Washington rather than informally aligned with Tehran. There are several relevant observations. Counterterrorism was at most a secondary goal of these wars. Furthermore, these wars were strategic failures on their own terms, failing either to become democracies or allies. And finally, as with the Vietnam War, the wrong lessons were learned. It was not realised that military intervention rarely succeeds, and only then at great costs, especially in post-colonial settings. In these settings native populations mount a national resistance that compensates for its battlefield weakness, displaying a strategic patience that dissipates the political will of its overseas intervener. It is hard to explain this America refusal to learn from past mistakes. The best explanations seem connected with the enormous investments made over many years in constructing the American military machine creating an ingrained bureaucratic reluctance to think outside the militarist box. And so instead of recognizing the limits of hard power, the prevailing approach has made it much harder to correct past mistakes and adapt to a new global security environment.

Another 9/12 issue that might have made a difference if handled more deftly is that of the nature of the enemy. George W. Bush repeatedly denounced al-Qaeda as inherently evil, as distinct from denouncing its tactics on 9/11 as evil, which the editor here does so effectively. Such a posture amounts to a refusal to examine the root causes of such political extremism and criminalized violence. When the root causes are examined it becomes evident that there are "legitimate grievances" that give rise to acute frustration and rage throughout the Arab world, eventuating in recourse to terror directed at the West. Two wrongs certainly don't make a right, especially here, but better grasping why the wrongs occurred may reduce the prospects of their repetition in the future. I recall that John Major, after being prime minister, let it be known that he only made progress in resolving the struggle in Northern Ireland when he stopped thinking of the IRA as a terrorist organization and starting conceiving of the IRA as a political actor with genuine grievances, limited goals, and a potential receptivity to political compromise. There are numerous other recent examples of converting terrorist organizations into diplomatic partners when the moment seemed right, but the lethal fusion of terrorist denunciation and Islamophobia have prevented to date any consideration in the post-9/11 world of whether political solutions might better achieve security and political normalcy than this War on Terror that threatens to be a war without end.

What makes this book so stimulating and significant is that it builds an intellectual foundation for exploring new paths to achieving genuine security in the face of terrorist threats without either devastating foreign countries or undermining liberty at home. The contributors to this volume show that counterterrorist policies and practices have not only collided with the most basic civilizational verities, but have violated several key international humanitarian law provisions, and contributed to putting once proud democracies on a rocky road leading straight to autocracy. In this regard, the secondary effects of intervention overseas in the form of massive refugee flows, pressures to close the borders and the hearts of sovereign states, and, in the process, create an open sesame for opportunistic leaders to scapegoat minorities and immigrants that inflict potentially fatal wounds on the body politic of democratic societies. It is late, but not too late, to have overdue dialogues on alternative approaches to counterterrorism and security in an age of terror. This book helps establish the kind of reflective atmosphere that should encourage citizens of good will to seek through dialogue an improved balance between security imperatives and ethical standards.

Richard Falk
Professor of International Law, Emeritus,
Princeton University
May 2018

Preface

Did the 9/11 atrocity ultimately prevail as an act of terror on the West? And is it perverse to suggest that it did? Some two decades after this monstrosity it is now clear that its enormity and insidiousness succeeded in dismantling some of the most highly venerated values of Western democracy. It needs hardly reminding how these coveted values arose from the 'Enlightenment' during what came to be known as the 'long eighteenth century' (a period from around 1685 to 1815). European politics, philosophy and science were radically transformed, in a movement that has come to be known as the 'Age of Reason' because it questioned traditional authority. There was then an indelible conviction that humanity could be refined and reformed through the agency of rational change. From free speech to religious tolerance, and from fair trials to freedom from torture, the cherished edifices of all have today been consciously and studiously disassembled following the Twin Tower attacks in New York on 11 September 2001. On reflection, what has surely been perverse is that this has been done by none other than our own democratically elected governments, and with the United States ahead of all others. This has consequences that are on the way to making us quite decidedly indistinguishable from those to whom we are opposed in this ill-fated 'War on Terror'.

As with all banalities of evil, it started off fairly innocuously. Following the outrage of 9/11 the US coalition forces, together with Britain, embarked on a conflict in Afghanistan and Iraq, causing it to become embroiled in fighting one disastrous war after another. In the determination to win these wars, there arose the official endorsement of torture and of imprisonment without trial. The result has been a ghastly mutation of our democracies into illiberal authoritarian states. Civil liberties have been disavowed and abandoned, individual rights disclaimed. Instead, a grotesquely colossal, extravagantly expensive, avoidably unnecessary, and recklessly extravagant armed forces and security organization has emerged from the ashes of the Twin Towers. In short, the abominable annihilation of the World Trade Center on 9/11 became the pretext for the remorseless enlargement of the security apparatus in the West. What followed thereafter was the NATO operation in 2011, which overthrew Colonel Gaddafi in Libya, only to leave the country deeply divided and unstable. This is not unsurprising given that in no less than three times in the decade after 9/11, the West toppled regimes in

Afghanistan, Iraq and Libya, without remotely planning for a new government, leading to the allied coalition of the dead and the injured which numbered in their tens of thousands, with countless thousands of civilian casualties, and three highly unstable Muslim countries now riven by Islamic terror. This, in turn, has invited even more of a War on Terror on those hapless lands and its peoples. Moreover, following the election of Donald Trump, it is now clear that the historical and political developments of the last two decades are now explicitly challenging the very basis of human rights; and that the war is now constructed consciously and calculatedly as a 'civilizational conflict' between a radical Islamist foe and a Judeo-Christian 'West'. A war that is now being waged exactly as Bernard Lewis and Samuel Huntington 'predicted'.

This is to say nothing of Syria, where after ISIS broke off from al-Qaeda in 2013, this Islamic State militant group spread itself into not just Iraq but also Syria, occupying half of those countries. A local insurgency that followed the so-called 'Arab Spring' (wishful thinking if ever there was one) has, as the *Washington Post* reminded us, metastasized into a 'mini world war', with now not just the USA but also Russia, together with regional actors, as well as radicalized fighters moving in, adding to the plight of a country that no longer exists as it once did, with its people disfigured, deprived and dislodged. Indeed, all three countries bear the scars of Western interventions undertaken without any proper intelligence analysis, unannounced regime change goals and a dodged moral responsibility, for a calamity left behind for someone else to clean up.

The countries bearing the brunt of the ill-crafted War on Terror are today mired in political and economic chaos, competing factions continue to fight for control and tens of thousands of refugees have been created who make perilous journeys to Europe, creating the biggest refugee crisis since the Second World War. If it were not for the fact that there has been, not a one-off failure here of a war going disastrously wrong, but no less than three wars in a ten years with Syria teetering on the brink, one could say that West does not know how 'to do war' (leave alone a 'just war'). That, however, is the present reality. The failure to plan, to wage and then to manage the aftermath suggests that our 'ways of the war' are seriously and pathologically flawed in what they reveal in the deep pattern that underlies its conduct. What emerges is that we are here today quite simply because of the way in which the vastly expanded network of security agencies have triumphed in embracing defective predispositions and biases, which have now become so deeply ingrained in our institutional structures that they dare not be discarded without the utter depletion and breakdown of institutional integrity, reliability and reputation.

Against this background, is it only a heretic who would question 'Western foreign policy' today? Taking our governments to task for drone attacks, for detentions at Guantanamo Bay, and for 'extraordinary renditions' where suspects are tortured in far-off lands out of sight and behind the scenes may be something that the common man or woman in our streets is blissfully unaware of. However, can a failure to make our governments accountable by asking them questions that make them feel awkward and uncomfortable be justified when we know that even an ordinary citizen in a Western democracy is now all too acutely aware of the myriad irreproachable lives lost, as a direct result of the West's War on Terror in the Islamic world? Yet, to raise such questions, and to seek governmental accountability from our elected leaders, is not to excuse the outrage of 9/11, any more than it is to excuse the London attacks of 2005 or the Boston Marathon terror attack of 2013, but only to explain the effect of what we do, both on ourselves and on others, as a result of ill-judged policies and their execution. Invoking the injustice and humiliation inflicted by the West on the Muslim world will not do as grounds for murder. But neither will invoking the necessities of the so-called War on Terror do as a justification for massacring the innocents.

With these questions in mind, the purpose of the essays in this compilation is to elucidate and unravel the persistent influence of the War on Terror in domestic and international laws and in explicating how the erosions into our civil liberties are now the 'new normal'. It is only when policy makers can see how much the liberties that we took for granted have been eroded that the roots of liberal democracy and universal human values can be salvaged and re-asserted. It is to be hoped that this approach will appeal to the increasing numbers rallying against the sweep to power of the 'alt-right'.

In the first essay, Victor Kattan explains how the concept of the much-touted 'pre-emptive action' gained favour in policy discussions in the West. This robust, proactive counter-terrorism strategy which centred on preventing the United States' enemies from striking first came soon after 9/11 in September 2002, when the Bush administration published *The National Security Strategy of the United States of America* (NSS-2002). This argued that the threat and consequences of inaction could not be tolerated, given the availability of WMD which meant that the traditional concepts of deterrence did not work against terrorists. What was required was 'taking anticipatory action' to defend the United States. Remarkably, this was 'even if uncertainty remains as to the time and place of the enemy's attack'. What is especially valuable of this exegesis by Kattan is that he traces the origins of what became known as the 'war on terrorism' to the US intervention in the Lebanon following Israel's 1982 invasion, when this 'Shultz doctrine' was taken from Israeli doctrine at the time.

In the second essay, Mileno Sterio explains how we have reached a stage where, some two decades after 9/11 in 2001, it is possible to say that, in its scope, expenditure and impact on international relations, the war on terrorism is comparable to the Cold War. This is because it represents the beginning of a new phase in global political relations. This, in turn, has important consequences for security, human rights, international law, cooperation and governance. Paradoxically, as she explains, the War on Terror began as an anti-terrorism response to the 9/11 attacks, but it has transmuted itself into an enormous campaign spanning military, intelligence, diplomatic and domestic dimensions, which when fathomed leave us in no doubt that the United States has overstepped its boundaries and has engaged in harmful behaviour – by infringing the sovereignty of other states and by curtailing the civil liberties of American citizens. The United States has been involved in major wars in Afghanistan and Iraq, covert operations in Yemen and elsewhere through the use of drones as well as other military tactics, large-scale military-assistance programmes for various friendly regimes and major increases in military spending. Thus, Sterio shows that in the examples of the use of drones, of mass surveillance and of detention at Guantanamo Bay, we see that the War on Terror's tangible anti-terrorism benefits have been outweighed by some of the War's most aggressive policies, violating both international law as well as civil liberties of Americans domestically. The result is that the War on Terror has shaped US law and policy in a manner that very few other world events have.

Against this background, Joseph Margulies undertakes a detailed and specific analysis in the third essay, of what 'Guantanamo Bay' represents to us, some two decades after 9/11, in a hard-hitting and yet difficult to challenge perspective. What scholars must do, he argues, is to 'detect the difference between symbol and substance', so that they can 'account for the chasm that separates the two' because the reality is that law at Guantanamo 'is an extravagant irrelevance', (and this is especially true of the law of military commissions) because what the law does is simply of almost no substantive purpose except to distract 'from the reality of unfettered global American power in the war on terror and the plight of the remaining prisoners at the base'. The result is that we overlook 'the scope of American hegemony'. The courts only provide the hollow hope of progressive social change. But the symbolism of Guantanamo matters. This is seen in the leading legal cases because although, as declarations of legal rights, *Rasul* and *Boumediene* had essentially no effect, nevertheless, as a salvo against official lawlessness, they were important contributors, because they became part of a much larger campaign against a particular form of presidential abuse. Although, the Bush administration conceived, designed and built the prison at Guantanamo to be the ideal interrogation chamber, inaccessible to the public and unsupervised by the judiciary, since the Supreme Court decision in *Rasul* the prison hasn't served that function. The result is that today Guantanamo is both historical artefact and exorbitant irrelevance, so that, paradoxically, as it became *less* important as a prison, it became *more* important as a symbol. What scholars need to do, he argues is not 'to obsess over every bolt and screw in the elaborate legal architecture that exists only to create the appearance of rule-of-law-regularity' because to do so is to overlook 'the reality of unfettered power'.

Taking these arguments further, the fourth essay by Martin Ewi acknowledges how the world changed after 9/11, and how the ensuing years have been a struggle by the international community to stem what has been regarded as 'terrorism', conceived of as what is a common threat to humanity. Martin shows how this new counter-terrorism world order has affected almost every aspect of life – communication, transportation, trade, social interaction, education, health, economic activities including banking, human rights and civil liberties, and democratic processes (just to name a few). New security regimes and norms have been adopted and populations are gradually (with difficulties) accepting as the new normal this new world order of securitization of everything. However, he argues that whether the world has become safer from terrorism and violent extremism since 9/11 remains heavily contested. What is known for sure is that in terms of number of attacks globally, terrorism has shown no signs of waning. Instead, the phenomenon has burgeoned.

On particularly insidious aspect of the War on Terror that the West has been most loath to own up to has been the use of torture, which sometimes has been euphemistically described as 'advanced techniques of interrogation'. This is why in the fifth essay Stephen Ellmann provides the most extensive chapter of this volume, critically analysing the role that lawyers should have played in preventing such actions, by asking what is torture, and how is it defined by the law. The question is important because it is not only 'torture' as so defined, but also other transgressions which violate other rules of international and domestic law that prohibit lesser, but still repellent, forms of mistreatment, given that Common Article 3 of the Geneva Conventions of 1949 prohibits not only torture but also 'violence to life and person, in particular murder of all kinds, mutilation, [and] cruel treatment' and 'outrages upon personal dignity, in particular humiliating and degrading treatment'. Moreover, the Convention Against Torture, to which the United States is a party, forbids torture and also 'other acts of cruel, inhuman or degrading treatment or punishment which do not amount to torture'. However, given that torture has a special horror, such that only those who wish to declare themselves ungoverned by law and mercy would want the label of 'torturer', what is to be done in cases where lawyers decide to instead embrace the concept of 'enhanced interrogation techniques', and to argue that one man's cruelty is another's justified severity? Given that if the focus were to shift from torture to 'cruel, inhuman or degrading', and given that the arguments marshalled for and against applying the latter label would much resemble those that have been brought to bear on the issue of torture, is it not time, he asks, that the question of how the prohibition of torture should be interpreted is pursued by lawyers?

No less serious violation than torture is the practice of 'extraordinary rendition' to another country, and into the hands of the security services of other nations, solely in order to be subjected to a form or interrogation, which would otherwise be considered beyond the pale in one's own country and by one's own government officials. This is the subject of discussion in the sixth essay by Margaret Satterthwaite and Alexandra Zetes, who remind us that the practice of rendition – the involuntary transfer of an individual across borders without recourse to extradition or deportation proceedings – is actually not new at all. For more than a hundred years, governments have been engaged in snatching a defendant for trial and thereby presenting him/her as 'rendition to justice'. In this respect, it has actually been celebrated as a crucial tool in the fight against impunity for grave crimes. However, what is worrisome today is that with nationalist governments growing in popularity and human rights guarantees weakening, leading to state practices such as moving to close borders, deport non-nationals, denaturalize their own citizens and use informal means to transfer suspects the mechanisms through which a state may transfer custody of an individual increasingly escape careful scrutiny. Satterthwaite and Alexandra Zetes accordingly argue that in this era of global realignment the human rights principles guiding inter-state cooperation in such matters must be reasserted, and set out to examine the legal norms governing informal transfers and detentions in this new era and aim to set out a minimum standard that must be upheld whenever a state renders an individual, no matter how extraordinary the times. In this they draw upon comparative jurisprudence, such as that of European human rights law, as seen in the *Abu Qatada* case, to support their argument that wherever individuals are subject to informal transfer, governments must ensure specific procedural and substantive protections against refoulement. They further suggest that the continuing lack of transparency related to the US use of informal transfer is extremely concerning.

Satvinder S. Juss takes up the theme in the seventh essay, of how the United States can learn from developments in other jurisdictions, this time in the United Kingdom, following the detention and torture of Abdul Hakim Belhaj in Diego Garcia, at the US 'black' site in the Chagos Islands. In 2013, he and his Libyan wife, Mrs Boudchar, decided to sue the United Kingdom's Security Intelligence Service (SIS) because, following his abduction in Malaysia, rendition flight assistance with transit facilities was provided by the British-owned, but American-operated base at Diego Garcia in the Indian Ocean. The full story would never have been known were it not for 'several extraordinary caches of secret British, American and Libyan intelligence documents that were discovered amid the chaos of the Libyan revolution in 2011, scattered around abandoned government offices, prisons and officials' private residences'. These not only confirmed covert CIA operations, but British complicity in them. By January 2015, as the pressure began to mount, a senior Bush administration official appears to have confirmed that 'Interrogations of US prisoners took place at a CIA black site on the British overseas territory of Diego Garcia'. It was said that, '[t]he island was used as a "transit location" for the US government's 'nefarious activities' post-9/11 when other places were too full, dangerous, insecure, or unavailable, according to Lawrence Wilkerson, Colin Powell's former chief of staff. This was significant as it 'was the first time a senior Bush administration official has stated on the record that the remote British territory was a part of the CIA's global network of black sites'. Yet, the long-established legal position was that the courts will not adjudicate upon acts done abroad by virtue of sovereign authority – what was to become known as the 'Foreign Act of State' doctrine – as is clear from the US Supreme Court's decisions in *Underhill v Hernandeez* (1897) and *Oetjen v Central Leather Co.* (1918). Belhaj, however, sued the UK government for its complicity in his human rights deprivations. Whilst the UK courts had themselves long decided to inherit the doctrine of the 'Foreign Act of State' from these earlier developments in American law, the UK Supreme Court in 2017 held that in deciding whether an issue is non-justiciable, English law will have regard to 'the extent to which the fundamental rights of liberty, access to justice and freedom from torture are engaged by the issues raised …'. Although the Court recognized traditional limitations, where judicial intervention will be inappropriate, such as the making of war and peace, making treaties with foreign sovereigns, and annexations and cessions of territory, the UK Supreme Court's decision is revolutionary and suggests for the USA a way forward, where fundamental human rights are violated by the actions of our governments abroad, such that the rule of law is preserved in all cases wherever possible.

In the eighth essay, Jonathan Hafetz returns to the question of how the continued impunity for torture and related human rights violations arising out of the extrajudicial detention of terrorism suspects after 9/11 has created an accountability gap. The absence of criminal or civil liability not only contradicts international human rights law's requirement of effective investigation and redress, but also has broader ramifications. It reinforces the perception that international human rights law and international criminal law are enforced in an uneven manner that protects the interests of the most powerful states. Hafetz argues that whereas other nations also participated in the US torture program and engaged in abuses on their own, it was the United States that remained exceptional in the chasm between the evidence of systematic torture and near complete absence of accountability. In fact, as he points out, several countries, including the United Kingdom, Sweden, Canada and Australia, have gone on to provide compensation to former detainees held by the CIA or US military in cases where their own public officials engaged in wrongdoing. However, Hafetz suggests that the greatest success in closing the accountability gap has actually been achieved through litigation in supranational human tribunals against other states for their complicity in US torture. He describes how in 2012 the European Court of Human Rights (ECtHR) issued a judgment against Macedonia, finding it in violation of the European Convention on Human Rights for its role in the torture and enforced disappearance of Khalid El-Masri. In 2014, the ECtHR issued judgments against Poland for similar abuses against two other detainees, Abd al-Rahim al-Nashiri and Abu Zubaydah, at secret CIA prisons (also known as 'black sites'). More recently, in 2016, the ECtHR issued a judgment against Italy for its role in the abduction and rendition of a terrorism suspect from Milan, and its subsequent failure to conduct an effective investigation. All three cases resulted in awards of monetary compensation to the victims. The cases have helped spur litigation against other countries for their participation in US torture and against states for participation in other US-led counter-terrorism operations. Consequently, these cases illustrate both the opportunities and challenges associated with holding states responsible for human rights violations in a pluralistic system with multiple centres of enforcement.

The final essay, by Steven R. Morrison and Annique M. Lockard, ends on a more sombre note. They explain that one reason why individuals' rights have been so completely violated is that once they are associated with groups that are deemed dangerous no reprieve for them is possible. The reason for this, they argue, is that the criminal law lacks a principled theory of group action. At its inception, the War on Terror was to be either a criminal issue or a war issue, so that when 9/11 happened the first choice was to decide whether to treat it as a crime or an act of war. The Bush administration chose the latter, which has shaped the United States' response to further acts of terrorism, and increasingly of other countries' responses too. What they argue is that, in part because of this choice, designating certain acts as 'terrorism' has become a political move, and that is despite the fact that the criminal law is intimately involved in addressing these acts. The result is a system in which the national security apparatus, the military apparatus and the domestic criminal justice system all play roles in addressing the War on Terror. Some people are tried in US federal courts as criminals, some are tried in Guantanamo Bay as combatants subject to military law and some are subject to targeted killing on the 'battlefield'. While the systems of criminal justice, national security and military operate very differently and are subject to different rules, they all have been marshalled to address what we call 'terrorism' and what really can mean different things in different contexts. Morrison and Lockard argue that this multi-pronged approach is not necessarily bad. However, it does lead to muddled political responses that do not necessarily give rise to just and measured outcomes. In addition, so many interest groups (domestic law-enforcement agencies, national security agencies, military sections) now rely on the War on Terror for their raison d'être that it appears the War on Terror will continue in perpetuity, not because terrorism will continue to be a problem (because it will), but because so many jobs everywhere rely on it continuing. As a result, American criminal law and, by extension, much of worldwide human rights, is on the cusp of a revolution away from individualistic norms of accountability and towards a more nuanced understanding of collectives. This revolution will produce systems of criminal law and of human rights that are more responsive to collective realities. They argue that law enforcement increasingly focuses on the groups and communities from which prior suspects have come. Because the 9/11 attackers were defined along religious-political lines, subsequent suspects overwhelmingly are Muslims who express discontent with American policies (but probably at a rate no higher than the American population at large). Therefore, when in the post-9/11 war on terror a complex of First Amendment-inspired and criminal due process human rights are threatened, they all share a basic assumption: that groups are particularly dangerous and, when faced with large-scale threats, the public safety imperative overrides individual rights norms and permits governments to pursue individuals for their connections with certain groups, whether those connections are real or perceived, and whether or not those connections reliably suggest criminal intent. What is necessary, according to Morrison and Lockard, is to stake out the border between criminal conduct and protected activity in the group context so as to generate an evidentiary regime capable of locating individuals on either side of that border.

I would like to thank my authors for so eagerly agreeing to participate in this project and I trust that readers will find these accounts informative, moving and disturbing in equal measure. I would like to record my praise and gratitude to Ghogi for the strategic support, delivered in such challenging circumstances. I would also like to thank my publishers, and especially Alison Kirk, Senior Editor at Routledge, for her unsparing support for the production of two edited books of mine on terrorism at the same time. The other book, the sequel to this, is *Beyond Human Rights and the War on Terror* and it tracks the development of anti-terror laws in the wider world following 9/11 and the impact of these on human rights elsewhere. I thank Alexandra Buckley for her careful overseeing of this project. I thank Seth Townley (Production Editor) and Alexandra Buckley for their careful overseeing of this project. And, finally, I would like to record my indebtedness to Richard Falk, Professor of International Law, Emeritus, at Princeton University, and the former United Nations Special Rapporteur for Human Rights, for his magnificent Foreword, written at my request at such short notice.

Satvinder S. Juss
10 May 2018

1 The "Netanyahu doctrine"

The National Security Strategy of the United States of America, and the invasion of Iraq

Victor Kattan

> Did Israel launch that preemptive strike because Saddam had committed a specific act of terror against us? Did we coordinate our actions with the international community? Did we condition this operation on the approval of the United Nations? No, of course not. Israel acted because, it understood, we understood, that a nuclear-armed Saddam would place our very survival at risk. And today the United States must destroy the same regime because a nuclear-armed Saddam will place the security of our entire world at risk.
>
> (Benjamin Netanyahu testifying before the US Congress at a hearing titled "Conflict with Iraq: an Israeli Perspective", 12 September 2002)

Introduction

The adoption of Article 51 of the Charter of the United Nations on 26 June 1945 marked a watershed as the first collective effort to provide a universal definition of self-defence in international law:

> Nothing in the present Charter shall impair the inherent right of individual or collective self-defence if an armed attack *occurs* against a Member of the United Nations, until the Security Council has taken measures necessary to maintain international peace and security....[1]

Coming after the German surrender but before the Trinity explosion and the bombings of Hiroshima and Nagasaki, the Charter's definition of self-defence soon provoked a wide-ranging debate as to whether force could be used by states in self-defence against an imminent attack with atomic weapons.[2] A similar debate took place in the USA following the 23 October 1983 bombing that killed 241 US Marines at their barracks in the Beirut International Airport, the largest loss of

1 Article 51 UN Charter (emphasis added).

2 For early debates, see C.H.M. Waldock, "The Regulation of the Use of Force by Individual States in International Law", *Recueil des Cours* 1952-II, p. 498. Derek Bowett, *Self-defence in International Law* (Manchester University Press, 1958), pp. 187–193. Ian Brownlie, "Some Legal Aspects of the Use of Nuclear Weapons" (14) *International and Comparative Law Quarterly* (1965), pp. 437–451.

Marines in a single incident since the battle of Iwo Jima.[3] Then the debate was whether force could be used by states in self-defence against attacks by non-state actors using sanctuaries in other states to launch their attacks.[4] After the attacks on the Twin Towers in New York City and the Pentagon in Washington, DC on 11 September 2001, these debates came together when scholars asked whether the UN Charter could cope with threats from weapons of mass destruction (WMD) in the event that a terrorist organisation was able to acquire WMD and had the means, and the intention, to deploy them.[5]

In September 2002, the Bush administration published *The National Security Strategy of the United States of America* (NSS-2002), which generated much commentary.[6] Coming after 9/11, NSS-2002 articulated a robust, proactive counter-terrorism strategy centred on preventing the USA's enemies from striking first.[7] Due to the availability of WMD and the claim that traditional concepts of deterrence did not work against terrorists, it was argued that the threat and the consequences of inaction made more compelling the case for "taking anticipatory action" to defend the USA, "even if uncertainty remains as to the time and place of the enemy's attack".[8] Accordingly, NSS-2002 announced that "[t]o forestall or prevent such hostile acts by our adversaries, the United States will, if necessary, act preemptively".[9]

As explained in this chapter, George P. Shultz articulated a broad pre-emptive counter-terrorism doctrine when he was Secretary of State in the Reagan administration when a "war against terrorism" was declared following the 1983 bombings of the US Embassy and Marine Corp barracks in Beirut.[10] The "Shultz doctrine" subsequently found expression in National Security Decision Directive 138 (NSDD-138), which was closely modelled on Israeli doctrine, and which was

3 Donald Rumsfeld, *Known and Unknown: A Memoir* (Penguin 2011), p. 9.
4 See the Symposium on Terrorism and International Law in volume 8, issue 3 of *The Whittier Law Review* (1986–1987). See also, Richard Falk, "The Decline of Normative Restraint in International Relations", 10 *Yale Journal of International Law* (1984–1985), p. 263.
5 See the Symposium on Rogue Regimes in volume 36(4) of the *New England Law Review* (2001–2002) and the Agora on the Future Implications of the Iraq Conflict in volume 97(3) of *The American Journal of International Law* (2003).
6 *The National Security Strategy of the United States of America* (17 September 2002). For contemporary commentary, see: "The Bush Doctrine", *The New York Post*, 21 September 2002; "The Bush Doctrine", *The New York Times*, 22 September 2002; Peter Beaumont, "Saddam's Secret Procurement Network: Now for the Bush Doctrine", *Observer*, 22 September 2002; Norman Podhoretz, "In Praise of the Bush Doctrine", *Commentary* (September 2002), pp. 19–28; John Lewis Gaddis, "A Grand Strategy of Transformation", 133 *Foreign Affairs* (Nov.–Dec. 2002), pp. 50–57.
7 NSS-2002, p. 15.
8 Ibid.
9 Ibid.
10 See David C. Wills, *The First War on Terrorism: Counter-Terrorism Policy during the Reagan Administration* (Rowman & Littlefield 2003), pp. 79–87; Mattia Toaldo, *The Origins of the US War on Terror: Lebanon, Libya and American Intervention in the Middle East* (Routledge 2014), pp. 96–97.

formulated following discussions between Shultz and Benjamin Netanyahu, then political attaché at Israel's Washington embassy. In contrast with NSS-2002, which was a public document, the policy enshrined in NSDD-138 was not published until 2010, and faced opposition, ironically, from the Pentagon and the Central Intelligence Agency (CIA). The Attorney-General and the Federal Bureau of Investigation (FBI) also expressed concern over the legality of the policy. Following the attacks on 9/11, many of Shultz's former colleagues in the State Department found themselves in the Pentagon where they would once more try to shape US policy. The counter-terrorism model they tried to shape in NSS-2002 was influenced by the difficulties they encountered in the Reagan administration while implementing NSDD-138. In short, the argument advanced here is that the Bush doctrine in NSS-2002 was taken from the Shultz doctrine, and that the Shultz doctrine in NSDD-138 was taken from Israeli doctrine.

To illustrate how the Shultz doctrine was taken from Israeli doctrine before it found expression in NSS-2002 this chapter revisits the origins of the "war on terrorism" during the US intervention in the Lebanon following Israel's 1982 invasion. Reference is made to the terrorism conference organised by the Jonathan Institute in Washington in 1984, to declassified documents from the Reagan Presidential Library on the drafting of NSDD-138 and to early drafts of NSS-2002 that have been published in *The Zelikow Papers* at the University of Virginia. The chapter also refers to documents from the British archives on Israel's raid on an Iraqi nuclear reactor in 1981 when the doctrine of pre-emption was first articulated at the UN, to *The Rumsfeld Papers* on the Iraq War, and to the report of the United Kingdom's Iraq Inquiry. The chapter has been further informed by discussions with senior officials from both the Reagan and George W. Bush administrations whom I interviewed in Washington.

The "Shultz doctrine" and the origins of the "war on terrorism"

In her leading study on international law and the use of force, Cambridge University Professor Christine Gray observed that the invocation of self-defence to justify using force in response to terrorist attacks was only invoked by a few states prior to 9/11. She mentions the USA and Israel before observing that most states regarded their responses as going beyond Article 51.[11] In one of the more detailed analyses of the US policy on counter-terrorism, Manchester University Professor Jackson Maogoto expressed his view that Israel's regular military incursions into Lebanon, Syria and Tunisia in the 1980s provided a practical manifestation of the tenet underlying the Reagan and Shultz doctrines.[12] Ghent University Professor Tom Ruys, perhaps comes the closest, however, with his trenchant observation

11 Christine Gray, *International Law and the Use of Force* (Oxford University Press 2008), p. 195.

12 Jackson Nyamuya Maogoto, "Walking an International Law Tightrope: Use of Military Force to Counter Terrorism—Willing the Ends", 31 *Brooklyn Journal of International Law* (2005–2006), p. 405, pp. 430–436 at p. 431. See also, Jackson Nyamuya Maogoto, *Battling Terrorism* (Ashgate 2005), p. 90.

that the Shultz doctrine "copied the reasoning hitherto defended by Israel, according to which a state unwilling to prevent terrorist attacks from its territory would be liable to a forcible response in self-defence".[13] But Ruys does not explore this observation any further.

The first shift in US policy on counter-terrorism began in response to the 1983 bombing of the US Marine barracks in Beirut. But that attack, despite its scale, and the manner of its commission, was not an act of terrorism, but an unconventional military assault against a military target – so argued Frederic Hof, who was awarded the Purple Heart for his services as US Army Attaché in Beirut, where he was injured. Hof was one of the authors of the Long report commissioned by President Reagan to look into the circumstances of those attacks.[14] Hof's views did not, however, prevail, because of the terms of reference that had been given to the commission, which obliged it to describe terrorism as an act of war:

> The commission believes that the most important message it can bring to the Secretary of Defense is that the 23 October 1983 attack on the Marine Battalion Landing Team Headquarters in Beirut was tantamount to an act of war using the medium of terrorism. Terrorist warfare, sponsored by sovereign states or organized political entities to achieve political objectives, is a threat to the United States ...[15]

According to Mattia Toaldo, the conclusions of the Long commission was the first time in US history that terrorism was defined as tantamount to an act of war.[16]

The deaths of so many Marines personally affected US Secretary of State for Defense Caspar Weinberger (1917–2006) and Secretary of State Shultz, both of whom had served in the Pacific theatre in the Second World War. Weinberger had served with the 41st Infantry Division and Shultz with the US Marine Corps where some of the fiercest fighting against Japan took place.[17] Yet, despite their experiences in the Pacific, both men responded very differently to the attack on the Marines' barracks. Whereas for Weinberger the lesson was never to send American soldiers into harm's way without a clear objective and clear national security goals, Shultz wanted to strike back at the terrorists even though it was not clear at the time who was responsible for the bombing.[18]

13 Tom Ruys, *"Armed Attack" and Article 51 of the UN Charter: Evolutions in Customary Law and Practice* (Cambridge University Press 2013), p. 422.
14 Frederic C. Hof, "The Beirut Bombing of October 1983: An Act of Terrorism?" XV (2) *Parameters: Journal of the US Army War College* (1985), p. 69.
15 US Department of Defense, *Report of the DOD Commission on Beirut International Airport Terrorist Act*, October 23, 1983, 20 December 1983, p. 4, para. 1.
16 Toaldo, *The Origins of the US War on Terror*, pp. 96–97.
17 Intriguingly, Shultz does not write much about the war in his memoir. See George P. Shultz, *Turmoil and Triumph: My Years as Secretary of State* (Macmillan 1993), p. 26. For Weinberger's recollections of the war, see Caspar W. Weinberger, *In the Arena: A Memoir of the Twentieth Century* (Regnery 2001), pp. 54–77.
18 A shadowy group called Islamic Jihad with Iranian links was reputedly behind the bombing, and it was claimed that Imad Mugniyeh was responsible. He was

The debate on how to respond to the Beirut bombings was deeply personal for both men as Weinberger opposed the decision to send the Marines to Beirut and clashed with Shultz who wanted to send the Marines back into Lebanon after they had already achieved their goal of evacuating Palestine Liberation Organization (PLO) fighters from Beirut. (Israel had demanded the evacuation of the PLO in exchange for agreeing to continue autonomy talks with the Palestinians at Camp David.)[19] However, following the Sabra and Chatila massacres that occurred less than two weeks after the Marines had left Lebanon, President Reagan, on the urging of the Israeli government and Secretary of State Shultz, decided to send the Marines back into Beirut.[20]

Despite the deteriorating security situation in Lebanon, with Israel refusing to withdraw, Shultz argued that the Marines had to stay in Beirut and have their rules of engagement relaxed so that they could assert themselves more forcefully, whereas Weinberger wanted to move the Marines out of Beirut altogether onto US warships offshore.[21] The problem was that the Marines had been used to secure an Israeli policy goal (the removal of the PLO from Lebanon), and therefore appeared to the warring militias as having taken Israel's side in the war and that of its Maronite ally.[22]

Shortly after the Beirut bombings, Shultz called his friend Donald Rumsfeld, whom he had first met in 1969 when they served in the Nixon administration.[23] Shultz told Rumsfeld that President Reagan needed to appoint a new special envoy to the Middle East to work on the Lebanon crisis and help with the American response to the terrorist attacks. He asked Rumsfeld if he would take a leave of absence from his job as CEO of a pharmaceutical company to serve his country. Rumsfeld accepted.[24] When it came to the debate between Weinberger and Shultz on using American force to pursue policy goals, Rumsfeld sided with Shultz in viewing the withdrawal of the Marines from Beirut after the attack as

assassinated on 12 February 2008 in a joint operation by the CIA and the Mossad. The authority for the killing was based on a presidential finding that Mugniyeh was a continuous and imminent threat to the USA. See Adam Goldman, "CIA and Mossad Killed Senior Hezbollah Figure in Car Bombing", *The Washington Post*, 30 January 2015. See also the account by Kai Bird in *The Good Spy: The Life and Death of Robert Ames* (Broadway, Penguin 2014), pp. 328–348.

19 Toaldo, *The Origins of the US War on Terror*, pp. 75–88.

20 Ibid., pp. 83–93; Caspar W. Weinberger, *Fighting for Peace: Seven Critical Years in the Pentagon* (Warner Books 1990), pp. 151–161; Shultz, *Turmoil and Triumph*, pp. 107–110.

21 Toaldo, *The Origins of the US War on Terror*, p. 92; Weinberger *Fighting for Peace*, p. 160, note 7.

22 This analysis is borne out by a declassified CIA intelligence assessment, which concluded that the reason the US Marines and French contingent of soldiers were attacked was because the USA had come to be perceived as pro-Maronite and pro-Israel. The British and Italian forces suffered fewer attacks because they were not seen to be so closely aligned with Israel and the Maronites. See Toaldo, *The Origins of the US War on Terror*, p. 96.

23 Rumsfeld, *Known and Unknown*, p. 11.

24 Ibid.

precipitous and similar to the American withdrawal from Saigon at the end of the Vietnam War.[25]

According to declassified government documents available at the Reagan Presidential Library in Simi Valley, California, the Attorney General, the FBI and the CIA remained opposed to an offensive counter-terrorism strategy even after the Beirut bombings.[26] William Smith, the Attorney-General, insisted that terrorism is a law-enforcement function and that it was unnecessary to have White House involvement in domestic law enforcement activity.[27] William Casey, the director of the CIA, agreed, and thought that forcible pre-emptive action is "difficult and very dangerous".[28] But Shultz persisted:

> We need to have agreement that when we know where terrorists are, we will act against them. It is recognised that there is a moral issue here in that evidence will never be conclusive enough to "win a Supreme Court case". Everyone in this room remembers what we went through after the attack on the Marines. At some point, we have to wrestle with the issue of how "sure" we have to be before we hit back.[29]

Weinberger repeatedly insisted on seeing evidence before he would consent to the use of American military forces in Grenada (1982), Lebanon (1983) and Libya (1986). This was in contrast with Shultz who was more willing to use military power to promote US foreign policy interests overseas, sometimes on the mere basis of "saving face" or maintaining "credibility".[30] In contrast to Shultz, Weinberger did not favour using the military as a tool of diplomacy. He did not want to risk the public's goodwill towards the Pentagon by engaging in a military disaster or prolonged operation, like those during the latter stages of the war in Vietnam when the American public turned against the military.[31]

David Wills explains that Casey would shift his view and consent to the pre-emptive neutralisation of anti-American terrorist groups following the kidnapping of William F. Buckley, the CIA station chief in Beirut on 16 March 1984.[32] This subsequently found expression in NSDD-138 on "Combatting Terrorism" (3 April 1984) that called on the director of Central Intelligence to "develop, in accordance with other friendly security services, capabilities for the pre-emptive neutralisation of anti-American terrorist groups which plan, support, or conduct hostile terrorist acts against US citizens, interests, and property overseas".[33]

25 Ibid., p. 28.
26 See Memorandum for Robert McFarlane, Summary of National Security Planning Group Meeting on Combatting Terrorism, 2 March 1984, 86–109, Box 3, Executive Secretariat, NSC: NSPG Collection, Ronald Reagan Library.
27 Ibid.
28 Ibid.
29 Ibid.
30 Wills, *The First War on Terrorism*, p. 28.
31 Ibid., p. 30.
32 Ibid., p. 83.
33 See National Security Decision Directive 138, 3 April 1984, p. 4.

Importantly, the strategy outlined in NSDD-138 went beyond the assassination context, which had been prohibited by Gerald Ford in 1976 following the recommendations of the Church Committee.[34] This is because NSDD-138 also called for developing "a military *strategy* that is supportive of an active, *preventive program* to combat state-sponsored terrorism *before* the terrorists can initiate hostile acts".[35] Accordingly, the adoption of NSDD-138 by the Reagan administration marked the first moment that US *policy* on pre-emptive self-defence emerged in the counter-terrorism context that would re-emerge in NSS-2002.

Despite the adoption of NSDD-138, there remained resistance in the US administration to an explicit pre-emptive counter-terrorism strategy that would involve using armed forces to attack terrorist groups in the territory of another state.[36] Although Congress was co-operative in ensuring there were sufficient resources for the counter-terrorism effort, Shultz felt the administration needed to do more.[37] This is when Netanyahu suggested that Shultz speak at a conference on terrorism organised by the Jonathan Institute, a foundation dedicated to public education on the nature of terrorism, which was founded by the Netanyahu family, and which is named after Benjamin's brother who was killed in the raid on Entebbe, the archetypal example of using force to combat terrorism.[38]

The Israeli connection to the Shultz doctrine

It is worth emphasising that Netanyahu approached Shultz *before* NSDD-138 was adopted as policy by the Reagan administration, as in his memoir Shultz appears to imply that Netanyahu only became involved in US counter-terrorism efforts after NSDD-138 was adopted on 3 April 1984.[39] According to Dov Zakheim, Deputy Undersecretary of Defense for Planning and Resources in the Pentagon, Shultz became an outspoken advocate of close ties with Israel when Syria torpedoed the 1983 Israel–Lebanon peace agreement that he had personally brokered.[40] So warm had Shultz's relationship with Israel become that "the Israelis viewed Shultz as the most friendly occupant of the seventh floor of the State Department since the creation of Israel, Henry Kissinger included".[41]

34 For analysis of how NSDD-138 overcame the prohibition on assassinations put in place by Gerald Ford in 1976 following the recommendations of the Church Committee see Markus Gunneflo, *Targeted Killing: A Legal and Political History* (Cambridge University Press 2016), pp. 109–127.
35 See National Security Decision Directive 138, 3 April 1984, p. 3 (emphasis added).
36 Shultz, *Turmoil and Triumph*, p. 645.
37 Ibid., p. 647.
38 Benjamin Netanyahu, *Fighting Terrorism: How Democracies Can Defeat the International Terrorist Network* (Farrar, Straus and Giroux, 2001 edition), pp. 67–68.
39 Shultz, *Turmoil and Triumph*, p. 647.
40 Dov S. Zakheim, *Flight of the Lavi: Inside a US–Israeli Crisis* (Brassey's 1996), p. 122. See also Bernard Gwertzman, "Reagan Turns to Israel", *The New York Times* (27 November 1983), p. SM62.
41 Zakheim, *Flight of the Lavi*, p. 150.

In his book *Fighting Terrorism*, Netanyahu explains that the Jonathan Institute's conference was part of a "political offensive" that had been "preceded by a deliberate intellectual effort spanning a number of years to persuade the West to change its policies regarding terrorism".[42] From the beginning of his involvement with the Jonathan Institute in the late 1970s, and later in his tenure as a diplomat in the early 1980s, Netanyahu believed that the key to the elimination of terrorism was having the USA lead the battle, in the hope that Washington would be able to persuade other states to adopt US policy.[43] Netanyahu explained that the effort to persuade the USA to change its counter-terrorism policy began as early as 1982 – the year of the Lebanon War – when Moshe Arens was appointed Israel's Ambassador to the United States.[44] According to Zakheim, Aren's was Prime Minister Shamir's closest advisor.[45] He was also the first ambassador to call on Shultz after Shultz was appointed Secretary of State.[46] Arens and Shultz knew each other from their days at the Massachusetts Institute of Technology (MIT), where Netanyahu had also studied.[47] Shultz told Arens and Netanyahu, then the political attaché at Israel's Washington embassy, that he needed Israel's help in shaping the debate on using armed force to counter terrorism because he was having difficulty changing US policy in the face of opposition from Weinberger, the Secretary of Defense, who at one point during the Lebanon War wanted to "cut off the pipeline of US assistance to Israel".[48]

The Jonathan Institute's terrorism conference took place at Washington's Four Seasons Hotel on 24 June 1984. For help with organising the conference in Washington, Netanyahu reached out to his friend Douglas Feith.[49] The conference was not the first terrorism conference organised by the Jonathan Institute. The first conference had been organised in Jerusalem in 1979. Then the speakers included George H.W. Bush and Henry Jackson.[50]

At the conference in Washington, Shultz explained that the time had come "to think long, hard, and seriously about more active means of defense—defense through appropriate preventive or preemptive actions against terrorist groups *before* they strike".[51] Shultz's speech was later republished by Netanyahu in a book published by Farrar, Straus, and Giroux titled *Terrorism: How the West Can Win*,

42 Netanyahu, *Fighting Terrorism*, p. 63.
43 Ibid., p. 65.
44 Ibid., pp. 66–67.
45 Zakheim, *Flight of the Lavi*, p. 11.
46 Shultz, *Turmoil and Triumph*, p. 39.
47 Shultz, *Turmoil and Triumph*, p. 49; Moshe Arens, *Broken Covenant: American Foreign Policy and the Crisis between the US and Israel* (Simon & Schuster, 1995), p. 26.
48 Netanyahu, *Fighting Terrorism*, p. 68; Shultz, *Turmoil and Triumph*, p. 60.
49 Ben Caspit and Ilan Kfir, *Netanyahu: The Road to Power* (Birch Lane Press 1998), p. 105.
50 See Benjamin Netanyahu (ed.), *International Terrorism: Challenge and Response: Proceedings of the Jerusalem Conference on International Terrorism*, Jerusalem 1979 (Transaction Books, 1981).
51 Benjamin Netanyahu, *Terrorism: How the West Can Win* (Farrar, Straus, and Giroux, 1986), p. 23 (emphasis in original).

along with articles by his father Benzion and by the newly formed neoconservative–Likud alliance: Daniel Patrick Moynihan, Jeane Kirkpatrick, Bernard Lewis, Moshe Arens, Charles Krauthammer, Yehuda Blum, Eugene Rostow and Meir Shamgar.[52] According to Shultz, Reagan read Netanyahu's book *Terrorism: How the West Can Win* on a trip to Tokyo "and had come back to the senior staff area several times from his cabin on *Air Force One* to read passages to us that he particularly liked".[53]

In addition to Shultz, the articles by Arens, Rostow, and Netanyahu called for a robust counter-terrorism strategy involving the use of force. Arens argued that

> we are in a state of war, an undeclared and broad war, a war against Western society. To force ourselves into a defensive posture, to exclude the option of taking the offensive, is as suicidal in the case of terrorism as it would be in any other form of warfare.[54]

Rostow was adamant that "our strategy against terrorism must move beyond the passive to the active and preemptive, as the Israelis did against the PLO in Lebanon in 1982".[55] Netanyahu argued that the right of self-defence always took precedence over territorial sovereignty: a terrorist war waged by armed bands from a neighbouring country was an act of aggression and the attacked state had "every right to take action against the terrorists or the government that shelters them. It may do so either in hot pursuit, in retaliation, or when faced with a *mounting threat*, in preemptive action."[56]

Shultz's speech at the Four Seasons was the first time a US official tried to influence US policy on counter-terrorism in public by aligning US counter-terrorism policy with Israeli policy.[57] Shultz would make several more speeches on terrorism that year calling for a more robust counter-terrorism policy, and in making the case he was supported by Rumsfeld who also delivered a similar speech.[58] Weinberger countered with speeches of his own.[59] After Shultz delivered a speech at the Park Avenue Synagogue in Manhattan on 25 October 1984, Vice President George H.W. Bush called Shultz to explain that the administration was irritated with his speech because he appeared to be trying to set US policy on his own "without going through the usual bureaucratic process—and that it was not a policy anyone else wanted".[60]

52 Yitzhak Rabin also spoke in his capacity as Defence Minister in the National Unity Government.
53 Shultz, *Turmoil and Triumph*, p. 790, footnote 5.
54 Netanyahu, *Terrorism*, p. 93.
55 Ibid., p. 147.
56 Ibid., p. 220 (emphasis added).
57 Shultz's speeches can be accessed in the files of Donald Fortier in Series I, Subject File, RAC 17–18, Box 9. Ronald Reagan Library.
58 Rumsfeld, *Known and Unknown*, p. 33.
59 See Text of Remarks by Secretary of Defense Caspar W. Weinberger to the National Press Club, 28 November 1984 in the Appendix to Weinberger, *Fighting for Peace*, pp. 433–445.
60 Shultz, *Turmoil and Triumph*, p. 648.

While the US had yet to formulate a policy that incorporated pre-emptive self-defence in its national security strategy, using force pre-emptively against terrorism had been a hallmark of Israeli policy long before the Beirut bombings. According to Toaldo, Ezer Weizman, Israel's Minister of Defence, announced a new policy of "preemptive attack" in Lebanon in 1979. He said that no longer would each Israeli attack be justified as revenge for a particular Palestinian action, but Israel would strike at its will and time of choice.[61] Menachem Begin then transformed pre-emption into a "semi-doctrine" with his speech at Israel's National Defence College on 8 August 1982, in the midst of the campaign in Lebanon that had begun on 6 June 1982. In this speech, Begin spoke of a war of choice, rather than a war of necessity.[62]

Israel's pre-emptive counter-terrorism doctrine was nicely summed up in a book on Israel's war with the PLO by William O'Brien, Professor of Government at Georgetown University. In the preface, O'Brien explained that the book was written with the co-operation of the government of Israel, including personal assistance from Netanyahu.[63] O'Brien explained that Israel's grand strategy involved striking pre-emptively at the *sources* of terrorism, and not at just the terrorists, so that the states harbouring armed groups were also hit:

> Israel's military grand strategy has been to deter, prevent and pre-empt PLO terrorist attacks and to contain them promptly and efficiently when they occur. Above all, from the early days of the *fedayeen* incursions and continuing throughout the war with the PLO, Israel's grand strategy has been to strike the sources of terrorism, not relying on passive defense alone. The purpose of these strikes has been to make the terrorists insecure as well as to inflict material damage on their personnel and facilities.[64]

O'Brien explained that although Israel would often attack groups believed to have been directly involved in terrorist attacks, "it may also attack other PLO targets, thought to be important, that have nothing to do with the terrorist actions recently experienced".[65]

Among O'Brien's many doctoral students at the University of Georgetown was John Bellinger Jnr, whose son, John Bellinger III, served in the Bush administration as Senior Associate Counsel to the President and Legal Adviser to the National Security Council when NSS-2002 was drafted.[66]

61 Toaldo, *The Origins of the US War on Terror*, p. 109.
62 Ibid.
63 William V. O'Brien, *Law and Morality in Israel's War with the PLO* (Routledge 1991), p. vii.
64 Ibid., p. 20.
65 Ibid., p. 25.
66 John B. Bellinger, Jr. passed away on 14 December 2011, and was interred at the Arlington National Cemetery. According to his biography, in the 1960s, Bellinger helped to persuade the Joint Chiefs of Staff to replace Massive Retaliation with the new strategy of a Flexible Response among strategic nuclear, theatre nuclear and

The drafting of *NSS-2002*

Following the adoption of NSDD-138 (1984),[67] the USA claimed that it needed to anticipate imminent threats in Libya (1986), Panama (1989), Iraq (1993) and Afghanistan (1998). However, the USA did not make a broad claim that pre-emption was a strategy recognised by international law until the publication of NSS-2002. Significantly, NSS-2002 did not limit pre-emption to the counter-terrorism context but included all types of threats – from forces that present an "imminent danger of attack" to states in possession of WMD "that can be delivered covertly, and without warning".

NSS-2002 was a conscious and deliberate effort to rewrite grand strategy for the coming decades, much in the way that Paul Nitze's historic NSC-68 provided the blueprint for the militarisation of the Cold War from 1950 to the collapse of the Soviet Union in 1991.[68] As Philip Zelikow, Executive Director of the 9/11 Commission and Counsellor to Secretary of State Condoleezza Rice, recalls, "For those who did not live through the 9/11 attacks, it is difficult now to conjure up the atmosphere of those times, especially as it affected the state of mind of those charged with leading the nation".[69] Published in the run-up to the Iraq War in March 2003, NSS-2002 also caught the world's headlines as the blueprint for the invasion:

> For centuries, international law recognized that nations need not suffer an attack before they can lawfully take action to defend themselves against forces that present an imminent danger of attack. Legal scholars and international jurists often conditioned the legitimacy of preemption on the existence of an imminent threat—most often a visible mobilization of armies, navies, and air forces preparing to attack. We must adapt the concept of imminent threat to the capabilities and objectives of today's adversaries. Rogue states and terrorists do not seek to attack us using conventional means.
>
> They know such attacks would fail. Instead, they rely on acts of terror and, potentially, the use of weapons of mass destruction—weapons that can be easily concealed, delivered covertly, and used without warning. The targets of these attacks are our military forces and our civilian population … As was demonstrated by the losses on September 11, 2001, mass civilian casualties is

conventional non-nuclear responses to aggression against US interests. In the 1970s, "under the mentorship of Dr. William O'Brien and Dr. Jeane Kirkpatrick, he completed his doctoral dissertation on decision-making in arms control, which explained how the perspectives of different U.S. agencies contributed to a balanced national decision". The testimonial for John B. Bellinger, Jr. can be read at the following link: http://apps.westpointaog.org/Memorials/Article/16534/.

67 See National Security Decision Directive 138, 3 April 1984, p. 3 (emphasis added).

68 Condoleezza Rice, *No Higher Honor: A Memoir of My Years in Washington* (Crown Publishers 2011), p. 153.

69 See Philip Zelikow, "US Strategic Planning in 2001–2" in Melvyn P. Leffler and Jeffrey W. Legro (eds), *In Uncertain Times: American Foreign Policy after the Berlin Wall and 9/11* (Cornell University Press, 2011), p. 104.

> the specific objective of terrorists and these losses would be exponentially more severe if terrorists acquired and used weapons of mass destruction.
>
> The United States has long maintained the option of preemptive actions to counter a sufficient threat to our national security. The greater the threat, the greater is the risk of inaction—and the more compelling the case for taking anticipatory action to defend ourselves, even if uncertainty remains as to the time and place of the enemy's attack. To forestall or prevent such hostile acts by our adversaries, the United States will, if necessary, act preemptively.[70]

This was a grand departure from the language used in Article 51 of the UN Charter, which requires an armed attack to have occurred before a state can respond in self-defence.[71] The Charter says nothing about using force pre-emptively to counter *threats* to national security. Using armed force against *threats* is something that is reserved for the Security Council.[72] States do not always have to wait to be attacked before they may defend themselves, however. The USA and the UK have long argued that a state may act in self-defence to anticipate an attack that is imminent; that has been launched before it hits its target.[73] But the UN Charter does not give states a right to use force against *threats* that have not materialised into armed attacks. Nor does the Charter give a right to states to *prevent* armed attacks that might arise at some point in the future. This is to safeguard against aggression.

For a document that acquired such infamy, it was perhaps not surprising that no one wanted to claim authorship of it. This did not stop scholars from speculating. Stefan Halper and Jonathan Clarke drew parallels between NSS-2002 and the *Defense Planning Guidance* drawn up by Paul Wolfowitz and I. Lewis "Scooter" Libby in 1992 when they were aides to Secretary of Defense Dick Cheney.[74] However, Zelikow, one of the drafters of NSS-2002, denies a connection.[75] Elisabeth Bumiller, author of a biography of Condoleezza Rice, then serving as the

70 *The National Security Strategy of the United States of America* (September 2002), p. 15.

71 See Art. 51 UN Charter (quoted in the introduction). According to Schlesinger, the USA rejected a British proposal to delete the word "armed attack" that would permit action against every sort of aggression, direct and indirect. The USA was worried that broader phraseology would allow states too great a leeway, including the right of preventive actions, which it was feared would wreck the organisation, given that the First and Second World Wars had both begun with preventive attacks. See Stephen C. Schlesinger, *Act of Creation: The Founding of the United Nations* (Westview Press 2004), pp. 184–185.

72 See Article 39 UN Charter.

73 See Waldock, "The Regulation of the Use of Force by Individual States in International Law", p. 498. See also Michael Wood, "International Law and the Use of Force: What Happens in Practice?" 53 *Indian Journal of International Law* (2013), p. 345 at p. 357.

74 Stefan Halper and Jonathan Clarke, *America Alone: The Neo-Conservatives and the Global Order* (Cambridge University Press 2004), pp. 145–146.

75 Ibid., p. 146. Interview with Philip Zelikow, University of Virginia, 12 November 2015.

National Security Advisor, pointed the finger at Zelikow for authoring the pre-emption language,[76] while Zelikow pointed the finger at John Bellinger, who was legal adviser to the National Security Council when NSS-2002 was drafted.[77]

Bellinger says that he edited the language in the first draft of NSS-2002 in an attempt to make it comport with the doctrine of anticipatory self-defence as reflected in the case of the *Caroline*.[78] This may explain why NSS-2002 uses the word "preemption" with "anticipatory action" and the verb "prevent" in the same paragraph. The confusion arises because many scholars associate pre-emption with prevention. As we shall see, this was also a confusion that befuddled Rice and Rumsfeld, with Rumsfeld asking William Haynes, General Counsel of the Department of Defense, for an info memo on whether there was "any significant difference" between "preemption", "preventive self-defense" and "anticipatory self-defence".[79] Haynes responded to Rumsfeld explaining that the DoD Dictionary of Military Terms defined pre-emptive attack as one "initiated on the basis of incontrovertible evidence that an enemy attack is imminent". Preventive war was defined as one "initiated in the belief that military conflict, while not imminent, is inevitable, and that to delay would involve greater risk". In Haynes' view, international law "recognizes no difference between 'preemption', 'preventive self-defense', and 'anticipatory self-defense'". He wrote "these terms all refer to the right to use force based on the existence of an imminent threat but prior to an armed attack".[80]

In her memoir, Rice explains that she asked Zelikow to take the pen for the first draft of the National Security Strategy, but that subsequent drafts were kept tightly under her control as it went through an interagency process piloted by Steve Biegun, the executive secretary of the National Security Council.[81] According to Zelikow, the initial draft of the National Security Strategy did not use the word pre-emption.[82] Rice and Hadley[83] inserted it, he explains, "but only to describe how the United States would deal with enemy terrorist groups such as al-Qaeda. The part of the strategy that discussed outlaw states thought to have WMD, such as Iraq, used a different verb: 'prevent'."[84] Zelikow adds that in July

76 See Elisabeth Bumiller, *Condoleezza Rice: An American Life* (Random House 2007), p. 193.
77 See Zelikow, "US Strategic Planning in 2001–2" in Leffler and Legro (eds), *In Uncertain Times*, p. 96 at pp. 113–114 and at p. 215 notes 61 and 64.
78 Interview with John Bellinger III, Arnold and Porter LLP, Washington, DC, 17 November 2015.
79 See Info Memo FOR: Secretary of Defense. FROM: William J. Haynes. SUBJECT: Legal Distinction between Preemption, Preventive Self-Defense, and Anticipatory Self-Defense. October 16, 2002, 4:00 PM. Available online at *The Rumsfeld Papers*.
80 Ibid. This conclusion is odd, given Haynes's own admission that the DoD Dictionary of Military Terms required of pre-emption "*incontrovertible evidence* of an armed *attack*", not just the *threat* of an attack.
81 Rice, *No Higher Honor*, p. 153.
82 Zelikow has usefully deposited the early drafts of the National Security Strategy (which are unclassified) on the website of the University of Virginia at http://faculty.virginia.edu/zelikow/documents/nationalsecuritypolicy.pdf (*The Zelikow Papers*)
83 Steven Hadley was the deputy national security adviser.
84 Zelikow, "US Strategic Planning in 2001–2", *In Uncertain Times*, p. 113.

2002, "Rice and some of her advisers, especially her lawyer, John Bellinger, became uncomfortable with saying that a possible war might be preventive. The phrase 'preventive war', had bad associations in nineteenth-century European and early 1950s Cold War history."[85] But to Rice, Zelikow explains, there was no other way to head off the menace. To her, pre-empting a WMD threat became identical with prevention and these terms were just semantic nuances.[86]

Significantly, the section on pre-emption was moved from the chapter on al-Qaeda and terrorism, its original home, to the chapter on WMD, when the link between terrorists and their use of WMD was made explicit.[87] These changes were made to the National Security Strategy when Zelikow was no longer involved in the drafting process, and was controversial, given that the case for invading Iraq was based on the claim that not only was Saddam Hussein still pursuing a weapons programme, but that he was also in direct communication with terrorist groups linked to al-Qaeda. These claims were false, and according to CIA director George Tenet were concocted by Douglas Feith and his team at the Pentagon.[88] In an email that Rumsfeld sent to Paul Wolfowitz and Feith dated 16 October 2002, Rumsfeld boasted that one of their "important accomplishments" after 9/11 was the "linkage of terrorist networks with WMD" and that self-defence against terrorism "requires preemption".[89] According to the Iraq Inquiry, as early as 18 March 2002, Wolfowitz told Sir Christopher Meyer, the United Kingdom's Ambassador to the United States, that the "WMD danger … was crucial to the public case against Saddam, particularly the potential linkage to terrorism".[90]

Given the link and subsequent criticism of the section on pre-emption in NSS-2002, Rice gave a lecture organised by the Manhattan Institute at the Waldorf Astoria Hotel in New York City on 1 October 2002.[91] In her speech, Rice explained that new technologies required new thinking about when a threat

85 Ibid.

86 Zelikow quotes an interview that Rice gave in 2002, in which Rice explained to a reporter for *The New York Times* that "preemption or anticipatory defense, self-defense or however you want to put it, by whatever name you want to call it … really means early action of some kind". See ibid. citing a transcript of an interview between Rice and *The New York Times* correspondent David Sanger.

87 Ibid., p. 114.

88 See George Tenet, *At the Center of the Storm: My Years at the CIA* (HarperCollins 2007), pp. 346–358.

89 While the email is dated 16 October 2002 the accompanying paper is undated but was obviously written earlier. SUBJECT: Important Accomplishments. FROM: Donald Rumsfeld. TO: Paul Wolfowitz, Doug Feith, Torie Clarke, Larry di Rita. October 16, 2002 8:46 AM. Available online at *The Rumsfeld Papers.*

90 See Section 3.2. Development of UK Strategy and Options, January to April 2002 – "Axis of Evil" to Crawford, p. 456, para. 395. *The Report of the Iraq Inquiry* chaired by Sir John Chilcot can be accessed online at the following link: www.iraqinquiry.org.uk/the-report/

91 See the Manhattan Institute 2002 Walter B. Wriston Lecture, Waldorf Astoria Hotel, 1 October 2002 by Condoleezza Rice, "A Balance of Power that Favors Freedom", which can be read online at www.manhattan-institute.org/html/2002-wriston-lecture-balance-power-favors-freedom-5566.html

becomes imminent and that as a matter of common sense the United States had to be prepared to take action, when necessary, before *threats* fully materialised. She added that pre-emption was not a new concept and that there had never been a moral or legal requirement that a state had to wait to be attacked before it could address existential threats.[92] Significantly, Rice quoted Shultz in support of pre-emption: "If there is a rattlesnake in the yard, you don't wait for it to strike before you take action in self-defense."

The hour of the hawks

Rice's decision to quote Shultz in her address at the Waldorf Astoria Hotel is intriguing. This is because Shultz was the most forceful proponent of pre-emption in the Reagan administration, and because Rice quoted a sentence from a commentary Shultz published in *The Washington Post* on 6 September 2002 – two weeks before the publication of NSS-2002 – calling for immediate military action against Iraq.[93] Earlier, Shultz had also advocated pre-emption at an address he gave to Foreign Service Officers to unveil the George P. Shultz National Foreign Affairs Training Center in Arlington, Virginia on 29 May 2002.[94] Shultz gave this speech three days before Bush's West Point speech (1 June 2002) where Bush used the word pre-emption for the first time.[95] In his address to the Foreign Service Officers on 29 May, Shultz recalled his speeches on pre-emption from his time as Secretary of State in 1984, quoting an interview that Secretary of Defense Donald Rumsfeld gave to Jim Lehrer that favoured taking the battle to the terrorists.[96] Shultz explained that, "we reserve, within the framework of our right to self-defense, the right to preempt terrorist threats *within a state's borders*".[97] Shultz also advocated going after the terrorists pre-emptively at a talk on global security that he delivered at the Stanford Institute for Economic Policy on 16 January 2002,[98] and one month after 9/11.[99]

92 Ibid. Bellinger, the NSC legal adviser, drafted this language. Interview with John Bellinger III, Arnold and Porter LLP, Washington, DC, 17 November 2015.
93 George Shultz, "Act Now: The Danger Is Immediate; Saddam Hussein Must Be Removed", *The Washington Post*, 6 September 2002, p. A25.
94 See George P. Shultz, "Hot Preemption", *Hoover Digest*, 2002. No. 3 (July) adapted from remarks delivered at the dedication of the George P. Shultz National Foreign Affairs Training Center in Arlington, Virginia on 29 May 2002. This can be accessed online at the following link: www.hoover.org/research/hot-preemption The speech was reported in the press: see William Safire, "Al Qaeda Provoking War", *The New York Times*, 30 May 2002, p. 25; Jim Hoagland, "Heading Off Terrorism", *The Washington Post*, 2 June 2002, p. B07.
95 See "Text of Bush's Speech at West Point", *The New York Times*, 1 June 2002. www.nytimes.com/2002/06/01/international/text-of-bushs-speech-at-west-point.html?_r=0
96 Shultz, "Hot Preemption", *Hoover Digest*, 2002. No. 3 (July).
97 Ibid. (emphasis added).
98 Mark Zavislak, "George Shultz Speaks at Hoover", *Stanford Review*, Volume XXVII, Issue 6, 30 January 2002.
99 George Shultz, "This Is an Act of War", *Hoover Digest*, 30 October 2001.

Shultz appeared to be echoing Netanyahu in these speeches. Recall that in his speech to the Jonathan Conference on International Terrorism in Washington in 1984, Netanyahu had spoken of the right to take action against terrorist threats in hot pursuit, retaliation or pre-emption.[100] Netanyahu had also articulated a broad doctrine of pre-emptive self-defence when, as Israel's UN Ambassador, he defended Israel's raid on Tunis in 1985 by insisting that the states that harboured terrorists were just as guilty as the terrorists.[101] This preceded the US raid on Libya in 1986 that was based on the same doctrine.[102] In his speech to Congress, one week after 11 September 2001, President Bush said the USA was going to "pursue nations that provide aid or safe haven to terrorism" as well as the terrorists.[103] Going after the states that harboured terrorism as well as the terrorists themselves, was the Netanyahu doctrine in all but name.[104] Writing in the immediate aftermath of 9/11, Netanyahu could confidently assert that:

> To win this war, we must fight on many fronts. The most obvious one is direct military action against the terrorists themselves. Israel's policy of pre-emptively striking at those who seek to murder its people is, I believe, *better understood today and requires no further elaboration.*[105]

In a speech that Netanyahu delivered to the American Enterprise Institute in March 2002, he claimed that two of the world's state sponsors of terrorism – Iran and Iraq – were rapidly acquiring nuclear weapons and warned Americans that "[t]hese weapons could mete out destruction on a scale that would dwarf even the towering tragedies of September 11".[106] Netanyahu repeated this warning in a commentary he published a month later in *The Wall Street Journal*, when he called for the terrorist regimes in the Middle East to be swept away.[107]

100 See Netanyahu, *Terrorism: How the West Can Win*, p. 220.
101 See United Nations Security Council Official Records, Fortieth Year, 2611th meeting, 2 October 1985, UN doc. S/PV.2611, at p. 6, paras 65–66.
102 See Christopher Greenwood, "International Law and the United States Air Operation against Libya", 89 *West Virginia Law Review* (1986–1987), p. 933. Mary Kaldor and Paul Anderson (eds), *Mad Dogs: The US Raids on Libya* (Pluto Press 1986); Daniel G. Partan and Francis Boyle, "Military Responses to Terrorism", 81 *Proceedings of the Annual Meeting (American Society of International Law)*, (1987), p. 288.
103 See the text of President Bush's address to a joint session of Congress and the nation on 20 September 2001 reprinted in *The Washington Post* (20 September 2001): www.washingtonpost.com/wp-srv/nation/specials/attacked/transcripts/bushaddress_092001.html.
104 See Benjamin Netanyahu, "The Strategy to End Terrorism", 18(4) *New Perspectives Quarterly* (Fall 2001), pp. 58–65.
105 Ibid., p. 64 (emphasis added).
106 See the remarks of former Israeli prime minister Benjamin Netanyahu at a recent discussion held at the American Enterprise Institute in Washington, DC, reprinted in 13 (2) *American Enterprise Institute* (March 2002), p. 47.
107 Benjamin Netanyahu, "The Root Cause of Terrorism", *The Wall Street Journal*, Eastern edition, 19 April 2002, p. A.18.

Rumsfeld also called for a pre-emptive strategy to combat terrorism in a speech he delivered at the National Defense University in Washington, DC on 31 January 2002.[108] This speech was delivered five months before Bush's West Point Speech. Rumsfeld said that "defending the U.S. requires prevention, self-defense, and sometime preemption".[109] In one of Rumsfeld's "snowflakes" dated 10 May 2002, Rumsfeld wrote "it is not possible to defend against terrorism in every place, at every time, against every conceivable technique. Self-defense against terrorism requires preemption—taking the battle to the terrorists wherever they are and to those who harbour terrorists."[110] This snowflake was subsequently shared with Vice President Cheney before the publication of NSS-2002.[111]

The timing of Shultz's address to the Foreign Service officers on 29 May and the timing of Bush's West Point speech on 1 June is striking *as days later* the following paragraph appeared in the mid-June draft of the National Security Strategy after White House discussions:

> For centuries, international law has recognized that nations need not suffer an attack before they can lawfully take action to defend themselves against forces that present an imminent danger of attack. Preemption can include any action to forestall or prevent hostile acts by our adversaries—from law enforcement actions to interdictions to use of force.
>
> The United States has long maintained the option to take preemptive actions if there is a sufficient threat to our national security. The contemporary threats of terrorism and weapons of mass destruction have rendered this option more important than ever before. The greater the threat, the greater the risk of inaction—and the more compelling the case for taking anticipatory action to defend ourselves, even if uncertainty remains as to the time and place of the enemy's attack. Where the capabilities and intentions of our foes are clear, the justification for acting promptly to thwart their plans is strong.
>
> Our Nation does not have a blanket policy of preempting emerging threats by force – nor does any Nation have a blank check under international law to invoke preemption as a pretext for aggression. Yet preemptive use of force can be justified when nations confront a clear and present danger of attack. And, in an age where the enemies of civilization itself are openly and actively

108 See Secretary Rumsfeld speaks on "21st Century Transformation" of US Armed Forces, National Defense University, Fort McNair, Washington, DC, 31 January 2002.

109 Ibid.

110 See Donald Rumsfeld SUBJECT: Major Directional Decisions 00 9/1//01 et seq. May 10, 2002 11:42 AM. Available online at *The Rumsfeld Papers.*

111 TO: Vice President Richard B. Cheney. FROM: Donald Rumsfeld. SUBJECT: Decisions. September 3, 3003 2:55 PM. "Attached is the paper I pulled together on threads, with respect to the war on terrorism". Available online in *The Rumsfeld Papers.*

seeking the world's most destructive technologies, the United States will not remain idle while dangers gather.[112]

Significantly, this was the first time pre-emption appeared in relation to terrorism and WMD. It was also the first draft to mention international law, although the claim that for centuries international law had recognised that nations need not suffer an attack before they can lawfully take action to defend themselves against forces that present an imminent danger of attack was not without controversy. There is some disagreement between Zelikow and Bellinger over who drafted the original pre-emption language in the mid-June draft of the National Security Strategy, which was inserted by Rice, and which is strikingly similar to the section that would finally appear in NSS-2002 with minor changes.[113] Zelikow had even struck out the first and third paragraphs quoted above, and they do not appear in the drafts of the National Security Strategy dated 24 June nor 12 July. But they reappeared in the final form of the National Security Strategy on 17 September, after Rice took sole control of the drafting process, and after the section had been edited by National Security Council (NSC) staff (including Bellinger).[114]

According to documents released by the UK's Iraq Inquiry, it would appear that the language on pre-emptive self-defence was reinserted into NSS-2002 to provide an alternative basis for military action against Iraq, in case the UN did not provide a basis for military action. In other words, it was the quid pro quo demanded by the hawks in the Bush administration for acquiescing to British pleas to seek authorisation from the UN Security Council through an ultimatum in a

112 Draft "Basic National Security Policy of the United States," undated (mid-June 2002) with annotations reflecting White House discussions of the draft at p. 11 in *The Zelikow Papers.*

113 Interview with Philip Zelikow, University of Virginia, 12 November 2015. Interview with John Bellinger III, Arnold and Porter LLP, Washington DC, 17 November 2015. Following my interviews there was an exchange of correspondence between Zelikow and Bellinger. In Zelikow's recollection, the revisions that Bellinger thought that he sent to Steve Beigun was actually sent to him while he was still holding the pen, even if Bellinger thought he was sending them to Biegun. Bellinger insists that he was not the primary drafter of the whole section. He wrote: "It's not clear to me whether he [Zelikow] is concerned about the whole preemption concept (that concerns me less as long as it is correctly stated), the language I added (which I believe helped to clarify the concept), or both. I continue to believe the language I added both in the NSS and in Rice's Wriston lecture is correct as a matter of international law. You will note that Obama Admin officials state in their officials [*sic*] defending drone strikes that the 'imminence' standard of anticipatory self-defense must be treated flexibly when dealing with terrorists planning threats." Email correspondence with Zelikow dated 25 November 2015. Email correspondence with Bellinger dated 1 December 2015.

114 See suggested insert from NSC staff (including legal adviser John Bellinger) for draft policy, "IV. Combatting the Threat of Weapons of Mass Destruction" undated (July 2002), in *The Zelikow Papers.*

resolution before undertaking military action.[115] On 12 September, five days before NSS-2002 was published, Netanyahu told Congress that it was time to launch a pre-emptive strike against Iraq to dismantle Saddam Hussein's regime because his nuclear programme had "fundamentally changed" since Israel's 1981 raid on Osirak.[116]

The spectre of nuclear terrorism

As mentioned, the section on pre-emption in the draft National Security Strategy was moved from the chapter on al-Qaeda and terrorism, its original home, to the chapter on WMD, where the link between terrorism and WMD was made explicit. This meant that pre-emption appeared in the chapter on terrorism and the chapter on WMD. In his memoir, Rumsfeld explains that he asked Feith (then number 3 in the Pentagon, after Wolfowitz) to consider the broader principles involved in planning the war in Iraq in light of the failure of the UN to contain Saddam's regional ambitions. Some of the questions Rumsfeld asked Feith to consider included the circumstances when the US could act alone, when it was reasonable to conclude that all means short of war had failed, and when pre-emptive action to forestall a threat was justified.

In response to Rumsfeld's request, Feith produced a memo titled "Sovereignty and Anticipatory Self-Defense".[117] The document, which can be downloaded from *The Rumsfeld Papers*, is dated 24 August 2002 – after pre-emption first appeared in the mid-June draft of the National Security Strategy – but before pre-emption was reinserted into the final draft of the National Security Strategy that was published on the 17 September 2002.[118] Unsurprisingly, given the title of the memorandum, Feith wrote that, although anticipatory self-defence introduced instability and unpredictability into the international system, "the source of that problem is the proliferation of weapons of mass destruction, of which the doctrine of anticipatory self-defense is the inevitable result".[119]

Rumsfeld had also asked William Haynes II, General Counsel of the Department of Defense, for an "Info Memo" on anticipatory self-defence, which Haynes submitted to the Secretary of Defense on 2 August 2002.[120] Haynes's memo

115 See Section 3.3. Development of UK Strategy and Options, April to July 2002 on the website of the report of *The Iraq Inquiry*. See also, Section 3.4 Development of UK Strategy and Options, Late July to 14 September 2002, p. 109, para. 86.

116 See "Benjamin Netanyahu Testified about Iraq to Congress", CNN Live Event, 12 September 2002, http://transcripts.cnn.com/TRANSCRIPTS/0209/12/se.07.html

117 "Sovereignty and Anticipatory Self-Defense, 24 August 2002, OSD Policy, available with *The Rumsfeld Papers* at http://papers.rumsfeld.com/. It is also reproduced by Feith in his book. See Douglas J. Feith, *War and Decision: Inside the Pentagon at the Dawn of the War on Terrorism* (HarperCollins, 2008), pp. 295–298.

118 "Sovereignty and Anticipatory Self-Defense", 24 August 2002, OSD Policy, ibid., p. 1.

119 Ibid., p. 3.

120 FOR: Secretary of Defense. FROM: William J. Haynes III, General Counsel. SUBJECT: Anticipatory Self-Defense, August 2, 2002, 10:30 AM. INFO MEMO. Available online at *The Rumsfeld Papers*.

explained that the UN Charter did not create the right of self-defence under customary international law, "nor does it limit it".[121] Haynes wrote that the 1837 *Caroline* case "is generally cited as establishing the right of 'anticipatory self-defense' under customary international law" and referenced US practice on anticipatory self-defence (including the Cuban Missile Crisis, Libya, Panama, Iraq and Afghanistan) to support the claim that this practice accorded with customary international law.[122] Haynes then drew attention to the problem of WMD and anticipatory self-defence:

> With the advent of nuclear and other sophisticated weapons and the potential for terrorists to obtain such weapons, the degree of imminence required to justify using force in anticipatory self-defense arguably should be seen differently: *the threat need not be as demonstrably imminent* if there is an increased risk of occurrence and an increased magnitude of harm.[123]

Significantly, this "Info Memo" preceded the publication of a similar opinion by the Office of Legal Counsel of the Department of Justice on the Iraq War, which argued in favour of a new standard of imminence for anticipatory self-defence.[124] It would therefore appear that the most forceful proponents of pre-emptive self-defence were within the Pentagon where Rumsfeld, Wolfowitz and Feith held sway. Yet there did not appear to be any dissension or push back from the other branches of the US government that were responsible for providing legal advice to the executive – such as the State Department Legal Adviser or the Legal Adviser at the NSC. Significantly, Bellinger was chairman of the interagency lawyers group when NSS-2002 was drafted, and presumably would have been privy to this exchange of advice.[125]

According to a classified Pentagon report that was shared with Congress on 8 January 2002 and obtained by the *Los Angeles Times*, the Bush administration had directed the military to prepare contingency plans to use nuclear weapons against seven countries (China, Russia, Iraq, North Korea, Iran, Libya and Syria) and to build smaller tactical nuclear weapons.[126] Arms control advocates explained that the report's directives on tactical nuclear weapons were a signal that the Bush

121 Ibid., p. 1.

122 Ibid., p. 2.

123 Ibid., p. 2 (emphasis added).

124 See "Authority of the President under Domestic and International Law to Use Military Force against Iraq" in *Opinions of the Office of Legal Counsel of the United States Department of Justice*, vol. 26 (2002) www.justice.gov/olc/file/623846/download, p. 194. The opinion was signed by Assistant Attorney General Jay S. Bybee (23 October 2002).

125 John Bellinger, "Charlie Savage and the NSC Lawyers Group", *Lawfare*, 8 November 2015. ("When I was NSC Legal Adviser from 2001–2005, I chaired the lawyers group and continued to use it to review numerous national security legal issues, including intelligence operations and counterterrorism matters.")

126 See Paul Richter, "U.S. works up plan for using nuclear arms", *LA Times*, 9 March 2002, p. A2.

administration was more willing to overlook the longstanding taboo against the use of nuclear weapons except as a last resort.[127] It was thought that the willingness to use such weapons would provide a credible deterrent against regimes involved in international terrorism and the development of WMD.[128]

In December 2002, *The National Security Strategy to Combat Weapons of Mass Destruction* was published.[129] The very first sentence of the strategy claimed that WMD in the possession of hostile states and terrorists "represent one of the greatest security challenges facing the United States".[130] The document claimed that because deterrence may not succeed, and because of the potentially devastating consequences of WMD use against our forces and civilian population, "U.S. military forces and appropriate civilian agencies must have the capability to defend against WMD-armed adversaries, including in appropriate cases through preemptive measures".[131]

We do not know whether the two memorandums on anticipatory self-defence written by Feith and Haynes were the only documents produced on the subject. Nor do we know whether the request for an opinion on anticipatory self-defence was connected to the classified Pentagon report, which suggested that the Bush administration was willing to use nuclear weapons against rogue regimes in the event of an imminent and grave threat. Nor do we know whether Feith and Haynes were involved in any of the earlier discussions with Rice and Steven Hadley at the NSC. Feith tells us that Rumsfeld would often bring Wolfowitz to meetings of the NSC, but that after Feith had been appointed Under Secretary the task increasingly became his.[132] According to Feith, Rumsfeld directed that Feith's paper on anticipatory self-defence be sent to Rice, who then distributed it to Vice President Dick Cheney, Secretary of State Colin Powell, General Myers, Tenet, White House Chief of Staff Andrew Card and Presidential Counsel Alberto Gonzales as background for the 27 August Principals Committee meeting on Iraq. Rice also sent copies to all the Deputies.[133] Given that Feith's memo was sent to Rice, Powell and their deputies, one might assume that the legal adviser at the NSC and State Department were privy to it. In any event, it would appear that Haynes's memo and Feith's paper on anticipatory self-defence would have strengthened the hand of those in the administration who wanted the section on pre-emption reinserted back into the National Security Strategy before it was published on 17 September. It is also significant that Feith's paper was shared with the Principals Committee in connection with the looming conflict in Iraq since it may have been requested to provide an alternative basis for the military invasion.

127 Ibid.
128 *LA Times*, 9 March 2002, p. A2.
129 *The National Security Strategy to Combat Weapons of Mass Destruction* (December 2002).
130 Ibid., p. 1.
131 Ibid., p. 3.
132 Feith, *War and Decision*, p. 54.
133 See the note with an asterisk at the bottom of p. 295 in Feith, *War and Decision*.

In addition to being close to Netanyahu,[134] Feith was an associate of Richard Perle who served six years in the Reagan administration as Assistant Secretary of Defense for Global Affairs in the Pentagon. Perle stepped in to rescue Feith's career when, by Feith's own account, Feith upset several people in the State Department's Near East Affairs bureau when he was a junior adviser at the National Security Council for the memos he wrote criticising their analyses and facts and sometimes changing them before they were seen by Reagan.[135] Perle was one of the few advisers who saw eye to eye with Shultz, when Perle worked at the Pentagon with Weinberger. Perle was also a trusted confidant of Rumsfeld.[136] One year before the 2000 elections, Rice asked Perle to join Bush's foreign-policy team when he was Governor of Texas "to represent the right-wing of the Republican foreign policy establishment".[137] When, following the election, Perle turned down the position of Undersecretary of Defense for Policy in the Bush administration, Feith was given the position after securing an interview with Rumsfeld, on the recommendation of Perle, Fred Iklé and Wolfowitz, while Perle accepted an appointment as chairman of the Defense Policy Board Advisory Committee.[138]

Like Feith, Perle looked to Israel as his model for US counter-terrorism policy, particularly Israel's 1981 preventive strike on Iraq's nuclear facilities. In an address to the Foreign Policy Research Institute in Washington on 30 November 2001, Perle told the audience that going after al-Qaeda and Taliban was not enough. The next phase in the war against terrorism had to be Iraq, and with the example of Israel's 1981 strike in Iraq in mind, Perle wanted the US to emulate Israel by taking pre-emptive action:

> So the question in my mind is do we wait for Saddam and hope for the best, do we wait and hope he doesn't do what we know he is capable of, which is distributing weapons of mass destruction to anonymous terrorists, or do we take some preemptive action. In 1981 the Israelis faced a similar question. The Iraqis were about to complete the construction of a French nuclear reactor at Osirak and they decided that the risk of waiting was just too great and so they destroyed that reactor in a breathtaking effective bombing run.[139]

Note the link that Perle makes between the contemporary threats of terrorism and WMD that rendered the option of pre-emption "more important than ever

134 See Benjamin Netanyahu, *A Durable Peace: Israel and its Place among the Nations* (Warner Books 1993), p. 465 where Netanyahu thanks Feith for suggesting "important revisions" to the manuscript.
135 Feith, *War and Decision*, pp. 35–36.
136 See Jacob Heilbrunn, *They Knew They Were Right: The Rise of the Neocons* (Doubleday, 2008), p. 232.
137 Rice, *No Higher Honor*, p. 4.
138 Feith, *War and Decision*, p. 42. See also Alan Weisman, *Prince of Darkness: Richard Pele* (Union Square Press 2007), p. 164.
139 See Richard Perle's speech, "Next Stop: Iraq", 30 November 2001, on the website of the Foreign Policy Research Institute at www.fpri.org/articles/2001/11/next-stop-iraq.

before" to paraphrase NSS-2002. The timing of Perle's speech to the Foreign Policy Research Institute is also intriguing. According to the UK's Iraq Inquiry, President Bush asked Rumsfeld to review existing battle plans for Iraq in November 2001, even though the UK's Joint Intelligence Committee concluded on 28 November 2001 "that Iraq had no responsibility for, or foreknowledge of, the attacks against the US on 11 November 2001".[140] Sir Kevin Tebbit, Permanent Under Secretary of State for the Ministry of Defence, told the Iraq Inquiry that Perle was one of the "most influential figures" on Secretary Rumsfeld's thinking.[141]

In his youth, Perle was close to Albert Wohlstetter, a giant in the field of strategic nuclear war,[142] through whom he came to know Paul Wolfowitz, when they left university in 1969 to work for the Committee to Maintain a Prudent Defense Policy in Washington.[143] Both men had been recruited by Wohlstetter, who was Wolfowitz's mentor at the University of Chicago, where Shultz was Professor of Industrial Relations, and Dean of the Graduate School of Business.[144] Wolfowitz's father was Professor of Mathematics at Cornell University (1951–1970) where Netanyahu's father was Professor of Judaic Studies (1962–1979).[145]

Whereas Wohlstetter argued for preventive deployment of weapons to enable a second strike capability in the event of a surprise nuclear attack from the Soviet Union,[146] Wolfowitz argued for pre-emptive action as the only way to assure order in a world in which it could no longer be assumed that nuclear-armed belligerents would behave rationally, especially in the chaos that might arise from disintegrating states with nuclear weapons in a post-Cold War world.[147] And the only country that had successfully resorted to pre-emptive strikes to destroy the nuclear capabilities of its enemies was Israel.[148]

140 See Section 3.1 of *The Report of the Iraq Inquiry*, 6 July 2016, pp. 352–353, paras 233 and 241.

141 Section 3.1 of *The Report of the Iraq Inquiry*, ibid. p. 377 para. 387.

142 Weisman, *Prince of Darkness*, pp. 16–17; Justin Vaïsse, *Neoconservatism: The Biography of a Movement* (Harvard University Press 2010), pp. 150–151; James Mann, *Rise of the Vulcans: The History of Bush's War Cabinet* (Viking 2004), p. 29. See also, Ron Robin, *The Cold World They Made: The Strategic Legacy of Roberta and Albert Wohlstetter* (Harvard University Press 2016), pp. 203–229.

143 Mann, *Rise of the Vulcans*, p. 31.

144 Ibid., p. 32; Shultz, *Turmoil and Triumph*, p. 28.

145 See Robin, *The Cold World They Made*, p. 204 and Caspit and Kfir, *Netanyahu*, p. 21. Benzion Netanyahu's tenure at Cornell overlapped with Jacob Wolfowitz's tenure between 1962 and 1970 when Wolfowitz retired. Wolfowitz passed away in 1981. See "Obituary: Jacob Wolfowitz, 71, Taught Math at Cornell and Columbia", *The New York Times*, 23 July 1981.

146 Albert Wohlstetter, "The Delicate Balance of Terror", 37 *Foreign Affairs* (1959), pp. 211–234.

147 See Khurram Husain, "Neocons: The Men Behind the Curtain", *Bulletin of the Atomic Scientists* November/December 2003, pp. 67–68.

148 Israel also destroyed a Syrian reaction in 2007. For the inside story see Elliott Abrams, *Tested by Zion: The Bush Administration and the Israeli–Palestinian Conflict* (Cambridge University Press, 2013), pp. 246–248.

Operation Opera

In his 18 November 2002 address to the Council on Foreign Relations, the State Department Legal Adviser William Taft explained that: "The President's National Security Strategy relies upon the same legal framework applied to the British in the *Caroline* and to Israel in 1981."[149] The *Caroline* was a reference to the Ashburton–Webster correspondence from 1837, which provided that anticipatory self-defence was limited to those instances where the necessity to act in self-defence was "instant, overwhelming, and leaving no choice of means, and no moment for deliberation".[150] Taft explained that the sole reason the United States voted in favour of the Security Council resolution condemning Israel's strike was because Israel had not exhausted all peaceful means for resolving its dispute with Iraq, not because the strike was viewed as going beyond the permissible scope of self-defence outlined in the *Caroline*.[151]

Taft's explanation of the US vote following Israel's bombing of Osirak as an example of "state practice" in support of the approach to self-defence taken by the Bush administration is intriguing because by Israel's own account, its actions went beyond anticipatory self-defence as outlined in the *Caroline*. Moreover, the United States came close to referring to Israel's actions as aggression when it voted in favour of the resolution that criticised Israel for bombing that reactor. That resolution strongly condemned "the military attack by Israel in clear violation of the Charter of the United Nations and the norms of international conduct".[152]

According to the UN record, the *Caroline* was mentioned in the Security Council debate to *distinguish* Israel's strike from anticipatory self-defence because it went beyond the necessity criteria identified in the *Caroline* correspondence. Although Israel resorted to pre-emptive strikes in the 1956 and 1967 wars, Israel did not justify these strikes by making a broad claim based on pre-emptive self-defence. Instead, Israel claimed that it had already been attacked – by Fedayeen incursions into the Gaza Strip from the Sinai in 1956 and by the regular Egyptian army in 1967 – arguments that were questionable on the facts but fully consistent with Article 51 of the UN Charter.[153] It was only following Israel's pre-emptive strike on an Iraqi nuclear reactor outside Baghdad in 1981 that Israel explicitly

149 Taft memorandum, CFR, 18 November 2002. This memorandum is available online at www.cfr.org/international-law/legal-basis-preemption/p5250.

150 Letter dated 27 July 1842, from Daniel Webster to Lord Ashburton (1841–1842) XXX *British and Foreign State Papers* 193–4, extract taken from Webster's earlier letter to Henry S Fox dated 24 April 1841, (1840–1841) XXIX *British and Foreign State Papers*, pp. 1137–8.

151 Taft memorandum, CFR, 18 November 2002 (no paragraph numbers).

152 See Security Council Resolution 487, 19 June 1981 (adopted unanimously).

153 On the Suez War, see the statement by Mr Eban, General Assembly, Official Records, First Emergency Special Session, 562nd Plenary Meeting, 1 November 1956, pp. 20–21 at para. 115. On the June 1967 war, see the statement by Mr Eban, Security Council, Official Records, Twenty-Second Year, 1348th Meeting, 6 June 1967, p. 15, para. 155. For analysis of Israel's role, see John Quigley, *The Six-Day War and Israeli Self-Defense: Questioning the Legal Basis for Preventive War* (Cambridge University Press 2013), pp. 59–112.

invoked its inherent right of self-defence to *abort* the Iraqi nuclear *threat* to Israel as a matter of *law*.[154] Significantly, during the Security Council debate, Israel rejected the concept of anticipatory self-defence in the *Caroline* correspondence as "emasculating" Israel's inherent right of self-defence.[155]

Yehuda Blum, Israel's UN Ambassador in 1981, explicitly *rejected* the *Caroline* standard of imminence[156] at the Security Council when he attempted to justify Israel's pre-emptive strike on Iraq's nuclear reactor, and was criticised for doing so by several of the council's members (especially for misquoting Waldock).[157] In other words, Blum was not claiming that Israel's actions amounted to anticipatory self-defence; he was making a wider claim and had difficulty justifying Israel's actions because there were few scholars he could cite and no instances of state practice.[158]

Perhaps Taft was trying to keep the NSS-2002 within existing law, hence the reference to the *Caroline*. The problem is we do not know if this was the intention of the lawyers at the NSC who advised Rice to insert the paragraph that appeared in the mid-June draft of the NSS-2002 who were probably trying to say something else. Moreover, Ambassador Jeane Kirkpatrick's speech to the Security Council was not an accurate reflection of the views of the State Department Legal Advisers.[159] In his memoir, Allan Gerson, Kirkpatrick's Legal Adviser at the US Mission to the UN, recalls that the State Department Legal Advisers had gone so far as to conclude that Israel's strike was an act of *aggression*, not an act of self-defence.[160]

The UK had also wanted to refer to the attack as aggression. According to a confidential telegram released in the British National Archives, the reason the UK did not refer to the attack as aggression was because Iraq sought to link such a

154 See the statement made by Ambassador Blum in the Security Council on 19 June 1981 in UN Doc. S/PV.2288, 19 June 1981, para. 79.

155 Ibid., para. 80.

156 See the statement made by Blum in Security Council, Official Record, 2288th meeting, 19 June 1981, UN Doc. S/PV.2288, para. 80.

157 Security Council, Official Record, 2288th meeting, ibid. para. 81. See the reply made by Ambassador Al-Qaysi in the same debate at paras 200–202. See also the comment by H G Darwin, Deputy Legal Adviser ("it appears from the recent New York telegram that the Israeli Representative in the Security Council quoted Sir Humphrey Waldock out of context ..."). See "Israeli Attack on Iraqi Nuclear Plant", FCO 93/2832. TNA. The reference to Waldock was a reference to a lecture he gave at The Hague Academy of International Law in 1952 that was published in *Recueil des Cours* 1952-II, p. 498.

158 The only scholars Blum could cite (apart from Waldock who he misquoted) were Stephen Schwebel and Myres McDougal. Tellingly, Blum did not refer to Israel's 1967 war as an example of "state practice", even though many scholars after 9/11 have referred to this case. See Quigley, *The Six-Day War and Israeli Self-Defense*, pp. 149–161.

159 See the speech by Kirkpatrick in Security Council, Official Record, 2288th meeting, 19 June 1981, UN doc. S/PV.2288, paras 20–36.

160 See Allan Gerson, *The Kirkpatrick Mission: Diplomacy without Apology America at the United Nations 1981–1985* (The Free Press 1991), p. 14. The State Department has not yet released its records on Osirak. My Freedom of Information Act request is pending.

finding to Chapter VII of the Charter that would have required enforcement measures against Israel. The Arab Bloc agreed to remove the reference to Chapter VII, until Kirkpatrick's intervention, when the reference to aggression was dropped from the resolution in exchange for a favourable US vote.[161] In other words, the only reason why the Security Council did not condemn Israel's strike on Osirak as *aggression* was because of Kirkpatrick's timely intervention.[162]

Conclusion

As a military strategy pre-emption may be justified as a deterrent, but to claim that pre-emption is a principle of law that is universally applicable to all states – friend and foe alike – is a dubious proposition at best and dangerous. Almost as soon as NSS-2002 was published, its paragraph on pre-emption was criticised for going beyond the UN Charter. The UK, usually so close to the USA in security matters, and one of the few countries to actively support and join the US military intervention in Iraq, even felt obliged to distance itself from NSS-2002. Peter Goldsmith, the Attorney-General, told Parliament: "international law permits the use of force in self-defence against an imminent attack but does not authorize the use of force to mount a pre-emptive strike against a threat that is more remote".[163]

The Report of the UN Secretary-General's High-Level Panel on Threats, Challenges, and Change likewise warned:

> in a world full of perceived potential threats, the risk to the global order and the norm of non-intervention on which it continues to be based is simply too great for the legality of unilateral preventive action, as distinct from collectively endorsed action, to be accepted. Allowing one to so act is to allow all.[164]

Indeed, almost as soon as NSS-2002 was published, India, Iran and Russia announced new doctrines of pre-emptive self-defence.[165] Unsurprisingly the *High-Level Panel* concluded that they "do not favour the rewriting or reinterpretation of Article 51".[166] Similarly, the UN's *World Summit Outcome* (2005) reaffirmed "that the relevant provisions of the Charter are sufficient to address the full range

161 See the correspondence in "Israeli Attack on Iraqi Nuclear Plant" in FCO 93/2829. TNA.
162 Gerson, *The Kirkpatrick Mission*, pp. 14–16.
163 See the statement by the UK's Attorney-General Lord Goldsmith on 21 April 2004 in Parliamentary Debates, House of Lords, (2004), pp. 370–371.
164 See *A More Secure World: Our Shared Responsibility, Report of the UN Secretary-General's High-Level Panel on Threats, Challenges, and Change* (United Nations 2004), p. 63, para. 191.
165 See W. Michael Reisman and Andrea Armstrong, "The Past and the Future of the Claim of Preemptive Self-Defense", 100(3) *The American Journal of International Law* (2006), pp. 545–546.
166 *A More Secure World*, p. 63, para. 192.

of threats to international peace and security".[167] However, despite these concerns, the USA (and, more recently, Australia and the UK) continues to espouse a broad doctrine of preventive self-defence with a view to persuading other states to repeal the language used in Article 51 of the UN Charter.[168]

As explained in this chapter, Shultz articulated a broad claim to pre-emptive self-defence when he was US Secretary of State in the Reagan administration after the attacks on the Marines in Lebanon, which found expression in NSDD-138. In making the case for pre-emptive self-defence, Shultz found support from Rumsfeld who had also been influenced by his personal experiences in the Middle East. The country they both identified with that directly influenced their views was Israel, which had a comprehensive pre-emptive counter-terrorism strategy already in place. However, it was only during Israel's 1981 raid on Osirak that a legal argument was advanced based on pre-emptive self-defence, although the Security Council rejected the argument. Netanyahu then embarked on a quest to convince American policymakers of the legitimacy of a pre-emptive strategy to deter acts of terrorism against the USA in the hope that other states would follow the US lead by emulating it.

Following the attacks on 9/11, pre-emption found its way into the NSS-2002 in the summer of 2002 after repeated calls from Shultz who had helped advance the careers of Rice, Rumsfeld and Wolfowitz by lobbying to get them positions in the Bush administration.[169] Five days before the publication of NSS-2002, Netanyahu called on the USA to eliminate the threat posed by Iraq by engaging in pre-emptive regime change in a hearing before the US Congress. In the fall of 2002, the Bush administration began advocating an invasion of Iraq on the spurious claim that Saddam Hussein's regime was a threat to the USA. The link between terrorism and WMD began to be articulated amidst claims circulating in the US press that Saddam's regime had connections to the 9/11 hijackers and other international terrorist organisations. In August 2002, William Haynes, General Counsel of the Department of Defense, prepared a legal opinion for Rumsfeld arguing that the concept of imminence had to be redefined with the advent nuclear and other sophisticated weapons and the potential for terrorists to obtain such weapons. Accordingly, Haynes explained that threats to the USA need not be as demonstrably imminent to enable it to attack another state in self-defence.

The pre-emption language in the draft National Security Strategy in July 2002 was objected to by Zelikow, and removed from subsequent drafts. But Rice reinserted pre-emption back into the National Security Strategy in August 2002 after the section had been edited by NSC staff (including by Bellinger), when the USA

167 General Assembly Resolution 60/1, 2005 Word Summit Outcome, 24 October 2005, p. 22 para. 79.

168 See Victor Kattan, "Furthering the 'war on terrorism' through international law: how the United States and the United Kingdom resurrected the Bush doctrine on using preventive military force to combat terrorism", 5(1) *Journal on the Use of Force and International Law* (2018), pp. 97–144.

169 Mann, *Rise of the Vulcans*, p. 116, pp. 225–226, pp. 250–251 and p. 269.

had committed itself to regime change in Iraq.[170] Following the publication of NSS-2002 on 17 September 2002, Rice gave a lecture at the Waldorf Astoria Hotel on 1 October in which she explained that new technologies required new thinking about when a threat becomes imminent and that as a matter of common sense the USA had to be prepared to take action, when necessary, before *threats* fully materialised. Two weeks later, Rumsfeld boasted to Wolfowitz and Feith that one of their important accomplishments in NSS-2002 was the linkage of terrorist networks with WMD and that self-defence against terrorism required pre-emption.

170 According to David Sanger, Chief Washington correspondent for *The New York Times*, "A legal adviser in the White House insisted Webster's elements are present in the Iraq confrontation. The threat is overwhelming, because his weapons could be used against American allies, including Israel, or slipped to a terrorist for delivery there." See David E. Sanger, "Beating Them to the Prewar", *The New York Times*, 28 September 2002, p. B7.

2 United States legal and policy approaches in the Global War on Terrorism

Milena Sterio[1]

> Every nation in every region now has a decision to make: Either you are with us or you are with the terrorists.[2]

Introduction

The War on Terror (WoT), also known as the Global War on Terrorism (GWoT), is a term invented by United States President George W. Bush in the wake of the 9/11 terrorist attacks on the World Trade Center.[3] These two terms have been used initially to refer to the international military campaign that started after the 9/11 attacks on the United States.[4] The Bush administration, as well as most Western media outlets, have since used these terms to designate a more global struggle, of a military, legal, and geopolitical nature, against terrorists, terrorist organizations, and various world regimes supporting them.[5] In 2013, President Barack Obama announced that the United States was no longer pursuing a War on Terror. According to President Obama, "We must define our effort not as a boundless 'Global War on Terror,' but rather as a series of persistent, targeted efforts to dismantle specific networks of violent extremists that threaten

1 I would like to thank the Cleveland-Marshall College of Law for its generous research support during this project.

2 George W. Bush Speech to Congress, September 20, 2001, available at www.washingtonpost.com/wp-srv/nation/specials/attacked/transcripts/bushaddress_092001.html.

3 President Bush coined the term "War on Terror" in his now famous speech, delivered on September 20, 2001, in which he emphasized the purportedly global nature of the fight against terrorism: "This is not … just American's fight. And what is at stake is not just America's freedom. This is the world's fights. This is civilization's fight. This is the fight of all who believe in progress and pluralism, tolerance and freedom." *Id.*

4 As a result of September 11, the United States attacked Afghanistan and drove out the Taliban, and in 2003, the United States invaded Iraq to remove Saddam Hussein. Lee Kuan Yew, *The United States, Iraq and the War on Terror: A Singaporean Perspective*, 86 *Foreign Affairs* 1 (January/February 2007).

5 *Encyclopedia Britannica*, War on terrorism, available at www.britannica.com/topic/war-on-terrorism.

America."[6] In reality, despite the change in presidential rhetoric, many of the policies and features of President Bush's War on Terror were continued under President Obama, and, for the purposes of this chapter, various War on Terror tactics will be discussed and evaluated regardless of whether they occurred under President Bush or President Obama.

While the original focus of War on Terror strategies was on al-Qaeda and countries associated therewith, as it will be demonstrated in this chapter, the War on Terror has resulted in multiple international and domestic policies, military campaigns, and enhanced intelligence efforts throughout multiple world regions, and several domestic laws, which have affected non-al-Qaeda affiliated regions and organizations, as well as the United States internally. Thus, it is the conclusion of this chapter that the War on Terror has been "fought" in an unnecessarily broad manner with few geographic, temporal, or legal boundaries. This chapter will first discuss the overall scope of the War on Terror and, in this section, it will introduce the most important legal and policy initiatives, domestically and abroad, which were developed as part of the War on Terror. Next, this chapter will focus on the most significant aspects of the War on Terror: the use of drones (internationally), the National Security Agency (NSA) surveillance program (domestically), and the detention of terrorism suspects at the United States military base at Guantanamo Bay in Cuba, as well as the ensuing litigation.

It will be this chapter's conclusion that the War on Terror, although it may have begun as an anti-terrorism response to the 9/11 attacks, has in fact resulted in an enormous campaign including military, intelligence, diplomatic, and domestic dimensions, through which the United States has overstepped its boundaries and has engaged in harmful behavior – by infringing upon the sovereignty on other states and by curtailing the personal freedoms of American citizens. This chapter will conclude that while the War on Terror has produced some tangible anti-terrorism results, its benefits may have been outweighed by some of the war's most aggressive policies, which have violated both international law as well as civil liberties of Americans domestically.

The large scope of the War on Terror

The War on Terror, which began as a counterterrorism operation in the wake of 9/11, relatively quickly morphed into a multidimensional campaign of almost limitless scope. Its first dimension has been military, and it has involved major wars in Afghanistan and Iraq, covert operations in Yemen and elsewhere through the use of drones as well as other military tactics, large-scale military-assistance programs for various friendly regimes, and major increases in military spending.[7] Most military efforts, which have embraced the use of military force by the United States in foreign countries, were domestically justified through the passage of an Authorization to Use Military

6 Paul D. Shinkman, "Obama: 'Global War on Terror' Is Over," *U.S. News & World Report*, May 23, 2013, available at www.usnews.com/news/articles/2013/05/23/obama-global-war-on-terror-is-over.

7 *Britannica, supra* note 5.

Force (AUMF) law in 2001.[8] The AUMF has been relied upon to justify direct military efforts in Afghanistan in the months following 9/11, but also remote and indirect military uses of force since 2001 and, until the present, in places such as Pakistan, Yemen, and Somalia. As the section below will discuss, the AUMF has been relied upon by both the Bush and the Obama administrations to justify the lethal use of drones in several countries, including in Pakistan, Yemen, and Somalia.

Its second dimension has focused on intelligence, and it has included efforts such as internal institutional reorganization, as well as considerable increases in the funding of America's intelligence-gathering capabilities.[9] In addition, the intelligence dimension has embraced a global program of capturing terrorist suspects and interning them at Guantanamo Bay, a United States military base located in Cuba, expanded cooperation with foreign intelligence agencies, and the tracking and interception of terrorist financing.

Its diplomatic dimension has included continuous efforts to construct and maintain a global coalition of partner states and organizations and an extensive public diplomacy campaign to counter anti-Americanism in the Middle East. Its domestic dimension has entailed new antiterrorism legislation, such as the USA PATRIOT Act, new security institutions, such as the Department of Homeland Security, the preventive detainment of thousands of suspects, surveillance and intelligence-gathering programs by the NSA, the Federal Bureau of Investigation (FBI), and local authorities, the strengthening of emergency-response procedures, and increased security measures for airports, borders, and public events.[10]

Thus, the War on Terror has shaped United States law and policy in multiple arenas over the past 15 years, in a manner which very few other world events have. It will be this chapter's ultimate conclusion that the War on Terror has been overbroad and may have in reality harmed American interests—by damaging America's reputation internationally, contributing to the rise of anti-American Islamist militant groups, and abridging important civil liberties domestically – while achieving relatively little. In order to demonstrate this point, the following sections will address the most significant aspects of the War on Terror, including the use of drones to conduct surveillance as well as killings, the NSA surveillance program, and the detention of terrorism suspects at Guantanamo Bay.

Use of drones

In the aftermath of the terrorist attacks of September 11, 2001, President Bush authorized dozens of drone strikes against terrorist suspects; President Obama

8 The Authorization to Use Military Force (AUMF) authorizes the President to "use all necessary and appropriate force against those nations, organizations, or persons" that he determines in some way aided the attacks of 9/11, in order to prevent any future acts of international terrorism against the United States. Authorization to Use Military Force, S. J. Res. 23, 107th Cong. (2001) (enacted), section 2(a); Pub. L. No. 107–40, § 2(a), 115 Stat. 224, 224 (2001).

9 *Britannica, supra* note 5.

10 *Id.*

continued this practice and expanded the scope of the United States' use of drones.[11] According to investigative reports, President Obama authorized a total of 373 drone strikes in Pakistan alone during his presidency, compared with 424 strikes in total, authorized by the Bush and the Obama administrations combined.[12] As part of the overall War on Terror, drone strikes have been conducted in traditional theatres of war, such as Afghanistan, Iraq, and Libya; in these places, drones have been operated by the Department of Defense. In addition, drone strikes have been used in other countries where the United States is not waging an armed conflict against state actors, but where terrorism suspects have been found, such as Pakistan, Somalia, and Yemen.[13] In the latter set of countries, drones are used in counter-terrorism operations; they are operated by the Central Intelligence Agency (CIA), and the contours of any drone policy in this paradigm remain vague.[14]

The CIA refused to acknowledge the existence of the drone program itself until recently,[15] and even after the Agency and the Obama administration admitted that drones are used in covert operations in places such as Pakistan and Yemen, unanswered questions remain regarding the official targeting policy, the intelligence

11 According to one commentator, "[u]nder Obama, drone strikes have become too frequent, too unilateral, and too much associated with the heavy-handed use of American power." See David Rohde, How Obama's Drone War Is Backfiring, Reuters.com, March 1, 2012, available at http://blogs.reuters.com/david-rohde/2012/03/01/how-obamas-drone-war-is-backfiring/.

12 The Bureau of Investigative Journalism, Get the data: Drone Wars, available at www.thebureauinvestigates.com/category/projects/drones/drones-graphs/. According to the Bureau of Investigative Journalism, between 2004 and 2016, the United States has conducted a total of 424 strikes in Pakistan, a total of confirmed 146–166 strikes in Yemen, and a total of possible 90–107 additional strikes, and a total of 32–36 confirmed strikes in Somalia. Id.

13 Ashley S. Boyle, Contextualizing the Drones Debate, American Security Project, August 2012, available at www.scribd.com/doc/102775947/Contextualizing-the-Drones-Debate.

14 Jane Mayer, The Predator War: What Are the Risks of the C.I.A.'s Covert Drone Program?, *New Yorker*, October 26, 2009, available at http://newyorker.com/reporting/2009/10/26/091026fa_fact_mayer.

15 The American Civil Liberties Union (ACLU) filed a Freedom of Information Act request in January 2010 with the Department of Defense, the Department of Justice (including the Office of Legal Counsel), the Department of State, and the CIA, asking for information regarding the legal and factual basis for the government's use of predator drones to conduct "targeted killings" overseas. The CIA denied the request by refusing to confirm or deny whether the CIA drone strike program existed. The ACLU filed a second lawsuit against the CIA in June 2010, arguing that the CIA's response was not lawful because the CIA Director and other officials had already publicly acknowledged the existence of the CIA's drone program. The District Court ruled in favor of the CIA, and the ACLU appealed to the DC Circuit Court of Appeals. In March 2013, the appellate court reversed the lower court's decision, ruling that the CIA could no longer deny its interest in the program. The DC Circuit Court of Appeals remanded the case to the district court, where the CIA will have to release documents that respond to the ACLU's request or legally justify withholding them. See ACLU, Predator Drones FOIA, available at www.aclu.org/national-security/predator-drones-foia.

information that forms the core of a targeting decision, and any appropriate oversight before each strike, as well as after-the-fact. This dimension of the American War on Terror has been particularly troublesome, and may have violated multiple international law provisions. What if the CIA is wrong about a significant number of its targets, and what if the American public simply does not know that the CIA is wrong? The executive branch's approach to this issue has been to argue that the American public needs to trust the president on national security issues—but in this case, trusting the president implies that he forms the judge, jury, and executioner regarding terrorism suspects who may be targeted via drone strikes. Ultimately, because very little information has been available about the CIA drone program, it is impossible to determine in which aspects the program may have violated international law.

The United States government, under the Bush and Obama administrations, has argued that the use of drones as part of the overall War on Terror is legal both internationally and domestically. The United States officials have argued that the use of drones is legal under international law, because the United States is exercising its right to self-defense against non-state actors, which operate out of sovereign nations that are unable or unwilling to combat such terrorism-inclined non-state actors. According to John Brennan, who at the time served as Assistant to President Obama on Homeland Security and Counterterrorism,

> The United States does not view our authority to use military force against al-Qa'ida as being restricted solely to "hot" battlefields like Afghanistan. Because we are engaged in an armed conflict with al-Qa'ida, the United States takes the legal position that—in accordance with international law—we have the authority to take action against al-Qa'ida and its associated forces without doing a separate self-defense analysis each time. And as President Obama has stated on numerous occasions, we reserve the right to take unilateral action if or when other governments are unwilling or unable to take the necessary actions themselves.[16]

According to this view, the battlefield against terrorism suspects knows no geographic boundaries, and drone strikes may be carried out both within a recognized theater of active armed conflict, such as Afghanistan and Iraq, but also in countries which either consent to drone strikes or appear unwilling or unable to combat non-state terrorist actors, such as Pakistan (consent), Somalia, and Yemen. "U.S. officials have argued that the fight with AUMF enemies is global, not confined to the territory of one country."[17] In other words, the United States government has argued that it is engaged in a non-international armed conflict with al-Qaeda, the

16 Remarks of John O. Brennan, Strengthening Our Security by Adhering to Our Values and Laws, Harvard Law School, September 16, 2011, available at www.whitehouse.gov/the-press-office/2011/09/16/remarks-john-o-brennan-strength ening-our-security-adhering-our-values-an [hereinafter Brennan Speech].

17 Ryan Vogel, Drone Warfare and the Law of Armed Conflict, 39 *Denv. J. Int'l L. & Pol'y* 101, 108 (2010–2011)

Taliban, and associated forces, and that almost any member of al-Qaeda, the Taliban, or associated forces is targetable. According to the legal rationale advanced by then Legal Advisor to the State Department Harold Koh, deciding

> whether a particular individual will be targeted in a particular location will depend upon considerations specific to each case, including those related to … The sovereignty of the other states, involved, and the willingness and ability of those states to suppress the threat the target poses.[18]

This rationale would arguably exclude the possibility of conducting drone strikes in countries that are able and willing to combat terrorist threats, but would allow the United States to use lethal force in self-defense, in the territory of countries that are not engaged in any armed conflict against the United States but which harbor al-Qaeda and Taliban associates. It is uncertain whether the United States would, under this rationale, choose to conduct drone strikes in "neutral states," such as Kenya, the Philippines and Saudi Arabia, which do appear willing and capable to combat terrorist groups within their borders, in a scenario where high-level terrorist suspects were located in these countries. What is unquestionable is that the United States has consistently argued that because it is engaged in an armed conflict of a global nature, the so-called War on Terror, the law of armed conflict applies in each instance, regardless of the location of each drone strike. It can be argued, therefore, that under the views of both the Bush and the Obama administrations, location of drone strike matters but it is not prohibitive. Location matters because drone strikes cannot be carried out in countries that have not consented or that are able and willing to combat terrorist threats; location is not prohibitive because drone strikes can be carried out in any country that has consented or that is not able or willing to combat terrorist threat. A scholar has described the United States' approach to defining lawful targets in the following manner: "that any military aged male in a kill zone is properly determined to be targetable".[19]

Thus, under the guise of War on Terror, the United States has engaged in aggressive and at times lethal behavior on the territory of multiple sovereign nations. This behavior has alienated many nations as well as contributed toward the rise of militant anti-American groups, which may someday engage in terrorist activity against the United States. Thus, while drone strikes have neutralized a number of al-Qaeda and Taliban operatives, they may have also violated international law and may have contributed to fueling future terrorist activity directed against the United States.[20]

18 Harold Koh, Legal Adviser, US Department of State, Address at the Annual Meeting of the American Society of International Law (March 25, 2010), available at www.state.gov/s/l/releases/remarks/139119.htm.

19 Gabor Rona, The Last Word (for now) on Targeted Killings: Rona Responds to Lewis, Opiniojuris.org, August 3, 2012, available at http://opiniojuris.org/2012/08/03/the-last-word-for-now-on-targeted-killings-rona-responds-to-lewis/.

20 For a discussion about whether drone strikes have produced anti-Americanism in Pakistan, see Madiha Afzal, Drone Strikes and Anti-Americanism in Pakistan,

As mentioned above, the Bush and the Obama administrations have also claimed that the use of drones in legal under domestic law—both under the Constitution as well as under federal law. The Bush and the Obama administrations have both cited the AUMF, a Congressional statute passed in the wake of September 11 terrorist attacks on the United States, which authorizes the use of force against leaders of al-Qaeda forces, to target or to kill enemies, as justification for the use of drones against terrorist suspects.[21] The argument that drone strikes are specifically authorized through the AUMF goes as follows: because members of al-Qaeda and the Talban can constitute a continuing threat to the safety of the United States, eliminating such continuing threat via drone strikes is a means to prevent future acts of international terrorism.[22] The AUMF specifically authorizes the president to do this, and this expansive reading of the AUMF would place almost no limitations on the president's authority to wage the so-called War on Terror.[23] While the Obama administration stopped using the term "War on Terror," it interpreted the AUMF in virtually the same way as the Bush administration.[24]

Many scholars have disagreed with this type of expansive interpretation of the AUMF.[25] Moreover, this rationale invites a host of legitimate questions regarding the localization of ongoing drone strikes. For example, how do we know that drone strikes conducted presently are truly linked to al-Qaeda forces responsible for the attacks of September 11 (because only those targets are contemplated through the AUMF)? What is the link between current terrorism suspects targeted through CIA drone operations and al-Qaeda and Taliban leaders present and engaged in the conflict back in 2001? And why does this conflict have no geographic boundaries? Accepting the AUMF as authorization for the use of lethal force by the United States against those responsible for the attacks of September 11 does not amount to

Brookings Institution, February 7, 2013, available www.brookings.edu/opinions/drone-strikes-and-anti-americanism-in-pakistan/.

21 See AUMF, *supra* note 8; see also Vogel, *supra* note 17, at 107–08 (noting that the Bush and Obama administrations have cited the AUMF as justification for the use of drones against terrorist suspects).

22 Vogel, *supra* note 17, at 108.

23 "War on Terror" was a term coined by the Bush administration, to describe the conflict that the United States entered as of September 11, 2001, against those responsible for the terrorist attacks of September 11, 2001. While the AUMF does not use the term "war on terror," it does provide the president with authority to use force against "nations, organizations, or person" which the president determined "planned, authorized, committed, or aided" the terrorist attacks of September 11, as well as those who "harbored such organizations or persons." See Vogel, *supra* note 17, at 108, n. 37. Moreover, the AUMF contemplates a global war against specific terrorist groups, such as al-Qaeda, the Taliban, and associated forces. *Id.* at 108.

24 Vogel, *supra* note 17, at 108.

25 One of the most vocal opponents of this type of rationale has been Professor Mary Ellen O'Connell. See, e.g., Mary Ellen O'Connell, Unlawful Killing with Combat Drones: A Case Study of Pakistan, 2004–2009, in *Shooting to Kill: Socio-Legal Perspectives on the Use of Lethal Force*, 263–92 (Simon Bronitt, Miriam Gani, and Saskia Hufnagel eds., 2011), Oxford: Hart Publishing.

accepting the AUMF as a perpetual statutory authorization to use deadly force through covert operations throughout the world against suspects who may have only circumstantial ties to the masterminds of September 11. Because most lethal drone strikes are conducted through covert CIA operations, we do not know whether suspects targeted today are those covered by the AUMF.

While some scholars have been sympathetic to the United States' rationale for the use of drones as part of its War on Terror[26]—because modern-day conflicts oppose state versus non-state actors, who often do not have a strict territorial nexus to any particular state—many others have been critical. Some scholars have criticized the United States for its expansive definition of the battlefield, arguing that

> the United States is engaged in armed conflict in Afghanistan. To lawfully resort to military force elsewhere requires that the country where the United States is attacking has first attacked the United States (such as Afghanistan in 2001), the U.N. Security Council has authorized the resort to force (Libya in 2011) or a government in effective control credibly requests assistance in a civil war (Afghanistan since 2002).[27]

According to this view, the battlefield where the United States could legally engage in military operations can lie in Afghanistan only pursuant to the self-defense rationale, and in Libya, pursuant to Security Council authorization. The battlefield may not lie in places such as Pakistan, Somalia, or Yemen, because the United States is not engaged in armed conflict in those places. The United States' government position, on the contrary, has consistently been that the battlefield follows al-Qaeda, Taliban, and associated forces members, and that, accordingly, the United States can launch a strike anywhere that such persons may be found. Others have criticized the covert nature of the CIA-led drone operations as an important facet of the War on Terror, and have called for more transparency and accountability regarding the drone program.[28] Finally, national security experts have questioned the perpetual reliance on the AUMF and have argued that the president should request contemporaneous Congressional authorization for the use of force.[29]

26 Laurie R. Blank, After "Top Gun": How Drone Strikes Impact the Law of War, 33 *U. Pa. J. Int'l L.* 675, 679 (2012). ("Once we are outside the belligerent–neutral framework that defined the traditional battlespace, determining the parameters of the contemporary battlefield or zone of combat becomes significantly more complicated.")

27 Mary Ellen O'Connell, When Are Drone Killings Legal?, CNN.com, August 16, 2012, available at www.cnn.com/2012/08/15/opinion/oconnell-targeted-killing/.

28 See, e.g., Milena Sterio, The Covert Use of Drones: How Secrecy Undermines Oversight and Accountability, 8 *Alb. Govt. L. Rev.* 129 (2015); Amos N. Guiora, The Importance of a Criteria-Based Reasoning in Targeted Killing Decisions, in *Targeted Killings: Law & Morality in an Asymmetrical World*, 303–25 (Claire Finkelstein, Jens David Ohlin, and Andrew Altman eds., 2012), Oxford: Oxford University Press.

29 See, e.g., Adam Jacobson, Obama Shouldn't Rely on 2001 AUMF for ISIL Fight, *Human Rights First*, March 12, 2015, available at www.humanrightsfirst.org/blog/obama-shouldn-t-rely-2001-aumf-isil-fight (arguing that President Obama should not

Because of the dubious legal rationale advanced by the United States for the use of drones, as part of its War on Terror—allowing the United States to pursue relentless drone strikes anywhere in the world and against any individual with tenuous links to al-Qaeda—it is this chapter's conclusion that the War on Terror has overstepped domestic and international legal boundaries, has encroached upon the sovereignty of foreign nations and has alienated potential United States' partners in the global fight against terrorism.

NSA surveillance program

In the wake of 9/11, as part of the overall War on Terror, the NSA began an electronic surveillance program entitled the Terrorist Surveillance Program. This specific program was part of the President's Surveillance Program, which was in turn conducted under the overall umbrella of the War on Terror.[30] Initially, NSA implemented the program to intercept al-Qaeda communications overseas where at least one party is not a US citizen. In reality, it appears that many purely domestic communications were intercepted and that the NSA may have stored billing and phone records of countless US citizens.[31]

The NSA's electronic surveillance program's legality is questionable because of the fact that the program had not been authorized or reviewed by a Foreign Intelligence Surveillance Act (FISA) Court, as well as because of the program's inherent secrecy. FISA explicitly applies to "electronic surveillance for foreign intelligence information" performed within the United States.[32] The most difficult

legally rely on the 2001 AUMF in his military efforts against ISIL and that, instead, President Obama should seek a new use-of-force authorization from Congress); Harold Hongju Koh, Ending the Forever War: One Year After President Obama's NDU Speech, *Just Security*, May 23, 2014, available at www.justsecurity.org/10768/harold-koh-forever-war-president-obama-ndu-speech/ ("Almost thirteen years after 9/11, it is increasingly problematic to rely on the 2001 AUMF to conduct all of America's counterterrorism operations. We should not use a broadly worded 13-year old AUMF text drafted for a prior situation to conduct perpetual armed conflict against a mutating group of terrorist networks").

30 Electronic Frontier Foundation, How the NSA's Domestic Spying Program Works, available at www.eff.org/nsa-spying/how-it-works.

31 See, e.g., Dana Priest & William Arkin, A Hidden World, Growing Beyond Control, *The Washington Post*, July 19, 2010, available at http://projects.washingtonpost.com/top-secret-america/articles/a-hidden-world growing-beyond-control/print/ (noting that the NSA intercepts and stores 1.7 billion emails, phone calls, and other types of communications every day).

32 Foreign Intelligence Surveillance Act of 1978, 50 U.S.C. ch. 36. Other legal sources relevant for the purposes of determining the legality of warrantless surveillance activities by the US government domestically include the Fourth Amendment to the US Constitution, Executive Order 12333, and United States Signals Intelligence Directive 18. For an excellent discussion of these legal sources and their applicability to the NSA surveillance program, see David Alan Jordan, Decrypting the Fourth Amendment: Warrantless NSA Surveillance and the Enhanced Expectation of Privacy Provided by Encrypted Voice Over Internet Protocol, 47 *Boston Coll L. Rev.* 1 (2006); *US Constitution, IV Amendment, and Katz v. United States*, 389 U.S. 347 (1978) (holding

and important legal issues regarding the NSA surveillance program include whether the parameters of the program are subject to FISA and, if so, whether President Bush had the authority to bypass FISA. No court decision or other explicit precedent exists supporting the argument that the president has constitutional authority to allow him to override statutory law itself (FISA). Thus, several prominent constitutional law scholars have argued that the president does not have authority to bypass a statute like FISA.

> The argument that conduct undertaken by the commander in chief that has some relevance to 'engaging the enemy' is immune from congressional regulation finds no support in, and is directly contradicted by, both case law and historical precedent. Every time the Supreme Court has confronted a statute limiting the commander in chief's authority, it has upheld the statute. No precedent holds that the president, when acting as commander in chief, is free to disregard an Act of Congress, much less a criminal statute enacted by Congress, that was designed specifically to restrain the president as such.[33]

Critics of the Bush administration have compared the current NSA surveillance program to those of Richard Nixon during the Vietnam War, such as Project Shamrock and Project Minaret.[34] According to these Bush administration critics, FISA was passed into law in response to widespread concerns over possible surveillance activities and abuses under President Nixon, in order to ensure that future presidents would be subject to judicial oversight when authorizing domestic surveillance programs.[35] Thus, according to this argument, President Bush did not

that the Fourth Amendment prohibition against unreasonable searches and seizures also applies to wiretapping); Executive Order 12333, United States Intelligence Activities, December 4, 1981, amended by Executive Order 13355, Strengthened Management of the Intelligence Community, August 27, 2004 and Executive Order 13470, July 30, 2008 (Executive Order 12333, and the two subsequent Executive Orders which amended it, has been regarded by the American intelligence community as a fundamental document authorizing the expansion of data collection activities, including the post 9/11 NSA surveillance program); see Spencer Ackerman, NSA Reformers Dismayed after Privacy Board Vindicates Surveillance Dragnet: Privacy and Civil Liberties Oversight Board Endorses Agency's So-called '702' Powers, Plus Backdoor Searches of Americans' Information, *Guardian*, July 2, 2014, available at www.theguardian.com/world/2014/jul/02/nsa-surveillance-government-privacy-board-report; see also Nat'l Sec. Agency/Cent. Sec. Serv., United States Signals Intelligence Directive 18 (July 27, 1993) [hereinafter USSID 18], available at http://www.gwu.edu/~nsarchiv/ NSAEBB/NSAEBB23/07–02.htm (declassified version with some language redacted by the NSA).

33 Letter to Members of Congress, February 2, 2006, available at https://balkin.blogspot.com/FISA.AUMF.ReplytoDOJ.pdf.

34 John W. Dean, George W. Bush as the New Richard M. Nixon: Both Wiretapped Illegally, and Impeachably; Both Claimed That a President May Violate Congress' Laws to Protect National Security, *Findlaw*, December 30, 2005, available at http://writ.news.findlaw.com/dean/20051230.html.

35 See, e.g., Ben O'Neill, FISA, the NSA, and America's Secret Court System, Mises Institute, February 22, 2014, available at https://mises.org/library/fisa-nsa-and-am

have authority to bypass FISA, the purpose of which was to limit presidential power by imposing court oversight over surveillance activities. In addition, the American Bar Association and the Congressional Research Service, as well as several former politicians and White House officials, have all criticized the Bush administration's justification for conducting electronic surveillance within the US without first obtaining warrants as contrary to FISA processes.[36] In addition, five former FISA Court judges have resigned in protest over this issue.[37]

The NSA surveillance program is thus legally problematic because it operated without the judicial oversight mandated by FISA. As a result, several legal challenges to the program have been brought and one case, a lawsuit brought by the Al-Haramain Foundation, is currently undergoing judicial review.[38] Another lawsuit brought by the American Civil Liberties Union (ACLU) on behalf of journalists, scholars, and lawyers was ultimately dismissed by an appellate court due to lack of standing.[39] At the initial trial, however, a US District Judge had ruled the program unconstitutional and had imposed an injunction on it.[40] In 2007, Attorney General Alberto Gonzales announced that the program would not be reauthorized by President Bush as such, but that any subsequent surveillance programs would be conducted subject to approval of the FISA Court.[41] In 2013, it was revealed that the original Terrorist Surveillance Program was replaced by a new NSA program under the code word PRISM.[42]

President Bush has defended the legitimacy of the surveillance program, despite its lack of FISA Court authorization. Bush claimed that he had reviewed and

erica%E2%80%99s-secret-court-system (noting that the FISA court was created as a result of intelligence scandals over the previous decades, and "as an additional safeguard against unlawful activity by US intelligence agencies, which had been found to have committed various kinds of unlawful surveillance activities").

36 See The American Bar Association Resolution, February 13, 2006, available at www.americanbar.org/content/dam/aba/migrated/op/greco/memos/aba_house302_0206.authcheckdam.pdf; Congressional Research Service Memorandum, January 5, 2006, available at https://fas.org/sgp/crs/intel/m010506.pdf; Dean, *supra* note 34.

37 Eric Lichtblau, Judges on Secretive Panel Speak Out on Spy Program, *The New York Times*, March 29, 2006, available at http://www.nytimes.com/2006/03/29/washington/judges-on-secretive-panel-speak-out-on-spy-program.html

38 Carol D. Leonnig & Mary Beth Sherridan, Saudi Group Alleges Wiretapping by U.S.: Defunct Charity's Suit Details Eavesdropping, *The Washington Post*, March 2, 2006, available at Carol D. Leoninig, Saudi Group Alleges Wiretapping by U.S.: Defunct Charity's Suit Details Eavesdropping.

39 Sarah Karush, Feds Appeal Ruling on Surveillance, *The Informational Blog*, August 18, 2006, available at https://unodude.wordpress.com/2006/08/18/days-of-my-life-feds-appeal-ruling-on-surveillance/.

40 *Id.*

41 Letter from Alberto Gonzalez, Attorney General, to Senators Patrick Leahy and Arlen Specter, January 17, 2007 (on file with author).

42 Barton Gellman & Laura Poitras, U.S. Intelligence Mining Data from Nine U.S. Internet Companies in Broad Secret Program, *The Washington Post*, June 7, 2013, available at www.washingtonpost.com/investigations/us-intelligence-mining-data-from-nine-us-internet-companies-in-broad-secret-program/2013/06/06/3a0c0da8-cebf-11e2-8845-d970ccb04497_story.html?utm_term=.3bb59fe6975b.

reauthorized the program approximately every 45 days since it was implemented. He also claimed that the leadership of the House and Senate intelligence committees had been briefed several times since the program's inception. In addition, it has come to light that several terrorists or potential terrorists were caught in the United States through NSA surveillance and communication interception. Thus, some terrorist attacks may have been thwarted through this NSA program.[43] These arguments do not on their own provide solid legal ground for the NSA surveillance programs. Although congressional leaders may have known about the basics of this program, a general briefing of such leaders does not equate to judicial oversight, which was mandated through FISA. Moreover, although a small number of potential attacks may have been thwarted through the surveillance program, it is questionable whether this seemingly small benefit outweighs the enormous cost of the surveillance program coupled with its continuous infringement upon the civil liberties of American citizens. Finally, the program's secrecy poses additional challenges.

It is difficult to assess the legality of the NSA surveillance program because of its inherent secrecy. The program's contours have remained confidential, and questions linger as to how the NSA intercepts communications, which communications are routinely tracked, and which may be stored indefinitely. Orin Kerr, a prominent legal scholar, has argued that the program is probably not a wiretap or call database, but more likely a pen register (or tap-and-trace) tap.[44] Unlike wiretaps, where the actual content of the call is monitored, or listened to, a pen register is a limited form of wiretap where only basic call data (metadata) such as originating and receiving telephone numbers, time of call, and duration are logged. Because of the limited nature of the data, frequently characterized as "outside the envelope," pen register taps have much lower legal standards than conventional wiretaps, and are not subject to Fourth Amendment protection. If the NSA is performing tap registers as opposed to traditional wiretaps, then the

43 For example, senior government officials have claimed that as many as 50 terrorist plots were foiled through NSA surveillance, in a hearing before the House Intelligence Committee in 2013. See Ellen Nakashima, Officials: Surveillance Programs Foiled More than 50 Terrorist Plots, *The Washington Post*, June 18, 2013, available at www.washingtonpost.com/world/national-security/officials-surveillance-programs-foiled-more-than-50-terrorist-plots/2013/06/18/d657cb56-d83e-11e2-9df4-895344c13c30_story.html?utm_term=.b05ad366cd6c. These claims have been disputed, however. See Jenna McLaughlin, U.S. Mass Surveillance Has No Record of Thwarting Large Terror Attacks, Regardless of Snowden Leaks, *The Intercept*, November 17, 2015, available at https://theintercept.com/2015/11/17/u-s-mass-surveillance-has-no-record-of-thwarting-large-terror-attacks-regardless-of-snowden-leaks/ (noting that "[d]espite the intelligence community's attempts to blame NSA whistleblower Edward Snowden for the tragic attacks in Paris on Friday, the NSA's mass surveillance programs do not have a track record—before or after Snowden—of identifying or thwarting actual large-scale terrorist plots").

44 Orin Kerr, Thoughts on the Legality of the Latest NSA Program, *The Volokh Conspiracy*, May 11, 2006, available at http://volokh.com/2006/05/11/thoughts-on-the-legality-of-the-latest-nsa-program/.

agency would not be subject to the Fourth Amendment.[45] Because little public information is available about the NSA surveillance program, it is impossible to determine whether the agency has been violating the Fourth Amendment or not. Some physical evidence supports the argument that the NSA may be performing pen registers—documents accidentally leaked to lawyers for an al-Qaeda affiliated group contain only logs of phone calls being placed, but not actual transcripts, suggesting that the wiretapping program may be a pen-register tap, as opposed to a traditional wiretap.[46] However, it is not entirely clear that NSA surveillance consists only of pen-register taps and not of traditional wiretaps and it is thus not clear that the Fourth Amendment does not apply. If the Fourth Amendment applies, it would seriously limit NSA's surveillance activity.

In sum, the NSA surveillance program which began as a counterterrorism operation in the wake of 9/11 has most likely been overbroad and has likely subjected American citizens to NSA surveillance, in violation of FISA and possibly the Fourth Amendment. The domestic harm inflicted on Americans through the NSA surveillance program has most likely outweighed the program's limited benefits (of having potentially intercepted some terrorist communication, which could have been intercepted anyhow had the surveillance program been overseen by FISA judges).

Guantanamo

The third facet of the War on Terror has been the indefinite detention of terrorism suspects at the Guantanamo Bay military base in Cuba. The first group of terrorism suspects arrived at Guantanamo in January 2002—a few months after 9/11. Although the Bush administration claimed that most of these detainees had been captured while fighting against the United States in Afghanistan, it appears that many were sold to the United States military in Afghanistan and Pakistan in exchange for monetary bounties.[47] Thus, the "capture" of at least some Guantanamo detainees is problematic and does not appear justified through any true anti-terrorism strategy. At that time, Secretary of Defense Donald Rumsfeld maintained that the purpose of the camp at Guantanamo was to detain extremely dangerous individuals, to interrogate high value suspects in an optimal setting and to prosecute

45 As a general matter, the Supreme Court has never authorized warrantless wiretapping within the United States, because of the Fourth Amendment's prohibition on unreasonable searches and seizures. See Letter, *supra* note 41. Because of the NSA surveillance program's inherent secrecy, it is very difficult to ascertain whether the program could be exempt from the Fourth Amendment. *Id.*

46 Ryan Singel, Top Secret: We're Wiretapping You, *Wired*, March 5, 2007, available at http://archive.wired.com/science/discoveries/news/2007/03/72811?currentPage=all.

47 Scott B. Horton, Law School Study Finds Evidence of Cover-Up After Three Alleged Suicides at Guantanamo in 2006, *The Huffington Post*, December 7, 2009, available at www.huffingtonpost.com/2009/12/07/law-school-study-finds-ev_n_382085.html.

some of the detainees for war crimes.[48] The initial allegation about Guantanamo's creation appeared somewhat credible as an anti-terrorism strategy. In reality, Guantanamo turned out differently and has served as a site used for indefinite and at times brutal detention of hundreds of detainees without trial.[49]

Guantanamo Bay was purposefully chosen as the site of terrorism suspects' indefinite detention: the Bush administration received advice from its own political appointees in the Office of Legal Counsel as well as the Department of Justice that the detention camp could be considered outside American legal jurisdiction. In addition, following such flawed legal advice, the Bush administration claimed that the detainees held at Guantanamo Bay were not entitled to any Geneva Convention protections.[50] This, at least initially, allowed the Bush administration to indefinitely detain hundreds of Muslim men from different countries, as a newly developed strategy of the War on Terror. At its peak, the Guantanamo Bay detention facility housed 779 detainees.[51] Of all detainees at Guantanamo, Afghans were the largest group (29 percent), followed by Saudi Arabians (17 percent), Yemenis (15 percent), Pakistanis (9 percent), and Algerians (3 percent). Overall, 50 nationalities were present at Guantanamo.[52]

The Bush administration has claimed that most of the men detained at Guantanamo Bay had been captured while fighting in Afghanistan. However, a 2006 report prepared by the Center for Policy and Research at Seton Hall University Law School debunked this claim. According to this report, which reviewed available Department of Defense data for the 517 men held at Guantanamo in 2005, over 80 percent of the prisoners had been captured by Pakistanis and Afghans, far from any real battlefield and often in exchange for bounty payments.[53]

48 US Department of Defense, DoD News Briefing—Secretary Rumsfeld and Gen. Pace, February 12, 2002, available at http://archive.defense.gov/Transcripts/Transcript.aspx?TranscriptID=263.

49 Although most Guantanamo detainees have by now been either released or prosecuted (either in the military commissions or in civilian courts), a small number of detainees continue to be held at Guantanamo, without facing any legal charges. These detainees have been dubbed by the press as "indefinite detainees"—too dangerous, according to the government, for release and not "prosecutable" because no concrete evidence against them is available. See Carol Rosenberg, FOIA Suit reveals Guantanamo's 'Indefinite Detainees,' *Miami Herald*, June 17, 2013, available at www.miamiherald.com/news/nation-world/world/americas/article1952557.html.

50 See, e.g., Amun Atum, Adeptus Exemptus Thesis 645 (2014); see also Human Rights Watch, Getting Away with Torture: The Bush Administration and Mistreatment of Detainees, July 12, 2011, available at www.hrw.org/report/2011/07/12/getting-away-torture/bush-administration-and-mistreatment-detainees.

51 Julia Preston, Judge Orders U.S. to Supply Prisoner Names, *The New York Times*, January 24, 2006, available at www.nytimes.com/2006/01/24/politics/judge-orders-us-to-supply-prisoner-names.html.

52 Emanuel Deutschmann, Between Collaboration and Disobedience: The Behavior of the Guantánamo Detainees and its Consequences, 60 *J. Conflict Res* 555, August 14, 2014, available at http://journals.sagepub.com/doi/abs/10.1177/0022002714545333.

53 The United States offered $5,000 per prisoner and distributed leaflets advertising this throughout Pakistan and Afghanistan. *USA Today*, Guantanamo Detainees Say Arabs,

The Guantanamo "program" has been problematic for several reasons, including the use of difficult and inhumane detention conditions, as well as the inability of detainees to meaningfully challenge the basis of their detention and seek judicial assistance.

First, detention conditions at Guantanamo Bay have been difficult. Current and former detainees have reported abuse and torture, and Amnesty International dubbed the facility the "Gulag of our times" in a 2005 report.[54] In another confidential report issued in July 2004 and leaked to *The New York Times* later in the same year, International Committee for the Red Cross inspectors accused the US military of using "humiliating acts, solitary confinement, temperature extremes, and use of forced positions" against prisoners.[55] The report concluded that "the construction of such a system, whose stated purpose is the production of intelligence, cannot be considered other than an intentional system of cruel, unusual and degrading treatment and a form of torture."[56] In addition, the report concluded that several activities routinely used at Guantanamo were "tantamount to torture."[57] These included exposure to loud noise or music, prolonged extreme temperatures, and beatings. Many of the released prisoners have confirmed that similar tactics have been used against them and have complained of beatings, sleep deprivation, prolonged use of stress positions and hooding, sexual and cultural humiliation, forced injections, and other physical and psychological mistreatment during their detention at Guantanamo.[58]

Second, the United States has attempted to hold some of the Guantanamo detainees indefinitely, without providing them with the opportunity to challenge their detention in a court of law. It appears that the Bush administration, in the wake of 9/11, most likely intended to hold Guantanamo suspects indefinitely without providing them with any opportunity to challenge the reasons of their detention. In fact, the Bush administration had contended that the laws and customs of war, including the Geneva Conventions, did not apply to the US armed

Muslims Sold for U.S. Bounties, May 31, 2005, available at http://usatoday30.usatoday.com/news/world/2005-05-31-bounties_x.htm.

54 Amnesty International, *Amnesty International Report 2005 Speech by Irene Khan at Foreign Press Association*, May 24, 2005, available at www.amnesty.org/en/documents/POL10/014/2005/en/.

55 Neil A. Lewis, Red Cross Finds Detainee Abuse in Guantánamo, *The New York Times*, November 30, 2004, available at www.nytimes.com/2004/11/30/politics/red-cross-finds-detainee-abuse-in-guantanamo.html?_r=0.

56 *Id.*

57 *Id.*

58 Julie Hyland, Britons Release Devastating Account of Torture and Abuse by U.S. forces at Guantanamo, World Socialist Web Site, August 6, 2004, available at www.wsws.org/en/articles/2004/08/guan-a06.html (reporting on the inhumane treatment of three British citizens detained at Guantanamo). By most accounts, the treatment of these detainees was consistent with the treatment of other detainees from other countries. See, e.g., Mark Denbeaux et al., Report on Guantanamo Detainees: A Profile of 517 Detainees, February 8, 2006, available at http://law.shu.edu/publications/guantanamoReports/guantanamo_report_final_2_08_06.pdf.

conflict with al-Qaeda fighters during the 2001 US invasion of Taliban-controlled Afghanistan—thus, Guantanamo detainees would not be entitled to prisoner-of-war status under this rationale, and would be held indefinitely.[59] The US Supreme Court litigation has fortunately prevented this result.

In 2004, the Supreme Court held in *Hamdi v. Rumsfeld* that detainees had the right to challenge detention before an impartial tribunal.[60] Following this ruling, the Bush administration established Combatant Status Review Tribunals, the purpose of which was to determine whether individual detainees were "enemy combatants."[61] In 2006, the Supreme Court held in *Hamdan v. Rumsfeld* that President Bush did not have authority to set up Combatant Status Review Tribunals, and that these Tribunals were illegal under both military justice law and the Geneva Convention.[62] The Supreme Court confirmed in Hamdan that Guantanamo detainees were entitled to the minimal protections listed under Common Article 3 of the Geneva Conventions, including the right to a fair trial. Following Hamdan, in September 2006, the US Senate and House of Representatives, respectively, passed the Military Commissions Act of 2006.[63] This controversial bill allowed the president to designate certain people with the status of "unlawful enemy combatants," thereby making them subject to military commissions, where they have fewer civil rights than in regular trials. Unsurprisingly, many Guantanamo detainees were designated as "unlawful enemy combatants."[64]

In 2008, the United States Supreme Court ruled in *Boumediene v. Bush* that the Guantánamo detainees were entitled to the protection of the United States Constitution.[65] Justice Kennedy's majority opinion held that existing Combatant Status Review Tribunals were "an inadequate substitute for habeas corpus" and that Guantanamo detainees should have access to federal courts.[66] In other words, Boumediene held that Guantanamo detainees could challenge their detention in civilian courts, including brining habeas corpus petitions. Boumediene thus overturned the Military Commissions Act of 2006, by holding that the act was unconstitutional for attempting to restrict the use of habeas corpus for Guantanamo detainees.[67]

59 See *supra* note 48 and accompanying text.
60 *Hadmi v. Rumsfeld*, 542 U.S. 507 (2004).
61 US Department of Defense, DoD to Review Status of All Guantanamo Detainees, July 11, 2004, available at http://archive.defense.gov/news/newsarticle.aspx?id=25741.
62 *Hamdan v. Rumsfeld*, 548 U.S. 557 (2006).
63 Military Commissions Act of 2006, Public Law 109–366 (2006).
64 For an excellent discussion of various cases involving Guantanamo detainees and their legal challenges regarding their detention, see Jennifer K. Elsea & Michael John Garcia, Enemy Combatant Detainees: Habeas Corpus Challenges in Federal Court, Congressional Research Service, February 3, 2010, available at https://fas.org/sgp/crs/natsec/RL33180.pdf.
65 *Boumediene v. Bush*, 553 U.S. 723 (2008).
66 *Id.*
67 *Id.*

Since the Boumediene ruling, dozens of Guantanamo detainees began to use habeas corpus petitions in US courts to seek freedom. While 15 federal judges have ordered the release of at least 30 detainees, for lack of government evidence against such detainees, a series of appellate rulings since 2010 have made it increasingly difficult for additional Guantanamo detainees to win their habeas corpus cases.[68]

It should be noted that while President Obama largely supported and continued President Bush's use of drones as a War on Terror tactic, Obama demonstrated a willingness to end the Guantanamo program. During his 2008 presidential campaign, President Obama referred to Guantanamo as a "sad chapter in American history" and promised to close it down.[69] As soon as he took office, in 2009, President Obama issued a request to suspend proceedings at Guantanamo military commission for 120 days and to shut down the detention facility that year. President Obama had planned to transfer Guantanamo detainees to US federal prisons and had designated potential sites for the transfer of hundreds of prisoners.[70] However, because of persistent Congressional opposition and unwillingness to accept Guantanamo detainees in American federal prisons, President Obama was unable to execute this promise.[71] Instead, the Obama administration, over the past eight years, managed to drastically decrease the number of detainees by transferring many of those who had been cleared for release to third countries. As of October 2016, the number of Guantanamo detainees had dropped to 60; out of these, 20 more had been cleared for transfer. According to President Obama, the prisoners not cleared for transfer should be brought to the United States to either stand trial in a civilian court or to be

68 Warren Richey, Supreme Court Deals Blow to Guantánamo Prisoners Challenging Their Detention, *The Christian Science Monitor*, June 11, 2012, available at www.csmonitor.com/USA/Justice/2012/0611/Supreme-Court-deals-blow-to-Guantanamo-prisoners-challenging-their-detention (noting that the federal appeals court has taken up 19 of the Guantanamo habeas cases and reversed or remanded every case in which a federal judge ordered a detainee's release).

69 Mary Bruce, Obama: Gitmo Likely Won't Close in First 100 Days, ABC News, January 11, 2009, available at http://abcnews.go.com/ThisWeek/Economy/story?id=6619291.

70 *Id.* (noting that President Obama had planned to transfer Guantanamo detainees to specific federal prisons).

71 It should be noted that while some have blamed Congress for the delay in closing Guantanamo, others have blamed President Obama for not being forceful enough in his efforts to close the camp. National Security Council spokesman Tommy Vietor said in a statement, "Obviously Congress has taken a number of steps to prevent the closure of the prison at Guantánamo Bay, but the President still believes it's in our national security interest and will keep trying." In the same interview, however, senior ACLU attorney Zachary Katznelson argued Obama had "enough control and power that he [could have gotten those] men out today if he [had] the political will to do so." Mike Negrin, Guantanamo Bay: Still Open, Despite Promises, ABC News, July 3, 2012, available at http://abcnews.go.com/Politics/OTUS/guantanamo-bay-open-promises/story?id=16698768.

prosecuted in a military commission.[72] As of January 2019, 41 prisoners remain at Guantanamo.[73]

It would be fair to conclude that President Obama remained opposed to the Guantanamo detention program in principle but that, despite his opposition, the somewhat diminished program remained an important facet of the United States War on Terror throughout the Obama administration.[74] The Guantanamo program has been controversial because the United States' position—that it could hold hundreds of foreign nationals indefinitely as part of its War on Terror, because these individuals had some tenuous links to al-Qaeda or other related terrorist organizations—does not have a sound legal basis in either domestic or international law. In addition, it appears that detention conditions at Guantanamo have been inhumane and some practices inflicted upon some detainees have amounted to torture. These detention conditions have unfortunately been a feature of the War on Terror, in a 15-year attempt to gather anti-terrorism intelligence information, through the repeated questioning of the detainees under inhumane conditions. Thus, it is this chapter's conclusion that the War on Terror has been overbroad and has resulted in questionable practices, such as the Guantanamo program. Many of the detainees could have been detained for a much shorter period of time, questioned under humane conditions, and either released or prosecuted in a court of law, if evidence against them was sufficient to warrant this course of action. Fighting terrorism does not justify the indefinite detention and inhumane treatment of hundreds of foreigners. Sadly, it appears that at least some of the released Guantanamo detainees have supported terrorist causes against the United States or have themselves engaged in terrorist activity.[75] And

72 Dan Lamothe, Obama Administration Approves Its Largest Single Release of Guantanamo Detainees Ever, *The Washington Post*, August 15, 2016, available at www.washingtonpost.com/news/checkpoint/wp/2016/08/15/obama-administration-its-largest-single-release-of-guantanamo-detainees-ever/?utm_term=.eea298fb2ec7.

73 Carol Rosenberg, Obama to Leave with 41 Captives Still at Guantanamo, Blames Politics, *Miami Herald*, January 19, 2017, available at www.miamiherald.com/news/nation-world/world/americas/guantanamo/article127473314.html. It is unclear what the Trump administration will do regarding Guantanamo. President Trump has vowed to keep the prison open and to use it to detain "bad dudes" including American ISIS supporters. Trump also announced that he was in favor of bringing back waterboarding and worse methods of torture. Connie Bruck, Why Obama Has Failed to Close Guantánamo, *The New Yorker*, August 1, 2016, available at www.newyorker.com/magazine/2016/08/01/why-obama-has-failed-to-close-guantanamo.

74 President Obama has stated that "[t]he executive branch must have the authority to determine when and where to prosecute Guantanamo detainees, based on the facts and circumstances of each case and our national security interests" and that Guantanamo Bay "is not who we are" and that it was "time to close Gitmo." David Jackson, Obama Wants to Try Gitmo Prisoners in U.S., *USA Today*, December 27, 2013, available at www.usatoday.com/story/theoval/2013/12/27/obama-guantanamo-bay-cuba-detainees-congress-bill-signing/4216855/.

75 In early 2009, the Pentagon said that it had evidence that 18 former detainees have had direct involvement in terrorist activities, but declined to provide their identities to the media. See David Morgan, Pentagon: 61 Ex-Guantanamo Inmates Return to Terrorism, Reuters, January 13, 2009, available at www.reuters.com/article/us-usa

the intelligence information obtained at Guantanamo does not seem to have resulted in significant terrorism prevention efforts. Thus, it may be that any benefits derived from the detention of foreigners at Guantanamo have been far outweighed by the program's violations of human rights and international law, and that Guantanamo will indeed remain a sad chapter in United States' history.

Conclusion

On the one hand, the War on Terror was successful in its first few years. Hundreds of terrorist suspects around the world have been arrested and the United States has not witnessed another large-scale terrorist attack on the American mainland. In addition, the Taliban regime in Afghanistan was toppled and many terrorist-training camps in Afghanistan have been closed.[76] Osama bin Laden as well as many other senior al-Qaeda members have been killed or captured, and we have witnessed increased levels of international cooperation in global counterterrorism efforts.[77]

On the other hand, many have argued that the failures and risks associated with the extraordinarily large scope of America's counterterrorism campaign have outweighed its successes. For example, some argue that the war in Afghanistan was ineffective, as it resulted in the scattering of the al-Qaeda network, thereby making it even harder to counteract against this organization. In addition, others believe that the American counterterrorism attacks in Afghanistan and Iraq, and particularly the use of drones, have increased anti-American sentiment among the world's Muslims.[78] This in turn has contributed toward the enhancement of militant Islam

-guantanamo-idUSTRE50C5JX20090113. In addition, in March 2016, Reuters reported that "111 of 532 prisoners released by the Republican administration of President George W. Bush are confirmed to have returned to the battlefield, with 74 others suspected of doing so." It further reported that "seven out of 144 Guantanamo prisoners who were freed since Obama took office in January 2009 have returned to fighting," with "number of former Guantanamo Bay prison inmates who are suspected of having returned to fighting for militants doubled to 12 in the six months through January." In summary, 118 of 676, or 17 percent, are confirmed to have returned to terrorism, with a further 86 (13 percent) suspected, for a grand total of 30 percent known or suspected of having returned to terrorism. Mark Hosenball, Ex-Guantanamo Prisoners Suspected of Rejoining Militants Increases: U.S, Reuters, March 8, 2016, available at http://ca.reuters.com/article/topNews/idCAKCN0WA003.

76 *Britannica, supra* note 5.

77 CNN, Death of Osama Bin Laden Fast Facts, April 17, 2016, available at www.cnn.com/2013/09/09/world/death-of-osama-bin-laden-fast-facts/ (reporting on the death of Osama bin Laden); Council on Foreign Relations, The Global Regime for Terrorism, available at www.cfr.org/terrorism/global-regime-terrorism/p25729 (reporting on the international community's increased attention and efforts to combat terrorism post-9/11).

78 See, e.g., DAWN, Imran Criticises US Drone Policy, January 22, 2013, available at www.dawn.com/2012/11/14/khan-urges-fia-to-initiate-asghar-khan-case-probe/imran-khan-afp-670-8/ (reporting on anti-American sentiment in Pakistan over the American use of drone strikes in Pakistan). For a discussion about whether drone strikes have produced anti-Americanism in Pakistan, see Afzal, *supra* note 20.

and a unification of small, disparate groups in a common (anti-American) cause. Some have argued that the United States has not been inclusive in its War on Terror strategies, and that the United States should have adopted a more multilateral approach in order to rally Europe, Russia, China, India, and other non-Muslim governments in a common anti-jihadist and anti-terrorism cause.[79] Larger cynics of American geopolitics allege that the war on terrorism is nothing but a smokescreen for the pursuit of a larger American geopolitical agenda, which includes controlling global oil reserves, increasing defense spending, expanding international military presence, and countering the strategic challenge posed by various regional powers.[80] Finally, many have pointed out that the War on Terror may have resulted in violations of international law abroad, as well as the curtailing of civil liberties domestically. As one commentator has argued, "[t]aken together, the Bush administration's anti-terrorism practices represent a stunning assault on basic principles of justice, government accountability, and the role of the courts."[81]

While this chapter does not go as far as the last statement in its overall conclusion and criticism of the American antiterrorism campaign post 9/11, it is certain that the breadth and scope of the War on Terror have influenced American law and policy both internationally and domestically and that, if the war's purpose was to simply combat terrorism, this goal could have been achieved through more narrowly construed initiatives. "The worldwide campaign has too often become an excuse for governments to repress opposition groups and disregard international law and civil liberties. Governments should address terrorism through international cooperation, using international law and respecting civil liberties and human rights."[82]

79 Yew, *supra* note 44, at 3 ("[a] world-wide coalition is necessary to fight the fires of hatred that the Islamist fanatics are fanning").

80 One commentator has argued that the United States' strategic goals in the Middle East, which have been pursued under the guise of the War on Terror, have included "the security of the lone regional nuclear power; Israel, control over the flow of Persian Gulf oil, and maintenance of regional stability to ensure the integrity of investment opportunities." Alex Carnes, The Global War on Terror: Unfolding the Static Approach of US Foreign Policy in the Middle East, *State of Nature*, October 15, 2010, available at www.stateofnature.org/?p=5658.

81 Anup Shah, *War on Terror*, GLOBAL ISSUES, October 7, 2013, available at www.globalissues.org/print/issue/245.

82 Global Policy, War on Terrorism, available at www.globalpolicy.org/war-on-terrorim.html.

3 Guantánamo

A well-studied trunk

Joseph Margulies

I

It is a curious but familiar feature of American public life that what matters most about a particular policy is often met with yawning indifference, while what matters least is frequently subjected to breathless scrutiny. Since early in the 21st century, for instance, much ink has been spilled about mass incarceration (e.g., Hinton, 2016). Under the benevolent influence of works like *The New Jim Crow*, the belief has become widespread that the crisis can be traced to the over-criminalization of drug use, especially among people of color (Alexander, 2010). Many people seem to think we can empty the prisons if we simply end the inhumane practice of locking up black and brown men and women for the possession of a small amount of drugs.

Yet this has never been remotely true. Most people in prison in this country have been convicted of either property crimes or crimes of violence (Wagner & Rabuy, 2017). Even if every person incarcerated for a drug offense were released tomorrow, the United States would still have the largest prison population the world has ever known. And those in prison on drug charges include a substantial number who were convicted not of possession but of distribution, as well as people for whom the current possession conviction comes atop a prior history of property or violent crimes (Pfaff, 2017; Sevigny and Caulkins, 2004). Trying to uncover the low level, non-violent drug offender incarcerated for mere possession—especially in the state system, which houses the great majority of inmates—is not quite like hunting for a snark, but it can begin to feel that way for those engaged in the task.[1]

Of course, there is nothing new in the recognition that social problems are socially constructed (Blumer, 1971; Schneider, 1985), and most readers can come up with other illustrations of this phenomenon that make the point as well or better than mine. Nor do I suggest that the war on drugs has been anything other than an abject failure, or that we should be indifferent to the fate of those few people who are imprisoned for mere possession of narcotics. But the interesting

1 One study put the total number of low-level, non-violent drug offenders at approximately 1–2% of the total prison population (Sevigny & Caulkins, 2004).

questions all have to do with why we so often train our attention on the trunk and not the elephant. Surely part of the answer must be that we are drawn to problems that seem to admit of simple solutions. Or perhaps more precisely, we are grateful when apparently intractable social problems can be framed in such a way as to permit prompt, painless resolution. If we produced mass incarceration by sending harmless addicts to prison, by all means let's stop. Problem solved. And if, along the way, we can help solve the problem of systemic racism in the criminal justice system, so much the better.

Responses like these relieve us of the distinctly unwelcome burden of hard work. They are the policy equivalent of a diet that tolerates unlimited pizza and ice cream. Besides, what's that old quip about the perfect being the enemy of the good (Arouet, 1772)? At least we can do some good, which is certainly preferable to doing more bad. And so we content ourselves with baby steps that are marginally better than standing still, but certainly do nothing to change the essential nature of things. We do not, for instance, take serious aim at the institutions and practices that most engorge and sustain the carceral state (e.g., Vitale, 2017). At times like this, we should recall a different quote from Voltaire: "A witty saying proves nothing" (Arouet, 1767).

I thought of all this when I began to write this review. If ever there were a well-studied trunk, it is the prison at Guantánamo.

II

By way of very brief review, the current Guantánamo saga began in November 2001, when President Bush announced plans to employ military commissions to prosecute people captured in connection with the newly minted war on terror (Bush, 2001). In time, the Bush administration announced it would hold these prisoners and conduct these trials at the US Naval Base at Guantánamo. The first prisoners reached the base in January 2002 (Margulies, 2006). The prison at Guantánamo eventually grew to hold 780 prisoners (Human Rights First, 2017), the majority of whom arrived in 2002 and 2003.

When the prisoners reached Cuba, the administration insisted that no court had jurisdiction to consider whether they were detained lawfully or treated humanely. Along with Michael Ratner and Steven Watt at the Center for Constitutional Rights, and Clive Stafford Smith at Reprieve, I brought the first lawsuit on behalf of imprisoned detainees in February 2002 in the United States District Court for the District of Columbia. We filed this initial case, *Rasul et al. v. Bush*, on behalf of three prisoners—two from Britain and one from Australia. We added a fourth—another Australian—a couple months later (Margulies, 2006).

As we first conceived the litigation, we imagined we would challenge the military commission system. We quickly realized, however, that if the administration could detain prisoners indefinitely with no process, they would not bother to hold trials (ibid.). Equipped with this insight, the litigation in *Rasul* became a challenge to the lawfulness of indefinite detention without legal process—or, as Michael Ratner used to quip, whether the Bush administration could create a prison beyond the law. In June 2004, the Supreme Court held that the prisoners at Guantánamo could seek a writ of *habeas corpus* to challenge the factual and legal basis of their detention in federal district court (*Rasul*, 2004). Congress responded by amending the habeas statute to eliminate statutory jurisdiction. More litigation followed, and in 2008, the Supreme Court clarified that the prisoners at the base had a constitutional right to *habeas* that could not be stripped away by mere statute (*Boumediene*, 2008).

As often happens, however, the Court announced the broad rule in *Rasul* and *Boumediene* but left it to the lower courts—in this case the Court of Appeals for the DC Circuit—to flesh out the particulars. Making the most of its opportunity, the DC Circuit fashioned a substantive standard and crafted a set of procedural rules that tilted heavily in favor of the government (e.g., Ahuja & Tutt, 2012; Wittes, Chesney, & Reynolds, 2012). Since then, the right to *habeas* has been more symbol than substance, creating the false impression that prisoners can challenge the lawfulness of their detention. It is closer to the truth to say they can file a lawsuit. They cannot, however, mount a serious challenge to their detention. Many observers celebrate the decisions in *Rasul* and *Boumediene* as great victories for the rule of law (e.g., Cole, 2016). Being more inclined to focus on substance than symbol, I have described the litigation in less flattering terms (Margulies & Metcalf, 2011).

Yet a funny thing happened as the litigation wended toward its predictably inconsequential conclusion (Rosenberg, 1991). During the Bush administration, the prison at Guantánamo became part of a powerful public narrative about the abuse of executive power. This narrative relied upon and fused together a number of very different executive branch policies of the post-9/11 era, including warrantless wiretapping; the torture, indefinite detention, and rendition of alleged terrorists; the rampant and reckless use of presidential signing statements; and an excessive fondness for executive secrecy. Taken together, these and related post-9/11 policies came to symbolize a dangerous hostility to constitutional governance and the rule of law. This narrative of presidential lawlessness gathered strength throughout the Bush administration and eventually became an important part of the change promised by Barack Obama during his successful campaign for the presidency in 2008 (Margulies, 2013).

The Guantánamo litigation thus tends to confirm the seminal work of both Gerald Rosenberg *and* Michael McCann: while the courts in this country provide only the hollow hope of progressive social change (Rosenberg, 1991), the fact that we live in an intensely legalistic society means that court decisions might do their most important work not in the courtroom, but in the streets (McCann, 1994). As declarations of legal rights, *Rasul* and *Boumediene* had essentially no effect; as a salvo against official lawlessness, they were important contributors. *Qua* litigation, they were failures; *qua* political contestation, they were—and remain—part of a much larger campaign against a particular form of presidential abuse (see generally Cole, 2016; Goldsmith, 2012; Lobel, 2004; Margulies, 2013; Margulies & Metcalf, 2011; Tarrow, 2015).

Still, the potency of a symbol can also be its unraveling. As Murray Edelman taught us more than 50 years ago, in its symbolic form, an event or phenomenon is almost infinitely elastic *so long as it is also remote* (Edelman, 1964). That is, so long as the public experiences an event as only (or principally) a remote symbol, it is subject to nearly endless manipulation by elites for political gain. As Guantánamo gained currency as a symbol, it became more flexible. Like a broken-in baseball glove, it could fit any hand that picked it up. So it was that immediately after President Obama announced his intention to shutter the island prison—a plan that enjoyed wide bipartisan support prior to his election—the right seized on Guantánamo as a symbol of a muscular American foreign policy and used Obama's proclamation as a symbol of his anti-American weakness (Margulies, 2013).

Once a phenomenon acquires this dual political significance—as potent symbol for both left and right—its symbolic importance quickly overtakes reality. Most people come to know it only for the work it does as a symbol, rather than for its actuality. When they conjure a mental image of the *thing*, they see in their mind's eye only the symbol. Ironically, the remote symbol becomes real as the reality becomes increasingly remote. The symbol becomes reality while reality is forgotten. I do not know whether it is invariably true, but at least in our hyper-partisan, politically charged environment, once a phenomenon takes on this Janus-faced symbolic role, any attempt to discuss it is like trying to have a serious conversation in a crowded bar; no one can hear a thing over the din, so you stop trying and order another drink.

For instance, speaking about Guantánamo during the 2016 campaign, Donald Trump promised "to load it up with some bad dudes." Of course, as of this writing in July 2018, he has not added a soul to the base since placing his hand on the Bible and vowing to "preserve, protect, and defend the Constitution of the United States." And because American counter-terror policy has largely shifted away from military campaigns on the ground to drone attacks from the air, and from human intelligence gathered by interrogations to signals intelligence gathered by surveillance, he will likely not add more than a handful—if any—during his entire time in office, however long that may be (Margulies, 2017).

Yet as with so much about this president, reality is beside the point. Wringing their hands over his stated intention to enlarge Guantánamo, most commentators overlooked the larger context of his remarks. Speaking at a rally in Sparks, Nevada, he said, "This morning, I watched President Obama talking about Gitmo, right, Guantánamo Bay, which by the way, which by the way, we are keeping open. Which we are keeping open … and we're gonna load it up with some bad dudes, believe me, we're gonna load it up" (Welna, 2016). The policy statement—"we're gonna load it up"—was simply an opportunity to reinforce a political message: President Obama is wrecking the country for people like you and me, but I will come to your rescue. Guantánamo is thus used symbolically to represent a muscular indifference to the effete whimpering of left-leaning intellectuals. In that respect, it is of a piece with the president's ridiculous vow to "build a wall" along the Mexican border. So long as his supporters believe he in fact stands for this message, what Trump actually does at Guantánamo is immaterial. The reality is far less important than the symbol, and for many years, the real work that Guantánamo does in American life has been symbolic.[2]

As its significance as a symbol has grown, its significance as a prison has diminished. The great majority of prisoners at the base have been released. Most were sent home by President Bush, when the public climate was most hostile to the facility; a much smaller number were repatriated by President Obama. By the time Obama left office, the prison held only 41 men (Human Rights First, 2017). Since his successor took over, one prisoner has been released, leaving 40 at the base in mid-2018. Having been confined for about 15 years and arrested during a very different security climate, these few prisoners are no longer a source of information, if they ever were. They are merely prisoners. Except that they, unlike other prisoners in the United States, have never been convicted of a crime.

Meanwhile, as the prison has shriveled, the cost to maintain it has remained high. By the end of 2015, the United States had spent nearly $5.7 billion on detention operations at Guantánamo. Costs in 2015 alone were nearly half a billion dollars. And that doesn't include the cost of Camp 7, where the so-called "high value" prisoners are held; those costs are not part publicly disclosed. Yet we have plenty of unused federal prison space on the mainland, where we could hold these 41 men in complete security at a fraction of the cost. We pay more than $10 million per inmate per year at Guantánamo; we safely house convicted terrorists at the Supermax facility in Florence, CO, for roughly $78,000 per inmate per year (ibid.). In the final analysis, therefore, Guantánamo is a minuscule but astronomically expensive prison.

Finally, it is important to differentiate the detentions at Guantánamo from other post-9/11 detention operations. The prisoners at Guantánamo are now held by the Department of Defense (DoD). Since 9/11, DoD has detained thousands of people in connection with the war on terror (Bush, 2006), and still detains an unknown number of suspects at facilities around the world, quite apart from the detentions at Guantánamo. The Central Intelligence Agency (CIA) also detained suspects after 9/11, and some of the CIA detainees were tortured in the course of "enhanced" interrogations. In the interest of full disclosure, I represent the first prisoner cast into the "enhanced interrogation" program, Zayn al Abedin Muhammad Hussain, known more widely as Abu Zubaydah. Abu Zubaydah was arrested at a home in Pakistan in late March 2002 and transferred to a CIA black site in Thailand, where he was tortured at great length by private psychologists under contract with the CIA. He was eventually held at a host of black sites before being shipped to Guantánamo and transferred to DoD custody in September 2006 (Bush, 2006). He remains at Guantánamo. President Obama ended the CIA

2 Of course, the problem with using symbols this way is that some people attach themselves to the substance, and think the president actually *intended* to "build a wall," just as he really planned to "repeal and replace" Obamacare. To assuage these voters, it becomes important for the president to blame someone else for his failure to make good on his campaign promises, which is why Republican legislators have become his scapegoat.

program in January 2009, though by that time, the CIA claimed it no longer held any prisoners (Obama, 2009).

In addition to the CIA and DoD detention programs, the United States rendered an unknown number of suspects to third countries for interrogation by foreign security services. This practice came to be known as "extraordinary rendition" to distinguish it from "rendition to justice," which involved kidnapping people abroad and bringing them back to the US to face trial. Again, in the interest of full disclosure, I represented one of the first people subjected to extraordinary rendition. Mamdouh Habib was born in Egypt but later took Australian citizenship. He was arrested in Pakistan and rendered by US agents to Egypt in late 2001, where he was subjected to an extended course of ingenious tortures, which I have elsewhere described in detail (Margulies, 2006). Egypt returned Habib to US custody in early 2002; the US shipped him to Guantánamo in April of the same year. We added him to the litigation in *Rasul* shortly after his arrival. The United States released him from prison in January 2005. Like the great majority of prisoners who have been released, he was never charged with any wrongdoing. At the request of the Australian government, I accompanied Mamdouh on the flight home from Guantánamo to Sydney. I am the only lawyer who has been allowed to accompany a client home from Guantánamo.

Many people do not differentiate among these various types of post-9/11 detentions. This conflation is certainly understandable. Though CIA, DoD, and US proxy detentions abroad were theoretically separate, in practice they overlapped a great deal. Like Habib, for instance, many prisoners who were rendered to third countries by the US were later also detained by the CIA or DoD. Like Abu Zubaydah, many prisoners tortured by the CIA were later held by DoD, and some—though not Abu Zubaydah—were also rendered to third countries. In addition, though the "enhanced" interrogation techniques adopted by the CIA were approved only for use on CIA prisoners, they quickly migrated to other agencies and were adapted for use by, among others, the DoD (Margulies, 2006). Still, when I refer to Guantánamo, in this review and elsewhere, I mean the prison in Cuba and not the other parts of the US detention policy in the post-9/11 world. When I refer to CIA detainees, I mean the prisoners held by the CIA at offshore black sites in the enhanced interrogation program from 2002–2006. And when I refer to extraordinary rendition, I mean only the practice of shipping prisoners to third countries for interrogation.

III

So, when it comes to Guantánamo, what is the elephant and what is the trunk? In a land where symbol has eclipsed substance, what is—and what ought to be—the subject of study? At the risk of some oversimplification, law is the trunk. The endless, obsessive, and arcane ruminations about the (il)legality of moves and counter-moves by the many layers of military and civilian courts that now have a hand in moving around the pieces at Guantánamo, to say nothing of the ever-changing collection of prison administrators and their handlers in the Bush,

Obama, and now Trump administrations, have long since come to remind me of Sayre's Third Law of Politics: the debates are so bitter because the stakes are so low. It is not simply that, as Don Henley wrote, "lawyers dwell on small details"; they're insignificant too.

Nothing illustrates the triumph of symbol over substance at Guantánamo better than the many books, articles, and news accounts devoted to the military commission system at Guantánamo. With inexplicable punctiliousness, serious scholars and journalists have devoted countless hours to chronicling the twists and turns, and debating the legality, of these much-maligned proceedings (e.g., Bravin, 2013; Ni Aoláin & Gross, 2013). From the sheer enormity of their output, we could almost conclude the commissions were a big deal. Then of course we are reminded that of the 780 people who have been brought to the prison since early 2002, only eight have been tried and convicted by the commissions—one fewer than the number of Guantánamo prisoners who have died in custody (including six who killed themselves), and one more than the number of military prosecutors who resigned from the commission system because they believed the process was unfair. And even this total overstates the success of these quasi-courts, since three convictions were reversed on appeal. Only one of the eight convictions involved a contested trial. Six other prisoners pleaded guilty in exchange for a promise to be released, and one defendant boycotted the proceedings (American Civil Liberties Union, 2017; Human Rights First 2017).

Looking to the future, only seven prisoners are currently being tried in the commission system. The Pentagon reports it has plans to prosecute 14 prisoners in total. Whether these trials will go forward is anyone's guess, but the odds are not good. As I write this, Brig. Gen. John Baker, the chief defense counsel for the commission system, has disbanded the defense team for Abd al Rahim al Nashiri, who is charged in connection with the attack on the USS *Cole*. Because the proceedings are classified, we cannot know why Baker felt the need to act as he did. Public reporting placed the blame on surreptitious monitoring by the government of privileged conversations between al Nashiri and his lawyers (Rosenberg, 2017). It seems the United States may have been eavesdropping on private conversations between al Nashiri and his lawyers, and could not assure anyone that the practice had ended. (I put the matter this way because there is a dispute about whether attorney–client conversations were *deliberately* monitored. Because the whole imbroglio is classified, we cannot know who has the better of the argument.)

This is bad enough, but the government made it far worse by forbidding the lawyers from telling al Nashiri about the eavesdropping. In logic fit for Lewis Carroll, the military says the fact that it may have secretly monitored privileged attorney–client communications is itself classified. Since al Nashiri does not have a security clearance, the lawyers cannot tell him whether his conversations with them were compromised, even though the thing at stake is al Nashiri's privilege. Nor could they assure him that their conversations with him going forward would be protected. This, of course, put the lawyers in an impossible bind. They could not have a private conversation with their client, and so were reduced to discussing trivialities. Yet they could not explain to their client, who faces a possible death sentence if convicted, why they would travel all the way to Cuba just to chat about the weather. Rather than maintain the charade, Brig. Gen. Baker disbanded the defense team.

If his trial had gone forward, al Nashiri would have been the first person to face capital charges in the Guantánamo military commission system. Now, of course, new counsel must be appointed, which means the entire proceeding is in limbo. In a real court, replacing trial counsel in a capital case and giving them time to come up to speed would delay the case by months if not years. In a case as complicated as the *Cole* bombing, involving classified investigations across the globe, the delay will almost certainly be two or more years. But even if new lawyers could be identified, and even if they were given enough time to prepare, they would labor under the same burden as the previous lawyers. If the problem is that the military has made it impossible to defend al Nashiri, bringing in a new set of lawyers won't make it better. And finally, even if the United States could recruit new counsel, and even if counsel could provide al Nashiri with effective representation, there is still one last hurdle to overcome. The United States has always maintained that even if a defendant in the commissions were acquitted, the military can still detain him indefinitely as an "enemy combatant," in the exact same cell under the exact same conditions. A military commission trial, therefore, literally changes nothing in the life of the accused.

Given their nearly unbroken record of futility and failure, the conclusion is irresistible that the commissions are all symbol and no substance—all trunk and no elephant. And yet we retain them and show no inclination to bring them to a merciful end. Why? Because their true purpose—their *raison d'être*—has nothing to do with whether they can dispense something like justice in something like a court pursuant to something like the rule of law. They exist because many Democrats, and especially President Obama, wanted to end them. They exist because the rest of the Western world despises them. They exist because they serve a partisan political function that has nothing to do with the law, and nothing to do with whether any proceeding is ever brought to a successful conclusion. And because that is why they exist, it is not important that they *do* anything. It is only important that they continue to exist.

Meanwhile, the United States has successfully prosecuted more than 600 terrorists in federal court since 9/11, including one who had previously been detained at Guantánamo (Human Rights First, 2017). For those keeping score at home, the commissions cost taxpayers more than $90 million a year (Human Rights First, 2017).

Yet the overwhelming majority of the academic literature about the commissions—at least so far as I can identify—is perfectly oblivious to this reality. Book after book and article atop article reads as though the commissions were an actual adjudicatory body bent on applying meaningful standards to resolve genuine disputes—as though, in short, they were *courts*—and therefore the sort of entity for which it matters whether, for instance, hearsay is admissible as substantive evidence, the Ex Post Facto Clause forbids criminalizing conduct that was once considered innocent, or whether prisoners at the base have a right to a trial by jury under the Sixth Amendment right (e.g., Frakt, 2007; Kris, 2011; McDonald, 2013). Most writers do not even pause to consider the possibility that the commissions have only a symbolic function—or at least, that the symbolic role of the commissions has long since dwarfed their substantive role.

As a result, there is virtually no discussion of why a quasi-court that doesn't actually do anything would come to acquire such bewildering significance. Surely it says something about the real and mythical role of legal rituals in American life—about legal consciousness and legalism—that writers devote so much attention to trial-like window dressing (Merry, 1990; Shklar, 1964). The commission building at Guantánamo was built to look like a real courtroom, which allows players in the game to engage, however infrequently and however impotently, in the gladiatorial drama of a genuine criminal case. Stern-looking defense lawyers march solemnly into the ring and take their seat next to an equally stern team of prosecutors. Briefs and books pile high around them, the weapons of lawyerly battle. The audience sits behind a railing, court watchers and journalists alongside military and civilian personnel, who scribble notes and carry on fevered electronic conversations with others elsewhere. Everyone stares intently as the accused, the image of all that is evil, is brought into the room and takes his place next to his lawyers. All rise as the judge enters and raps the familiar gavel. Though nothing of substance takes place, the trappings of seeming legal regularity, entwined with the barely concealed prospect of no-holds-barred combat, is apparently irresistible.

Though nothing matches the discussion of the military commissions for its obsessive irrelevance, the literature on the law of detention is a close second. Some authors, for instance, seem intent on maintaining the fiction that the law serves as a meaningful check on executive detention authority. For example, when officials at the University of Kent at Canterbury in England invited retired Supreme Court Justice Sandra Day O'Connor to speak about Guantánamo, they helpfully fashioned a title for her talk: "Guantánamo Bay: Legal Black Hole." The Justice insisted on adding a question mark to the end of the title, and concluded the question should be answered in the negative. After reviewing the Supreme Court jurisprudence regarding the island prison, she said, "I think you must acknowledge that the United States Courts have taken a rather firm stand on the status of prisoners held at Guantánamo Bay. Hopefully, you will reconsider the appellation of 'legal black hole'" (O'Connor, 2008). We might forgive a former Supreme Court justice for focusing rather too much on the importance of legal pronouncements by the Supreme Court, but her view seems to be widely shared. One scholar, for instance, described the same line of cases as "a watershed of American jurisprudence as to separation of powers, the vitality of the writ of habeas corpus, and the rule of law as to due process deriving from both the Constitution and international law" (Sherman, 2010). Yet *habeas* is almost literally a dead letter at Guantánamo. Since the DC Circuit Court of Appeals gutted *Boumediene*, prisoners have lost every case (Denbeaux, 2012).

To be sure, some scholars have recognized that the law of detentions at Guantánamo has been much ado about nothing. In a lengthy article in the *Boston University Law Review*, for instance, Kim Lane Scheppele reviews the same decisions as Justice O'Connor. But unlike the Justice, Scheppele points out, quite rightly, that detainees have won in the Supreme Court but lost at Guantánamo. The decisions, in other words, have given the prisoners only the empty comfort of lofty language and not the hard benefit of protectable rights (Scheppele, 2012). Even Scheppele, however, does not take up the symbolic role that the law and the prison have come to play. Though she demonstrates at great length the difference between law in the books and law in action, she is the first to acknowledge that this divergence is hardly unusual. The important questions have to do with why scholars have focused so intently on what doesn't matter rather than what does and have given the law such unjustifiable prominence, despite its evident impotence. (In the same spirit, see Huq, 2010.)

IV

If law is the trunk, what is the elephant? As elephants tend to be, the substance of Guantánamo is both more profound and more prosaic than the law could ever be. Two things now matter about (and at) Guantánamo. Ironically, they are the same two things that mattered in 2002, when the first prisoners arrived. The first is the fate of the men imprisoned. In the relentless partisan pot-banging, we cannot hear their voice and no longer recognize their humanity. They have come to share the fate of the disappeared in every age, for whom the greatest fear is to be forgotten. In that respect, some of the most important scholarship currently underway comes from medical ethicists, who have written eloquently about the dilemmas arising from physician assistance in the forced feeding of Guantánamo prisoners who protest their detention by engaging in hunger strikes (e.g., Annas, 2017; Garasic, 2015; Garasic, 2013).

The second is the extent to which the United States—and especially the executive branch—has achieved an absolutely unfettered power in the war on terror. As a practical matter, there are no external constraints on US action, anywhere in the world. Despite the occasional legal successes, the United States has as much authority to act as it ever did. There is only the discretionary choice to restrain itself in any given case, if and as it sees fit. This is precisely what the architects of the post-9/11 response within the Bush administration sought (e.g., Yoo & Delahunty, 2001). They have been astoundingly successful, perhaps more than they ever imagined.

Here perhaps it is time to ask why we should care that so much effort is expended on symbol instead of substance. To begin with, I suggest there is an intrinsic value to studying what *is* rather than what one imagines. But even if I am wrong about this, the fact remains that scholars who write about Guantánamo seem to believe they are studying the elephant, and not the trunk. They behave as though, contrary to all the evidence, their research involves something terribly important about a genuine system of rules intended and determined to resolve real disputes. We are in apparent agreement, therefore, that the academy should address *both* symbol and substance. They have simply mistaken the two. Both are worth scholarly comment, but until we correctly distinguish one from the other, we lose all hope of thoughtful analysis.

But the confusion of symbol for substance is more than simply an academic mistake. It perpetuates dangerous myths and occludes problems that deserve far more scrutiny. Focusing on the victories in *Rasul* and *Boumediene*, for instance, without looking beyond them to the reality of *habeas* in Guantánamo, perpetuates the liberal illusion that litigation alone can be an effective tool to achieve social change (Rosenberg, 1991). Nothing in the history of post-9/11 litigation remotely supports this interpretation. In fact, it is only the recognition that *Rasul* and *Boumediene* contributed to *political* struggles that rescues them from the conclusion that they were both near-total failures (McCann, 1994).

Likewise, pretending that *Rasul* and *Boumediene* "solved" the problem of post-9/11 detentions blinds us to the reality of how US detention practices changed *precisely because of those decisions.* Since *Boumediene*, the United States has brought almost no prisoners to Guantánamo. Yet it continues to capture and detain an unknown number of prisoners in facilities beyond Guantánamo. To date, the courts have held that prisoners held by the United States in overseas facilities other than Guantánamo cannot challenge their detention in federal court unless they are US citizens (*Munaf*, 2008). So the net effect of *Rasul* and *Boumediene* was to create a perverse incentive for the United States to detain prisoners outside Guantánamo. Foreign nationals held outside the country are thus every bit as much beyond the law as the prisoners at Guantánamo ever were. At best, therefore, the litigation in *Rasul* and *Boumediene* did nothing to end the practice of wartime detentions beyond judicial supervision. It simply carved out Guantánamo as a curious space where a very limited, ineffectual form of supervision takes place. At worst, *Rasul* and *Boumediene* contributed—albeit unintentionally—to the erroneous conclusion that Guantánamo is *the* place where bad things happen in cages, particularly since the CIA closed its black sites.

This focus on Guantánamo blinds us to post-9/11 detentions taking place elsewhere and in other forms. For instance, during the latter part of the Bush administration and accelerating during the Obama administration, the United States began to form detention partnerships with allies, especially in the Horn of Africa. Terrorism suspects are nominally held by third countries like Uganda or Ethiopia, typically but not always on domestic criminal charges. In exchange for training, resources, and materiel provided by the United States, the third country grants US agents access to the prisoner as needed for interrogation and intelligence-gathering. Because the prisoner is at least nominally held by the third country, no federal court has jurisdiction and no reporter has access. The detentions are thus completely beyond supervision (Associated Press, 2007; Associated Press, 2008[3]

There is evidence these operations will continue and expand under President Trump. Recently, Defense Secretary Mattis met with Senators Lindsey Graham (R-SC) and John McCain (R-AZ), senior members of the Senate Armed Services Committee, and told them the United States will be shifting its counter-terror role

3 To be fair, a small number of scholars have written about detentions elsewhere (e.g., Hajjar, 2011; Sidhu, 2011).

to place more emphasis on Africa. After the meeting, Graham told reporters, "You're going to see more actions in Africa, not less; you're going to see more aggression by the United States toward our enemies, not less." Among the changes being considered include a revision of targeting policy to allow US troops to use deadly force against a target even if the person does not pose an immediate threat (Demirjian, 2017).

I stress that I am taking no position on whether this counter-terror shift to Africa is a good or bad thing. Likewise, I take no position on the shift from human intelligence gathering to signals intelligence, or from aerial assaults and ground troops to drone attacks. My point is simply that the obsessive focus on Guantánamo—and especially on aspects of Guantánamo that are utterly insignificant, like the military commissions and the law of detentions—threatens to consume all the oxygen in the room, leaving us unable and unwilling to unearth and critique the current state of unrestrained executive power in an increasingly global war. To the extent Guantánamo exemplifies and reveals this power, it is important. But to the extent it *conceals* this power by suggesting either that the power has been curbed when it has not, or that it is exercised only in Cuba when in fact it is global, Guantánamo has become a serious threat to the truth.[4]

Conclusion

The Bush administration conceived, designed, and built the prison at Guantánamo to be the ideal interrogation chamber—inaccessible to the public and unsupervised by the judiciary. But since the Supreme Court decision in *Rasul*, the prison hasn't served that function. Today, Guantánamo is both historical artefact and exorbitant irrelevance. It serves no substantive purpose except to drain the public fisc. Yet paradoxically, as it became *less* important as a prison, it became *more* important as a symbol. And because symbol has long since eclipsed substance, it is errant foolishness to obsess over every bolt and screw in the elaborate legal architecture that exists only to create the appearance of rule-of-law-regularity. Sadly, however, that is where most scholars have trained their attention. But those who stare at only a

4 I cannot close this review without at least mentioning some of the many self-serving accounts written by former players in the Bush administration. With rare but refreshing exceptions (e.g., Goldsmith, 2009), these are transparent attempts to pander to partisan crowds. Carrying titles like *Courting Disaster: How the CIA Kept America Safe and How Barack Obama is Inviting the Next Attack* (Thiessen, 2009), *Hard Measures: How Aggressive CIA Actions After 9/11 Saved American Lives* (Rodriguez & Harlow, 2012), and *Enhanced Interrogation: Inside the Minds and Motives of the Islamic Terrorists Trying to Destroy America* (Mitchell & Harlow, 2016), they disclose no important details and add nothing to the literature. On the other hand, they provide an enlightening window into the apparently limitless human capacity for self-justification. Many of these books defend the CIA torture program and thus do not focus exclusively on Guantánamo. I mention them because the CIA torture program and the prison at Guantánamo were two legs in the three-legged stool that made up the Bush administration's detention policy (the third being extraordinary rendition), and because several of the prisoners tortured by the CIA are now housed at Guantánamo.

single point eventually see nothing else, and the single-minded focus on the law threatens to rob us of the ability to see what now matters most—the fate of those imprisoned and the reality of unfettered power.

Acknowledgments

Many thanks to my colleagues Aziz Rana and Sid Tarrow for their helpful comments on an earlier draft of this review.

Disclosure statement

The author has no financial interest that might be favorably or adversely affected by this review. He does, however, represent *pro bono* Zayn al Abedin Muhammad Hussein, known more widely as Abu Zubaydah, a prisoner at Guantánamo and former prisoner at a CIA black site. He has also been involved in a number of legal challenges to post-9/11 detention policies around the world since late 2001.

Works cited

Ahuja, J. K. & Tutt, A., 2012. Evidentiary Rules Governing Guantánamo Habeas Petitions: Their Effects and Consequences. *Yale Law & Policy Review*, 31(1), pp. 185–226.

Alexander, M., 2010. *The New Jim Crow: Mass Incarceration in the Age of Colorblindness.* New York: New Press.

American Civil Liberties Union, 2017. *Guantánamo by the Numbers.* New York: American Civil Liberties Union.l

Annas, G. J., 2017. Force-feeding at Guantánamo. *J. Med. Ethics*, January, 43(1), p. 26.

Arouet, F.-M., 1767. *Le dîner du comte de Boulainvilliers: Deuxième Entretien.*

Arouet, F.-M., 1772. "La Bégueule," in *Contes* (*Tales*).

Blumer, H., 1971. Social Problems as Collective Behavior. *Social Problems*, 18, pp. 298–306.

Boumediene v.Bush. 2008. 553 U.S. 723.

Bravin, J., 2013. *Terror Courts: Rough Justice at Guantánamo Bay.* New Haven, CT: Yale University Press.

Bush, G. W. 2001. Detention, Treatment, and Trial of Certain Non-Citizens in the War Against Terrorism. November 13. [Online] Available at: Gerhard Peters and John T. Woolley, *The American Presidency Project.* www.presidency.ucsb.edu/ws/?pid=63124 [Accessed October 30, 2017].

Bush, G. W. 2006. Remarks on the War on Terror. September 6. [Online] Available at: Gerhard Petersand John T. Woolley, *The American Presidency Project.* http://www.presidency.ucsb.edu/ws/?pid=779. [Accessed 30 October 2017].

Cole, D., 2016. *Engines of Liberty: The Power of Citizen Activists to Make Constitutional Law.* New York: Basic Books.

Daskal, J., 2008. *Why Am I Still Here? The 2007 Horn of Africa Renditions and the Fate of Those Still Missing*, New York: Human Rights Watch.

Demirjian, K. Oct. 21, 2017. "U.S. counterterrorism efforts to grow in Africa," *Washington Post.*

Denbeaux, M. & Hafetz, J., 2012. *No Hearing Habeas: D.C. Circuit Restricts Meaningful Review*, Newark, NJ: Seton Hall University Law School, Center for Policy and Research.

May 1. [Online] Available at: http://law.shu.edu/ProgramsCenters/PublicIntGovServ/policyresearch/upload/hearing-habeas.pdf.

Edelman, M., 1964. *The Symbolic Uses of Politics.* Champagne-Urbana: University of Illinois Press.

Frakt, D. J. R., 2007. An Indelicate Balance: A Critical Comparison of the Rules and Procedures for Military Commissions and Courts-Martial. *American J. of Criminal Law*, 34(3), pp. 315–367.

Garasic, M. D., 2015. *Guantánamo and Other Cases of Forced Medical Treatment: A Biopolitical Analysis.* Heidelberg: Springer.

Goldsmith, J., 2012. *Power and Constraint: The Accountable Presidency after 9/11.* New York: W.W. Norton.

Gross, M. L., 2013. Force-Feeding, Autonomy, and the Public Interest. *New England J. of Medicine*, 11 July, 369, pp. 103–105.

Hajjar, L., 2011. Bagram: Obama's Other Gitmo. *Middle East Report*, October, 41(3), pp. 8–17.

Hinton, E., 2016. *From the War on Poverty to the War on Crime: The Making of Mass Incarceration in America.* Cambridge: Harvard University Press.

Human Rights First, 2017. *Guantánamo by the Numbers*, Washington, D.C.: Human Rights First.

Huq, Aziz. 2010. What Good Is Habeas? *Constitutional Commentary.* Summer, 26(3), pp. 385–432.

Kris, D. S., 2011. Law Enforcement as a Counterterrorism Tool. *Journal of National Security Law and Policy*, 5(1), pp. 1–104.

Lobel, J., 2004. *Success Without Victory: Lost Legal Battles and the Long Road to Justice in America.* New York: New York University Press.

Margulies, J., 2006. *Guantánamo and the Abuse of Presidential Power.* New York: Simon & Schuster.

Margulies, J., 2013. *What Changed When Everything Changed: 9/11 and the Making of National Identity.* New Haven, CT: Yale University Press.

Margulies, J., 2017. *Donald Trump and the National Security State.* [Online] Available at: https://verdict.justia.com/2017/01/09/donald-trump-national-security-state [Accessed October 30, 2017].

Margulies, J. & Metcalf, H., 2011. Terrorizing Academia. *Journal of Legal Education*, 60, pp. 433–471.

McCann, M., 1994. *Rights at Work: Pay Equity Reform and the Politics of Legal Mobilization.* Chicago: University of Chicago Press.

McDonald, T., 2013. A Few Good Angry Men: Application of the Jury Trial Clause of the Sixth Amendment to Non-Citizens Detained at Guantánamo Bay. *American University Law Review*, 62(3), pp. 701–737.

Merry, S. E., 1990. *Getting Justice and Getting Even: Legal Consciousness Among Working-Class Americans.* Chicago: University of Chicago Press.

Mitchell, J. E. & Harlow, B., 2016. *Enhanced Interrogation: Inside the Minds and Motives of the Islamic Terrorists Trying To Destroy America.* New York: Crown Publishing.

Munaf v.Geren. 2008. 553. U.S. 674.

Ní Aoláin, F. & Gross, O. eds., 2013. *Guantánamo and Beyond: Exceptional Courts and Military Commissions in Comparative Perspective.* New York: Cambridge University Press.

Obama, B., 2009. Executive Order 13491—Ensuring Lawful Interrogations. January 22, 2009. [Online] Available at: Gerhard Petersand John T. Woolley, *The American*

Presidency Project. www.presidency.ucsb.edu/ws/?pid=85669 [Accessed October 30, 2017].

O'Connor, S. D., 2008. Guantánamo Bay: Legal Black Hole. *Canterbury Law Review*, 14(2), pp. 207–216.

Pfaff, J., 2017. *Locked In: The True Causes of Mass Incarceration and How to Achieve Real Reform*. New York: Basic Books.

Press, A., 2007. *U.S. Interrogating at Africa's Secret Prisons*. Nairobi, Kenya: NBC News.

Rasul v.Bush. 2004. 542. U.S. 466.

Rodriguez, J. A. & Harlow, B., 2012. *Hard Measures: How Aggressive CIA Actions After 9/11 Saved American Lives*. New York: Threshold Editions.

Rosenberg, C., Oct. 14, 2017. "Guantanamo's USS Cole death-penalty case in limbo after key defense lawyer quits," *Miami Herald*.

Rosenberg, G., 1991. *The Hollow Hope: Can Courts Bring About Social Change?*Chicago: University of Chicago Press.

Scheppele, K. L., 2012. The New Judicial Deference. *Boston University Law Review*, 92(1), pp. 89–179.

Schneider, J. W., 1985. Social Problems Theory: A Constructionist View. *Am. Rev. Sociol.*,11, pp. 209–229.

Sevigny, E. L. & Caulkins, J. P., 2004. Kingpins or Mules: An Analysis of Drug Offenders Incarcerated in Federal and State Prisons. *Criminology and Public Policy*, 3, pp. 401–434.

Sherman, E. F., 2010. Terrorist Detainee Policies: Can the Constitutional and International Law Principles of the Boumediene Precedents Survive the Political Pressures? *Tulane Journal of International and Comparative Law*, 19(1), pp. 207–246.

Shklar, J., 1964. *Legalism: Law, Morals, and Political Trials*. Cambridge, MA: Harvard University Press.

Sidhu, D. S., 2011. Shadowing the Flag: Extending the Habeas Writ Beyond Guantánamo. *William and Mary Bill of Rights Journal*, 20, pp. 39–79.

Tarrow, S., 2015. *War, States, and Contention: A Comparative Historical Study*. Ithaca, NY: Cornell University Press.

Thiessen, M. A., 2009. *Courting Disaster: How the CIA Kept America Safe and How Barack Obama Is Inviting the Next Attack*. Washington, DC: Regnery.

Vitale, A., 2017. *The End of Policing*. New York: Verso Books.

Wagner, P. & Rabuy, B., 2017. *Mass Incarceration: The Whole Pie 2017*, Northampton, MA: Prison Policy Initiative.

Welna, D., Nov. 14, 2016. "Trump has Vowed to fill Guantanamo with 'Some Bad Dudes'—But Who?," *National Public Radio*.

Wittes, B., Chesney, R. M., & Reynolds, L., 2012. *The Emerging Law of Detention 2.0: The Guantánamo Habeas Cases as Lawmaking*, Cambridge, MA: Harvard Law School National Security Research Committee.

Yoo, J. & Delahunty, R., 2001. The President's Constitutional Authority to Conduct Military Operations Against Terrorists and Nations Supporting Them. Department of Justice, Office of Legal Counsel. [Online] Available at: www.justice.gov/sites/default/files/olc/opinions/2001/09/31/op-olc-v025-p0188_0.pdf [Accessed 30 October 2017].s

4 Experimentative counter-terrorism strategies after 9/11

Limitations of military responses to terrorism and violent extremism

Martin Ewi

Introduction

Sixteen years ago, the international community, shocked by the 9/11 attacks, undertook under the aegis of the United Nations, never again to witness such atrocious acts against humanity, and called upon states to "combat by all means, in accordance with the Charter of the United Nations, threats to international peace and security caused by terrorist acts." The sweeping nature of the international response that ensued, particularly following the adoption of the United Nations Security Council resolution 1373, signaled that 9/11 was indeed a cataclysmic act of terror to end terrorism. During this period, counter-terrorism emerged as the most dominant if not preponderant political discourse that has shaped international relations profoundly. The world changed after 9/11, and the past 16 years have been a struggle by the international community to stem terrorism, conceived as a common threat to humanity.

This new counter-terrorism world order has affected almost every aspect of life—communication, transportation, trade, social interaction, education, health, economic activities including banking, human rights, and civil liberties, and democratic processes (just to name a few). New security regimes and norms have been adopted and populations are gradually (with difficulties) accepting as the new normal, this new world order of securitization of everything. Whether the world has become safer from terrorism and violent extremism since 9/11 remains heavily contested. What is known for sure is that in terms of number of attacks globally, terrorism has shown no signs of waning. Instead, the phenomenon has burgeoned.

This chapter focuses on violent extremism and seeks to identify challenges and opportunities for countering such a form of extremism. It contends that among the various strategies that have been developed and implemented, a focus on countering violent extremism offers a silver lining in the fight against terrorism. It is argued that the debate on violent extremism offers a larger and inclusive framework from which to address the undercutting issues of terrorism such as motivation, radicalization, and violent extremist ideologies. Such an approach helps to map the ecological system in which violent extremism or terrorism grows. In other words, it explains how the interplay of environmental, social, economic, and political factors breeds or prevents terrorism. The purpose of this chapter is not to have an exhaustive definitions or debate, but rather to clarify the context in which they are used, and to provide an overview of the threat of terrorism since 9/11, with a view to discern trends in the threat of terrorism. It will undertake an examination of some of the major counter-terrorism strategies employed by the international community since 9/11. The chapter will discern some of the challenges and reasons why counter-terrorism strategies fail and succeed. Focus is then turned to countering violent extremism and the opportunities it presents. The chapter concludes with some lessons learned from the 16 years of counter-terrorism and countering violent extremism.

Terrorism

The first major attempt to define terrorism at the international level was under the League of Nations.[1] Numerous definitions exist, some of which focus on the perpetrators and targets or victims, others on objectives or purposes of the acts or perpetrators, while others focus on the acts and tactics and their outcome.[2] This definitional problem is largely confined to the United Nations (UN) level[3] and does not affect the entire international system.[4] Significant progress has been made towards defining terrorism at the regional and other organized interstate levels. For example, organizations such as the African Union (AU) with 55 member states,[5] European Union (EU) with 28 member states,[6] the Arab League with 22 member states,[7] and Association of Southeast Asian Nations (ASEAN) with 10 member states[8] all have instruments in which terrorism or its acts are defined.

1 The closest the international community has come to defining terrorism was under the League of Nations, which in 1937 defined terrorism as "criminal acts directed against a state and intended or calculated to create a state of terror in the minds of particular persons, or a group of persons or the general public." The key aspects of the League's definition included the notions of willfulness, attempting to, and supporting the commission of acts of terrorism. See Article 2(1–5) of the Convention for the Prevention and Punishment of Terrorism, adopted on November 16, 2017.

2 J. Stern, *The Ultimate Terrorists* (London: Harvard University Press, 1999), 11.

3 This is perhaps due to the fact that the UN comprises a vast diversity of states from all the regions of the world, each of which may have its own unique acquaintance and experience with terrorism.

4 Organizations such as the Organization of American States (OAS) with 35 member states have not been able to find consensus on a common definition, but have adopted legal instruments to address the crime of terrorism.

5 See Articles 1 and 3 of the OAU Convention on the Prevention and Combating of Terrorism, adopted in July 1999.

6 See Article 1 of the Council of Europe Framework Decision of June 13, 2002, on Combating Terrorism, and Article 1 of the Council of Europe Convention on the Prevention of Terrorism, adopted in Warsaw, Poland, on May 16, 2005.

7 See Article 1(2) of the Arab Convention on the Suppression of Terrorism, signed at Cairo, Egypt, on April 22, 1998.

8 See Article II of the ASEAN Convention on Counter-terrorism, adopted on January 13, 2007.

Despite the lack of a universal definition, studies on terrorism in the past two centuries have discerned certain elements and features common to most definitions.[9] These include the methods, targets, purpose or objectives, and perpetrators.[10] Progress made towards the conclusion of the UN Comprehensive Convention Against International Terrorism, demonstrates that international law has moved away from a purely academic definition to one that seeks to define or categorize the act. This means that there is a general understanding of what acts of terrorism are but not the concept.[11] The key challenge to international law is to separate terrorism from armed conflicts, and to determine as to whether the definition of terrorism should include state-sponsored terrorism and the activities of freedom fighters.[12] For the purpose of this report, the term "terrorism" shall be understood in the context defined by the United Nations Security Council resolution 1566 (2004). In that resolution, the Council recalls that terrorism refers to

> criminal acts, including against civilians, committed with the intent to cause death or serious bodily injury, or taking of hostages, with the purpose to provoke a state of terror in the general public or in a group of persons or particular persons, intimidate a population or compel a government or an international organization to do or to abstain from doing any act, which constitute offences within the scope of and as defined in the international conventions and protocols relating to terrorism, are under no circumstances justifiable by considerations of a political, philosophical, ideological, racial, ethnic, religious or other similar nature, and calls upon all States to prevent such acts and, if not prevented, to ensure that such acts are punished by penalties consistent with their grave nature.[13]

9 See, for example, S. Mahn and P.L. Griset, *Terrorism in Perspective* (Thousand Oaks, CA: Sage Publications, Inc., 2008), 5.

10 A.P. Schmid, Frameworks for Conceptualising Terrorism, *Terrorism and Political Violence*, Vol. 16:2, Winter 2004, 197–221. See also: A.P. Schmid, A Jongman et al., 1988, cited in L. Weinberg, A. Pedahzur, & S. Hirsch-Hoefler, The Challenges of Conceptualizing Terrorism, *Terrorism and Political Violence*, Vol. 16:4, Winter 2004, 781. See also, L. Weinberg, A. Pedahzur, & S. Hirsch-Hoefler, The Challenges of Conceptualising Terrorism, in J. Horgan & K. Braddock (eds.), *Terrorism Studies: A Reader* (New York: Routledge, 2012), 76–90.

11 Due to the lack of a general definition of terrorism, the UN has adopted 19 universal instruments on different acts of terrorism. For a comprehensive list of the 19 universal counter-terrorism instruments, see United Nations Office on drugs and Crime (UNODC) website: www.un.org/en/counter-terrorism/legal-instruments.shtml, accessed March 17, 2017.

12 E.S. Bates, *Terrorism and International Law: Accountability, Remedies, and Reform*, a report of the IBA Task Force on Terrorism (Oxford: Oxford University Press, 2011), 2.

13 See operative paragraph 3 of the United Nations Security Council resolution 1566, Security Council's document *S/RES/1566 (2004)*, dated 8 October 2004.

Violent extremism

For the purpose of this report, violent extremism is understood as "an ideology that accepts the use of violence for the pursuit of goals that are generally social, racial, religious and/or political in nature."[14]

Counter-terrorism (CT)

The online *Oxford Advanced Learner's Dictionary* defines counter-terrorism as "action taken to prevent the activities of political groups who use violence to try to achieve their aims."[15] This definition would have been largely sufficient had it not limited the action to prevention, and terrorists to political groups. Counter-terrorism therefore from an inclusive perspective can be defined as encompassing all offensive and defensive actions including diplomatic, political, economic, legal and judicial, social, and military and/or security measures taken to prevent, neutralize and/or combat terrorist-related activities. It is not limited to the actions of governments but also include such actions by civil society, civil society organizations, private sector, academic and research institutions, and nongovernmental organizations (NGOs).

Countering violent extremism (CVE)/preventing violent extremism (PVE)

Countering violent extremism (CVE) is generally understood as efforts aimed at reducing the support for or participation in violent extremism through non-coercive means by identifying and addressing factors conducive to the spread of terrorism.[16] It refers to interventions designed to respond to a particular extremist threat or community vulnerability.[17] In this context, CVE refers to any action taken to address the pull and push factors including psychopathological, socioeconomic, political, and environmental factors that lead individuals to participate in violent extremism. Preventing violent extremism (PVE) refers to specific non-coercive measures taken to thwart the development or escalation of conditions and drivers of violent extremism. It emphasizes the need to create conditions that engender peace and security such as good governance and equal opportunity to both economic and political resources. While CVE seeks to prevent and counter violent extremism activities in order to return society to normality, PVE aims specifically

14 See J.L. Striegher, Violent-Extremism: An Examination of a Definitional Dilemma, Edith Cowan University Research Online, January 2015, 79, available electronically at: http://ro.ecu.edu.au/do/search/?q=Jason-Leigh%20Striegher&start=0&context=1738305&facet, accessed May 11, 2017.

15 See *Oxford Advanced Learner's Dictionary*, www.oxfordlearnersdictionaries.com/definition/english/counter-terrorism?q=Counter-terrorism, accessed April 12, 2017.

16 See "Countering Violent Extremism and Promoting Community Resilience in the Greater Horn of Africa: An Action Agenda," a report by the Global Center on Cooperative Security, May 2015, 2.

17 Ibid.

at strengthening society's resilience against violent extremism by addressing its fragility to the phenomenon. CT and CVE/PVE are often confused and are sometimes used interchangeably. The key distinguishing factor is that CT is much broader and may involve both military and non-military strategies, while CVE/PVE are largely non-military in nature and are much deeper in their scope as they deal with preconditions and secondary factors that result in terrorism.

The global terrorist threat since 9/11

There are not many ways of determining the level of the threat of terrorism that confronts the world since 9/11. Approaching it quantitatively often poses many problems due partly to the fact that there is no universally accepted definition of terrorism. As a result, what is considered a terrorist incident may differ from one data source to another. This problem is further complicated by the fact that most data sources on terrorism rely on media-reported incidents, which often lack consistency and accuracy of facts. Despite these shortcomings, data remains the closest indicator for determining the global scale of terrorism. In this context, in order to determine the level of global terrorism since 9/11, data is used only as an indicator. It is also important to note that the data used here reflects only the global macro picture and not the micro picture at the state level, which may be different. For example, global data show increasing trends in terrorist attacks since 9/11, whereas the data for the United States of America demonstrate decreasing trends. According to various data sources, there has been an unprecedented surge in global terrorist attacks since 9/11, with a record number of casualties since recorded data began in 1968.[18] Figure 4.1 illustrates these trends. It makes clear the dramatic increases in terrorist incidences worldwide after 9/11, reaching a peak in 2014, when over 16,860 incidences were recorded that year. After dipping in 1998, stagnating in 1999 and 2000, recording a sharp rise in 2001 and 2002.

Figure 4.2 shows the rising trends in fatalities from terrorist incidents since 9/11, reaching their highest mark in 2014, which recorded over 30,000 deaths. These fatalities were largely concentrated in three countries—Iraq, Nigeria, and Afghanistan as the figure shows. Deaths from terrorist attacks since 9/11 have mimicked the same trends seen in the number of attacks, as demonstrated in Figure 4.1. According to the Consortium for the Study of Terrorism and Responses to Terrorism (START), which maintains the largest database of terrorist incidences, 65,000 people died from terrorist attacks during the first decade after 9/11, averaging 7,258 deaths per year.[19] This represents a

18 See, for example, M. Roser and M. Nagdy, Terrorism, Our World in Data online data on terrorism: https://ourworldindata.org/terrorism/#terrorism-after-911, accessed June 8, 2017.

19 START Background Report: 9/11, Ten Years Later, 5, www.start.umd.edu/gtd/, accessed April 10, 2017.

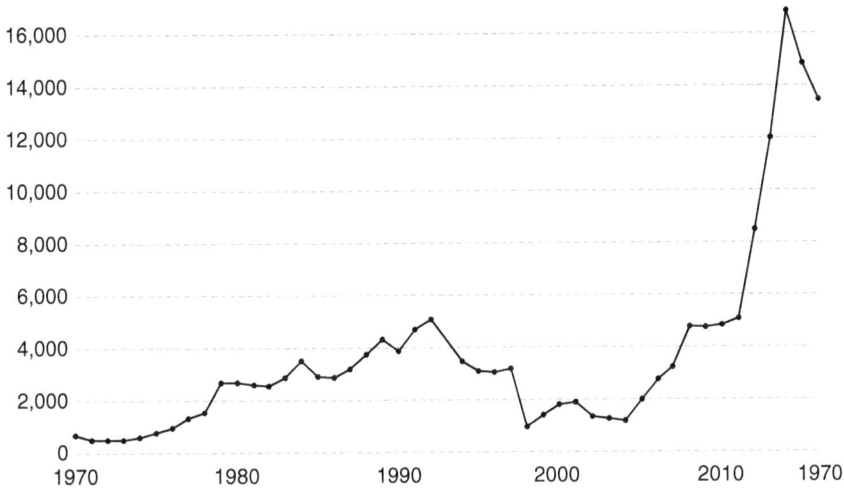

Figure 4.1 Total incidences of terrorist attacks worldwide, 1970–2016[20]

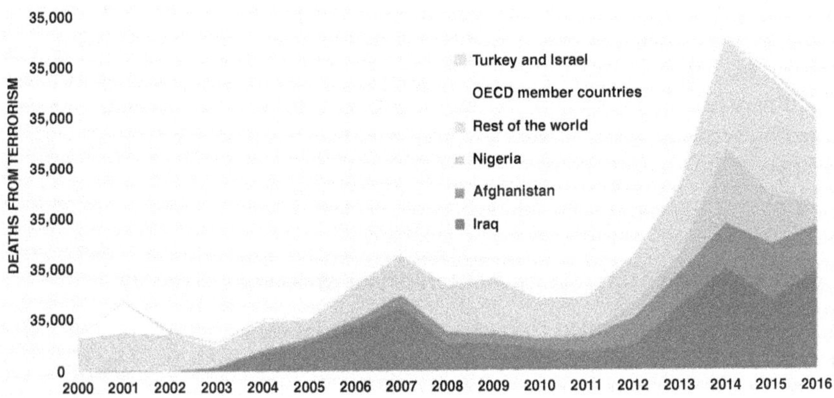

Figure 4.2 Trends in fatalities caused by terrorism 2000–2016
Source: Institute of Economics and Peace (IEP) 2017 Global Terrorism Index p.16[21]

20 Our World in Data: https://ourworldindata.org/terrorism
21 See Institute of Economics and Peace (IEP) Global Terrorism Index Report for 2016, http://economicsandpeace.org/reports/, accessed May 15, 2017.

dramatic increase from the previous decade, which recorded a total of 61,000 deaths with an annual average death of 6,825.[22] The Institute for Economics and Peace (IEP), a think-tank organization that measures the global economic impact of terrorism, provides in its 2017 Global Terrorism Index (GTI) a comprehensive view of the trends of terrorism since 9/11. The figure "Trends in deaths caused by terrorism 2000–2016" summarizes the trends in deaths from terrorist attacks between 2000 and 2016.[23]

According to IEP, deaths in terrorism have grown from 3,361 in 2012 to 29,376 in 2015. Since 9/11, the deadliest year has been 2014, which recorded 32,685 deaths from 14,000 attacks. The figure "Trends in deaths caused by terrorism 2000–2016" illustrates the distribution of the deaths by target category. As shown, private citizens have been targeted more than any other category reaching its peak in 2014, which is also considered the year with the highest terrorist deaths since record began. This is followed by others including business, police, military, and government, in that order. These data also show the expansive nature of terrorism since 9/11, with 85 countries experiencing attacks in 2012, 88 in 2013, and 93 in 2014.

It can therefore be concluded from the above data that the terrorist threat has intensified, become more deadly and widespread. In theory, it also means that global responses to terrorism have not had an impact. From a micro perspective, this conclusion may be misleading given that the global data on terrorism was dominated by a few countries, particularly the top ten countries, namely, Iraq, Afghanistan, Nigeria, Pakistan, Syria, Yemen, Somalia, India, Egypt, and Libya, which accounted for over 90% of the attacks and deaths. What cannot be contested however, is the fact that more countries have been affected by terrorism in the post 9/11 period, making terrorism more global than it has ever been in history.

Failed experimentative counter-terrorism strategies after 9/11

This section is not intended to evaluate counter-terrorism strategies and measures after 9/11.[24] The purpose here is to identify broad strategies that have not worked and those that have worked. The 9/11 attacks caught the world unprepared for anything of that magnitude. Security issues were not a priority of the UN at the time, as the Cold War rivalry had ended and conflicts had become localized or internalized. The focus was on the new millennium and its promise for humanity, with priority accorded to human rights, development, and the consolidation of democracy. In fact, less than a year earlier (before 9/11), 106

22 Ibid.

23 See the IEP Global Terrorism Index Report for 2016, Global Terrorism Index Report for 2016, http://economicsandpeace.org/reports/, accessed May 15, 2017.

24 For readers interested in an evaluation of the counter-terrorism since 9/11, see N. Adams, T. Nordhaus, and M, Shellenberger, *Counter-terrorism Since 9/11: Evaluating the Efficacy of Controversial Tactics*, (Oakland, ON: Breakthrough Institute, Spring 2011), accessible at: www.thebreakthrough.org, accessed June 21, 2017.

countries had met in Warsaw, Poland, in June 2000, to sign the Warsaw Declaration, which outlined what was described as the "core democratic principles and practices"[25] that its signatories committed to uphold. Democracy was hailed as a panacea to post-Cold War internal conflicts and insurgencies in Africa and other developing countries. The adoption of the Millennium Development Goals by the UN, which set out clear targets and timelines for eradicating extreme poverty,[26] was a historic achievement that further emphasized the new focus on development.

Military invasion of countries perceived to be harboring terrorists

Most post-9/11 responses have been conducted at ad hoc, without proper planning. No one really knew what effective CT strategies are and which ones are not. It has therefore been a learning curve for the international community, as to how to effectively and efficiently fight terrorism. As a result, various experimentative strategies have been developed and implemented. At the outset, the strategy was to go with brute force, which became the fulcrum of the so-called global war on terror, to tear down countries that were believed to be harboring terror or posed a threat to the civilized world, known in American parlance as the "axis of evil." This strategy saw the United Nations Security Council (UNSC) approve invasion of Afghanistan in 2001,[27] the controversial American–British invasion of Iraq in 2003, and the UN tacit approval of North Atlantic Treaty Organization (NATO)-backed military operations in Libya in 2011.[28] This use of force did not augur well for the fight against terrorism as it backfired, creating more enemies and destabilizing more states, which became safe havens for terrorists.[29] The military operations in Libya helped Islamist militants to destabilize Mali, where in 2012 they controlled three-quarters of the country's territory—the vast northern region.[30] Research also indicated that arms from Libya helped Boko

25 See the Warsaw Declaration, www.community-democracies.org/values/warsaw-declaration/, accessed March 20, 2017.

26 See Millennium Summit, UN website, www.un.org/en/events/pastevents/millennium_summit.shtml, accessed July 11, 2017.

27 See UNSC resolution 1386, Security Council's document *S/RES/1386 (2001)*, dated December 20, 2001.

28 See, for example, UN Security Council resolution 1973, Security Council's document *S/RES/1973 (2011)* dated March 17, 2011.

29 For an in-depth assessment of the counter-terrorism operations in Afghanistan, Iraq, and Libya, see, D. Held and K.C. Ulrichsen, Wars of Decline: Afghanistan, Iraq and Libya, *Open Democracy*, December 12, 2011, www.opendemocracy.net/david-held-kristian-coates-ulrichsen/wars-of-decline-afghanistan-iraq-and-libya, accessed April 28, 2017.

30 See, for example, L. Dearden, How David Cameron's Intervention in Libya is Fueling War and Terror around the World, *Independent*, September 15, 2016, www.independent.co.uk/news/world/africa/libya-report-britain-uk-gaddafi-civil-war-david cameron-responsible-terrorism-isis-al-qaeda-mali-a7309821.html, accessed July 7, 2017.

Haram to seize large swathes of land in Nigeria estimated to be more than the size of Belgium.[31] The biggest legacy of the invasion of Iraq and Syria was the creation of the world's largest, fiercest, and deadliest terrorist group—known variously as the Islamic State of Iraq and Syria (ISIS), Islamic State of Iraq and Levant (ISIL), Islamic State (IS), Da'esh, and so on, which declared an Islamic Caliphate after taking over control of several territories in Syria and Iraq, including Mosul—Iraq's second largest and richest city.[32] ISIS has also recruited several thousands of youths, which in the UN's modest estimate amounted to 30,000 from over 100 countries.[33] The emergence of ISIS has further inspired the creation of numerous terrorist groups, estimated to be over 5,000 around the world, which have been more deadly than those that existed during the pre-9/11 period.[34]

Hardline military strategies

Despite various resolutions of the UN such as Security Council resolution 1373 (2001) as well as the General Assembly Global Counter-Terrorism Strategy (2006), which obligate states to address the conditions conducive to terrorism, states' instinctive reaction to a terrorist attack is through the deployment of coercive and excessive military operations, which violate human rights and civil liberties. This is evident in several countries where terrorism is pervasive. For example, Nigeria's instinctive military response to Boko Haram's riots in July 2009, provoked the largest and deadliest terrorist insurgency the country had ever known. US's instinctive military attacks in Afghanistan and Iraq strengthened the Taliban and inspired the creation of ISIS, two of the world's fiercest terror groups. Heavy military responses in Cameroon, Pakistan, India, Kenya, Egypt, Bangladesh, and Somalia have not resolved the issues of terrorism in those countries. Lengthy and ferocious military campaigns against the Tamil Tigers in Sri Lanka did not end terrorism, but negotiations and other soft measures did.

This instinctive military response to terrorism seems to arise principally from the fact that the executive branch of government has absolute monopoly over counter-terrorism responses. The executive sees a terrorist attack as a test of toughness, of the resilience of the administration, and reacts nervously with fear of losing. Counter-terrorism experts have warned that responses to terrorism that are based on fear lead to bad policy and practice because they prompt basic human instincts

31 L. Charbonneau, Arms from Libya could reach Boko Haram, al Qaeda: UN, *Reuters*, January 26, 2012, www.reuters.com/article/us-libya-un-arms-idUSTRE80P1QS20120126, accessed March 29, 2017.

32 D Filkins, Did George W. Bush Create ISIS? *The New Yorker*, May 15, 2015, www.newyorker.com/news/news-desk/did-george-w-bush-create-isis, accessed February 18, 2017.

33 See "Report of the Secretary-General on the Threat Posed by ISIL (Da'esh) to International Peace and Security and the Range Of United Nations Efforts in Support of Member States in Countering the Threat," Security Council's document *S/2016/92* dated January 29, 2016, 7.

34 See, for example, K. Leigh, J. French, and J. Juan, Islamic State and Its Affiliates, WSJ, http://graphics.wsj.com/islamic-state-and-its-affiliates/, accessed 12 July 2017.

of fight or flight.[35] No military has ever won a war against terrorism. In Algeria for example, despite the military's instrumental role and targeted killing of militants, the fight against the Salafi Group for Preaching and Combat (GSPC), which would later become the al-Qaeda in the Islamic Maghreb (AQIM), only achieved significant results after the government diversified its approach and involved communities, as well as introducing a reward system. The excessive military force is based on a faulty doctrine that by out-powering terrorists with more fighters and bigger and advanced weapons, the military can crush them. When the military becomes tougher terrorists go for softer targets. Because of their flexibility, terrorists will always adapt to new security conditions.

This excessive military force has gone unchecked in the post-9/11 period because of the emergence of a counter-terrorism exceptionalism emanating from the preeminence or the political exigency of the fight against terrorism. States have interpreted this as a blanket check for them to do anything in the name of counter-terrorism. The results have been massive violations of human rights as states have used counter-terrorism to justify extrajudicial killings of terrorist suspects, rendition and extraordinary rendition, torture of terrorist suspects, and the curtailment of democratic norms and practices. To sustain this coercive military response to terrorism and violent extremism, many states have suspended democratic constitutions and declared lengthy state of emergencies.[36] For example, the United States remains under the state of emergency declared in 2001;[37] France has been under a state of emergency since November 2015;[38] Egypt, Algeria, and Tunisia battling ISIS, al-Qaeda, and their affiliates have been under lengthy state of emergencies; Nigeria in its struggle against Boko Haram declared a state of emergency in three northern states in April 2014, which remains in place (as of July 31, 2018); and Iraq has declared numerous state of emergencies since 2004.

Other countries that have declared state of emergencies granting extraordinary counter-terrorism powers to security forces, thereby significantly limiting political freedom and civil liberties, include but are not limited to Pakistan, Nepal, Syria,

35 See for example, A. Du Plessis, In Counterterrorism, Good Evidence Trumps Bad Instinct, *Daily Maverick*, September 19, 2016, www.dailymaverick.co.za/article/2016-09-19-op-ed-in-counterterrorism-good-evidence-trumps-bad-instinct/, accessed September 20, 2016.

36 Although international law does permit the declaration of state of emergency to allow states pursue national security objectives, particularly to reestablish public order and safety, this limitation, however, does not apply to absolute rights such as right to life, prohibition of torture and cruel, inhuman or degrading treatment or punishment. For a comprehensive discussion, see E.S. Bates, *Terrorism and International Law: Accountability, Remedies, and Reform*, A report of the IBA Task Force on Terrorism (Oxford: Oxford University Press, 2011), 147.

37 See G. Korte, Special Report: America's Perpetual State of Emergency, *USA Today*, October 22, 2014, www.usatoday.com/story/news/politics/2014/10/22/president-obama-states-of-emergency/16851775/, accessed April 1, 2017.

38 See R. Zaretsky, France's Perpetual State of Emergency, *Foreign Policy*, July 16, 2016, http://foreignpolicy.com/2016/07/16/frances-perpetual-state-of-emergency/, accessed March 19, 2017.

Philippines, Ethiopia, Kenya, Serbia, Belgium, Mali, Burkina Faso, Cote d'Ivoire, Chad, and Niger. As discussed further below, states have used this constitutional emergency clause to carry out gross violations of political rights and civil liberties. In some cases, states have created no man's lands such as Guantanamo Bay, to evade constitutional and criminal justice requirements for fair trial, no torture and the respect of the human rights of terrorist suspects, including during interrogation in contradiction to the Warsaw principles and practices, particularly principles 8, 9, 10, and 11.[39] Furthermore, human rights organizations have accused the US government of operating "floating prisons" to illegally detain those arrested in its war on terror.[40]

In some cases, the US president has detained suspects abroad and revoked their habeas corpus right, which denies them justice.[41] As Theresa May, the British prime minister, revealed in her reaction to a series of terrorist attacks in London and Manchester in the first half of 2017, the executive seems to see counter-terrorism as incompatible with human rights. The prime minister spoke of "longer prison sentences for anyone convicted of terrorism offences, and making it easier to deport foreign terrorist suspects back to their own countries," and about "doing more to restrict the freedom and movements of terrorist suspects when we have enough evidence to know they are a threat, but not enough evidence to prosecute them in full in court,"[42] and she added that "If our human rights laws stop us from doing it, we will change the laws so we can do it."[43] In other words, May, like most executives when faced with terrorism, is basically saying that she is ready to compromise human rights for the sake of counter-terrorism. By nature, military strategies are incompatible with human rights and studies on violent

39 Principles 8, 9, 10, and 11 enumerates civil liberties and political rights equal protection of the law, and the rights to be free from arbitrary arrest or detention; to be free from torture and other cruel, inhumane or degrading treatment or punishment; and to receive due process of law, including to be presumed innocent until proven guilty in a court of law.

40 See, for example, D. Campbell and R. Norton-Taylor, US Accused of Holding Terror Suspects on Prison Ships, *Global Policy Forum*, June 2, 2008, www.globalpolicy.org/component/content/article/154/26822.html, accessed February 23, 2017. See also M. Porges, America's Floating Prisons, *The Atlantic*, June 27, 2014, www.theatlantic.com/international/archive/2014/06/americas-floating-prisons/373577/, accessed April 15, 2017.

41 See, for example, Sudeshna Sen, 9/11: Ten Years of Towering Terror, *The Economic Times*, September 12, 2011, http://blogs.economictimes.indiatimes.com/LettersfromLondon/9-11-ten-years-of-towering-terror/?sortBy=mostThreaded, accessed February 7, 2016.

42 Cited in S. Allison, Dear Theresa May: a Counter-Terrorism Lesson from Africa, *Daily Maverick*, June 12, 2017, www.dailymaverick.co.za/article/2017-06-12-dear-theresa-may-a-counter-terrorism-lesson-from-africa/#.WXWFl4pLc_U, accessed June 18, 2017.

43 Cited in Martha Spurrier, Theresa May Has Said She'll Rip Up Human Rights. We Should All Be Afraid, *Guardian*, June 7, 2017, www.theguardian.com/commentisfree/2017/jun/07/theresa-may-human-rights-european-charter-terrorists, accessed July 3, 2017.

extremism have shown that the military option is not effectual in addressing the complex undercutting issues that lead youths to violent extremism. Hughes, for example, argues that one of the problems of deploying military in CT/CVE tasks is that armed forces are doctrinally trained for warfare, and not for the hard task of identifying and tracking terrorists, who hide among the civilian population.[44]

The challenge is that the military cannot replace the police, which is the civilian force for dealing with social problems.[45] Empirical evidence on the role of the military has been mixed. Examples from Pakistan,[46] Nigeria[47] and Indonesia[48] have shown that military operations can play a significant role in reducing violent extremism, and at the same time they often result in backlash that fuels or inflames terrorism and violent extremism.[49] Excessive military operations often end up hurting more innocent people, whose urge for revenge pushes them to participate in violent extremism.[50] For Fukuyama, "[c]oercion remains central to the functioning of the state, which is why state power so often generates fear and hatred."[51]

Draconian and repressive anti-terrorism legislations

A record number of 140 states adopted or amended legislations on CT/CVE between 2001 and 2012.[52] Many of these legislations are adopted on the basis of

44 G. Hughes, The Military's Role in Counter-terrorism: Examples and Implications for Liberal Democracies, *The Letort Papers*, May 2011, 47.

45 See, for example, D.K. Gupta, The World After 9/11: What Have We Learned, *India Quarterly*, Vol. 68:1, 2012, 11.

46 M. Nazir, Daesh in South Asia, *Journal of Current Affairs*, Vol. 1:1&2, 2016, 7.

47 For example, a study by the CLEEN Foundation found that excessive military force by the Nigerian government against Boko Haram has not been a major factor in youth radicalization. See CLEEN Foundation, Youths, Radicalisation and Affiliation with Insurgent Groups in Northern Nigeria, *Monograph Series*, No. 20, 2014, xi; see also A. Botha, M. Ewi, U. Salifu, and M. Abdile, Understanding Nigerian citizens' perspectives on Boko Haram, ISS Monograph Series, No. 196, 2017, 48–49.

48 D. Timberman, Violent Extremism and Insurgency in Indonesia: A Risk Assessment, a report of the Management Systems International, reviewed by USAID, January 7, 2013.

49 S. Hellsten, Radicalisation and Terrorist Recruitment among Kenya's Youth, the Nordic Africa Institute *Policy Note*, No. 1, February 2016, 3–4. See also A. Botha, Assessing the Vulnerability of Kenyan Youths to Radicalisation and Extremism, *ISS Paper*, No. 245, April 2013, 6–7.

50 Mockaitis et al. cite the case of Israel's military intervention in Lebanon, in response to Hezbollah rocket attacks in 2006, which failed to put an end to rocket attacks, as an example of how an "overly militarily focused 'kinetic operation'" can make a bad situation even worse. See T.R. Mockaitis, C. Tucker Jr., and A. Invictus, The Military and the Role of Law in Countering Terrorism, in A.M.S. De Frias, K.L.H. Samuel, and ND White (eds.), *Counter-Terrorism: International Law and Practice* (New York: Oxford University Press, 2012), 392.

51 F. Fukuyama, Why Is Democracy Performing so Poorly? In L. Diamond and M.F. Plattner (eds.), *Democracy in Decline?* (Baltimore, MD: Johns Hopkins University Press, 2015), 14.

52 See In the Name of Security: Counter-terrorism Laws Worldwide since September 11, *Human Rights Watch*, June 29, 2012, www.hrw.org/report/2012/06/29/name-security/counter-terrorism-laws-worldwide-september-11, accessed April 21, 2017.

the principle of *salus reipublicae suprema lex*, or the principle that the safety of the state is supreme, instead of the *salus populi suprema lex*, which accords supremacy to the people. This means that states have approached the post-9/11 terrorist threat as a national security, rather than a human security, issue. Responses to the latter often emphasize a focus on the basic needs of people that so often underlie the genesis of terrorism and violent extremism, whereas a focus on national security often elicits hard security measures and a powerful executive branch at the detriment of other branches of government, which are key for a functional democracy. This has also encouraged repressive and draconian measures, which often limit citizens' political rights, and civil liberties. For example, Turkey perceived the failed coup plot in July 2016 and a series of terrorist attacks as a national security issue. As a result, the government arrested and detained thousands of people as suspects, and subsequently organized a referendum in April 2017, which gave the president more constitutional powers,[53] including the ability to enact certain laws by decree.[54] It has become evident that counter-terrorism legislations have been used to extend the executive powers and to legalize human rights violations by states. Human Rights Watch has summarized the eight major features of the post–9/11 CT/CVE laws that raise human rights concerns.[55] These include:

1 definitions of terrorism and terrorist acts;
2 designations of terrorist organizations and banning membership in them;
3 restrictions on funding and other material support to terrorism and terrorist organizations;
4 limitations on expression or assembly that ostensibly encourage, incite, justify, or lend support to terrorism;
5 expansions of police powers that undermine basic rights, including powers to conduct warrantless arrests, searches, surveillance, and property seizures, and to detain suspects incommunicado and without charge; as well as restrictions on challenging wrongful detention or seeking accountability for police abuses;
6 creation of special courts and modifications of trial procedures (including evidentiary rules) to favor the prosecution by limiting defendants' due process rights;
7 imposition of the death penalty for terrorism-related offenses; and
8 creation of administrative detention and "control order" mechanisms.

53 See Why Did Turkey Hold a Referendum? *BBC News*, April 16, 2017, www.bbc.com/news/world-europe-38883556, accessed April 18, 2017.
54 See Does Erdogan Expect Trump to Ditch Syrian Kurds?, *Al Monitor*, April 23, 2017, www.al-monitor.com/pulse/originals/2017/04/erdogan-trump-hopes-iran-tempers-iraqi-saudi-rapprochement.html?utm_source=Boomtrain&utm_medium=manual&utm_campaign=20170423&bt_ee=heVk3QUkGgWs6GgXpolKXAY7QjctRleaq35nRCdQ5Zeqptn75kyL74eA3szTG/hP&bt_ts=1493022922535, accessed April 24, 2017.
55 See In the Name of Security: Counter-terrorism Laws Worldwide since September 11, Human Rights Watch, June 29, 2012, www.hrw.org/report/2012/06/29/name-security/counter-terrorism-laws-worldwide-september-11, accessed April 21, 2017.

One indicator of the repressive nature of post-9/11 CT/CVE legislation is the resurgence of the death penalty, which is strongly discouraged in international law. Its revival reflects the retributive and draconian nature of post-9/11 CT/CVE strategies, in all the countries where terrorism is considered a capital offence. Of the 140 countries with CT/CVE legislation, 82 or 58.57% of them have capital punishment or death penalty.[56] Of the 24 172 death sentences between 2007 and 2012, 6,221 or 25.74% were executed, with 38.42% of the executions occurring in 2008.[57]

Rendition, extraordinary rendition, illegal deportation, and extrajudicial killings

The Warsaw Declaration requires states to refrain from extra-constitutional actions. Nonetheless, because of the exigency of the counter-terrorism exceptionalism, some states have indulged in various extra-judicial activities. International law requires states to cooperate in the fight against terrorism, and there are clear principles upon which such cooperation should be conducted. These include the principles of extradition and mutual legal assistance. The former defines state jurisdiction and the basis upon which states may extradite or surrender terrorist suspects to one another. The latter deals with the technical support that states may need from each other to facilitate prosecution or a terrorist suspect. States may also legally deport individuals who violate immigration rules and other national laws as provided under the constitution. Several states unlawfully arrest and render terrorist suspects to others through covert operations that flagrantly violate their own constitutions. Such suspects are often exposed to torture, unlawful detention in secret prisons, or special detention facilities, and cruel interrogative techniques and other inhuman and degrading treatment. In one such case, a judge in Kenya ruled that the Kenyan government's deportations of Somali immigrants from Kenya to Somalia and finally to Ethiopia in 2007 were unlawful, and ordered the government to pay the sum of nearly $460,000 as restitution.[58] Hillebrand has cited the US government's Guantanamo Bay and Abu Ghraib facilities as typical examples of such facilities.[59] In covert operations, several states have also carried out unlawful mass deportations of terrorist suspects and refugees, and have used intelligence agencies to carry out decapitations and extrajudicial executions of

56 See Amnesty International, www.amnesty.org/en/who-we-are/, accessed April 26, 2017.

57 Data provided by Amnesty International, cited in *Guardian*: www.theguardian.com/news/datablog/2011/mar/29/death-penalty-countries-world#data, accessed April 26, 2017.

58 See Kenya to Pay $460k to Rendition Victims," News24, August 2, 2013, www.news24.com/Africa/News/Kenya-to-pay-460k-to-rendition-victims-20130801, accessed March 26, 2017

59 C. Hillebrand, The CIA's Extraordinary Rendition and Secret Detention Programme: European Reactions and the Challenges of Future International Intelligence Co-Operation, a report by The Hague, Netherlands Institute of International Relations Clingendael, March 2009.

terrorist suspects. These practices have significantly undermined democracy. Recently, President Trump's counter-terrorism strategy, built on the effective control of immigration, attracted global condemnation[60] when the president signed an executive order that effectively denied entry to people from seven Muslim-majority countries, including those with green cards, who otherwise have permanent residence in the US.[61]

Successful experimentative strategies

Use of drones and other precision military equipment

The military is not generally recommended for counter-terrorism operations; however, when it is used responsibly, not in an excessive manner, and when its operations are surgical and guided by intelligence, the military can be an important force for counter-terrorism. On April 13, 2017, President Trump ordered the use of the largest non-nuclear bomb also known as the mother of all bombs (MOAB) or GBU-43 in Afghanistan in order to smoke out ISIS's militants from their tunnel complexes in the province of Nangarhar.[62] The airstrike was symptomatic of the preponderant military approach to the fight against terrorism since 9/11, which has been characterized by air bombardments and ground military operations. The blueprint of this approach is embodied in the so-called "Coalition of the Willing" comprising 46 countries, created by the administration of George W. Bush in 2003, which was later succeeded by the Global Coalition to defeat ISIS in August 2014,[63] comprising 68 countries (including France, the United Kingdom, Germany, and several Gulf countries), under the Obama administration.[64]

As of July 21, 2017, the date this chapter was finalized, the Coalition had carried out 29,786 airstrikes, in which 108,107 bombs and missiles were dropped in Iraq and Syria.[65] This is excluding similar military operations in Afghanistan,

60 See O. Douliery, World Leaders Condemn Donald Trump's "Muslim Ban," *Al Jazeera*, January 28, 2017, www.aljazeera.com/news/2017/01/world-leaders-condemn-donald-trump-muslim-ban-170128134635041.html, accessed March 30, 2017.

61 See Trump Signs Executive Order Banning Syrian Refugees," *Al Jazeera*, January 28, 2017, www.aljazeera.com/news/2017/01/trump-signs-executive-order-banning-syrian-refugees-170128033811131.html, accessed March 30, 2017.

62 E. Tamkin & P. MCleary, United States Drops "Mother of All Bombs" on ISIS in Afghanistan, *Foreign Policy*, April 13, 2017, http://foreignpolicy.com/2017/04/13/united-states-drops-mother-of-all-bombs-on-isis-in-afghanistan/?utm_source=Sailthru&utm_medium=email&utm_campaign=Ed%20pix%204-13&utm_term=%2AEditors%20Picks

63 J.S. Robbins, Fighting the Islamic State: The U.S. Scorecard, *The Journal of International Security Affairs*, No. 30, Winter 2016, www.securityaffairs.org/issues/number-30/fighting-islamic-state-us-scorecard, accessed April 12, 2017.

64 For details about the Coalition's activities, see www.defense.gov/News/Special-Reports/0814_Inherent-Resolve/, accessed April 20, 2017.

65 See Airwars, a website that monitors the Global Coalition's activities with a view to assessing civilian casualties, https://airwars.org/, accessed April 26, 2017.

Somalia, Libya, Egypt, Nigeria, Mali, Cameroon, Niger, Pakistan, India, and Yemen, which have become the expanded theaters or frontlines in the global campaign to defeat ISIS, al-Qaeda, and their affiliates in these countries. Typical with such military operations, civilians have been caught in the line of fire, which conservative estimates put the total number as 3,111 civilian casualties[66] from the Coalition's, not ISIS's bombings. Beside the civilian and humanitarian cost of the operations, the Coalition has incurred huge financial cost, which as of February 28, 2017, was estimated to be US$11.9 billion, an average daily cost of US$12.8 million.[67] The cost of military operations cannot be overstated and doubt remains whether they can be sustained over a long period. Taking the use of drones as an example, it cost the US government about US$ 314 million to develop MOAB[68] and a single bomb is estimated to cost US$16 million.[69]

Figure 4.3 illustrates the success of the drones programme and how civilian casualties have been kept minimal while the number terrorists killed has been increasing with the number of strikes. A total of 4,926 strikes were conducted in the four countries, in which 7,715 terrorists and their supporters were neutralized, which resulted in 751 civilian deaths. This provides an average of 1 civilian death per 7 drone strikes. By comparison, an average of 2 terrorists were killed per drone strike.

Figure 4.3 Drone use in four countries heavily affected by terrorism

66 Ibid.

67 See US Department of Defense, Operation Inherent Resolve: Targeted Operations Against ISIS' Terrorists, www.defense.gov/News/Special-Reports/0814_Inherent-Resolve/, accessed April 20, 2017.

68 For a detailed discussion of MOAB and the reasons President Trump ordered its first use in Afghanistan, see M. Menon, The MOAB Mystery: Why Trump Bombed Afghanistan, *Harvard Political Review*, April 23, 2017, http://harvardpolitics.com/world/moab-mystery-trump-bombed-afghanistan/, accessed April 23, 2017.

69 B. Roggio, US Military Drops MOAB on Islamic State in Afghanistan, *Long War Journal*, April 13, 2017, www.longwarjournal.org/archives/2017/04/us-military-drops-moab-on-islamic-state-in-afghanistan.php?utm_source=feedburner&utm_medium=email&utm_campaign=Feed%3A+LongWarJournalSiteWide+%28FDD%27s+Long+War+Journal+Update%29<AQ: access date?>

Using foreign aid to fight terrorism

The emergence of a counter-terrorism (CT) exceptionalism after 9/11 however, has bequeathed states with unfettered powers to eradicate the phenomenon at all cost. In reality, this meant that international norms, particularly human rights, civil liberties, and other democratic principles were not accorded priority. Instead they have been viewed by many states as impediments to robust CT and countering violent extremism (CVE) programs. The shift in US policy focus from that of promoting democracy to CT/CVE may bear the greatest responsibility for the decline in democracy after 9/11. This shift was evident in US foreign assistance, which benefited mostly countries involved in the GWoT and not necessarily those making progress towards democracy, such as Iraq, Afghanistan, Pakistan, Egypt, Ethiopia, Uzbekistan, Sudan, and Turkey.[70] Mickey et al. argue that the waning of democracy in the US has been taking place since 1980 due to deepening polarization and the radicalization of the Republican Party.[71] They also, however, point out that the election of President Donald Trump, "who has praised dictators, encouraged violence among supporters, threatened to jail his rival, and labeled the mainstream media as 'the enemy,'" considered more dangerous than the threat of terrorism during the past decades, raising fears that the US is heading towards authoritarianism.[72]

Assessing states' counter-terrorism strategies and their implications on democracy after 9/11

The virulent spread and intensity of terrorist attacks and violent extremist groups are the direct consequences of the choices that states have made in reaction to 9/11. At its inception in 2001, post-9/11 responses were described as a "global war on terror (GWoT)." Indeed, in his declaration of GWoT, President George W. Bush gave the world two options: either to be with America or with the terrorists. As he put it, "Every nation, in every region, now has a decision to make. Either you are with us, or you are with the terrorists."[73] In reality, this meant an invitation to all nations to follow the US's lead on GWoT. This global war began in earnest with the military invasions in Afghanistan and Iraq in 2001 and 2003, respectively. The Obama's administration extended the war to Libya, Syria, and Yemen. France, the

70 For a detailed discussion on US foreign assistance after 9/11, see T. Moss, D. Roodman, and S. Standley, The Global War on Terror and U.S. Development Assistance: USAID allocation by country, 1998–2005, Centre for Global Development *Working Paper*, No. 62, 2005.

71 R. Mickey, S. Levitsky, and L.A. Way, Is America Still Safe for Democracy? Why the United States Is in Danger of Backsliding, *Foreign Affairs*, May/June 2017, www.foreignaffairs.com/articles/united-states/2017-04-17/america-still-safe-democracy<AQ: access date?>

72 Ibid.

73 Voice of America, Bush: "You Are Either with Us, or with the Terrorists," 2001-09-21, *VOA News*, October 27, 2009, www.voanews.com/a/a-13-a-2001-09-21-14-bush-66411197/549664.html, accessed February 3, 2017.

UN, and the African Union brought it to Mali, Somalia, and to some extent the Lake Chad Basin. By conceptualizing the global efforts to address, prevent, and eliminate the crime of terrorism, in militaristic terms, states chose hard military strategies over soft and effective criminal justice strategies. As a result, counter-terrorism acquired a new exceptionalism and became the fulcrum of international politics, or what Daniel Benjamin describes as "the prism through which everything is evaluated and decided."[74] As war, it further radicalized more people around the world and gave the terrorists a new justification, casting themselves as warriors, liberators that would boost their recruitment and foreign terrorist fighters (FTFs) to record numbers.[75]

The problem therefore lies in the nature of states' responses. By deviating from the Warsaw principles and practices and fallaciously believing that the preponderant military strategies can indeed eradicate the scourge of terrorism and violent extremism by crushing or neutralizing terrorist groups, states have gotten it wrong. In his famous book published in 2004, Richard Clarke, a US policy expert, warned presciently about the pernicious implications of these so- called 9/11 wars. As he averred:

> Many thought that the Bush administration was doing a good job of fighting terrorism when, actually, the administration had squandered the opportunity to eliminate al Qaeda and instead strengthened our enemies by going off on a completely unnecessary tangent, the invasion of Iraq. A new al Qaeda has emerged and is growing stronger, in part because of our own actions and inactions. It is in many ways a tougher opponent than the original threat we faced before September 11 and we are not doing what is necessary to make America safer from that threat.[76]

The new al-Qaeda Clarke referred to is actually ISIS, which was formed in 2004 as a result of US invasion of Iraq, and which today is the world's most dangerous terrorist group. Several other dangerous and ferocious terrorist organizations formed after 9/11 include Boko Haram in Nigeria, which was ranked the world's deadliest group in 2014; al Shabaab in Somalia, formed in 2006; and hundreds of others around the world. Today there are more dangerous terrorist groups, more terrorist attacks, and more terrorist fatalities than there were prior to 9/11. In

74 D. Benjamin, Strategic Counter-terrorism, Foreign Policy at Brookings *Policy Paper*, No. 7, October 2008, 2.

75 In a 2016 report, the UN estimated that around 30,000 foreign terrorist fighters came from over 100 countries, and actively engaged in the activities of al-Qaida, Islamic State of Iraq and Syria, as well as associated groups. For details see Report of the Secretary-General on the Threat Posed by ISIL (Da'esh) to International Peace and Security and the Range of United Nations Efforts in Support of Member States in Countering the Threat, Security Council's document *S/2016/92* dated January 29, 2016, 7.

76 R. Clarke, *Against All Enemies: Inside America's War on Terror* (New York: Free Press, 2004), ix.

addition, some of the groups that were existing before 9/11, such as al-Qaeda and the Taliban, have become more powerful or resilient to military strategies. The paradox is that, while violent extremism is a psychological war, which is spread through an appeal to hearts and minds, states' strategies seek to counter it through the use of force.

Opportunity for addressing violent extremism

Lessons drawn from states practices and strategies in the past 16 years offer opportunities for reversing the current trends in terrorism and violent extremism. One lesson learned is that democracy is a key requirement for effective CT/CVE. The gradual shift from CT to C/PVE provides an opportunity to effectively counter terrorism and violent extremism and still protect democracy. The notion of CT connotes state security, often dominated by militarized state actors. This approach is costly, inefficient, and unsustainable. The new emphasis on CVE brings back the focus on human security, which involves various actors from all strata of society, including government, civil society, academia or intelligentsia, and the private sector. The same elements that are emphasized in a CVE/PVE framework are the same as those required in a democracy.

The UN Global Counter-terrorism Strategy's four pillars remain relevant for a holistic approach to CVE/PVE.[77] The key attributes of this CVE/PVE framework as contained in the UN Secretary-General's Action Plans for preventing and countering violent extremism include dialogue and conflict prevention; strengthening good governance, human rights, and the rule of law; engaging communities; empowering youths; gender equality and empowering women; education, skills development, and employment facilitation; strategic communications, the Internet and social media.[78] These attributes, which are in consonance with the Warsaw Declaration, are anchored on states' capacity-building and international cooperation.

Conclusion

This chapter has argued that the erosion of democracy in the past 16 years of CT/CVE has been the result of states' reaction to terrorism. A key lesson learned is that when national security is threatened, states' choices and strategies are not often in conformity with democratic values.[79] Fukuyama believes that this is so

77 See UN General Assembly Resolution *A/RES/60/288* on the United Nations Global Counter-Terrorism Strategy, dated September 20, 2006, 4–9.

78 See Report of the Secretary-General, Plan of Action to Prevent Violent Extremism, General Assembly document *A/70/674* dated December 24, 2015.

79 See, for example, D.B. Prieto, War about Terror: Civil Liberties and National Security After 9/11, Council on Foreign Relations Working Paper, February 2009, vi; www.cfr.org/content/publications/attachments/Civil_Liberties_WorkingPaper.pdf, accessed February 9, 2017.

because "[c]oercion remains central to the functioning of the state, which is why state power so often generates fear and hatred."[80] While military strategies are not necessarily incompatible with democracy, excessive and unregulated military strategies can severely curtail political rights, civil liberties, and human rights. The view espoused in this brief is that military strategies should be intelligence-guided and constitute part of a broader criminal justice response led by the police. States' practices since 9/11 have also confirmed the fallacious belief that, with bigger and more powerful guns, states can effectively address the threat of violent extremism. The biggest challenge in the post-9/11 period has been the unbridled states' responses to terrorism arising from the exceptionalism of counter-terrorism, which gave little consideration to international law and other states' international obligations. The decline in democracy in the past decade has not helped the cause against terrorism. It is therefore cogent to argue that states can only effectively counter terrorism and violent extremism in a healthy democratic environment. Terrorism cannot be defeated if states' strategies against it end up hurting innocent people whom they are meant to protect.

Lessons learned:

- fear leads to bad counter-terrorism measures
- huge disparity between written strategies and states' counter-terrorism operational practices
- the monopoly of counter-terrorism by the executive branch of government creates high risks of militarization of counter-terrorism

States' practices and strategies in countering violent extremism in the aftermath of the tragic attacks in the United States of America on September 11, 2001, commonly referred to as 9/11, illustrate certain key trends, challenges, and opportunities for addressing terrorism and violent extremism. The political exigency of the fight against terrorism brought an unnecessary hierarchy to global issues, catapulting counter-terrorism to the fore of the global agenda. Terrorism has since then been regarded as the most pressing threat to international peace and security. The implication is that states, acting on the basis of undue peer pressure, have adopted draconian measures that contravene international law, including human rights and humanitarian laws. This new counter-terrorism imperative has been implicit in states' foreign policy shift after 9/11. The shift suggests an abandonment of the aggressive pursuit of global democracy and human rights that had characterized the period prior to 9/11, in favor of aggressive counter-terrorism efforts.

Prior to 9/11, democracy was promoted around the world as the ultimate weapon for the maintenance of world order, based on the theoretical proposition that democracies are more stable and more resilient to conflict and instability. As a

80 F. Fukuyama, Why Is Democracy Performing so Poorly? In L. Diamond and M.F. Plattner (eds.), *Democracy in Decline?* (Baltimore, MD: Johns Hopkins University Press, 2015), 14.

result, democracy was hailed and promoted as a panacea to post-Cold War internal conflicts and insurgencies in Africa and other developing countries. This universal recognition of democracy brought together 106 countries in Warsaw, Poland, in June 2000, to sign the Warsaw Declaration, which outlined what was described as the "core democratic principles and practices"[81] that its signatories committed to uphold. The advent of 9/11 has been a litmus test for the Warsaw Declaration.

The preeminence of the so-called global war on terror (GWoT) seems to have tacitly given states a license to suppress civil liberties and other democratic values, all in the name of fighting terror. The consequence is that ordinary citizens are often caught between indiscriminate terrorist attacks on the one hand and ruthless states' responses on the other. Evidence from Kenya, Nigeria, the United States, Iraq, and Pakistan has demonstrated that gross human rights violations and the suppression of civil liberties and other democratic values have been the recipes for the spread of violent extremism around the world. It is therefore no coincidence that at a time that the world has witnessed the highest number of states committed to counter-terrorism, it has also paradoxically seen a record rise in the numbers of terrorist attacks and fatalities, resulting in the growing perception that "Our reaction to terrorism is more dangerous than the terrorists."[82]

Recommendations

- The responses to terrorism should focus on CVE and PVE issues in order to effectively address radicalization and the undercutting social, economic and political factors that give rise to violent extremism.
- Prioritize the implementation of the existing international legal framework adopted at the regional, continental, and international levels; including regional CT strategies—all of which should be harmonized to ensure synergies.
- Universalize international criminal justice as the fundamental basis for CT/CVE responses, with a view to empower law-enforcement agencies to play a more central role, and to be complemented by intelligence-guided military operations including the use of drones as the need may arise. In this context, ensure that all military and drone strikes are conducted in full compliance of human rights and civil liberties.
- The United States and other powerful/influential nations should refocus attention on the promotion of democracy as a foreign-policy priority and model the approach that they expect from others, particularly when conducting CT/CVE operations. The Community of Democracies should play an increased role in CT/C/PVE by developing guidelines to help states respect their democratic obligations while pursuing their CT/C/PVE goals.

81 See the Warsaw Declaration, www.community-democracies.org/values/warsaw-declaration/, accessed March 20, 2017.

82 See, for example, D. Rothkope, Our Reaction to Terrorism Is More Dangerous than the Terrorists, *Foreign Policy*, November 25, 2015, http://foreignpolicy.com/2015/11/25/our-reaction-to-terrorism-is-more-dangerous-than-the-terrorists-trump-obama-eu-isis/, accessed February 2, 2017.

- Promote and support a pro-human security approach to CT/CVE, by developing and strengthening the role of community and civil society actors in CT/CVE, and community–law-enforcement partnership.
- Promote the use of targeted sanctions against individuals and states suspected of committing or supporting the commission of terrorist acts.
- Prioritise capacity-building to states in need under conditions that ensure that states do not use such capacity and equipment to commit gross human rights abuses and disregard for humanitarian law against its own people.

5 Interpreting—again—the prohibition of torture

Stephen Ellmann[1]

Are there any legal rules that govern, or constrain, interpretation of the prohibition against torture? This question at once raises another: interpretation *by whom*? A lawyer representing a defendant facing criminal charges for committing the crime of torture surely is entitled, indeed obliged, to interpret the torture statute extremely aggressively, so as to discern within it any possible argument in her client's behalf. The fact that the readings she offers might undercut the broad social purpose of preventing torture is not much her concern; her job is to defend her client as effectively as the law can be read to permit. Conversely, but for the same reasons, a lawyer needing to show that her client was the victim of torture at the hands of his interrogators must seek every possible line of argument supporting the contention that what happened to the client during the interrogation was torture. So, really, there are very few interpretive rules that bind all lawyers called upon to read the prohibition of torture, because lawyers' interpretive work is so heavily an exercise in the pursuit of clients' interests.

So let us narrow the question, to the role of lawyers for the United States government, charged with interpreting the obligations of US government officials and employees so as to lay out for those actors the extent of their legal powers. The lawyers who play this role most authoritatively are the attorneys in the Justice Department's Office of Legal Counsel (OLC), whose opinions are regarded within the federal government as authoritative resolutions of uncertain questions of law. Jack Goldsmith says that on most questions of "executive branch conduct related to war and intelligence ... the executive branch determines for itself what the law requires, and whether its actions are legal."[2] OLC opinions issued during

1 I'm grateful to participants in a New York Law School scholarship lunch workshop, and in a University of Cape Town faculty seminar, for their comments on this chapter. I also presented an earlier draft at a panel meeting at the Law & Society Association annual meeting in Chicago in May 2010; thanks to Peter Margulies, who organized the panel, and to other participants and attenders for their comments. Thanks also to Oliver Tobias for research assistance; to Carolyn Hassellmann and Michael McCarthy of the Mendik Law Library; to Sheldon Bach for helpful discussions of these issues; and as always to Teresa Delcorso-Ellmann.

2 Jack Goldsmith, *The Terror Presidency: Law And Judgment Inside The Bush Administration* (New York: W.W. Norton & Company, 2007), 32.

the Bush presidency on the meaning of torture[3] were important and controversial, indeed notorious. But while the OLC's institutional role gives its opinions special power, there are in fact many other lawyers in the federal government—lawyers for the Department of Defense, for example, or for the Department of State, or in the White House—whose views may play a part in shaping the US government's understanding of its authority. This chapter asks what limits, if any, there are on the interpretations these lawyers can offer.

We want to know, then, how these lawyers, as advisors to the US government, should answer the question "what is torture?" or rather, and more precisely, the question "what is torture as it is defined in US law?" But is this a question that really deserves our attention? It can certainly be argued that focusing on the exact definition of torture is a mistake, because it diverts attention from whether actions taken in our name violated other rules of international and domestic law that prohibit lesser, but still repellent, forms of mistreatment. After all, Common Article 3 of the Geneva Conventions of 1949 prohibits not only torture but also "violence to life and person, in particular murder of all kinds, mutilation, [and] cruel treatment" and "outrages upon personal dignity, in particular humiliating and degrading treatment."[4] The Convention Against Torture, to which the United States is a party, forbids torture and also "other acts of cruel, inhuman or degrading treatment or punishment which do not amount to torture."[5] Moreover, many federal and state criminal and civil laws seem to forbid a wide range of mistreatment even if it falls short of torture.[6]

3 See, in particular, Jay S. Bybee, Memorandum for Alberto R. Gonzales—Counsel to the President, Re: Standards of Conduct for Interrogation under 28 U.S.C. 2340–2340A (August 1, 2002), available at www.justice.gov/olc/file/886061/download [hereinafter cited as Memorandum on Standards of Conduct for Interrogation]; Jay S. Bybee, Memorandum for John Rizzo—Acting General Counsel of the Central Intelligence Agency, Interrogation of al Qaeda Operative (August 1, 2002), available at www.justice.gov/sites/default/files/olc/legacy/2010/08/05/memo-bybee2002.pdf [hereinafter cited as Memorandum on Interrogation of al Qaeda Operative]. Goldsmith writes that Bybee "had little expertise in war-related issues" and "largely delegated OLC's war-on-terrorism responsibilities to [John] Yoo and another of his deputies, Patrick Philbin." Goldsmith, *supra* note 2, at 23. He also notes that the "Standards of Conduct for Interrogation" memo, "according to press reports and John Yoo's public comments, … was drafted by Yoo himself." *Id.* at 142. See also [Department of Defense] Working Group Report on Detainee Interrogations in the Global War on Terrorism: Assessment of Legal, Historical, Policy, and Operational Considerations (April 1, 2003); Goldsmith reports that yet another memo from Yoo, still classified, was the "controlling authority" for this document. Goldsmith, *supra*, at 143.

4 For the text of Common Article 3, so called because it appears in all four of the Geneva Conventions of 1949, see, e.g., Geneva Convention Relative to the Treatment of Prisoners of War art. 3, August 12, 1949, 6 U.S.T. 3316, 75 U.N.T.S. 135.

5 Convention Against Torture and Other Cruel, Inhuman or Degrading Treatment or Punishment art. 16.1, Dec. 10, 1984, 1465 U.N.T.S. 85.

6 Immediately after taking office, President Obama signed Executive Order No. 13,491, "Ensuring Lawful Interrogations," 74 Fed. Reg. 4893 (issued January 22, 2009). In addition to setting out "Standards and Practices for Interrogation of Individuals in the Custody or Control of the United States in Armed Conflicts," this order revoked any

But of course torture has a special horror. Only those who wish to declare themselves ungoverned by law and mercy would want the label of "torturer." Otherwise, no one, and no nation, wants to be called a torturer; very possibly no one wants even to admit to himself that he is a torturer. Far better to embrace the use of "enhanced interrogation techniques," and to argue that one man's cruelty is another's justified severity. And, of course, if the focus were to shift from torture to "cruel, inhuman or degrading," no doubt the arguments marshaled for and against applying the latter label would much resemble those that have been brought to bear on the issue of torture. So let us pursue the question of how the prohibition of torture should be interpreted.

A prologue: why does the prohibition on torture need to be interpreted?

If there were no doubt about the meaning of the prohibition on torture, it would not need interpretation. Even if there were doubt, there would have been little need for interpretation if United States policy had been to stay away from anything that even remotely resembled torture. If you need to ask, this policy would have said, you're already too close. I would have applauded this policy, but it was far from the approach the US government chose under President George W. Bush. It is certainly far from the inclination of President Trump as well. During his campaign, Trump notoriously promised to bring back waterboarding and "a hell of a lot worse"; fortunately he does not seem (yet) to have done so, and his recent appointment to head the CIA, Gina Haspel, a CIA veteran who had herself been involved in CIA enhanced interrogations, only secured Senate confirmation after declaring not only that no similar program would be undertaken in the future but also that the CIA's program was a mistake even when it was undertaken. Still there is no reason for complacency on this score.[7] I do not in any way mean to approve

elements inconsistent with its provisions in "[a]ll executive directives, orders, and regulations" issued from September 11, 2001 to January 20, 2009. It concluded, in section 6, with a list of laws which the order was *not* to be taken to affect the force of, "including but not limited to: the Fifth and Eighth Amendments to the United States Constitution; the Federal torture statute, 18 U.S.C. 2340–2340A; the War Crimes Act, 18 U.S.C. 2441; the Federal assault statute, 18 U.S.C. 113; the Federal maiming statute, 18 U.S.C. 114; the Federal "stalking" statute, 18 U.S.C. 2261A; articles 93, 124, 128, and 134 of the Uniform Code of Military Justice, 10 U.S.C. 893, 924, 928, and 934; section 1003 of the Detainee Treatment Act of 2005, 42 U.S.C. 2000dd; section 6(c) of the Military Commissions Act of 2006, Public Law 109-366; the Geneva Conventions; and the Convention Against Torture."

7 For Trump's campaign promise, see Paul McLeary, *In Stunning Reversal, Trump Scraps His Calls to Bring Back Torture*, Foreign Policy, November 22, 2016, http://foreignpolicy.com/2016/11/22/in-stunning-reversal-trump-scraps-his-calls-to-bring-back-torture/. After his election, he selected several senior officials who appeared to hold similar views. See Dan de Luce et al., *Trump's Team Could Bring 9/11 Mindset Back to the White* House, Foreign Policy, November 18, 2016, http://foreignpolicy.com/2016/11/18/trumps-team-could-bring-911-mindset-back-to-the-white-house/. Senator Jeff Sessions, now Trump's Attorney General, voted

of the Bush administration's brutal interrogation techniques, or of any similar techniques the Trump administration may adopt, but I nevertheless believe that it is legitimate for the president to want to treat a captured alleged terrorist as harshly *as the law permits*, in order to get information from the captive.[8] This proposition is not self-evident, but it does follow from a very conventional way that we think about law: our obligation to the law is to obey it, but it is not part of our obligation to do more than the law requires. Certainly we accept this in many circumstances: the law requires us to drive safely, to take due precautions, but not to take more precaution than is due. We can drive as fast as the law permits; we need not remain silent as we drive; we can listen to the radio. We can structure

against an amendment to the 2016 National Defense Authorization Act that moved limitations on interrogation that President Obama had imposed by Executive Order in 2009 into statute. Conor Friedersdorf, These 21 Republicans Voted Against a Torture Ban, *The Atlantic*, June 28, 2015, www.theatlantic.com/politics/archive/2015/06/these-21-republicans-voted-against-a-torture-ban/396095/; see Joshua Keating, Will the U.S. Finally, Actually, Once and for All Outlaw Torture?, *Slate*, June 16, 2015, www.slate.com/blogs/the_slatest/2015/06/16/senate_votes_to_ban_torture_will_it_stick_this_time.html. Representative Mike Pompeo, originally director of the CIA and now Secretary of State, criticized President Obama for "ending our interrogation program in 2009." Mike Pompeo, Press Release: Statement of Rep. Mike Pompeo on ISIS Vote, September 17, 2014, http://pompeo.house.gov/news/documentsingle.aspx?DocumentID=394228. McLeary reports that retired Lt. General Mike Flynn, who briefly served as National Security Advisor and has since pled guilty, refused to rule out "killing family members of suspected terrorists," though he also "express[ed] some misgivings" about "enhanced techniques." McLeary, *supra*. But Trump also selected, as his Secretary of Defense, retired Marine General James "Mad Dog" Mattis. General Mattis opposes torture, and President-elect Trump declared that he was "very impressed" by Mattis's views. McLeary, *supra*. In addition, Senator Sessions, in his confirmation hearing, declared that waterboarding is "absolutely improper and illegal." Eric Lichtblau & Matt Apuzzo, Jeff Sessions Says He Would Be Independent and Stand Up to Trump, *The New York Times*, January 10, 2017, www.nytimes.com/2017/01/10/us/politics/jeff-sessions-attorney-general.html.

For Gina Haspel's statements about the CIA's program of enhanced interrogation, see Charlie Savage, Gina Haspel Likely to Be Confirmed as C.I.A. Chief After Repudiating Torture, *The New York Times*, May 15, 2018, www.nytimes.com/2018/05/15/us/politics/gina-haspel-cia-torture-letter-senate.html.

8 I should emphasize again that a determination that conduct is not "torture" is not a determination that it is lawful, because it might still violate a range of other prohibitions that honor US international obligations to also avoid cruel, inhuman, or degrading treatment of prisoners. But a showing that conduct is not torture is one step towards a showing that it is lawful, and, as I've already suggested, the kinds of interpretive arguments that would be deployed in subsequent steps of the analysis would fundamentally resemble those we will be examining in the context of torture. Nevertheless I agree with those who deplore this question; I argue here that a President is entitled to ask it and to have it answered, but she is hardly obliged to ask it and would be better off shaping US policies so that the question need never be reached. For a cogent argument against the legitimacy of seeking precision in the definition of torture, see Jeremy Waldron, *Torture, Terror and Trade-Offs: Philosophy for the White House* (Oxford: Oxford University Press, 2010), 198–207.

our transactions so as not to incur tax liability (though we cannot do so in ways that amount to illegal tax evasion). And so on.

One might respond by saying that behavior like this, which seems like the calculating behavior of the "bad man" who does not care for the intrinsic value and purposes of the law but only for the success of his own enterprises, is not the behavior that a president or a democracy should engage in.[9] It may well be that a nation should not treat its legal obligations as the calculating "bad man" would. But here the president is not seeking some selfish extra-legal goal, while indifferent to her legal obligations—or at least the president's decision to ask how harshly detainees may be treated does not in itself demonstrate that kind of disregard for the law.[10] The president, after all, has a constitutional duty to protect the nation and must meet that responsibility along with all other legal responsibilities. For the president to say that we will treat detainees as harshly as the law permits is not necessarily an expression of contempt for the law, but may instead reflect a view that the law's command to protect the country must shape the right understanding of the law's simultaneous command not to mistreat detainees.

This is not an argument for a presidential power to violate one law in order to implement another, or to take away constitutional protections for the sake of preserving the nation. No less a figure than Abraham Lincoln suggested arguments of this sort, writing that "measures otherwise unconstitutional, might become lawful, by becoming indispensable to the preservation of the constitution, through the preservation of the nation."[11] I am not borrowing that logic here, however, for Lincoln's point seems best understood as a rationale for law violation *in extremis* rather than an approach to law interpretation. My claim is only that it is legitimate for the president, while acknowledging the obligation to obey the law, at the same time to go no further than the law requires, with respect to detainee rights, in order to go as far as she can with respect to protection of the nation.

Perhaps surprisingly, this position—rather than an assertion that the president could simply violate what actually was the law—seems to have been the Bush administration's stance. Much as that administration sought to minimize what law required, and to deny the binding force of seemingly binding laws, it shrank from deliberate lawbreaking. So Jack Goldsmith, a conservative legal scholar who served—courageously—as head of the elite OLC, found when he suggested to his

9 Oliver Wendell Holmes, Jr., spoke of this "bad man" in 1897, when he wrote that "[i]f you want to know the law and nothing else, you must look at it as a bad man, who cares only for the material consequences which such knowledge enables him to predict, not as a good one, who finds his reasons for conduct, whether inside the law or outside of it, in the vaguer sanctions of conscience." Oliver Wendell Holmes, The Path of the Law, 110 *Harv. L. Rev.* 991, 993 (1997) (first published 1897).

10 For ease of reading, I frequently refer to the president as "she," and to each of the president's lawyers as "he"; both pronouns refer to people of every gender.

11 Abraham Lincoln, Letter to Albert G. Hodges (April 4, 1864), in *Abraham Lincoln, Addresses and Letters Collected Works* (Charles W. Moores ed.) (New York: American Book Company, 1914), 204, 205.

White House counterparts that the president could choose to violate the law: "Gonzales and Addington [counsel to Bush and Cheney, respectively] looked at me as if I were crazy."[12] There probably were exceptions, perhaps not readily acknowledged to the head of the OLC.[13] But the predominant attitude seems to have been the one Goldsmith quotes Michael Hayden, then head of the Central Intelligence Agency (CIA), as embracing in 2004: that he was "'troubled if [he was] not using the full authority of the law' after 9/11, and that he was 'going to live on the edge,' where his 'spikes will have chalk on them.'"[14]

If it is legitimate to take this attitude towards the treatment of detainees, then it must also be legitimate to ask for a legal opinion on how harshly a prisoner actually can be treated within the law. Note that this is not an argument for a right to receive advice focused merely on what one can get away with. There is, of course, a legal realist argument that what one can get away with—at least if one's conduct is actually capable of being identified and assessed by the lawful authorities—*is* what the law permits. But this idea seems particularly unpersuasive when the party asking what the lawful authorities will actually do is the chief executive of those very authorities; it devolves toward the proposition that what the president chooses to do is law.[15]

To be sure, it can certainly be argued—and without embracing legal realist jurisprudence in this fashion—that in a system of laws, in which clients depend on lawyers to understand the system's operation, lawyers are ethically entitled, even in many circumstances obliged, to answer the client's question of "what will happen to me if I do such and such?"[16] Presidents too have the right to understand how to stay out of trouble. But I take it as a premise that a president mindful of her obligation to obey the law would want to know what the law means, and not only what she can get away with. My point is simply that if it is legitimate for the president to want to treat detainees as harshly as the law permits, then it must be legitimate for her to ask for legal advice on just how harsh that is.[17]

12 Goldsmith, *supra* note 2, at 80.

13 Jane Mayer reports the shock that one participant in a meeting felt when he heard "Scooter" Libby, Cheney's chief of staff, say of the CIA's secret program of detention and interrogation that "Ninety-nine percent of what we do is legal"—a statement which might mean that Libby, and others, knew that one percent was not. *Jane Mayer, The Dark Side: The Inside Story of How the War on Terror Turned Into a War on American Ideals* (New York: Doubleday, 2008), 305.

14 Goldsmith, *supra* note 2, at 78.

15 See Holmes, *supra* note 9. For reporting on the suggestions by President Trump's lawyers that he *cannot* obstruct justice because he himself determines what the law requires, see Charlie Savage, Trump and His Lawyers Embrace a Vision of Vast Executive Power, *The New York Times*, June 4, 2018, www.nytimes.com/2018/06/04/us/politics/trump-executive-power-russia-investigation.html.

16 For a thoughtful exploration of this issue, see Stephen Pepper, Counseling at the Limits of the Law: An Exercise in the Jurisprudence and Ethics of Lawyering, 104 *Yale L.J.* 1545 (1995).

17 See Goldsmith, *supra* note 2, at 147–148.

A word of explanation is in order: I've just referred to the president's asking questions of "her lawyers." Strictly speaking, this phrasing is incorrect. The president may have a personal lawyer—to handle the purchase of a vacation home, for instance, or to defend the president against personal civil or criminal liability. But the lawyers of the Department of Justice are not the president's personal lawyers. Rather, they represent the US government.[18] True as this is, however, it does not directly affect what I am exploring here. The president, as the chief executive, has extensive authority to make decisions for the US government as long as those decisions are within the law—and the question I have imagined the president asking is precisely a question about what the law's limits are. When the president asks the government's lawyers to articulate the boundaries of the law, the question surely is entitled to an answer.

Does that mean the lawyers must answer? Not quite. Lawyers, in the federal government as elsewhere, generally have a choice: they may perform their functions, or resign their role. A lawyer who found the question of "how harshly can detainees be treated?" repellent could, perfectly legitimately, refuse to answer it and leave the government.[19] What a lawyer could not, legitimately, do is to deliberately answer the president's question in a way that satisfies the lawyer's conscience but ignores the demands of legal interpretation as the lawyer reasonably understands them. But this does not mean that the lawyer's moral convictions can play no role in the answer he gives to the president. Those moral convictions may well play a legitimate part in the work of legal interpretation itself—and it is also true, with the president as with other clients, that "[p]urely technical legal advice" may not meet the lawyer's professional responsibility as an advisor.[20]

Interpretation, uncertainty, and the role of the client's wishes

If the meaning of statutory language was entirely clear, then the boundaries of interpretation would be clear as well. It might take sophisticated legal reasoning to discern that clear meaning, but once the task of discernment was complete then

18 For the view that "a government lawyer may not assert the government attorney–client privilege against the government, because the government lawyer works for the government as an incorporeal entity," rather than "for any particular public official," see Ronald D. Rotunda & John S. Dzienkowski, *Professional Responsibility: A Student's Guide* (St. Paul, MN: West Group, 2010), 261.

19 *See* Model Rules of Prof'l Conduct R. 1.16(b)(4) (2017) (permitting withdrawal, with the approval of a tribunal where required by law, when "the client insists upon taking action that the lawyer considers repugnant or with which the lawyer has a fundamental disagreement").

20 *Id.* R. 2.1 cmt. ("Advice couched in narrow legal terms may be of little value to a client, especially where practical considerations, such as cost or effects on other people, are predominant. Purely technical legal advice, therefore, can sometimes be inadequate. It is proper for a lawyer to refer to relevant moral and ethical considerations in giving advice. Although a lawyer is not a moral advisor as such, moral and ethical considerations impinge upon most legal questions and may decisively influence how the law will be applied.")

the only remaining function for the lawyer would be to report the results. But in the nature of things it seems likely that the answer to most interpretive questions will be in some respects uncertain. Textual language will be imprecise; interpretive conventions applicable to that language may point in conflicting directions; and the context and purpose of the enactment may be complex and disputable.

What is the lawyer's duty in the face of such uncertainty? A straightforward answer is that the lawyer should ascertain the *most likely* meaning of the law, explain the basis for choosing this meaning to the client, and address any substantial arguments against this chosen interpretation. Perhaps this answer seems little more than a truism, but it is not. Implicit in this definition of the lawyer's role is the requirement that the lawyer must competently deploy the tools of legal interpretation to reach his or her answer. The rules of legal ethics demand no less, simply as a matter of competence, and as a matter of morality I agree with Bradley Wendel that "lawyers have an obligation to do right with regard to the law."[21] An answer that disregards obviously relevant legal principles, for example, or draws on irrelevant materials as a basis for interpretation, is not legitimate legal interpretation. The OLC memos of the early Bush administration, when they finally saw the light of day, were sharply criticized for just such errors as these.[22]

But what if the client—here, the president—wants the lawyer to argue for an interpretation of the law that is *not* the most likely meaning of the law? For three reasons, it seems to me that if the lawyer can make such an argument based on a competent deployment of the tools of legal interpretation, then she may ethically do so. First, the government's lawyers are not judges; though I will argue that their duties *are* affected by the extent to which they in effect make law for the executive branch, nevertheless these lawyers are also advocates, with a responsibility to promote their client's interests as the client defines them.[23]

21 *Id.* R. 1.1 ("A lawyer shall provide competent representation to a client. Competent representation requires the legal knowledge, skill, thoroughness and preparation reasonably necessary for the representation"); W. Bradley Wendel, Legal Ethics and the Separation of Law and Morals, 91 *Cornell L. Rev.* 67, 72 (2005).

22 *See* Goldsmith, *supra* note 2, at 165 ("How could [these opinions] reflect such bad judgment, be so poorly reasoned, and have such a terrible tone?"); Harold Hongju Koh, *The Nomination of the Honorable Alberto R. Gonzales as Attorney General of the United States Before the Senate Judiciary Committee* at 3 (January 7, 2005), available at www.judiciary.senate.gov/imo/media/doc/koh_testimony_01_06_05.pdf ("the August 1, 2002 OLC Memorandum is perhaps the most clearly erroneous legal opinion I have ever read"); Waldron, *supra* note 8, at 212 ("a disgrace"); Wendel, *supra* note 22, at 68–71 & n.2, 81–85.

23 Goldsmith quotes Robert Jackson, an Attorney General under Franklin Roosevelt, later a Supreme Court justice and a Nuremberg prosecutor, observing that "[t]he Attorney General should not 'act as a judge and foreclose the Administration from making reasonable contentions,' … a view that applies equally to OLC today." Goldsmith, *supra* note 2, at 35. Just how far government lawyers should take this deference to their client is a difficult question; Goldsmith notes, for example, the sharp criticism that has been levelled against an opinion written by Jackson himself to validate "Franklin Roosevelt's destroyers-for-bases deal in the tense summer of 1940." *Id.* at 168.

Second, it's long been recognized that clients in litigation must have the right to test the scope of the law. We are not speaking directly of litigation here, but the analogy seems sound: a client seeking to govern itself by law in a context where courts will not be resolving what the law is should be able to assert a reasonable view of what the law should be. Model Rule 1.2(d), which forbids a lawyer to "counsel a client to engage … in conduct that the lawyer knows is criminal or fraudulent," also says that a lawyer "may counsel or assist a client to make a good faith effort to determine the validity, scope, meaning or application of the law."[24] The comment to this provision (comment [12]) says that it "recognizes that determining the validity or interpretation of a statute or regulation may require a course of action involving disobedience of the statute or regulation or of the interpretation placed upon it by governmental authorities."[25] In principle, it seems reasonable to say that the president might challenge an interpretation placed on a matter by some authorities by asking her lawyers to articulate a different interpretation—if that can be done within the bounds of reasonable argumentation.

Third, the president's right to ask counsel to assert a particular interpretation is all the stronger if the president's own interpretation is legally entitled to some degree of deference. That is, presumably, the case with the interpretation of US obligations under international treaties such as the Convention Against Torture.[26] It might also be the case, by virtue of the president's responsibility as commander in chief, with the judgment of what treatment of detainees is justified by military necessity.[27] Simply as the elected chief executive, responsible for taking care that the laws are faithfully executed, the president might also be entitled to some deference to her assessment of what the complex task of faithful execution of the laws requires. Clearly, deference on any of these grounds would not be unlimited,[28] but it would add to some extent to the weight her preferred interpretation should receive.

If the president may legitimately ask her lawyers to defend, within the bounds of legitimate legal argumentation, an interpretation that is to her liking, it

24 Model Rules of Prof'l Conduct R. 1.2(d) (2017).

25 *Id.* cmt.

26 Cf. *Medellin v. Texas*, 552 U.S. 491, 513 (2008) ("It is … well settled that the United States' interpretation of a treaty 'is entitled to great weight'").

27 Cf. *Holder v. Humanitarian Law Project*, 561 U.S. 1, 33–34 (2010) (noting the "sensitive and weighty interests of national security and foreign affairs," and arguing that "[o]ne reason" for "respect for the Government's conclusions" about the impact of "contributions to foreign terrorist organizations" is "that national security and foreign policy concerns arise in connection with efforts to confront evolving threats in an area where information can be difficult to obtain and the impact of certain conduct difficult to assess").

28 See *Zivotovsky v. Kerry*, 135 S. Ct. 2076, 2089–90 (2015) (while upholding exclusive presidential power to recognize foreign states, the Court rejects the idea of an "unbounded" presidential foreign affairs power, and emphasizes that "it is Congress that makes laws, and in countless ways its laws will and should shape the Nation's course. The Executive is not free from the ordinary controls and checks of Congress merely because foreign affairs are at issue").

becomes all the more important to understand what those bounds of legitimate legal argumentation are. I've said that the lawyer must not ignore relevant legal principles and materials, but this point can and should be taken further: the lawyer cannot assert clarity where he does not believe clarity can reasonably be claimed. A client—the president—may wish to be told that the law clearly supports a particular course of action. Those about to test the limits of law want a legal shield; they naturally crave clear advice, on which they can rely, that tells them that what they are about to do is lawful.[29] But a statement by a government lawyer that the law clearly supports the client's inclination, when in fact the lawyer knows or should know that the law is less than clear, is hard to square with the requirements of good practice. If the client is unaware that the lawyer is misstating the law, the lawyer has violated his ethical obligation to "render candid advice." Even if the client herself is in effect a willing collaborator in the misstatement, the lawyer's claim may violate Rule 4.1(a) of the Model Rules of Professional Conduct, which bars a lawyer "[i]n the course of representing a client" from "knowingly … mak[ing] a false statement of material fact or law to a third person."[30] Assuming the client herself is not misled, the only apparent function of the lawyer's false description of the state of the law is to mislead other third persons—judges, for example—into believing that those who acted in accordance with it were genuinely guided by the advice of counsel. Nor can it be argued that one government official has the right to ask a lawyer to deceive another government official, since, as noted earlier, the lawyer ultimately represents the government itself rather than any particular official.

But perhaps it's enough simply to say that it is legitimate for the president to ask her lawyers to say how harshly a prisoner can be treated, and for the lawyers to give an answer that can be sustained within the bounds of legitimate legal argument. The rest of this chapter will be, in essence, an effort to identify the boundaries of legitimate legal argument in this context. Thus the question I want to ask is: how far can the scope of what the prohibition on torture outlaws be narrowed by legal interpretation? Assuming that it is legitimate for the government to go all the way up to (but not over) the legal lines marked by the prohibition on torture, what are they? In the following section I will first explore the textual possibilities within the current prohibition on torture and then illustrate the non-textual interpretive moves that US legal culture might recognize. Once we have a sense of the range

29 For a statute making "[g]ood faith reliance on advice of counsel" an "important factor" in a defense "that such [person] did not know that the practices were unlawful and a person of ordinary sense and understanding would not know the practices were unlawful," see Section 1004 of the Detainee Treatment Act, Pub. L. 109–148, Div. A, Title X, § 1004, Dec. 30, 2005, 119 Stat. 2739, codified at 42 U.S.C. § 2000dd-1 (2017). [The dates of statutory citations in this chapter are given as 2017, based primarily on review of these sources in Westlaw in January 2017.] I discuss this statute further in note 160 *infra*.

30 Model Rules of Prof'l Conduct R. 2.1 ("render candid advice"); *id*., R. 4.1(a) (2017). [The dates of Model Rules citations in this chapter are given as 2017, based on review of these Rules on the American Bar Association website in January 2017 or thereafter.]

of possibilities, we will be in a position to ask whether any principles limit how far a lawyer can go in narrowing the scope of what the prohibition on torture prohibits.

Textual and non-textual possibilities

Let's start from the core definition of torture embodied in the "torture statute," which was enacted as part of US implementation of the Convention Against Torture. This statute defines torture as "an act committed by a person acting under the color of law specifically intended to inflict severe physical or mental pain or suffering … upon another person," and prohibits it, with no provision for excuse or justification, by making those who inflict or attempt to inflict it—outside of the United States—guilty of a crime.[31] What interpretive issues does this language present?

First, specific intent. This requirement is not in the statute by accident. It was added in consonance with an "understanding" that the United States made a condition of its ratification of the international Convention Against Torture, which required that torture be "intentionally inflicted" but didn't specify what kind of intent was called for. The US "understanding" declared that "in order to constitute torture, an act must be specifically intended to inflict severe physical or mental pain or suffering."[32] What's "specific intent"? No one quite knows, but here's what the en banc Third Circuit said in *Pierre v. Attorney General*, in the course of rejecting a claim that returning a person to Haiti where he might well die as a result of the abysmal medical care he would receive in its prisons would be returning him to face "torture": "In our view, a petitioner cannot obtain relief under the CAT unless he can show that the prospective torturer will have the goal

31 18 U.S.C. §§ 2340(1), 2340A (2017). The statute does not have a formal name, but its three sections (18 U.S.C. §§ 2340–2340B) make up Chapter 113B of Title 18 of the United States Code, whose name is "Torture." This statute's definition of torture is not the only one in the US statutes, and in fact the torture statute applies only to acts committed "outside the United States," 18 U.S.C. § 2340A(a) (2017); since "United States" is defined to include "the commonwealths, territories, and possessions of the United States," 18 U.S.C. § 2340(3) (2017), it seems arguable that the torture statute does not apply to the US base at Guantanamo. The War Crimes Act, 18 U.S.C. § 2441(d)(1)(A) (2017), applies to acts committed anywhere, and defines torture as "[t]he act of a person who commits, or conspires or attempts to commit, an act specifically intended to inflict severe physical or mental pain or suffering (other than pain or suffering incidental to lawful sanctions) upon another person within his custody or physical control for the purpose of obtaining information or a confession, punishment, intimidation, coercion, or any reason based on discrimination of any kind." While this definition adds a purpose requirement not present in the torture statute, it otherwise is largely similar, and 18 U.S.C. § 2441(d)(2)(A) (2017) explicitly incorporates the torture statute's definition of "severe mental pain or suffering," which I discuss in the text below.

32 US Senate Resolution of Ratification (containing Reservations, Declarations, and Understandings), Convention Against Torture and Other Cruel, Inhuman or Degrading Treatment or Punishment, 136 Cong. Rec. 36,198 (October 27, 1990).

or purpose of inflicting severe pain or suffering."[33] That at least seems to mean that if an interrogator does not believe that what he is doing will inflict severe pain or suffering, and does not mean to inflict that, then even if he *does* inflict it he has not committed torture.[34]

Second, severe pain or suffering. The torture memoranda suggested that severe physical pain or suffering was equivalent to what would be suffered at death or major organ failure; as critics have pointed out, this definition is both too narrow and too confusing.[35] But the word "severe" can't be ignored. It's obvious that "severe" pain is more than, say, "moderate" pain, or "mild" pain. The European Court of Human Rights drew a similar inference in *Ireland v. United Kingdom*, saying that the difference between torture and inhuman or degrading treatment is that the term "torture" "attach[es] a special stigma to deliberate inhuman treatment causing very serious and cruel suffering."[36] How "severe" is severe? One scholar has commented that "[i]t is notoriously difficult to determine at what point ill-treatment moves from being *inhuman* and becomes *torture*."[37] But one plausible approach begins from the fact that we are talking about "torture." The pain we associate with the common understanding of torture is intense.[38] "Severe," then, is a word to be taken seriously. The upshot would be that some rather large range of pain or suffering *could* be imposed, *with specific intent*, and still not be torture. And if the amount of suffering exceeded what was specifically intended, as of course it might, it still wouldn't be torture because that extra suffering wasn't specifically intended.

Third, severe mental pain or suffering. Obviously torture can be accomplished by imposing mental agony rather than physical; the "Chinese water torture" is an

33 *Pierre v. Att'y Gen.*, 528 F.3d 180, 190 (3rd Cir. 2008) (en banc).

34 I put aside, as beyond the realm of plausibility, the argument that the interrogator lacks the specific intent to torture because what he actually wants is to extract information rather than to inflict pain—though this argument has been made. See Stephen Dycus et al., National Security Law (New York: Aspen Publishers, 4th ed. 2007), 761 (reporting an opinion given by an army lawyer).

35 Goldsmith, *supra* note 2, at 145.

36 *Ireland v. United Kingdom*, 25 Eur. Ct. H.R. (ser. A) 1 (1978), at ¶ 167. The court drew this distinction even without the textual reference to severity in the US definition (which in turn is derived from the Convention Against Torture). Article 3 of the European Convention simply states that "no one shall be subjected to torture or to inhuman or degrading treatment or punishment." It has been argued that the line between torture and inhuman or degrading treatment should not be (and in European jurisprudence is not) based on intensity of suffering, but it seems hard to avoid the view that suffering of some intensity is an essential element of the definition of torture. See Malcolm D. Evans, Getting to Grips with Torture, in *Association for the Prevention of Torture, The Definition of Torture: Proceedings of an Expert Seminar* (Geneva: Association for the Prevention of Torture, 2001).

37 Evans, *supra* note 36, at 36.

38 For an impassioned statement of this view, see *Ireland v. United Kingdom, supra* note 36, separate opinion of Fitzmaurice J., at ¶ 35 (insisting on the distinction between "the mere aches, pains, strains, stresses and discomforts" of five techniques considered by the Court, "which pale into insignificance in comparison with the searing, unimaginable, agony of" true torture).

old example. But "severe mental pain or suffering" has its own statutory definition,[39] derived from further language in the "understanding" that the United States attached to its ratification of the Convention Against Torture.[40] This is important to keep in mind: the US government—the president and the Senate in the ratification process, then the full Congress in the enactment of the torture statute—chose not to leave the concept of "severe mental pain or suffering" to stand unmodified; the United States wanted to narrow its compass, and it did. So this narrowing has to be reckoned with.

This definition is quite long, but it begins with this: "'severe mental pain or suffering' means the prolonged mental harm caused by or resulting from" four subsequently specified sources. There are at least two definitional questions here: first, what's "mental harm" and, second, what's "prolonged"? As for "mental harm," is "being terrified" a mental harm or is it simply a very unwelcome mental "experience"? As for "prolonged," the obvious question is, "how long is prolonged?" The statute doesn't say; again, it seems perfectly reasonable to say, since we're talking about *torture*, that prolonged means quite a long time. Hours? Days? Months?

Then, of course, there are questions about the meaning of the specified sources from which the severe mental pain or suffering must result.[41] The first is the use or threat of physical torture—which thus incorporates by reference the ambiguities in that concept.[42] Next is "the administration or application, or threatened administration or application, of mind-altering substances or other procedures calculated to disrupt profoundly the senses or the personality";[43] what, in particular, is required to say that a "procedure" is "calculated to disrupt profoundly … the personality"? Is terror by itself such a profound disruption? The third is "the threat of imminent death."[44] This one seems straightforward enough, until one asks whether the threat must exist in the eye of the perpetrator or the victim, and whether the threat must be explicit or can be implicit: if a procedure causes someone to fear for his life, and is meant to have that effect, has he been threatened with imminent death? Finally, the last recapitulates the first three, providing that a threat of any of these three directed at *another person* (a loved one, to

39 18 U.S.C. § 2340(2)(2017) defines this term to mean: "the prolonged mental harm caused by or resulting from— (A) the intentional infliction or threatened infliction of severe physical pain or suffering; (B) the administration or application, or threatened administration or application, of mind-altering substances or other procedures calculated to disrupt profoundly the senses or the personality; (C) the threat of imminent death; or (D) the threat that another person will imminently be subjected to death, severe physical pain or suffering, or the administration or application of mind-altering substances or other procedures calculated to disrupt profoundly the senses or personality…."

40 US Senate Resolution of Ratification (containing Reservations, Declarations, and Understandings), Convention Against Torture and Other Cruel, Inhuman or Degrading Treatment or Punishment, 136 Cong. Rec. 36,198 (October 27, 1990).

41 18 U.S.C. § 2340(2)(A)-(D) (2017).

42 *Id.* § 2340(2)(A).

43 *Id.* § 2340(2)(B).

44 *Id.* § 2340(2)(C).

name the obvious example) can satisfy the "severe mental pain or suffering" requirement.[45]

In short, the torture statute's text seems to introduce two central lines of interpretive limitation. The first is that it naturally imparts the idea of torture as something uniquely horrible—so lesser wrongs will not qualify. The second, paradoxically, is that for mental torture the text turns from "torture-as-horror" to "torture-as-precisely-identified": again, only some harms suffice, but now these harms must be caused in certain particular ways or they do not count. Once a lawyer sets out to interpret the torture statute, he can hardly disregard any of these matters.

Nor can he ignore what isn't written down. Suppose that we agree that the text of the statute, despite its ambiguities in some respects, is also quite clear in others, and by its terms seems plainly to treat certain kinds of conduct as torture. Does the clarity of the language compel the conclusion that these acts *are* torture? The answer, in US statutory interpretation law, is "no." Consider, in this regard, the classic case of *Church of the Holy Trinity v. United States.*[46] This vintage statutory interpretation case declares that "[i]t is a familiar rule, that a thing may be within the letter of the statute and yet not within the statute, because not within its spirit, nor within the intention of its makers."[47] While *Holy Trinity* has fallen out of fashion as American statutory interpretation has become more textualist, interpretive departures from the text in fact persist nonetheless.

So, for example, in *Bond v. United States,*[48] the Supreme Court narrowed the meaning of the text of a statute, the Chemical Weapons Convention Implementation Act,[49] enacted to implement a treaty to which the United States is a party, the Convention on the Prohibition of the Development, Production, Stockpiling, and Use of Chemical Weapons and on Their Destruction.[50] Under the terms of the statute, it was a felony to possess or use "any chemical weapon."[51] The term "chemical weapon," in turn, was defined to mean "[a] toxic chemical and its precursors, except where intended for a purpose not prohibited under this chapter."[52] "Toxic chemical" was defined as well; this term meant "any chemical which through its chemical action of life processes can cause death, temporary incapacitation or permanent harm to humans or animals. The term includes all such chemicals ...."[53] Finally, "purpose not prohibited under this chapter" was defined, in relevant part, to mean "[a]ny peaceful

45 *Id.* § 2340(2)(D).
46 143 U.S. 457 (1892).
47 *Id.* at 459.
48 134 S. Ct. 2077 (2014).
49 18 U.S.C. §§ 229–229F (2017).
50 Convention on the Prohibition of the Development, Production, Stockpiling and Use of Chemical Weapons and on Their Destruction, 1974 U.N.T.S. 45, 32 I.L.M. 800 (1993).
51 18 U.S.C. § 229(a)(1) (2017).
52 *Id.* § 229F(1).
53 *Id.* § 229F(8)(A).

purpose related to an industrial, agricultural, research, medical, or pharmaceutical activity or other activity."[54]

Carol Anne Bond, a microbiologist, sought to take revenge against her former best friend, who was having an affair with Bond's husband, by acquiring two chemicals, both toxic and "in high enough doses, potentially lethal" to humans, and spreading them on surfaces that the friend would likely touch, including the friend's "car door, mailbox, and door knob."[55] Bond's goal was not to kill her former friend but to cause her to "develop an uncomfortable rash," and on one occasion the victim did "suffer[] a minor chemical burn on her thumb, which she treated by rinsing with water."[56]

It's quite clear that the chemicals Bond stole fitted the terms of the definition of "toxic chemical." It also seems difficult (perhaps not impossible, but difficult) to assert that Bond's purpose in acting as she did was a "*peaceful* purpose related to an industrial, agricultural, research, medical or pharmaceutical activity or other activity" (emphasis added). Accordingly, Bond's action was the use of a chemical weapon, and a federal felony. Or so the text seems to indicate. But Chief Justice Roberts, writing for a majority of the Supreme Court, ruled otherwise. Reminding us that "[p]art of a fair reading of statutory text is recognizing that 'Congress legislates against the backdrop' of certain unexpressed presumptions,"[57] the Court invoked "the well-established principle that 'it is incumbent upon the federal courts to be certain of Congress' intent before finding that federal law overrides' the 'usual constitutional balance of federal and state powers.'"[58] Emphasizing that applying the statute to Bond would federalize "local criminal conduct," the Court decided that the statute was ambiguous—despite the seeming clarity of its language.

> In this case, the ambiguity derives from the improbably broad reach of the key statutory definition given the term—"chemical weapon"—being defined; the deeply serious consequences of adopting such a boundless reading; and the lack of any apparent need to do so in light of the context from which the statute arose—a treaty about chemical warfare and terrorism. We conclude that, in this curious case, we can insist on a clear indication that Congress meant to reach purely local crimes, before interpreting the statute's expansive language in a way that intrudes on the police power of the States.[59]

Though the Court was at pains in this passage to limit the generalizability of its decision, this case is not unique in recent Supreme Court jurisprudence. Perhaps the most striking case on these lines in recent years is *King v. Burwell*, the case that at least for a time preserved the system of health insurance that came to be

54 *Id.* § 229F(7)(A).
55 *Bond*, 134 S. Ct. at 2085.
56 *Id.*
57 *Id.* at 2088, quoting *EEOC v. Arabian American Oil Co.*, 499 U.S. 244, 248 (1991).
58 *Bond*, 134 S. Ct. at 2089 (some internal quotation marks omitted).
59 *Id.* at 2090.

called Obamacare.[60] In *King v. Burwell* the Court addressed the question of whether people in states which did not operate their own health insurance exchange markets, but instead had left that function to the federal government, were eligible to receive the tax credits that were essential to make their purchase of insurance affordable—and thus to keep the Affordable Care Act's complicated health insurance system functioning.[61] As explained by the Court, the Act "allowed an individual to receive tax credits only if the individual enrolls in an insurance plan through 'an Exchange established by the State" under the statute.[62] Since the statute itself defined "State" to mean "each of the 50 States and the District of Columbia,"[63] it might seem that an Exchange established not by any of the 50 States or the District of Columbia but instead by the federal government could not qualify.

But the Court concluded that "when read in context, 'with a view to [its] place in the overall statutory scheme,' the meaning of the phrase 'established by the State' is not so clear."[64] After an extensive demonstration that there was indeed ambiguity,[65] the Court then resolved it, by "turn[ing] to the broader structure of the Act.... Here," the Court decided, "the statutory scheme compels us to reject petitioners' interpretation [which would have meant that no tax credits were available except in states that had established their own exchanges] because it would destabilize the individual insurance market in any State with a Federal Exchange, and likely create the very 'death spirals' that Congress designed the Act to avoid."[66] Aware that interpretation such as this was "'a subtle business, calling for great wariness lest what professes to be mere rendering becomes creation and attempted interpretation of legislation becomes legislation itself,'"[67] the Court insisted that here "the context and structure of the Act compel us to depart from what would otherwise be the most natural reading of the pertinent statutory phrase."[68] Despite its cautionary words, it is clear that *King v. Burwell* stands as a guidepost illuminating a path of interpretation that quite consciously departs from the text—and that path could be followed in statutes dealing with torture as in statutes dealing with health insurance.[69]

60 135 S. Ct. 2480 (2015).
61 *See id.* at 2486–87.
62 *Id.* at 2489.
63 *Id.* at 2490, citing 42 U.S.C. § 28024(d) (2017).
64 *Id.*
65 *Id.* at 2489–92.
66 *Id.* at 2492–93.
67 *Id.* at 2495–96, quoting *Palmer v. Massachusetts*, 308 U.S. 79, 83 (1939).
68 *Id.* at 2495.
69 Another, much less momentous, Supreme Court departure from the strictest literalism is *Yates v. United States*, 135 S. Ct. 1074 (2015). Here the Supreme Court had to decide the meaning of the phrase "tangible object" in a statute, 18 U.S.C. § 1519 (2017), providing that "[w]hoever knowingly alters, destroys, mutilates, conceals, covers up, falsifies, or makes a false entry in any record, document, or tangible object with the intent to impede, obstruct, or influence the investigation or proper administration of any matter" within federal jurisdiction was guilty of a felony. The statute,

Indeed, we do not need to leave the boundaries of currently conventional statutory interpretation[70] to say that even seemingly plain language may turn out, on analysis, not to be so plain as first thought—especially if that language seems out of kilter with other important legal considerations. A classic example, part of the background of Lon Fuller's parable of law and interpretation, *The Case of the Speluncean Explorer*,[71] was the centuries-old availability of the defense of "self-defense" against the charge of murder, even though the statute Fuller hypothesized said nothing at all about this defense.[72]

Fuller's example was a hypothetical, but in fact the possible availability of a non-textual necessity defense against charges of torture is a live and present question. OLC lawyers argued in one of the "Torture Memos" for the recognition of exactly this defense.[73] It's arguable, though not certain, that the default reading of

enacted as part of the Sarbanes-Oxley Act of 2002, Pub. L. 107–204, 116 Stat. 745 (2002), was presumably aimed at protecting the financial markets that were the concern of that Act. In Yates, however, the alleged tangible objects were *fish*, thrown overboard in an effort to evade prosecution for catching undersize fish. *Yates*, 135 S. Ct. at 1079–80 (plurality opinion of Ginsburg, J.). Despite the fact that fish are tangible, the Court concluded that they were not, within the meaning of this statute, "tangible objects." As the plurality put the point, "'Tangible object' in § 1519, we conclude, is better read to cover only objects one can use to record or preserve information, not all objects in the physical world." *Id.* at 1081.

70 For a rare example of a judge almost explicitly going beyond conventional boundaries, see *United States v. Marshall*, 908 F.2d 1312 (7th Cir. 1990) (en banc), *aff'd sub nom. Chapman v. United States*, 500 U.S. 453 (1991). There, in a case dealing with the tremendously disparate penalties then at least potentially applicable to sellers of LSD, as compared to those for sellers of other illegal drugs, Judge Posner in dissent was prepared to depart sharply from the seeming meaning of the text to correct its acute unfairness. He maintained "[t]he words of the statute [should be] interpreted against a background that includes a … constitutional commitment to rationality," 908 F.2d at 1337 (Posner, J., dissenting), and that the judges "should not make Congress's handiwork an embarrassment to the members of Congress and to us." *Id.* at 1338 (Posner, J., dissenting). This kind of judicial role might be condemned as usurping democratic self-government. But it can also be defended as a form of fidelity to democratic choice that takes into account the inevitable imperfections of statute-making and seeks to honor the basic goals of the lawmakers even when they themselves have not succeeded in doing so. For a brief exposition of such an argument, suggesting that the work of statutory interpretation might be analogous to the task of a domestic employee who has been given instructions by her employer that become more and more problematic during a period while the employer is away, see William N. Eskridge, Jr., *Dynamic Statutory Interpretation* (Cambridge, MA: Harvard University Press, 1994), 125–128); John F. Manning & Matthew C. Stephenson, *Legislation and Regulation: Cases and Materials* (St. Paul, MN: Foundation Press, 2nd ed. 2013), 74–75 (discussing Eskridge's argument). But, again, the interpretive arguments I make in the text do not rely on such unconventional approaches.

71 Lon L. Fuller, The Case of the Speluncean Explorers, 62 *Harv. L. Rev.* 616 (1949).

72 *Id.* at 624.

73 In the August 1, 2002 Memorandum on Standards of Conduct for Interrogation, *supra* note 3, at 42–45, the OLC also suggested "self-defense" and "defense of another" and exercise of "the nation's right to self-defense" as possible limits on the torture statute's reach.

US criminal statutes is that they include an implied necessity defense unless they provide to the contrary.[74] If that's right, can it apply to torture? One strong reason it should not is that the Convention Against Torture says there is no justification for torture: "No exceptional circumstances whatsoever, whether a state of war or a threat of war, internal political instability or any other public emergency, may be invoked as a justification of torture."[75] That's plain enough. But it's puzzling, then, that Congress did not include these words, or any like them—such as "The defense of necessity is not available in prosecutions under this statute"—in the torture statute. Still, a venerable canon of interpretation, the *Charming Betsy* rule,[76] says that statutes should be read to accord with international law if that's reasonably possible,[77] and surely a reading that Congress meant to adhere to international law is reasonably possible here, since Congress enacted the torture statute pursuant to US obligations under the Convention.

But it is quite arguable that a defense of necessity is available—with no breach of US international law obligations—even though no system of torture can be justified on any basis. This is an argument that David Margolis makes in his memorandum of decision overturning the Justice Department Office of Professional Responsibility's finding of professional misconduct by John Yoo and Jay Bybee for their authorship of the torture memos.[78] It's not a frivolous position—and it finds some support in a 1999 decision by the Israeli Supreme Court, *Public Committee Against Torture in Israel v Israel*.[79] The legal distinction is between a

74 David Margolis, Memorandum for the Attorney General [and] the Deputy Attorney General, Memorandum of Decision Regarding the Objections to the Findings of Professional Misconduct in the Office of Professional Responsibility's Report of Investigation into the Office of Legal Counsel's Memoranda Concerning Issues Relating to the Central Intelligence Agency's Use of "Enhanced Interrogation Techniques" on Suspected Terrorists (January 5, 2010), at 50, available at www.aclu.org/files/pdfs/natsec/opr20100219/20100105_DAG_Margolis_Memo.pdf.

75 Convention Against Torture and Other Cruel, Inhuman or Degrading Treatment or Punishment, *supra* note 5, art. 2(2).

76 *Murray v. Charming Betsy*, 6 U.S. (2 Cranch) 64, 118 (1804) ("It has also been observed that an act of Congress ought never to be construed to violate the law of nations if any other possible construction remains ....").

77 But for an argument that international laws of war impose no limit on "the war powers granted by the AUMF and other statutes," see *Al-Bihani v. Obama*, 590 F.3d 866, 871–72 (D.C. Cir. 2010). Judge Kavanaugh, the author of this panel decision, and now a nominee for a Supreme Court seat, elaborated on the reasons for rejecting the *Charming Betsy* canon in a "statement" regarding the petition for rehearing in this case, *Al-Bihani v. Obama*, 619 F.3d 1, 32–42 (D.C. Cir. 2010), *cert. denied*, 563 U. S. 929 (2011) (statement of Kavanaugh, J.). But Judge Kavanaugh's views did not prevail, as a result of the judgment, endorsed by a majority of the en banc court on petition for rehearing, that "the panel's discussion of [the role of international law-of-war principles in interpreting the AUMF] is not necessary to the disposition of the merits." Al-Bihani, 619 F.3d at 1 (statement of Chief Judge Sentelle and Judges Ginsburg, Henderson, Rogers, Tatel, Garland, and Griffith).

78 Margolis, *supra* note 74, at 42–43, 56.

79 *Public Committee Against Torture in Israel v. Israel*, HCJ 5100/94 (Israel Supreme Court, sitting as the High Court of Justice, 1999) (in English translation in

system that authorizes torture—forbidden—and a system that may excuse torturers on the ground that their actions fitted the defense of necessity—possibly not forbidden.[80] That may be a distinction that makes a difference, the difference between treating torture as prohibited but in very limited circumstances perhaps excusable, or as a fundamentally permissible part of interrogation practice. In saying all this, I should emphasize, I am not trying to demonstrate that the necessity defense ultimately should be recognized in torture cases—I would argue that it should not be[81]—but to illustrate the range of potential interpretive moves that might narrow the scope of the torture statute. And that range is substantial.

Interpretation applied—the case of waterboarding

How far can these narrowing interpretations of one sort or another take us? Obviously quite a ways. Let me take a particularly troubling example, namely waterboarding. I believe waterboarding is torture; it is a horror, carefully engineered[82] to terrify and appall and thus overwhelm those subjected to it. I also think that the torture statute as written should be interpreted to forbid waterboarding, for the simple reason that, as David Luban explains, it causes "severe physical or mental pain or suffering," as the torture statute requires. Luban quotes a veteran instructor from the army's SERE school (where waterboarding was used to train US soldiers in what they might face if they were captured); this instructor describes the "agonizing feeling of the water overpowering your gag reflex, and then feel your throat open and allow pint after pint of water to involuntarily fill your lungs."[83]

Judgments of the Israeli Supreme Court: Fighting Terrorism within the Law 23 (n.d.), available at www.mfa.gov.il/MFA/Government/Law/Legal+Issues+and+Rulings/Fighting+Terrorism+within+the+Law+2-Jan-2005.htm).

80 Public Committee Against Torture in Israel, ¶¶ 34–38.

81 I am concerned that once it is understood that a necessity defense exists, those state agents considering whether to torture will view the existence of this defense as an implied authorization to do whatever they believe is necessary—so that in practice the existence of the necessity defense will institutionalize the practice of torture. Yet I find it troubling to say that a state agent who believed that only torture would enable him to stop a "ticking bomb," and who in fact did stop that bomb by the exercise of torture, should now be punished for his actions. If such a case ever arises, I would accommodate it not by establishing a generally available necessity defense, but by recognizing that the president can exercise her pardon power to meet the demands of an individual, special case.

82 Though torture need not be elaborately engineered, there is force to the idea, discerned by Malcolm Evans in the work of the European Committee for the Prevention of Torture, Inhuman or Degrading Treatment or Punishment, that torture "has required some form of 'preparation', such as the use of electric shock, falaka [foot-whipping], suffocation with bags over heads, beating prisoners in tethered positions, etc.—what have elsewhere been called 'exotic' methods, for the want of any better description." Evans, *supra* note 36, at 40.

83 David Luban, "The Fundamental Trick: Pretending That 'Torture' is a Technical Term (Update)", *Balkinization*, February 26, 2010, http://balkin.blogspot.com/2010/02/fundamental-trick-pretending-that.html. In the third of its "Findings and

It seems to me that this *has* to be torture. But it is possible to argue otherwise, and I want to explore these arguments in order to ask what legal rules might constrain the government lawyer not to accept the arguments that could exempt waterboarding from the statute. It's especially important to do so because even if waterboarding's status were settled, there would undoubtedly be other techniques that interrogators could devise that would, like waterboarding, seek to skirt the limits of the definition of torture while terrorizing those subjected to them just as traditional methods of torture did. This point, it bears mentioning, is not hypothetical. One of the torture memos devoted itself to defending the legality of an array of other techniques—placing detainees terrified of poisonous insects in small spaces with insects they believed were poisonous, for example.[84] The interpretive problem that the government lawyers face will always be with those techniques that might, just barely, be said to escape the category of "torture"—and the issue will be whether the interpretive techniques that could effectuate that escape are legitimate.

So let us begin with the concept of physical pain, or in the statute's terms "severe physical ... pain."[85] The army instructor uses the phrase "agonizing feeling" and undoubtedly waterboarding produces exactly that. If this is a description of physical agony, then of course it meets the statute's "severe physical pain or

Conclusions," the Senate Select Committee on Intelligence study confirms the accuracy of this description, concluding that "[t]he waterboarding technique was physically harmful, inducing convulsions and vomiting. Abu Zubaydah, for example, became 'completely unresponsive, with bubbles rising through his open, full mouth.' Internal CIA records describe the waterboarding of Khalid Shaykh Mohammad as evolving into a 'series of near drownings.'" Senate Select Committee on Intelligence, Committee Study of the Central Intelligence Agency's Detention and Interrogation Program, Findings and Conclusions 3 (2014), available at www.amnestyusa.org/pdfs/sscistudy1.pdf [hereinafter Senate Committee Study].

84 Memorandum on Interrogation of al Qaeda Operative, *supra* note 3. The ten techniques which the CIA wanted to use on Abu Zubaydah were listed as "(1) attention grasp, (2) walling, (3) facial hold, (4) facial slap (insult slap), (5) cramped confinement, (6) wall standing, (7) stress positions, (8) sleep deprivation, (9) insects placed in a confinement box, and (10) the waterboard." *Id.* at 2. Technique (9) was described as follows. "You would like to place Zubaydah in a cramped confinement box with an insect. You have informed us that he appears to have a fear of insects. In particular, you would like to tell Zubaydah that you intend to place a stinging insect into the box with him. You would, however, place a harmless insect in the box. You have orally informed us that you would in fact place a harmless insect such as a caterpillar in the box with him." *Id.* at 3 (the remainder of the description, covering one full line and parts of two others, is blacked out, presumably because it remains classified). "Cramped confinement," meanwhile, "involves the placement of the individual in a confined space, the dimensions of which restrict the individual's movement. The confined space is usually dark. The duration of confinement varies based upon the size of the container. For the larger confined space, the individual can stand up or sit down; the smaller space is large enough for the subject to sit down. Confinement in the larger space can last up to eighteen hours; for the smaller space, confinement lasts for no more than two hours." *Id.* at 2–3.

85 18 U.S.C. § 2340(1) (2017).

suffering" requirement.[86] But what if waterboarding is agonizing because it produces desperation, as one's gag reflex is overcome and water pours into one's lungs, rather than because those events produce unbearable physical pain?

The result could still be torture, but this conclusion would depend on the meaning of the statutory language "severe physical … pain or suffering." If the phrase "pain or suffering" in the statute is understood to refer to two different things, pain *and* suffering, then the "agonizing feeling" of one's gag reflex being overcome certainly sounds like the sort of physical suffering the statute has in mind. *Does* "pain or suffering" mean to identify two separate kinds of physical experience? It is possible to argue that "pain or suffering" is simply a legal cliché, really referring to just one thing, namely pain. But the phrase "pain or suffering" by its terms suggests that either pain or suffering will suffice, though Congress's choice of a conjunction (such as "or") is not always dispositive. Moreover, it makes sense to include pain *or* suffering, since intense physical suffering that isn't pain still surely is abhorrent in the same way that intense physical pain is. As Luban writes, "there are forms of physical suffering that aren't pain"[87]—with waterboarding, if indeed it is painless, a paradigm case.

But another statute might now be employed to define "physical suffering" narrowly. In the Military Commissions Act of 2006, Congress also amended the War

86 Of course—unless the torture statute should be read to require that physical pain or suffering, in order to count as "severe," must be of a certain duration, longer than the time that waterboarding takes. So the OLC later argued, in an opinion cutting back on the earlier torture memos. Daniel Levin, Memorandum for James B. Comey—Deputy Attorney General, Re: Legal Standards Applicable Under 18 U.S.C. §§ 2340–2340A (December 30, 2004), at 12, available at www.aclu.org/files/torturefoia/released/082409/olcremand/2004olc96.pdf (arguing that "'*severe* physical suffering' would have to be a condition of some extended duration or persistence as well as intensity"). Luban, *supra* note 83, contends that the fact that the statute only explicitly requires "prolonged" *mental* suffering indicates that it does not require any extended period of physical suffering, and invokes the statutory interpretation canon *expressio unius est exclusio alterius* to support this. (The *expressio unius* canon infers from the statute's mention of certain items its intention to exclude those not mentioned; here the failure to mention any requirement of "prolonged" physical pain or suffering suggests that no such requirement was imposed.) "Some extended duration or persistence" need not be as long as "prolonged," however, and so it is possible to argue that *some* duration is required for physical suffering as well—but surely Luban is right that "forty seconds of suffocation" is quite enough. (The CIA had represented to the OLC "that 40 seconds was the maximum length of a single waterboard application." Senate Committee Study, *supra* note 83, at 423 n. 2377.) Marty Lederman forcefully makes a similar point about the torturous quality of brief, horrific, subjection to the waterboard, in Marty Lederman, Lowering the Bar: Well, At Least We're Not as Barbaric as the Spanish Inquisition, *Balkinization*, February 14, 2008, http://balkin.blogspot.com/2008/02/lowering-bar-well-at-lest-were-not-as.html. It is worth adding that a "single waterboard application" seems to have been quite an unlikely event; of the three people the CIA is acknowledged to have waterboarded, one was subjected to this technique at least 183 times (Khalid Shaykh Mohammad), and another at least 83 times (Abu Zubaydah). *Id.* at 118 n. 698.

87 Luban, *supra* note 83.

Crimes Act to make clear, among other things, that only certain violations of Common Article 3 of the Geneva Conventions would constitute "grave breach[es]" of the Conventions and be punishable war crimes.[88] Among those crimes was torture, defined in this act as entailing "severe physical or mental pain or suffering."[89] Also included was "cruel or inhuman treatment," which the amended statute defined as entailing "severe or serious physical or mental pain or suffering."[90] "Serious physical pain or suffering," in turn, was defined as:

> meaning bodily injury that involves –
> (i) a substantial risk of death;
> (ii) extreme physical pain;
> (iii) a burn or physical disfigurement of a serious nature (other than cuts, abrasions, or bruises); or
> (iv) significant loss or impairment of the function of a bodily member, organ, or mental faculty.[91]

This definition appears to imply that "suffering" can be distinct from pain—for example, physical disfigurement without serious pain presumably would be characterized as serious physical suffering. But it's striking that "serious physical suffering" other than "extreme physical pain" (which is specifically referenced in subsection (ii)) is here being given a quite precise definition, encompassing bodily injury producing one of three kinds of harm (those listed in subsections (i), (iii), and (iv)): substantial risks of death; serious burns or disfigurement; or significant loss or impairment of a function of the body or mind.

Does waterboarding cause any of these three kinds of "serious physical suffering"? It doesn't seem to involve physical disfigurement. Nor does it involve the significant loss or impairment of the function of a bodily organ—as long as that concept is understood to refer to some lasting effect. The person waterboarded cannot breathe, so his lungs' function is obviously impaired at that time, but once his lungs empty again they will resume their work unimpaired. Nor, it may be argued, does waterboarding necessarily involve a substantial risk of death—provided the process is carefully, "professionally" monitored. The person waterboarded will experience the horrifying, and physical, sensation of drowning, but if that experience is only a terrifyingly vivid simulation of drowning, then perhaps what he is experiencing is not serious physical suffering *as defined in the War Crimes Act*. It might then be argued that this definition should be applied to the torture statute as well, using the interpretive canon of *in pari materia*,[92] and it

88 *See* 18 U.S.C. § 2441(c)(3) (2017).
89 *Id.* § 2441(d)(1)(A).
90 *Id.* § 2441(d)(1)(B).
91 *Id.* § 2441(d)(2)(D).
92 One formulation of the *in pari materia* canon understands it to require that "similar statutes should be interpreted similarly, unless legislative history or purpose suggests material differences." William N. Eskridge, Jr., Philip P. Frickey, & Elizabeth Garrett,

would seem to follow that he also couldn't be experiencing the "severe" (not just "serious") physical suffering that's required under the torture statute.

A lawyer exploring the application of the torture statute to waterboarding might also ask whether the pain or suffering is actually physical or mental. There's no doubt that this is a very physical experience—the victim is, the same instructor says, being subjected to "controlled drowning … as the lungs are actually filling with water."[93] But is what makes it awful physical suffering or mental suffering? On this, the instructor's words quoted by Luban leave some room for debate: "Waterboarding is slow motion suffocation with enough time to contemplate the inevitability of black out and expiration—usually the person goes into hysterics on the board."[94] This could be taken as a description of mental suffering more than physical. So could the instructor's comment that "[a] team doctor watches the quantity of water that is ingested and for the physiological signs which show when the drowning effect goes from painful psychological experience, to horrific suffocating punishment to the final death spiral."[95]

I would not endorse the effort to draw a line between physical and mental pain and suffering, which here seem thoroughly intermingled. But suppose one said, not altogether implausibly, that the principal suffering of waterboarding is mental pain. Then the torture statute would present a big problem, because conduct that causes mental pain is only torture if it causes "prolonged mental harm."[96] If the victim of waterboarding rises from the board at the end shaken, but not suffering "prolonged mental harm," then it turns out he hasn't been tortured after all. Now, roughly a decade after the worst instances of "enhanced interrogation techniques," we have substantial evidence that in fact these techniques so traumatize their targets that there is plenty of "prolonged" mental harm,[97] but we can imagine, at least, that ten years ago these effects were unrecognized. And if they weren't recognized, and weren't sought, then it's quite arguable that the people administering waterboarding did not—as the statute also requires—specifically intend them.[98]

Finally, even if waterboarding is understood to produce prolonged mental difficulties, it is possible that these do not constitute "prolonged mental pain or suffering" as required by the statute because they do not result from one of the specific causes of such harm that the statute insists be responsible.[99] The first of

Legislation and Statutory Interpretation (New York: Foundation Press, Thomson/West, 2nd ed. 2006), 395.

93 Luban, *supra* note 83. Luban emphasizes the physical suffering it entails. *Id.*

94 *Id.*

95 *Id.*

96 18 U.S.C. § 2340(2) (2017).

97 See Matt Apuzzo, Sheri Fink, & James Risen, How U.S. Torture Left a Legacy of Damaged Minds, *The New York Times*, October 8, 2016, www.nytimes.com/2016/10/09/world/cia-torture-guantanamo-bay.html?action=click&contentCollection=Americas&module=RelatedCoverage&region=Marginalia&pgtype=article.

98 See text at notes 32–34 *supra*.

99 See 18 U.S.C. § 2340(2) (2017).

these is, in essence, the use or threat of physical torture,[100] but if the kinds of arguments sketched above are accepted then waterboarding isn't physical torture. The second is the use of "mind-altering substances or other procedures calculated to disrupt profoundly the senses or the personality."[101] Waterboarding is calculated to terrify its subjects; but that effect may not rely at all on disrupting the target's personality in the way that, say, hallucinogenic drugs might. The third is "the threat of imminent death"—but as much as waterboarding may convey such a threat, it is quite possible that no such threat is ever voiced, and arguable that only a clear, or at least a clearly intended, threat is required.[102] (The fourth, the threat of applying any of the first three to another person, isn't applicable here.[103]) So it might be that even if it in fact results in prolonged mental harm, waterboarding isn't one of the statutorily specified causes of such harm that must be present for that harm to constitute, under the torture statute, "severe mental pain or suffering."

Again, I think Luban is right: here, the physical suffering is part and parcel of the horror, and on that ground waterboarding is torture under the statute. But suppose it was, somehow, a little different, or suppose the US government had devised some other method whose impact was more unmistakably to cause mental harm, but, again, mental harm that could plausibly be said not to be prolonged or not to be caused by one of the specific mechanisms the statute requires. And yet we know—essentially, because almost everyone breaks under it—that it is torture.

What I've tried to describe is a technique that is torture and yet that might not, under conventional legal interpretive analysis, fall clearly within the torture statute. With such a technique, the boundaries of proper interpretation may determine the outcome, just as, in a dispute over contested facts, the assignment of the burden of proof may predetermine the result. The question, then, is whether there is a way, from within the law, to say that methods of interpretation that will narrow the meaning of the prohibition of torture so as to make techniques of this sort lawful are themselves impermissible or at any rate unpersuasive. That question is the subject of the following section.

Limits on the interpretive minimization of torture

Let me start with one possible limit, one that Luban emphasizes—namely, that the meaning of the statute is clear.[104] I think there is force to this; deliberately

100 See *id.* § 2340(2)(A).
101 *Id.* § 2340(2)(B).
102 *Id.* § 2340(2)(C).
103 *Id.* § 2340(2)(D).
104 Case law can also limit interpretive invention, and Luban rightly points to the decision in *United States v. Lee*, 744 F.2d 1124 (5th Cir. 1984), in which a federal appellate court seemed to take for granted that a technique Luban reports was almost identical to water-boarding was "torture." David Luban, David Margolis Is Wrong: The Justice Department's Ethics Investigation Shouldn't Leave John Yoo and Jay Bybee Home Free, *Slate* (updated February 22, 2010), available at www.slate.com/toolbar.aspx?action=print&id=2245531 (last visited May 25, 2010). But this decision, while

subjecting someone to agonizing experiences has to be torture. Moreover, I concur with the underlying implication of saying that the statute has a clear core of meaning, namely that legal language is not, after all, completely indeterminate. But even though the torture statute has a core meaning that is indeed clear, there remain—as the preceding section sought to show—a range of ways that this statute's meaning is *not* entirely clear. And, as we have seen, even seemingly clear language may turn out to be susceptible to interpretation that takes its meaning a considerable distance from what its words at first blush appeared to convey. For the kinds of techniques that I am focusing on, we need something more than the words alone to confirm that they are torture.

Perhaps this is a vain effort, and we should dispense with the notion of limits to be found within the law. There are, to be sure, many recognizable techniques of legal reasoning, but perhaps there is no real way to draw guidance from them. For every interpretive move, there is another equal and opposite one,[105] and so in the end there is only will and power, not anything that could be called objective interpretation. Certainly the extent to which human perceptions and reasoning are influenced by preconceptions and self-interest gives one pause in asserting that objective interpretation is a meaningful touchstone for a legal system.

But the argument that the torture statute has clear meaning is, necessarily, an argument that there is such a thing as objective interpretation, which is what will enable a reader to discern that clear meaning. It seems to me that it is hard to aspire to a "government of laws and not of men" unless we also aspire to objective interpretation of those laws. And in fact lawyers in the government who were moved by their view of the importance of objective interpretation took decisive action to combat the minimization of the torture prohibition in the Bush years. This is the attitude reflected in this account by Jack Goldsmith of his own response to an earlier OLC opinion on which the CIA's interrogation techniques relied:[106]

> [I]n contrast to my sense of the Defense Department techniques [techniques he considered lawful], I wasn't as confident that the CIA techniques could be approved under a proper legal analysis. I didn't affirmatively believe they were

instructive, could still be parsed; it is not, after all, a decision about what torture is under the torture statute.

105 The classic article on the "dueling canons" is Karl Llewellyn, Remarks on the Theory of Appellate Decision and the Rules or Canons About How Statutes Are to Be Construed, 3 *Vand. L. Rev.* 395 (1950). For the first of a series of articles developing the argument that in fact the canons do not contradict each other, but instead make up a coherent body of legal guidelines, see Michael Sinclair, "Only a Sith Thinks Like That": Llewellyn's "Dueling Canons," One to Seven, 50 *N.Y.L. Sch. L. Rev.* 919 (2006).

106 Goldsmith, *supra* note 2, at 155–156. Earlier in his book, Goldsmith invokes the idea of "a government of laws, and not of men," to explain why the OLC "has developed powerful cultural norms about the importance of providing the President with detached, apolitical legal advice, as if OLC were an independent court inside the executive branch." *Id.* at 33.

> illegal either, or else I would have stopped them. I just didn't yet know. And I wouldn't know until we had figured out the proper interpretation of the torture statute, and whether the CIA techniques were consistent with that proper legal analysis.

Another head of the OLC, Daniel Levin, went so far as to have himself waterboarded in an effort to determine whether the technique truly was torture.[107] I suspect that this same commitment to finding the true meaning of the law underlies the impressive opposition to torture expressed by many soldiers and military lawyers over recent years.[108] We need the common ground between lawyers of different political views that the aspiration to find a "proper legal analysis" provides, and so I believe it is worthwhile to seek reasons "within the law" for constraining the interpretation of the torture statute.

Exploring higher authority as a source of limitation

Our interpretive task would be easier if we could find some overarching source of authority that prescribes to us that "*this* legal interpretation is well-founded and *that* one is not." This is not an unreasonable aspiration. Much legal reasoning is about which legal sources take precedence over which; the Supreme Court's decisions, for example, take precedence over those of lower courts. I do not want to reject the relevance of the search for authoritativeness in the interpretation of the torture statute, but I do argue that the possible sites of such authority turn out, on examination, to be less cogent than might have been expected. These problems emerge as we look at the possibility that presidential directives can shape interpretation; the alternative notion that popular sentiments might determine the meaning of statutes; and finally the suggestion that the "interpretive community" will provide us with the bearings that we need. If we look not to legal actors such as the president or the people or the interpretive community, but instead to the law itself and its overarching essence—whether determined as a matter of moral philosophy or as the product of synthesis of the many disparate strands that make up the US legal system—again we will find ourselves with less conclusive guidance than we might have wished.

One possible source of interpretive clarity—presidential directive—was offered by the OLC in its memorandum withdrawing the original torture memos. This memo, responding to the debate over the correct interpretation of "specific intent," said:

107 Mayer, *supra* note 13, at 298–299. Mayer reports that Levin concluded that waterboarding "could definitely be classified as illegal torture unless … it was strictly limited in terms of time and severity and was closely monitored in a very professional way." *Id.* at 299.

108 See Josh White, Military Lawyers Fought Policy on Interrogations: JAGs Recount Objections to Definition of Torture, *Washington Post*, July 15, 2005, www.washingtonpost.com/wp-dyn/content/article/2005/07/14/AR2005071402187_pf.html.

> We do not believe it is useful to try to define the precise meaning of "specific intent" in section 2340. In light of the President's directive that the United States not engage in torture, it would not be appropriate to rely on parsing the specific intent element of the statute to approve as lawful conduct that might otherwise amount to torture.[109]

This is an argument that, essentially, the president's directives dictate that "parsing" the statute to find loopholes to permit torture not be engaged in. Since the president certainly has authority to shape executive branch activity, and arguably has some interpretive discretion with respect to foreign affairs and military matters, it is quite reasonable for his lawyers to defer to some extent to his directives. But the guideline the OLC lawyers professed to find was an ambiguous one indeed. The meaning of President Bush's directives was itself deeply controversial, since he had also approved of waterboarding.[110] Perhaps more important, whatever is directed today could be differently directed tomorrow—and we know now, in 2018, that this is a real possibility.

Another source of interpretive clarity might be the views of the American people about torture. I would not deny that the views of the American people are part of the source of statutory meaning, as of constitutional understanding.[111] But what are those sentiments? According to Dahlia Lithwick, "[a] 2009 poll revealed that 53 percent of the public believes torture is at least sometimes justified to gain important information from terror suspects." And she adds that "[t]hese numbers rise every few months."[112] (Other data, however, suggest much greater American skepticism about torture).[113] A recent survey conducted for the International

109 Daniel Levin, Memorandum for James B. Comey—Deputy Attorney General, Re: Legal Standards Applicable Under 18 U.S.C. §§ 2340–2340A (December 30, 2004), at 16–17 (footnote omitted) (cited at note 86 *supra*).

110 Bush on Waterboarding: Damn Right, *CNNpolitics* (November 5, 2010 7:13 p.m. EDT), www.cnn.com/2010/POLITICS/11/05/bush.book/. But another insider from this era, John Rizzo, maintains that Bush is mistaken in remembering himself as directly involved with the decision on waterboarding. Steve Coll, The C.I.A.'s Lawyer: Waterboarding and Memory, *The New Yorker*, January 1, 2014, www.newyorker.com/news/daily-comment/the-c-i-a-s-lawyer-waterboarding-and-memory.

111 If the legal community consists not just of legal professionals but of all those who are concerned with the law, and if the legal community's views of what the law rightly means inevitably affect which legal arguments are accepted and which rejected, then it must follow that the views of the public affect the arguments that in turn generate authoritative statutory and constitutional interpretations.

112 Dahlia Lithwick, Torture Bored: How We've Erased the Legal Lines around Torture and Replaced Them with Nothing, *Slate*, February 22, 2010, www.slate.com/toolbar.aspx?action=print&id=2243737. See also Chris Kahn, Exclusive: Most Americans Support Torture Against Terror Suspects—Reuters/Ipsos Poll, Reuters, March 30, 2016, www.reuters.com/article/us-usa-election-torture-exclusive-idUSKCN0WW0Y3 (reporting on a March, 2016 poll which found that "[n]early two-thirds of Americans believe torture can be justified to extract information from suspected terrorists").

113 Paul Gronke, Darius Rejali, & Peter Miller, No, Americans Aren't "Fine with Torture." They Strongly Reject It, *Washington Post*, December 11, 2014, www.washingtonpost.com/posteverything/wp/2014/12/11/no-americans-arent-fine-with-tor

Committee of the Red Cross shows that a growing percentage—but still a minority—of the citizens of other Western nations also accept torture as a legitimate step in wartime.[114] It seems safe to say that the issue of torture is one on which Americans (and others) are sharply divided, and so there seems likely to be little clear guidance to be had from this source either. At the same time it is important to keep in mind that while the views of the people may well be part of the dialogue that shapes the meaning of US laws, the requirement that statutes be formally enacted makes the unenacted inclinations of the people less than authoritative. Indeed, the processes of representative, as opposed to direct, democracy amount to a deliberate institutional limit on the weight to be given to sentiments not yet formally made into law. Lawmaking is *hard*—and so the laws that make it all the way through the legislative process to enactment have a weight that popular sentiments do not.[115]

For similar reasons I do not think we can look to the bounds of the "interpretive community" to tell us our answer, despite the frequent suggestion that interpretations find their legitimacy in good part through their acceptance by this entity. The interpretive community is not monolithic—witness the existence of the torture memos in the first place. Nor does it have ways to express its views authoritatively; there is no voting in the interpretive community. Nevertheless, its views may be felt, and the community need not be of exactly one mind for its judgment that some ideas are beyond the bounds to make itself felt. To some extent that may be what has happened in the response to the torture memos.[116] But the interpretive community is also in perpetual motion, and what it rejects today it may accept tomorrow. Moreover, what it accepts or rejects presumably depends at least to some extent on the strength of what it is presented with. Strong legal arguments tend to shape the boundaries of the interpretive community that then validates them as strong legal arguments—and we haven't yet identified the legal arguments that would strongly argue against complete interpretive freedom in reading the torture statute.

ture-they-strongly-reject-it/?utm_term=.c8b25b606081 (finding Americans "deeply ambivalent about the use of torture," and noting that "when Americans are asked about specific techniques … public support is far lower," with 84–89% disapproving of "sexual humiliation" and 58–81% opposed to waterboarding).

114 Kenneth Watkin, The ICRC Survey and Torture: A Glass Two-Thirds Full?, *Just Security*, December 23, 2016, 9:16 AM, www.justsecurity.org/35816/icrc-survey-torture-glass-two-thirds-full/ ("only two-thirds of all those asked [17,000 people from 16 nations] say torture is wrong, and 27 percent see it as a 'part of war'").

115 See Frank H. Easterbrook, The Role of Original Intent in Statutory Construction, 11 *Harv. J.L. & Pub. Pol'y* 59, 64–65 (1988) (emphasizing that the results of an "opinion poll of Congress" would not thereby "become the law").

116 For an account of the movement among lawyers—largely unaccompanied by a broader social mobilization—to challenge US mistreatment of detainees, see Lisa Hajjar, Lawyers, Litigation and the US Anti-Torture Campaign (American Political Science Association 2010 Annual Meeting Paper), available at https://papers.ssrn.com/sol3/papers.cfm?abstract_id=1642413.

If we look not to legal actors but to the essence of law itself for authoritative limitations, we again find less clarity than we might have hoped. Inspired by Lon Fuller, we might argue that any law, or legal interpretation, that permits conduct that should be prohibited as torture is inconsistent with the very nature of law as a set of rules infused with the protection of human rights and dignity.[117] Fuller wrote, for example, that "Law, considered merely as order, contains, then, its own implicit morality. This morality of order must be respected if we are to create anything that can be called law, even bad law."[118] Elsewhere he described "the theory of natural law … in its most modest form" as fundamentally affirming

> the role of human reason in the design and operation of legal institutions. It asserts that there are principles of sound social architecture, objectively given, and that these principles, like those of physical architecture, do not change with every shift in the details of the design toward which they are directed.[119]

Interpretation infused with this understanding can be a powerful tool against injustice; it is possible to see much of the work of anti-apartheid lawyers and judges in South Africa, for instance, as embodying this stance. But as appealing as this conception of law is, it offers us limited succor when we confront legal materials that in fact exist and yet do not protect human rights and dignity; in the end, within the world in which these dispiriting laws exist, they seem to have force. We face a similar problem when we confront legal interpretations which seek to deprive laws of their potential capacity to protect rights and dignity; in a clash between rights-minded and, say, security-minded interpretations, we seem to be cast back to moral philosophy rather than law to say which interpretations should be honored.

We might respond by arguing that the "legal materials that in fact exist" in American society do confirm the unacceptability of torture, that indeed acceptance of torture is simply incompatible with a host of legal decisions firmly embodied throughout the US legal system. This is the argument of Jeremy Waldron in his thoughtful book *Torture, Terror and Trade-Offs: Philosophy for the White House.*[120] Waldron makes a cogent and wide-ranging case for his thesis that "narrowing or otherwise undermining the definition of torture might deal a body blow to the *corpus juris* that would go beyond the immediate effects on the mentality of torturers and the terror and suffering of their victims."[121] But Waldron's argument that the rule against torture is an "archetype" of the US legal system moves us from a focus on what torture is to a perhaps more uncertain

117 I am grateful to Catherine Powell of the University of Cape Town Faculty of Law for showing me the relevance of Fuller's thinking to my work in this article.
118 Lon L. Fuller, Positivism and Fidelity to Law—A Reply to Professor Hart, 71 *Harv. L. Rev.* 630, 645 (1957).
119 Lon L. Fuller, *Anatomy of the Law* (New York: New American Library, 1968), 181.
120 Waldron, *supra* note 8, at 186–260.
121 *Id.* at 191.

inquiry into the relation between the rule against torture and much broader legal and social concerns.

Eric Posner and Adrian Vermeule urge that "Waldron errs by attempting to derive concrete conclusions from premises that are too general or abstract to cut between policy choices on the ground."[122] If the legal system is committed to rejecting brutality and savagery, they urge, it might still accept laws permitting brutal treatment when it is sufficiently justified; in that case

> their symbolic meaning falls by the wayside, in part because that meaning is qualified: a brutal law that does good no longer expresses brutality in unambiguous form. Indeed, such laws do no more than symbolize the government's willingness to produce the greatest possible good overall.[123]

This rebuttal is surely overstated; it seems very likely that as torture, or something like torture that by virtue of legal interpretation goes by another name, becomes part of our repertoire in one area it will spread insidiously to others as well—so that soon we will see abuse become widespread, as it did at Abu Ghraib in 2003.[124] But whether the prohibition on torture is in a more general sense archetypal, as Waldron contends, will remain a complex, perhaps simply unanswerable, empirical question.[125]

The elements of lawyers' work as interpretive limits

For the reasons just discussed, I am hesitant about the likelihood of finding definitive guidance either in some authoritative figure in the legal system or in broad conceptions of the fundamental nature of this system. Though I do not mean to disregard any of these sources entirely, I suggest that we can find firmer interpretive footing on more traditional doctrinal ground. If we want to interpret laws bearing on torture, we should look, first, at the meaning of the word "torture" itself and at what makes it so abhorrent. Then, second, we should consider what the legal system has actually had to say about torture, especially in the multiple statutes Congress has enacted in this field. Third, and finally, we should consider

122 Eric A. Posner & Adrian Vermeule, *Terror in the Balance: Security, Liberty and the Courts* (Oxford: Oxford University Press, 2007), 204–05.

123 *Id. at* 205.

124 See Seymour M. Hersh, Torture at Abu Ghraib: American Soldiers Brutalized Iraqis. How Far Up Does the Responsibility Go?, *The New Yorker*, May 10, 2004, available at www.newyorker.com/magazine/2004/05/10/torture-at-abu-ghraib. For indications of direct links between abuse at Abu Ghraib and the earlier interrogation of a terrorist suspect at Guantanamo, see Josh White, Abu Ghraib Tactics Were First Used at Guantanamo, *Washington Post*, July 14, 2005, www.washingtonpost.com/wp-dyn/content/article/2005/07/13/AR2005071302380.html. Posner & Vermeule, however, maintain that "the evidence of a causal relationship at the time of this writing is thin." Posner & Vermeule, *supra* note 122, at 201.

125 Waldron acknowledges that "[t]he case I am making is in part an empirical one, and it is open in principle to empirical refutation." Waldron, *supra* note 8, at 243.

again the responsibilities that the president's lawyers have to the potential victims of torture, in light of the lawyers' role in essentially, and often secretly and unreviewably, determining what the law of torture will actually be. Some of what I will say in undertaking these inquiries may echo to the broader sources of interpretation that I've just surveyed and found problematic, but I do not regret that overlap; rather it seems to me that those broader perspectives may best be brought to bear through a closer focus on the more traditional details of lawyers' interpretive work.

The meaning of the word "torture"

In *Babbitt v. Sweet Home Chapter of Communities for a Great Oregon*,[126] the Supreme Court debated the meaning of the word "take" in the context of the *taking* of wildlife. Faced with a statutory definition (and an agency regulation based on that definition) that could be read to very broadly construe the meaning of "take," Justice Scalia argued that:

> if the terms contained in the definitional section are susceptible of two readings, one of which comports with the standard meaning of "take" as used in application to wildlife, and one of which does not, an agency regulation that adopts the latter reading is necessarily unreasonable, for it reads the defined term "take"—the only operative term—out of the statute altogether.[127]

The majority resisted Scalia's attempt to narrow what it saw as the meaning of the statutory definition, declaring that "Congress explicitly defined the operative term 'take' … no matter how much the dissent wishes otherwise."[128] But if Scalia's argument overstates the weight to be given to traditional meanings in the face of explicit text, he surely is correct that traditional meanings remain of some value in interpretation.

Let us therefore look again at the meaning of torture. Posner and Vermeule write that "the only strong argument against torture is that it causes pain."[129] This assessment is at least too quick. As we have already seen some forms of torture do not cause *physical* pain; for example, it can be torture to threaten to torture a third party whom the threatened person loves. Indeed, if torture can be accomplished, as the words of its statutory definition suggest, by the imposition of either pain *or* suffering, then "pain" itself is not a requirement. Moreover, torture is by no means the only thing governments do that causes pain—most obviously, cruel, inhuman and degrading treatment may also cause serious pain.[130] It seems to me that the strongest argument against torture, or put differently the factor that makes torture so distinctively awful, is not that it is painful, but that it causes the

126 515 U.S. 687 (1995).
127 *Id.* at 718 (Scalia, J., dissenting).
128 *Id.* at 696 n. 10.
129 Posner & Vermeule, *supra* note 122, at 205.
130 See text at note 90 *supra*.

person tortured to believe that there is no limit at all on what his torturers may do to him. He is cast beyond the limits of mercy and of law, and may be subjected to whatever tyranny his torturers desire.[131]

That torture is about tyranny intersects with an understanding of the Eighth Amendment's "cruel and unusual punishment" clause that the Supreme Court articulated a century ago, in *Weems v. United States.*[132] Though the Supreme Court has decided that this clause only regulates "punishments,"[133] and some instances of torture—such as torture during interrogation—may not be punishments,[134] it is surely clear that instances of torture that are part of punishment are among the paradigmatic cases to which any prohibition of torture should apply. So it is instructive to consider what the Supreme Court said in *Weems*, in explaining what those who supported adoption of the Eighth Amendment were concerned with:[135]

> Their predominant political impulse was distrust of power, and they insisted on constitutional limitations against its abuse. But surely they intended more than to register a fear of the forms of abuse that went out of practice with the Stuarts. Surely, their jealousy of power had a saner justification than that. They were men of action, practical and sagacious, not beset with vain imagining, and it must have come to them that there could be exercises of cruelty by laws other than those which inflicted bodily pain or mutilation.... [W]hat more potent instrument of cruelty could be put into the hands of power? And

131 See Waldron, *supra* note 8, at 233 (the prohibition on torture is "vividly emblematic of our determination to sever the link between law and brutality, between law and terror, and between law and the enterprise of trying to break a person's will").

132 217 U.S. 349 (1910). The case applied the Eighth Amendment to a punishment imposed by the Philippines, then a United States colony. This penalty—for the falsification of a public document—required a minimum of "confinement in a penal institution for twelve years and one day, a chain at the ankle and wrist of the offender, hard and painful labor, no assistance from friend or relative, no marital authority or parental rights or rights of property, no participation even in the family council." Even after the term of imprisonment, the convicted person would face "perpetual limitation of his liberty." The Court summed up: "No circumstance of degradation is omitted. It may be that even the cruelty of pain is not omitted." *Id.* at 366.

133 See *Ingraham v. Wright*, 430 U.S. 651, 666 (1977) ("every decision of this Court considering whether a punishment is 'cruel and unusual' within the meaning of the Eighth and Fourteenth Amendments has dealt with a criminal punishment").

134 In *Bell v. Wolfish*, 441 U.S. 520 (1979), the Court cited the following list of "the tests traditionally applied to determine whether a governmental act is punitive in nature": "Whether the sanction involves an affirmative disability or restraint, whether it has historically been regarded as a punishment, whether it comes into play only on a finding of *scienter,* whether its operation will promote the traditional aims of punishment—retribution and deterrence, whether the behavior to which it applies is already a crime, whether an alternative purpose to which it may rationally be connected is assignable for it, and whether it appears excessive in relation to the alternative purpose assigned are all relevant to the inquiry, and may often point in differing directions." *Id.* at 537–38, quoting *Kennedy v. Mendoza-Martinez*, 372 U.S. 144, 168–69 (1963).

135 *Weems*, 217 U.S. at 372–373.

> it was believed that power might be tempted to cruelty.... [T]here was more to be considered than the ordinary criminal laws. Cruelty might become an instrument of tyranny; of zeal for a purpose, either honest or sinister.

If the essence of torture is tyrannical power over others, then we have one limit on the correct interpretation of statutes defining torture: they should not be interpreted so as to permit tyranny. Techniques such as waterboarding clearly create this kind of tyrannical power, exercised by men and women filled with "zeal for a purpose"—that is why those subjected to these techniques break so predictably—and that is a very strong reason not to read the ambiguities of the torture statute to permit these techniques.[136]

The legal system's statements about torture

All legal rules are subject to interpretation. If a particular rule is asserted only obliquely, or incompletely, or inarticulately, then its interpretation may justly be said to be up for debate. But if a rule is declared repeatedly and clearly, the sheer multiplication of these declarations reinforces the clarity of each separate iteration. This argument is frankly positivist; I am not asking here whether the law necessarily must embody a firm prohibition on torture, or even whether the prohibition on torture is an archetype of American law, but only whether the actions of US lawmakers have in fact repeatedly buttressed the strength of that prohibition in the law. The answer is that even during the early years of the Bush administration, the United States' commitment to the prohibition of torture was embodied in multiple authoritative sources. In the years since then, this commitment has been underlined even more emphatically.

First, we can begin with the Convention Against Torture.[137] The Convention provides that "Each State Party shall take effective legislative, administrative, judicial or other measures to prevent acts of torture in any territory under its jurisdiction."[138] It continues: "No exceptional circumstances whatsoever, whether a

136 Although waterboarding evidently overpowers almost everyone subjected to it, Khalid Shaykh Muhammad manifestly suffered from it, yet proved unusually capable of coping with it. Senate Committee Study, *supra* note 83, at 426 ("CIA personnel concluded the waterboard was not an effective interrogation technique against KSM"), 494 ("The on-site medical officer [reported] ... that KSM 'hated it but knew he could manage.'") But if Muhammad was a remarkable exception to the rule about waterboarding's impact, that should not change our understanding of the overall status of this technique.

137 Convention Against Torture and Other Cruel, Inhuman or Degrading Treatment or Punishment, *supra* note 5. While this Convention focuses specifically on torture, and supplies a definition of that term that forms a basis for the US statutory definitions, the International Covenant on Civil and Political Rights also prohibits torture. International Covenant on Civil and Political Rights, art. 7, December 16, 1966, 999 U.N.T.S. 171, 6 I.L.M. 368 (1967). Waldron begins his list of the "texts and the prohibitions" with this Covenant. Waldron, *supra* note 8, at 191.

138 Convention Against Torture, *supra* note 5, art. 2.1.

state of war or a threat of war, internal political instability or any other public emergency, may be invoked as a justification of torture."[139] The United States signed this convention in 1988 and the Senate ratified it in 1994,[140] so it is part of US law.

Second, the United States adopted in 1994 the "torture statute,"[141] meant to implement the nation's obligation under the Convention Against Torture to prevent torture in any territory under its control.[142] This statute applies to acts of torture committed in any place "outside the United States" by any US national, or by anyone else found present in the US.[143] (A range of ordinary criminal laws already made acts of torture criminal when committed inside the United States.)[144] As we have already seen, this statute defines torture as "an act committed by a person acting under the color of law specifically intended to inflict severe physical or mental pain or suffering (other than pain or suffering incidental to lawful sanctions) upon another person within his custody or physical control."[145] That definition offers considerable room for lawyers' interpretive maneuvers, as we have discussed at length, but it is worth remarking that it is largely similar to the definition in the Convention Against Torture[146]—as would be expected of an implementing statute.[147]

139 *Id.*, art. 2.2.
140 United Nations Treaty Collection, Status of Treaties, Convention Against Torture and Other Cruel, Inhuman or Degrading Treatment or Punishment, https://treaties.un.org/Pages/ViewDetails.aspx?src=IND&mtdsg_no=IV-9&chapter=4&clang=_en (accessed January 5, 2017). The Convention went into force in 1987, *id.*
141 18 U.S.C. §§ 2340–2340B (2017).
142 The enacting law designated the section containing the torture statute as "Torture Convention Implementation." Foreign Relations Authorization Act, Fiscal Years 1994 and 1995, Pub. L. 103–236, April 30, 1994, 108 Stat. 382, § 506.
143 18 U.S.C. § 2340A(a) (2017).
144 Several of these laws were listed by President Obama in Executive Order No. 13,491 (issued January 22, 2009), quoted in note 6 *supra*.
145 18 U.S.C. § 2340(1) (2017).
146 The Convention defines "torture" as "any act by which severe pain or suffering, whether physical or mental, is intentionally inflicted on a person for such purposes as obtaining from him or a third person information or a confession, punishing him for an act he or a third person has committed or is suspected of having committed, or intimidating or coercing him or a third person, or for any reason based on discrimination of any kind, when such pain or suffering is inflicted by or at the instigation of or with the consent or acquiescence of a public official or other person acting in an official capacity. It does not include pain or suffering arising only from, inherent in or incidental to lawful sanctions." Convention Against Torture, *supra* note 5, art. 1.1. As we have already seen, the US statute also includes an elaborate definition of the component term "severe mental pain or suffering," 18 U.S.C. § 2340(2) (2017), to which the Convention contains no analogue.
147 Three years before enacting the torture statute, Congress had also adopted the Torture Victim Protection Act of 1991, Pub. L. 102–256, Mar. 12, 1992, 106 Stat. 73, codified as 28 U.S.C. § 1350 Note (2017), which provides a cause of action for victims of torture against their torturers. Section 3(b) defines torture much as the torture statute and the subsequently enacted War Crimes Act do.

Third, even before ratifying the Convention and implementing it by statute, the United States had long since ratified the Geneva Conventions of 1949 and adopted implementing legislation for those treaties. The most broadly relevant provision of the Geneva Conventions of 1949 is Common Article 3.[148] Common Article 3 prohibits a range of profound offenses against humanity, specifically including "torture."[149] The United States implemented the Geneva Conventions through the War Crimes Act of 1996. As originally enacted, this statute made it a crime to commit a grave breach of the Geneva Conventions, and defined "grave breach of the Geneva Conventions" to mean "conduct defined as a grave breach" in any of those Conventions.[150] Article 130 of the Third Geneva Convention defines grave breach to include "willful killing, torture or inhuman treatment."[151]

In 2006, during the Bush administration, the War Crimes Act was amended in considerable detail,[152] but grave breaches remained federal crimes, and the definition of grave breaches continued to track the Geneva Conventions' definitions.[153] The amended statute did circumscribe the definition of torture in non-international conflicts (to which only Common Article 3 of the Geneva Conventions applied).[154] It even declared that the new provisions, including this definition of torture, fully implemented the Third Geneva Convention's requirement of "effective penal sanctions for grave breaches" of Common Article 3 in non-international armed conflicts,[155] and also barred invoking any of the Geneva Conventions in any American court "as a source of rights" in cases involving the United States or its personnel.[156] But the new definition actually did not

148 Common Article 3 is cited in note 4 *supra*. Common Article 3 by its terms applies only to "armed conflict not of an international character" but other provisions of the Prisoner of War convention, Geneva Convention Relative to the Treatment of Prisoners of War art. 3, August 12, 1949, 6 U.S.T. 3316, 75 U.N.T.S. 135, impose even more extensive protections for those involved in international armed conflicts. See, e.g., *id.* art. 17 ("No physical or mental torture, nor any other form of coercion, may be inflicted on prisoners of war to secure from them information of any kind whatever.")

149 *Id.* art. 3(1)(a).

150 War Crimes Act of 1996, Pub. L. 104–192, § 2(a), August 21, 1996, 110 Stat. 2104, codified at 18 U.S.C. § 2441 (2017).

151 Geneva Convention Relative to the Treatment of Prisoners of War art. 130, August 12, 1949, 6 U.S.T. 3316, 75 U.N.T.S. 135.

152 Military Commissions Act of 2006, Pub. L. 109–366, § 6(b)(1), October 17, 2006, 120 Stat. 2600, 2633.

153 See 18 U.S.C. §§ 2441(a) & (c)(1) (2017).

154 The new definition specified that torture constituting a grave breach of Common Article 3 was "the act of a person who commits, or conspires or attempts to commit, an act specifically intended to inflict severe physical or mental pain or suffering (other than pain or suffering incidental to lawful sanctions) upon another person within his custody or physical control for the purpose of obtaining information or a confession, punishment, intimidation, coercion, or any reason based on discrimination of any kind." 18 U.S.C. § 2441(d)(1)(A) (2017).

155 Military Commissions Act of 2006, Pub. L. 109–366, § 6(a)(2), October 17, 2006, 120 Stat. 2600, 2633, codified as 18 U.S.C. § 2441 Note (2017).

156 *Id.*, § 5(a), codified as 28 U.S.C. § 2241 Note (2017); see also *id.* § 6(a)(2), codified as 18 U.S.C. § 2441 Note (2017) ("No foreign or international source of law shall

narrow the definition of torture more than the one already incorporated in the torture statute.

It is worth noting that the War Crimes Act definition adds a purpose requirement not present in either the US torture statute or the Geneva Conventions. Purpose surely has some part in the definition of torture, but this list of purposes is quite comprehensive. In the context of interrogation of suspected terrorists—surely a context much on the minds of the drafters of the War Crimes Act—the list seems less like a narrowing of the reach of the prohibition of torture than a confirmation that there are no purposes for which true torture is justified. This reading is confirmed if we look at the Convention Against Torture, whose definition of torture includes a very similar (though non-exclusive) list of purposes, while another of its provisions explicitly bars any justification of torture.[157] That explicit bar is not reiterated in the torture statute, and its omission, read in light of the *expressio unius* canon, might have seemed to suggest that the torture statute did not rule out torture in all conceivable circumstances. Though the point is not free from doubt, the *in pari materia* canon supports the inference that the *implicit* confirmation of the complete prohibition of torture in the War Crimes Act, a statute dealing with the same subject matter as the torture statute, indicates that the absence of a reiteration of the unavailability of justifications in the torture statute was not significant. Instead, it would seem, the unqualified prohibition on torture that the torture statute does contain was meant to be taken literally.

Fourth, in a dramatic effort to reform US interrogation practices, Congress enacted the Detainee Treatment Act of 2005.[158] This statute provides that "No individual in the custody or under the physical control of the United States Government, regardless of nationality or physical location, shall be subject to cruel, inhuman, or degrading treatment or punishment."[159] It is an effort to short-circuit debate about the definition of torture, by making clear that not only torture but also "cruel, inhuman or degrading treatment" are everywhere prohibited. It is fair to say that this approach implies a recognition that some

supply a basis for a rule of decision in the courts of the United States in interpreting the prohibitions enumerated in" the new statutory definition of grave breaches under Common Article 3).

157 Convention Against Torture, *supra* note 5, arts. 1, 2.2. For a brief discussion of the role of purpose in the definition of torture, see Christina Kosin, The Difference Between Torture and Other Ill-Treatment: Cestaro v. Italy and the "Prohibited Purpose" Requirement, *EU Law Analysis*, April 14, 2015, http://eulawanalysis.blogspot.com/2015/04/the-difference-between-torture-and.html.

158 Pub. L. 109–148, Div. A, Title X, §§ 1001–05, December 30, 2005, 119 Stat. 2739. Originally codified as a Note to 10 U.S.C. § 801, provisions of the current version of the Act are now codified at 42 U.S.C. § 2000dd *et seq.* (2017).

159 42 U.S.C. § 2000dd-0(1) (2017). Section 2 defines "cruel, inhuman, or degrading treatment or punishment" as "cruel, unusual, and inhumane treatment or punishment prohibited by the Fifth, Eighth, and Fourteenth Amendments to the Constitution of the United States, as defined in the United States Reservations, Declarations and Understandings to the United Nations Convention Against Torture and Other Forms of Cruel, Inhuman or Degrading Treatment or Punishment done at New York, December 10, 1984." *Id.*, § 2000dd-0(2).

abhorrent techniques of interrogation are not torture, but that was always clear. It is also fair to say that this statute further reduces the chance that torture will take place, by removing the potential argument that a given technique, however, abhorrent, is not quite torturous.[160] In effect, this statute provides a practical limitation on interrogation in the same vein as the limits on interpretation of the torture statute that this chapter is identifying.

Fifth, and most recently, a section of the National Defense Authorization Act for Fiscal Year 2016 extended the Detainee Treatment Act's reach. The new law, instead of relying on the always somewhat uncertain contours of the Constitution, provides that any individual held in US custody or in a US facility "shall not be subjected to any interrogation technique or approach, or any treatment related to interrogation, that is not authorized by and listed in the Army Field Manual 2–22.3."[161] In urging the adoption of this provision, David Cole argued that it was needed precisely to prevent the kinds of misinterpretation that had pervaded the Bush administration's torture memos:

> The existing torture and cruel treatment bans include broad definitions of banned activity, and Justice Department lawyers showed that these broad bans can be willfully misinterpreted to permit what they are designed to prohibit. The Anti-Torture Amendment addresses the challenge differently. Instead of expressing a broad prohibition, it confines interrogators to a set list of expressly approved techniques. That approach, already used by the military for

160 Section 1004 of the Detainee Treatment Act, Pub. L. 109–148, Div. A, Title X, § 1004, December 30, 2005, 119 Stat. 2739, codified at 42 USC § 2000dd-1 (2017), did also provide a defense for those who might be accused of unlawful detention or interrogation in connection with suspected international terrorism. If their actions "were officially authorized and determined to be lawful at the time that they were conducted, it shall be a defense that such [person] did not know that the practices were unlawful and a person of ordinary sense and understanding would not know the practices were unlawful. Good faith reliance on advice of counsel should be an important factor, among others, to consider in assessing whether a person of ordinary sense and understanding would have known the practices to be unlawful." This provision underlines that the Act was more concerned with bringing abusive interrogation to an end than with punishing those who might have carried it out in the past. It also confirms how important it is that the advice the president's lawyers give be based on legitimate legal argument. See text at notes 29–30 *supra*.

161 National Defense Authorization Act for Fiscal Year 2016, Pub. L. 114–92, Div. A, Title X, § 1045, November 25, 2015, 129 Stat. 977, codified at 42 U.S.C. § 2000dd-2(a)(2)(A) & (B) (2017). Section 1002 of the Detainee Treatment Act, Pub. L. 109–148, Div. A, Title X, § 1002, December 30, 2005, 119 Stat. 2739, had imposed this same rule on those held in the custody or in a facility of the Department of Defense, but the new statute extends the binding power of the Army Field Manual to all United States detainees, no matter which agency holds them. The text of the Army Field Manual, Headquarters, Department of the Army, FM 2–22.3, Human Intelligence Collector Operations, September 2006, is available at https://fas.org/irp/dod dir/army/fm2-22-3.pdf [hereinafter cited as Army Field Manual FM 2–22.3].

their interrogations, avoids ambiguity; if a technique is not affirmatively approved, it is banned.[162]

Like the Detainee Treatment Act, the new law acknowledges—and avoids—the debate over exactly what the boundaries of "torture" are. But like the Detainee Treatment Act, its practical import is to bar evasion of the prohibition on torture, just as the interpretive limitations I am discussing seek to do.[163]

Of course, if all of these statements are of no legal weight, then their mere repetition does not add much to their force. It could be, and in fact was, argued that limitations like these, if applied to the president's conduct of interrogations in the midst of the war on terrorism, were either unconstitutional or raised such serious constitutional questions that they should be interpreted to have no force. One of the August 1, 2002 torture memos argued that "Congress may no more regulate [the president's] ability to detain and interrogate enemy combatants than it may regulate his ability to direct troop movements on the battlefield," and that we should "construe [the torture statute] to avoid this constitutional difficulty, and conclude that it does not apply to the President's detention and interrogation of enemy combatants pursuant to his Commander-in-Chief authority."[164] There is undoubtedly support in American law for deference to the president's authority in the field of war.[165] In fact, I have already argued in this chapter that such deference adds to the president's authority to ask his lawyers to offer an interpretation of the torture statute that is to his liking.[166]

162 David Cole, No Torture Means No Torture—Why We Need the McCain-Feinstein Anti-Torture Amendment, *Just Security*, June 10, 2015, www.justsecurity.org/23678/torture-means-torture-mccain-feinstein-anti-torture-amendment/.

163 The provisions of the Army Field Manual are themselves subject to critique, notably with respect to Appendix M, which permits techniques of isolation and sleep deprivation that are problematic themselves. See Human Rights First, The U.S. Army Field Manual on Interrogation: A Strong Document in Need of Careful Revision, at 2–3, www.humanrightsfirst.org/wp-content/uploads/pdf/Army_Field_Manual.pdf (last accessed January 5, 2017); Army Field Manual FM 2–22.3, *supra* note 161, Appendix M ("Restricted Interrogation Technique—Separation"). I discuss Appendix M in the text below, at notes 193–95. The new law, however, does require a review of the Manual every three years and revisions "as necessary to ensure that Army Field Manual 2–22.3 complies with the legal obligations of the United States and the practices for interrogation described therein do not involve the use or threat of force." 42 U.S.C. § 2000dd-2 (6)(A)(i) (2017).

164 Memorandum on Standards of Conduct for Interrogation, *supra* note 3, at 35.

165 See The Prize Cases, 67 U.S. (2 Black) 635, 670 (1863) ("Whether the President in fulfilling his duties, as Commander-in-Chief, in suppressing an insurrection, has met with such armed hostile resistance, and a civil war of such alarming proportions as will compel him to accord to them the character of belligerents, is a question to be decided *by him*, and this Court must be governed by the decisions and acts of the political department of the Government to which this power was entrusted. 'He must determine what degree of force the crisis demands.'")

166 *See* text at notes 26–28 *supra*.

But I confess that I find it inconceivable that the rest of the US government is without authority to prevent the president from ordering the use of torture. Such decisions as *Hamdi*,[167] *Hamdan*,[168] and *Boumediene*,[169] all handed down in the years since 2002, make clear that the Supreme Court finds such a notion of unconstrained executive power inconceivable as well.[170] One way to restate the core claim of this Article, indeed, is to say that the sources of interpretive guidance that I am surveying here are, in aggregate, strong enough to outweigh such force as the idea of deference to presidential authority should have.

There are, in fact, canons of statutory interpretation that point in precisely the opposite direction. I have already noted the longstanding *Charming Betsy* principle that US laws should ordinarily be interpreted so as to be in harmony with international law—including, therefore, the provisions of the Geneva Conventions and the Convention Against Torture that outlaw torture.[171]

A second relevant canon is the presumption in favor of liberty, or more precisely the interpretive presumption against finding that Congress or the president has intended to invade constitutional rights. In the World War II internment case of *Ex parte Endo*,[172] as described many years later by Justice Souter,[173]

> [t]he petitioner was held entitled to habeas relief in an opinion that set out this principle for scrutinizing wartime statutes in derogation of customary liberty:
>
> "In interpreting a wartime measure we must assume that [its] purpose was to allow for the greatest possible accommodation between … liberties and the exigencies of war. We must assume, when asked to find implied powers in a grant of legislative or executive authority, that the law makers intended to

167 *Hamdi v. Rumsfeld*, 542 U.S. 507 (2004) (finding that the government has the power to detain even a U.S. citizen as an enemy combatant under the law of war, but also finding that due process requires procedural protections for decision that the detainee is in fact an enemy combatant).

168 *Hamdan v. Rumsfeld*, 548 U.S. 557 (2006) (refusing to find that Congress had suspended the writ of habeas corpus as to Guantánamo detainees, and holding that procedures for trial of Hamdan by military commission were inconsistent with the Uniform Code of Military Justice and with Common Article 3 of the Geneva Conventions, and were therefore unlawful). See generally Stephen Ellmann, The 'Rule of Law' and the Military Commission, 51 *N.Y.L. Sch. L. Rev.* 761 (2006/07).

169 *Boumediene v. Bush*, 553 U.S. 723 (2008) (finding that alleged alien enemy combatants detained at Guantánamo were constitutionally entitled to the protection of the writ of habeas corpus).

170 But for an argument that decisions like these do not reflect the rejection of deference in the midst of true emergency, but rather are the result of the justices' perception that the emergency has eased, see Posner & Vermeule, *supra* note 122, at 42–43, 50–51.

171 See text and notes at notes 76–77 *supra*.

172 323 U.S. 283, 300 (1944). For a thoughtful discussion of this case, see Patrick O. Gudridge, Remember Endo?, 116 *Harv. L. Rev.* 1933 (2003).

173 In his separate opinion in *Hamdi*, 542 U.S. at 544 (Souter J., joined by Ginsburg, J., concurring in part, dissenting in part, and concurring in the judgment).

place no greater restraint on the citizen than was clearly and unmistakably indicated by the language they used."

Exactly how firm the status of this rule of interpretation is has not been definitively settled. The *Hamdi* plurality found that the Authorization for Use of Military Force (AUMF), which initiated the United States' use of force in response to the 9/11 attacks, *did* "clearly and unmistakably authorize[] detention in the narrow circumstances presented here," but did not declare that *Endo* was the operative standard.[174] The Fourth Circuit in *Padilla v. Hanft*[175] argued that another Supreme Court decision, *Ex parte Quirin*,[176] did not follow this approach and if anything seemed to call for a much more deferential interpretive stance, when it said that "the detention and trial of petitioners—ordered by the President in the declared exercise of his powers as Commander in Chief of the Army in time of war and of grave public danger—are not to be set aside by the courts without the clear conviction that they are in conflict with the Constitution or laws of Congress constitutionally enacted."[177] Moreover, it must be acknowledged that under current law it is by no means clear that alleged alien enemy combatants, confined outside the United States, enjoy most constitutional rights at all (the sole established exception being those individuals detained at Guantánamo—*almost* the United States—who do enjoy at least one constitutional protection, the guarantee of habeas corpus embodied in the Suspension Clause).[178] But the idea that courts should be specially zealous on behalf of individual liberty obviously has deep

174 *Hamdi*, 542 U.S. at 519 (plurality opinion). The Authorization for Use of Military Force, Pub. L. No. 107-40, 115 Stat. 224, September 18, 2001, is codified at 50 U.S.C. § 1541 Note (2017).

175 423 F.3d 386, *cert. denied*, 126 S. Ct. 1649 (2006).

176 317 U.S. 1 (1942). *Quirin* held that German saboteurs, including one person assumed to be a US citizen, could be tried by military commission for violations of the law of war.

177 317 U.S. at 25. *Quirin* reflects that interpretive canons can be adjusted to suit judges' perceptions of social needs. So, in apartheid South Africa, the Appellate Division decided in a case concerning detention without trial "that in interpreting [the law] this Court should accord preference neither to the 'strict construction' in favour of the individual … nor to the 'strained construction' in favour of the Executive referred to by Lord Atkin in *Liversidge*'s case … but that it should determine the meaning of the section upon an examination of its wording in the light of the circumstances whereunder it was enacted and of its general policy and object." *Rossouw v. Sachs*, 1964 (2) SA 551, 563–64 (A). But it is striking that despite this decision, in the midst of apartheid South Africa's state of emergency in the 1980s, it was still possible to assert as a rule of South African statutory interpretation that "where a statute is reasonably capable of more than one meaning, a court will give it the meaning which least interferes with the liberty of the individual." *Tshwete v. Minister of Home Affairs*, 1988 (4) SA 586, 612G (A) (dissenting judgment of Nestadt JA); see Stephen Ellmann, *In a Time of Trouble: Law and Liberty in South Africa's State of Emergency* (Oxford: Clarendon Press (Oxford University Press), 1992), 44–53.

178 *Boumediene*, 553 U.S. 723 (2008).

resonance,[179] and it is not odd to say that lawyers when they interpret, or perhaps more accurately make, the law—and especially when they must reason in secret (a point we will take up in a moment)—should be similarly guided.

A third substantive legal principle points in this same direction. The Department of Justice's Office of Professional Responsibility, in assessing the conduct of the authors of the torture memos, made the following argument:

> [W]e looked at the circumstances surrounding these particular requests for legal advice, to assess whether the requirements of the applicable professional rules and Department regulations were met. In doing so, we began with the premise that "the right to be free from official torture is fundamental and universal, a right deserving of the highest status under international law, a norm of *jus cogens*." *Siderman de Blake v. Republic of Argentina*, 965 F.2d 699, 717 (9th Cir.), cert. denied, 507 U.S. 1017 (1993). *See also, e.g., Filartiga v. Pena-Irala*, 630 F.2d 876, 884 (2d Cir. 1980). We thus determined that Department attorneys considering the possible abrogation or derogation of a *jus cogens* norm such as the prohibition against torture must be held to the highest standards of professional conduct.[180]

Associate Deputy Attorney General Margolis, reviewing (and overturning) the Office of Professional Responsibility's decision, did not quarrel with the possible value of this standard, though he decided it had not been in place as an unambiguous obligation at the time the memos were written.[181] But in effect the Office of Professional Responsibility's argument is simply the one I have made throughout this section. The fact that the prohibition on torture has repeatedly been incorporated into US law, by statute, by treaty and perhaps as a matter of customary *jus cogens*, does indeed, as the Office of Professional Responsibility argued, add to the responsibilities of attorneys. The legal force of the prohibition on torture—manifested in the international legal consensus, but also, and more directly, in the United States' repeated enactment of statutory limits on the use of torture—constrains the legitimate range of government interpretative maneuver.

The implications of the secret role of the president's lawyers

The third factor we should assess is a process consideration, responding to the secrecy of the discussions that shaped the OLC's torture opinions and the secrecy of the opinions themselves—and to lawyers' special responsibility as guardians of

179 See *Greene v. McElroy*, 360 U.S. 474, 506–07 (1959); *Kent v. Dulles*, 357 U.S. 116, 129–30 (1958).

180 Office of Professional Responsibility, Investigation into the Office of Legal Counsel's Memoranda Concerning Issues Relating to the Central Intelligence Agency's Use of "Enhanced Interrogation Techniques" on Suspected Terrorists, at 24–25 (July 29, 2009) (footnote omitted), as quoted in Margolis, *supra* note 74, at 12.

181 Margolis, *supra* note 74, at 12–13, 25–26.

fair process.[182] The methods of interrogation were not intended to be made public, nor were the arguments that justified those methods. Actually, this is a partial overstatement, for administration officials may not have been shy about saying that after 9/11 "the gloves came off,"[183] but it is at least correct that the details—both of interrogation and of legal argument—were kept secret. Much that was written, and much that was done to detainees, has since become public, but more despite the government's best efforts than because of them.

In fact, even other lawyers within the administration were sometimes deliberately kept out of the loop of consultation in the preparation of terrorism opinions.[184] In perhaps the most bizarre extension of this approach, lawyers for the National Security Agency, which as is now well known was conducting a highly secret "terrorist surveillance program" that arguably disregarded the Foreign Intelligence Surveillance Act (FISA), were not allowed access to the OLC opinion upholding the legality of their program.[185] Goldsmith writes that after September 11, 2001 Cheney, Addington "and other top officials in the administration dealt with FISA the way they dealt with other laws they didn't like; they blew through them in secret based on flimsy legal opinions that they guarded closely so no one could question the legal basis for the operations."[186] This is abuse, rather than good faith legal practice.

But secrecy in national security is sometimes necessary, and legal opinions dealing with secret operations may legitimately need to be kept secret as well. Even when secrecy is entirely justifiable, it remains inevitable that the more is kept secret, the less the resources of the legal system can be brought to bear to properly constrain what is said and done. As lawyers are under special ethical responsibilities

182 The Preamble to the Model Rules of Professional Conduct begins: "A lawyer, as a member of the legal profession, is a representative of clients, an officer of the legal system and a public citizen having special responsibility for the quality of justice." Model Rules of Professional Conduct, Preamble (2017).

183 Cofer Black, Director of the Counterterrorist Center of the CIA from 1999 through May 2002, testified before a congressional inquiry in September 2002 that "After 9/11 the gloves come off." See Joint Inquiry into Intelligence Community Activities Before and After the Terrorist Attacks of September 11, 2001, Report of the U.S. Senate Select Committee on Intelligence and U.S. House Permanent Select Committee on Intelligence Together with Additional Views 14 (2002). Black's testimony is available at https://fas.org/irp/congress/2002_hr/092602black.html (last accessed January 13, 2017).

184 Goldsmith describes the "secretive five-person group with enormous influence over the administration's antiterrorism policies. The 'War Council,' as the group called itself, included the White House Counsel, Alberto Gonzales; the Vice President's Counsel, David Addington; [William J.] Haynes ['the Pentagon's top lawyer']; Tim Flanigan [a 'very experienced national security lawyer' in the White House]; and [John] Yoo. The War Council met every few weeks .... It would plot legal strategy in the war on terrorism, sometimes as a prelude to dealing with lawyers from the State Department, the National Security Council, and the Joint Chiefs of Staff who would ordinarily be involved in war-related interagency legal decisions, and sometimes to the exclusion of the interagency process altogether." Goldsmith, *supra* note 2, at 22, 20, 171.

185 *Id.* at 181–182.

186 *Id.* at 181.

in ex parte court proceedings to "inform the tribunal of all material facts known to the lawyer that will enable the tribunal to make an informed decision, whether or not the facts are adverse,"[187] so lawyers engaged in secret interpretation might be under a special responsibility not to parse the law too far against those who are unrepresented in the process.[188] Robert Chesney has suggested in a somewhat related context that a "quasi-judicial process ... within the executive branch" is already functioning in connection with decisions to kill enemy combatants who are also US citizens.[189] I am not suggesting the creation of tribunals to review lawyers' opinions, but urging that the government's lawyers themselves accept the burden of protecting the wholly unrepresented targets of their power.

But does this draw too much from the fact of secrecy? Goldsmith considers secrecy a relevant consideration, but does not take it as far as I've just suggested. He writes, in responding to the torture memos' ill-supported assertion of presidential primacy as against congressional statutes, that:

> when one concludes that Congress is disabled from controlling the President, and especially when one concludes this in secret, respect for separation of powers demands a full consideration of competing congressional and judicial prerogatives, which was lacking in the interrogation opinions.[190]

This formulation fits well with the ethics' rules mandate of disclosure in ex parte proceedings. But the duty Goldsmith identifies here seems quite close to the duty of somewhat disinterested judgment that Goldsmith believes that the OLC always has.[191] If Goldsmith believes that secrecy adds something to that responsibility, that "something" would seem to be an obligation to pay closer attention to the arguments for the other side than would otherwise be required. That proposition is one that I endorse.

Conclusion

These arguments—based on a close focus on understanding the meaning of "torture," attention to the reiteration of the US legal system's rejection of such

187 Model Rules of Prof'l Conduct r. 3.3(d) (2017).

188 All the more would this be so if the government lawyers in a broad sense actually represent the subjects of interrogation as well as the interrogators. Where the targets of interrogation are US citizens, lawyers for the government do in a broad sense represent them, as the government represents all of the people. Whether lawyers have any comparable responsibility towards noncitizens interrogated outside the United States is a difficult question. As noted earlier in the text, however, we do know that those noncitizens held as enemy combatants at Guantanamo have at least one constitutional right, access to the privilege of habeas corpus. *Boumediene*, 553 U.S. 723 (2008).

189 Robert Chesney, Written Statement, United States House of Representatives, Committee on the Judiciary, "Drones and the War on Terror: When Can the United States Target Alleged American Terrorists Overseas?," at 6 February 27, 2013.

190 Goldsmith, *supra* note 2, at 149.

191 *Id.* at 33, 37–39.

conduct, and an emphasis on lawyers' special responsibility for fair process—are not irrefutable. For a lawyer convinced of the central importance, in wartime, of a sweeping understanding of presidential power, none of these considerations would be persuasive, and such a lawyer, in entire good faith, could reject their implications. In truth, there are few absolutely irrefutable answers in law, and the reality of American war powers law is that it is pervasively inconclusive. But that is no reason to abandon the field; instead, it is important for us to recognize and invoke the powerful array of legal arguments that do support an interpretation of the prohibition on torture that gives full force to this rule of law.

Preventing torture is not, of course, a task accomplished solely or even primarily at lawyers' desks—though what happens there can play a surprisingly important role, in a national security world as heavily lawyered as the United States' is,[192] and as filled with law, national and international, as today's world is. I am impressed by the deep opposition to torture expressed by many soldiers and Judge Advocate General military lawyers, and I take them to be an important—hopefully increasingly important—part of the interpretive community. The shameful transmission of prisoner mistreatment through the detention facilities of the US war on terror, however, points to the importance of institutional controls that help sustain legal rules. Standard operating procedures that ensure that detainees are monitored may help protect them. Requirements of explicit approval from senior officers will help block low-level misconduct. Insisting that the senior officer making the decision consciously consider whether the treatment in question is lawful may also be of value.[193]

It is ironic, however, that all of these potentially valuable institutional arrangements can be found in the most problematic portion of the Army Field Manual, Appendix M.[194] There, in a ten-page discussion titled "Restricted Interrogation Technique—Separation," the Manual provides, in effect, for solitary confinement and for something approaching sleep deprivation.[195] I don't support this controversial provision, and would characterize it as at least opening the door to cruel and inhumane treatment. This troubling feature confirms that even when institutional safeguards meant to reduce the risk of abuse are in place, it matters very much which techniques are authorized and which are not.

192 *Id.* at 91.

193 I've benefited from hearing Professor Diane Amann discuss the significance of safeguards of this sort, in a presentation at an AALS Annual Meeting, and from conversations with Professor Jethro Lieberman.

194 Army Field Manual FM 2–22.3, *supra* note 161, Appendix M ("Restricted Interrogation Technique—Separation").

195 See id. ¶¶ M-26 through M-31. Normally, "separation" is accomplished by separate confinement, but when this is not feasible, "goggles or blindfolds and earmuffs" may be used. ¶ M-28. "Use of separation must not preclude the detainee getting four hours of continuous sleep every 24 hours"—a limitation that might not be violated if the detainee sleeps for four hours at the start of one 24-hour period, and then is kept awake for the next 40 hours, until he is permitted to sleep for four hours at the end of the second 24-hour period.

For that reason, again, the work of interpretation is needed; lines need to be drawn. I doubt that it is enough to simply say "stay away from anything close to improper treatment": for some people, that injunction will bar even techniques that in fact are proper, while for others it may not bar anything at all. So it remains important to reason as lawyers do, and to find bounds on the potential destructive force of that reasoning when unchecked. The arguments I have made, which focus on articulating the considerations shaping the "ordinary work" of lawyers engaged in interpretation, do, I hope, provide a pathway for this important reasoning to proceed as it should.

The course of the past decade has not been kind to the idea that harsh treatment is the preferred solution to the threat of terrorism. It suggests, instead, that the effort to treat detainees as harshly as the law permits is a very perilous one, likely to infuriate the watching world and to generate not just harsh but ultimately illegal conduct as well. But if a President asks what the law's limits are, as I believe she can, the President's lawyers owe the President an answer. My argument is that in answering this question they should be guided by the principles articulated here, so that they would have strong reasons to provide the President with an answer that fully honored the crucial importance of preventing torture in the United States' name.

6 Rendition in extraordinary times

Margaret L. Satterthwaite and Alexandra M. Zetes

Introduction: rendition as a counter-terrorism tool

The practice of rendition—the involuntary transfer of an individual across borders without recourse to extradition or deportation proceedings—is not new. Indeed, the practice of snatching a defendant for trial—"rendition to justice"—has been used by governments for more than a century.[1] Although rendition has been controversial in human rights circles, it has been celebrated by many as crucial in the fight against impunity for grave crimes.[2]

Former US President George W. Bush was criticized for the "novel" practice of "extraordinary rendition"—the transfer of suspects to locations known for the systematic use of torture, including secret Central Intelligence Agency (CIA) prisons (this set of practices is hereinafter referred to as the "Extraordinary Rendition Program").[3] US officials at the time defended the practice, relying on justifications developed to support "rendition to justice" and arguing that the US Extraordinary Rendition Program was legal.[4] Despite these justifications, international human rights bodies and intergovernmental organizations including the Council of Europe, the European Union, and human rights bodies of the United Nations

1 M.L. Satterthwaite, The Legal Regime Governing Transfer of Persons in the Fight Against Terrorism, in *Counter-Terrorism Strategies in a Fragmented International Legal Order: Meeting the Challenges* 589, at 590–91 (Larissa van den Herik and Nico Schrijver, eds., Cambridge University Press, 2013).

2 For a defense of rendition to justice, see G. S. McNeal & B. J. Field, Snatch and Grab Ops: Justifying Extraterritorial Abduction, 16 *Transnat'l L. & Contemp. Probs.* 491 (2007).

3 For a discussion of these criticisms, see M. Satterthwaite, Rendered Meaningless: Extraordinary Rendition and the Rule of Law, 75 *Geo. Wash. L. Rev.* 1333 (2007). See also Satterthwaite, *supra* note 1 at 601, fn. 50.

4 See C. Rice, US Sec'y of State, US Dep't of State, Remarks upon Her Departure for Europe (Dec. 5, 2005), www.state.gov/secretary/rm/2005/57602.htm (in which Secretary Rice defends the US use of rendition), and The Charlie Rose Show: Interview with Director Michael Hayden (PBS television broadcast, Oct. 22 & 23, 2007), www.cia.gov/news-information/press-releases-statements/press-release-archive-2007/interview-with-charlie-rose.html (in which former CIA Director Michael Hayden explains the continuation of the US program of rendition and CIA detention).

determined that the extraordinary form of rendition was unlawful under human rights law.[5] Although individuals have faced significant legal hurdles in fighting the practice through the US legal system,[6] there is little doubt among international law experts that extraordinary rendition is prohibited.[7] Indeed, the European Court of Human Rights (ECtHR) has found that multiple European states violated their human rights obligations by cooperating with the US Extraordinary Rendition Program.[8]

5 See UN Committee Against Torture, *Concluding observations on the combined third to fifth periodic reports of the United States of America*, U.N. Doc. CAT/C/USA/CO/3–5 (Dec. 19, 2014); UN Committee Against Torture, *Consideration of Reports Submitted by States Parties Under Article 19 of the Convention: Second Periodic Reports of States Parties Due in 1999: Addendum: United States of America*, 5, U.N. Doc. CAT/C/48/Add.3 (2005) (considering US report submitted May 6, 2005); UN Human Rights Committee, *Concluding Observations of the Human Rights Committee: United States of America*, U.N. Doc. CCPR/C/USA/CO/3/Rev.1 (2006); European Parliament, *Report on the Alleged Use of European Countries by the CIA for the Transportation and Illegal Detention of Prisoners*, Eur. Parl. Doc. A6–0020/2007(2007), www.europarl.europa.eu/comparl/tempcom/tdip/final_report_en.pdf; European Parliament, *Draft Interim Report on the Alleged Use of European Countries by the CIA for the Transportation and Illegal Detention of Prisoners*, Eur. Parl. Doc. A6–0213/2006 (2006), www.statewatch.org/cia/reports/ep-cia-interim-report-english.pdf; European Parliament Ass. Comm. on Legal Affairs and Human Rights, *Alleged Secret Detentions in Council of Europe Member States*, Doc.No. AS/Jur (2006), http://assembly.coe.int/CommitteeDocs/2006/20060124_Jdoc032006_E.pdf; European Parliament Ass. Comm. on Legal Affairs and Human Rights, *Secret Detentions and Illegal Transfers of Detainees Involving Council of Europe Member States: Second Report*, 64, Doc. No. 11302 rev. (2007), http://assembly.coe.int/Documents/WorkingDocs/Doc07/edoc11302.pdf; Press Release, Inter-American Commission on Human Rights, IACHR Calls on the United States to Investigate and Punish Acts of Torture Established in the Senate Intelligence Committee Report (Dec. 12, 2014) www.oas.org/en/iachr/media_center/preleases/2014/152.asp

6 See M. Satterthwaite, Human Rights and Humanitarian Law in the "War on Terror": The Story of *El Masri v. Tenet*, in *Human Rights Advocacy Stories* (Hurwitz & Satterthwaite, with Ford, eds., 2009). The US government has repeatedly blocked rendition-related cases in US courts. (See *Mohamed v. Jeppesen Dataplan, Inc.*, 586 F. 3d 1108 (9th Cir. 2009); see also *Mohamed v. Jeppesen Dataplan, Inc.*, 614 F. 3d 1070 (9th Cir. 2010) (en banc).

7 For legal analyses of the prohibitions relevant to extraordinary rendition, see Satterthwaite, *supra* note 1; D. Weissbrodt and A. Bergquist, *Extraordinary Rendition: A Human Rights Analysis*, 19 Harv. Hum. Rts. J. 123 (2006); D. Weissbrodt & A. Bergquist, Extraordinary Rendition and the Torture Convention, 46 *Va. J. Int'l L.* 585 (2006); and D. Weissbrodt and A. Bergquist, Extraordinary Rendition and the Humanitarian Law of War and Occupation, 47 *Va. J. Int'l L.* 295 (2007).

8 The United States sought cooperation from dozens of other states to facilitate its Rendition Program. While the actual numbers are unknown, it is believed that over 50 states assisted the United States with this program. See Globalizing Torture: CIA Secret Detention and Extraordinary Rendition, Open Society Justice Initiative, 5–6 (2013). For specific examples of ECtHR jurisprudence on the issue, see *El-Masri v. "The former Yugoslav Republic of Macedonia"* App. no. 39630/09, (Eur. Ct. H.R., 2012); *Al Nashiri v. Poland*, App. no. 28761/11 (Eur. Ct. H.R. 2014), *Husayn (Abu*

Soon after former President Barack Obama was inaugurated in January 2009, he promised to end the most severe human rights violations carried out by the US government in the name of fighting terrorism, including the use of torture and secret detention facilities.[9] While this move was a positive signal that the United States planned to bring its practice into line with international norms, the Obama administration in fact retained a number of problematic tools developed by previous administrations. Although Obama signed executive orders ending the use of torture and secret detention, he did not order the cessation of all informal transfers, nor did he pursue accountability for those who designed and implemented the Extraordinary Rendition Program. Instead, his administration continued to quash rendition-related cases with the argument that such cases dangerously threatened to reveal "state secrets," and formed a task force to examine transfers and to compile recommendations about how the process could be brought back in line with US law and international obligations.[10] Although it is impossible to know precisely how many informal transfers were carried out by the Obama administration,[11] the number plainly was significantly smaller than those conducted by the Bush administration during the Extraordinary Rendition Program. Instead, President Obama increased the use of drones to target and kill suspected terrorists outside of the United States, and continued the use of proxy detention in the name of fighting terrorism.[12] The Obama administration also engaged in

Zubaydah) v. Poland, App. no. 7511/13 (Eur. Ct. H.R. 2014), *Nasr and Ghali v. Italy*, App. no. 44883/09 (Eur. Ct. H.R. 2016); *Al Nashiri v. Romania*, App. no. 33234/12 (Eur. Ct. H.R 2018); *Abu Zubaydah v. Lithuania*, App. no. 46454/11 (Eur. Ct. H.R 2018).

9 See Exec. Order No. 13,491, 74 Fed. Reg. 4893 (Jan. 22, 2009).

10 See *id.* The Task Force's report, which was made publicly available in 2016, indicated that the United States should continue to rely on rendition as a counter-terrorism tool, and focused on ways to improve the practice, including strengthening the requirements for diplomatic assurances (discussed later in this chapter). The unclassified portions of the Task Force Report was released in December of 2016; see Department of Justice, Report of the Special Task Force on Interrogation and Transfer Policies (2009) (hereinafter "Task Force Report"), www.justice.gov/oip/foia-library/2009_report_special_task_force_interrogation_and_transfer_policies/download. See M. Lederman, President Obama's Report on the Legal and Policy Frameworks Guiding and Limiting the Use of Military Force [UPDATED], *Just Security* (Dec. 5, 2016), www.justsecurity.org/35239/president-obamas-report-legal-policy-frameworks-guiding-united-states-military-force-related-national-security-operations/.

11 See, e.g. C. Whitlock, Renditions Continue Under Obama, Despite Due-Process Concerns, *The Washington Post* (Jan. 1, 2013), www.washingtonpost.com/world/national-security/renditions-continue-under-obama-despite-due-process-concerns/2013/01/01/4e593aa0-5102-11e2-984e-f1de82a7c98a_story.html?utm_term=.2781bd83ca4c

12 Proxy detention has been called "rendition light" by some (N. Baumann, *Locked Up Abroad – for the FBI*, Mother Jones (Sept./Oct. 2011), www.motherjones.com/politics/2011/07/proxy-detention-gulet-mohamed/). It entails a state (in this case the United States) effectuating or arranging for the transfer of an individual to a partner state that has agreed to detain and interrogate the individual in question and return the fruits of that interrogation to the transferring state. Proxy detention raises a variety

other forms of problematic terrorism-related detentions. For example, in several cases, individuals suspected of crimes of terrorism were detained and interrogated on US Navy ships before they were transferred to custody on US territory.[13]

The Trump administration presents alarming new risks: in addition to the anti-terrorism tools left in place by the Obama administration,[14] President Trump has promised to use torture and said he would fill Guantánamo Bay with "bad dudes" captured in the fight against al-Qaeda and the Islamic State in Iraq and Syria (ISIS). While some of President Trump's most disturbing campaign promises have not yet come to fruition,[15] the administration's lack of transparency surrounding counter-terrorism measures, the ongoing US military engagements in Afghanistan, Syria, and Iraq, and the hunt for al-Qaeda in Yemen present opportunities for the US government to return to—or worsen—the abusive practices it pioneered as part of the Extraordinary Rendition Program. With the publication of the National Security Strategy in December 2017, the Trump administration renewed its commitment to fighting terrorism in aggressive terms with little consideration for human rights.[16] These risks are made more severe by the administration's lack of a clear detention

of human rights concerns, especially as receiving states often employ methods of interrogation that amount to torture and cruel and inhuman treatment under international law. Proxy detention will not be discussed in depth in this chapter. For further discussion of proxy detention and its relation to extraordinary rendition, see J. Hafetz, *Habeas Corpus After 9/11: Confronting America's New Global Detention System* (New York: New York University Press, 2011).

13 Two known cases are Ahmed Abdulkadir Warsame in 2011 and Anas al-Liby in 2013. Both were held aboard US navy ships before being sent to face criminal charges in the United States. Warsame was detained on the U.S.S. *Boxer* for two months; Al-Liby was detained on the U.S.S. *San Antonio* for more than a week. See S. Ackerman, *Drift: How This Ship Became a Floating GITMO*, WIRED (July 6, 2011), www.wired.com/2011/07/floating-gitmo/ (discussing Warsame's detention on the U.S.S. *Boxer*); and B. Weiser and E. Schmitt, U.S. Said to Hold Qaeda Suspect on Navy Ship, *The New York Times* (Oct. 6, 2013), www.nytimes.com/2013/10/07/world/africa/a-terrorism-suspect-long-known-to-prosecutors.html (discussing Al-Liby's detention on the U.S.S. *San Antonio*). For further analysis regarding the legal implications from this kind of detention, see R. Goodman and S. Knuckey, The Case of Abu Anas al-Libi: International Law Q & A, *Just Security* (Oct. 9, 2013), www.justsecurity.org/1827/case-abu-anas-al-libi-international-law/#notarmed.

14 See Task Force Report (2009).

15 Although President Trump has repeatedly indicated his plans to send new detainees to Guantánamo, at the time of writing, he had not sent any newly captured individuals there. The most recent example at the time of writing was Mustafa al-Imam, a suspect in the 2012 Benghazi attacks. Al-Imam was captured by US commandos on October 30, 2017, and taken to the United States to face criminal charges, see A. Goldman and E. Schmitt, *Benghazi Attacks Suspect Is Captures in Libya by U.S. Commandos*, N. Y. Times (Oct. 30, 2017), www.nytimes.com/2017/10/30/world/africa/benghazi-attacks-second-suspect-captured.html.

16 The Trump administration released in December 2017 a National Security Strategy (touted as "America First" (i-ii)), which detailed the administration's priorities for national security, including significant emphasis on the fight against terrorism, specifically ISIS, al-Qaeda, and Hizbollah (i, 7–11, 53), an increased military presence in Afghanistan (29, 49–50), and an enhanced role for the intelligence community in

and transfer policy. Reports surfacing in 2017 of individuals being tortured while in United Arab Emirates custody in Yemen with the alleged collusion of the United States suggest that conditions are ripe for violative handover practices.[17] In September 2017, a US citizen who had allegedly been fighting for ISIS surrendered to Syrian rebel forces and was later handed over to US officials in Iraq. He was then held without access to counsel for over three months, despite his express request for an attorney, until a US district court ordered that he be allowed to remotely access an attorney.[18] When news reports suggested that the US government was considering transferring the individual to Saudi Arabia, the judge ordered the government to provide 72 hours' notice before any such transfer;[19] the government subsequently notified the court that it planned a forcible transfer to Saudi Arabia.[20] On appeal, the DC Circuit Court of Appeals upheld both of the district court's rulings, prohibiting the planned transfer because the detainee had not been afforded due process and requiring notice before transfer to another country.[21] Perversely, the US government then notified the district court that it planned to release the detainee—in Syria, where his attorneys argue he is at risk of being killed. The legality of this plan was being litigated at the time of writing.[22]

The threat that counter-terrorism measures will become more abusive is made more stark by the rise in nationalist governments pursuing protectionist policies

national security (32). These priorities, combined with the self-proclamation that the strategy is "guided by outcomes, not ideology" (1) presents a troubling picture for those concerned about maintaining a balance between human rights and national security. See The White House, National Security Strategy of the United States of America, Dec. 2017, www.whitehouse.gov/wp-content/uploads/2017/12/NSS-Final-12-18-2017-0905.pdf.

17 M. Michael, In Yemen's Secret Prisons, UAE Tortures and US Interrogates, AP News (Jun. 22, 2017), https://apnews.com/4925f7f0fa654853bd6f2f57174179fe; see also L. Hartig, Reported Emirati Abuse of Detainees and the Perils of U.S. Partnerships, *Just Security* (Jun. 22, 2017), www.justsecurity.org/42459/reported-emirati-abuses-detainees-perils-u-s-partnerships/; see also S. Vladeck, The Potential Legal Implications for the U.S. in the PA's Disturbing UAE Torture Scoop, *Just Security* (Jun. 22, 2017), www.justsecurity.org/42428/u-s-law-implications-aps-disturbing-uae-torture-scoop/.

18 See *Doe v. Mattis*, No. 17-cv-2069 (D.D.C. Dec. 23, 2017), www.aclu.org/legal-document/doe-v-mattis-memorandum-opinion.

19 See, e.g., C. Savage, E. Schmitt, and A. Goldman, Officials Weigh Sending American Detainee to Saudi Arabia, *The New York Times*, Dec. 20, 2017, www.nytimes.com/2017/12/20/us/politics/american-detainee-saudi-arabia.html.

20 See *Doe v. Mattis*, No. 18-5032 (D.C. Cir. May 7, 2018), www.aclu.org/legal-document/doe-v-mattis-appeals-court-opinion-barring-transfer.

21 See *id.* For a compilation the filings relating to the ongoing *habeas* case, see ACLU, *Doe v. Mattis – Challenge to Detention of American by U.S. Military Abroad*, www.aclu.org/cases/doe-v-mattis-challenge-detention-american-us-military-abroad.

22 See J. Hafetz, *The Trump Administration Wants to Dump a Detained American into One of the Most Dangerous Places on Earth*, Speak Freely (June 7, 2018), www.aclu.org/blog/national-security/detention/trump-administration-wants-dump-detained-american-one-most.

with weakening regard to human rights guarantees. With governments moving to close borders,[23] deport non-nationals,[24] denaturalize their own citizens,[25] and use informal means to transfer suspects,[26] the mechanisms through which a state may transfer custody of an individual—and the permissible purposes for such handovers—have escaped careful scrutiny. In this era of global realignment, the human rights principles guiding inter-state cooperation in such matters must be reasserted. This chapter examines the legal norms governing informal transfers and detentions in this new era and sets out a minimum standard that must be upheld whenever a state renders an individual, no matter how extraordinary the context.

Rendition: definition and scope

Rendition is the transfer of an individual from the custody of one state to another without the benefit of a regular process by the rendering country. In the contemporary context, such transfers include the movement of individuals captured in the fight against ISIS and al-Qaeda, transfers to the detention facility at Guantánamo, the handover of individuals captured in a variety of settings to secret proxy detention, the transfer of individuals detained by one state to the custody of the detainee's national state, and the transfer of individuals to the territory of the transferring state to stand trial before a regular criminal court. While there is continuing controversy over the legality of many of these forms of rendition, other forms have escaped scrutiny in the face of grave concern over the abuses committed by ISIS and other terrorist groups.[27] In all of these contexts, the absence of

23 See, e.g., B. Frelick, I. M. Kysel, and J. Podkul, The Impact of Externalization of Migration Controls on the Rights of Asylum Seekers and Other Migrants, 4 *Journal on Migration and Human Security* 190 (2016).

24 M.D. Shear and R. Nixon, New Trump Deportation Rules Allow Far More Expulsions, *The New York Times* (Feb. 21, 2017), www.nytimes.com/2017/02/21/us/politics/dhs-immigration-trump.html?mcubz=0.

25 K. Bennhold, *Britain Increasingly Invokes Power to Disown Its Citizens, The New York Times* (Apr. 9, 2014), www.nytimes.com/2014/04/10/world/europe/britains-power-to-disown-its-citizens-raises-questions.html?mcubz=0&_r=0.

26 *Transnational Injustices, National Security Transfers and International Law*, International Commission of Jurists, 64–69, 2017, www.icj.org/wp-content/uploads/2017/09/Europe-Transnational-Injustices-Publications-Reports-Thematic-reports-2017-ENG.pdf (hereinafter *Transnational Injustices*).

27 Indeed, although many governments have engaged in discussion aimed at clarifying the legal status of some transfers, (for example, European governments, led by the government of Denmark, have participated in the Copenhagen Process concerning battlefield transfers; see Satterthwaite, *supra* note 1 at 593) confusion has continued. European governments and Canada have endured critique for the transfer of detainees held by their armed forces in Afghanistan and Iraq to the custody of the home state or to the United States. (See, e.g., Amnesty International, *Afghanistan: Detainees Transferred to Torture: ISAF Complicity?*, AI Index ASA 11/011/2007, Nov. 13, 2007, www.amnesty.org/en/library/info/ASA11/011/2007/en (critiquing the transfer activities of European, US, and Canadian forces in Afghanistan under the rubric of ISAF forces and calling for a temporary halt of such transfers to ensure ISAF countries were living up to their international obligations pertaining to transfer). A

formal procedures places individuals at grave risk, and the abandoning of human rights protections risks eroding the rule of law at the moment it is needed most.

A minimum standard for the transfer of alleged terrorists

Because they are carried out in a wide variety of settings, the legal regime applicable to the transfer of terrorism suspects can vary. However, a close examination of the norms governing such transfers reveals important protective principles that apply across settings. This section draws on relevant rules of international human rights law, international refugee law, and international humanitarian law to distil a minimum standard that must be upheld in all settings.

These regimes of law, as a general rule, apply extraterritorially and concurrently,[28] though some states challenge this approach. For example, the United States acknowledges it is legally bound by the obligations of *non-refoulement* domestically, but only enforces the obligation extraterritorially as a matter of policy.[29] In addition, as a general rule, the *lex generalis* of international human rights law sets out basic norms that apply in all situations, including during armed conflict.[30] Where there is a direct conflict of norms during armed conflict, the *lex*

number of European governments, as well as Canada and the United States, have faced litigation by individuals and groups challenging the legality of informal transfers. See *Al-Saadoon and Mudfhi v. United Kingdom*, App. No. 61498/08, para. 140 (Eur. Ct. H.R. 2010); *Othman (Abu Qatada) v. United Kingdom*, App No. 8139/09 (Eur. Ct. H.R., 2012). See also *Belhaj and another v. Straw and others*, UKSC 2014/0264 (Jan. 17, 2017). Additionally, the rendition litigation before the ECtHR has included the question of transfer as integral in assessing the relevant State's violations of its convention obligations. See *El-Masri; Al Nashiri v. Poland* (2014) and *Husayn (Abu Zubaydah) v. Poland* (2014); *Nasr and Ghali v. Italy* (2016); *Al Nashiri v. Romania* (2018); *Abu Zubaydah v. Lithuania* (2018). See also Press Release, Amnesty International, UK holds off on detainee transfers to Afghan authorities (Nov. 30, 2012), AI Index: PRE01/585/2012.

28 On the concurrent application of international humanitarian law and international human rights law, see Legality of the Threat or Use of Nuclear Weapons, Advisory Opinion, 1996 I.C.J. 226, para. 25 (Jul. 8, 1996) (holding that international human rights law continues to apply in times of armed conflict). For a discussion of the concurrent application of international humanitarian law and international refugee law, see S. Jaquemet, The Cross-Fertilization of International Humanitarian Law and International Refugee Law, *83 Int'l Rev. Red Cross* 651 (2001). Although there have been debates over the circumstances in which international human rights treaties have extraterritorial effect, human rights bodies have found that such norms apply whenever states have effective control over territory or when they exercise effective control over an individual. For discussion and citations, see Satterthwaite, *supra* note 1.

29 The White House, Report on the Legal and Policy Frameworks Guiding the United States' Use of Military Force and Related National Security Operations, December 2016; see also Task Force Report (2009).

30 This general rule is relevant to those rights considered to be non-derogable under human rights law. Such non-derogable rights include, *inter alia*, the right to be free from torture and cruel, inhuman, or degrading punishment and the right to life. See, e.g., ICCPR, art. 4. See also *Abu Zubaydah* § 499; *Al Nashiri v. Poland* § 507; *Nasr and Ghali* § 280; *El Masri* §195 (indicating that the prohibition of torture is non-

specialis of international humanitarian law may displace or modify a particular rule of human rights law.[31] In the context of transfer, specific humanitarian protections concerning transfer are consistent with—though often more protective than—the *lex generalis* of human rights law, meaning that the humanitarian law norms complement the generally applicable human rights rules on transfer.

The applicability of the protections concerning transfers of custody from one state to another in the context of armed conflict in which states are cooperating pursuant to collective defense regimes or peacekeeping operations within the borders of a single state have been subject to intense debate. However, recent decisions by human rights bodies affirm that because international law protects individuals within the effective control of a state or its agents regardless of the location of that custody, the protections of human rights law should apply to any handover of an individual from the jurisdiction of one state to another, even in the context of armed conflict.[32] This is especially relevant today in light of the ongoing fight against ISIS, which has prompted both unilateral action and a United Nations (UN) call for international cooperation to defeat the organization.[33]

Examining human rights law, refugee law, and humanitarian law norms together allows for the identification of a minimum standard to be applied whenever

derogable). See also Legality of the Threat or Use of Nuclear Weapons, Advisory Opinion, 1996 I.C.J. 226, para. 25 (Jul. 8, 1996). See also Legal Consequences of the Construction of a Wall in the Occupied Palestinian Territory, Advisory Opinion, 2004 I.C.J. 131, para. 106 (Jul. 9, 2004) (explaining that some rights are regulated by either human rights or humanitarian law while “others may be matters of both these branches of international law”).

31 For a discussion on the different ways international human rights law and international humanitarian law interact during armed conflict, see O. Hathaway, R. Crootof, P. Levitz, H. Nix, W. Perdue, C. Purvis, and J. Spiegel, *Which Law Governs During Armed Conflict? The Relationship Between International Humanitarian Law and Human Rights Law*, Faculty Scholarship Series. Paper 4724 (2012), http://digitalcommons.law.yale.edu/fss_papers/4724.

32 For further discussion see Satterthwaite *supra* note 1, at 602–03, fn. 55.

33 The UN Security Council has passed a number of Resolutions regarding the crisis in Syria and the fight against ISIS. Key resolutions include S.C. Res. 2170 (2014), U.N. Doc. S/RES/2170 (Aug. 15, 2014); S.C. Res. 2178 (2014), U.N. Doc. S/RES/2178 (Sept. 24, 2014), S.C. Res. 2199 (2015), U.N. Doc. S/RES/2199 (Feb. 12, 2015); S.C. Res. 2249 (2015), U.N. Doc. S/RES/ (Nov. 20, 2015); S.C. Res. 2253 (2015), U.N. Doc. S/RES/2253 (Dec. 17, 2015); and S.C. Res. 2332 (2016), U.N. Doc. S/RES/2332 (Dec. 21, 2016). Almost all of these Resolutions require member states “that have the capacity” to “take all necessary measures, *in compliance with international law … including international human rights, refugee and humanitarian law* … to redouble and coordinate their efforts to prevent and suppress terrorist acts committed specifically by ISIL also known as Da’esh as well as ANF, and all other individuals, groups, undertakings, and entities associated with Al Qaeda, and other terrorist groups, as designated by the United Nations Security Council … and to eradicate the safe haven they have established over significant parts of Iraq and Syria.” S. C. Res. 2249, ¶ ¶ 5–6 (Nov. 20, 2015) (emphasis added). Although this language doesn’t speak specifically to rendition or transfer, it makes clear that any action taken by member states against ISIS must be in accordance with international law.

states carry out the transfer of an individual within their effective control, including clandestine, informal procedures such as extraordinary rendition.[34] While certain individuals facing transfer have greater protections than those set out here (for example, specific categories of people under international humanitarian law), no individual would have less protection.[35] The minimum standard is derived from both procedural and substantive norms set out in the major international human rights treaties. The relevant substantive norms concern protections from transfer to a risk of certain types of grave human rights violations, including torture or cruel, inhuman or degrading treatment, enforced disappearance, persecution, or arbitrary deprivation of life, as well as specific rules concerning wartime transfers. Relevant procedural norms have been articulated in the context of detention and formal transfer as well as in relation to the substantive norms concerning transfers to a risk of grave abuse.[36]

Domestic courts have largely avoided the substantive questions relating to informal transfer, either by examining the case at hand as a jurisdictional issue, or in some cases by invoking rules concerning state secrets or national security to avoid any substantive discussion of the case.[37] International human rights bodies, however, have viewed the issue of rendition differently. In recent years, the ECtHR has found European states culpable for their complicity and facilitation of the US Extraordinary Rendition Program through activities on their territory.[38] These cases have provided some clarity about state obligations regarding transfers under the European Convention on Human Rights and other relevant instruments.[39] A similar case is pending before the African Commission on Human and

34 See C. Droege, Transfers of Detainees: Legal Framework, Non-Refoulement, and Contemporary Challenges, 90 *Int'l Rev. Red Cross* 669, at 677 (2008).

35 Individuals entitled to specific additional guarantees, whether due to *lex specialis* or where relevant states have ratified more protective conventions, must be given those protections as well.

36 See, e.g. *Abu Qatada* (2012); see also *Boumediene v. Bush*, 476 F. 3d 981 (2008).

37 The majority of US cases that have attempted to address issues of extraordinary rendition and secret detention have been dismissed after the government has invoked the state secrets privilege. See, e.g., *Mohamed v. Jeppesen Dataplan, Inc.*, 586 F. 3d 1108 (9th Cir. 2009); see also *Mohamed v. Jeppesen Dataplan, Inc.*, 614 F. 3d 1070 (9th Cir. 2010) (en banc). But see *Salim v. Mitchell*, 183 F.Supp.3d 1121 (2016) (this case settled after surviving dismissal attempts based on the state secrets privilege).

38 See *El-Masri*, *Al Nashiri v. Poland*, *Husayn (Abu Zubaydah) v. Poland*, *Nasr and Ghali*.

39 In recent years, the European Court of Human Rights has heard six relevant cases. This set of cases has started to illustrate a framework for addressing informal transfer and the procedural and substantive norms at risk in such circumstances. See generally *El-Masri*, *Al Nashiri v. Poland*, *Husayn (Abu Zubaydah) v. Poland*, *Nasr and Ghali v. Italy*, *Al Nashiri v. Romania*, and *Abu Zubaydah v. Lithuania*. Specifically, regarding transfer to torture, *see Abu Zubaydah* §451; *Al Nashiri v. Poland* § 454; *Nasr and Ghali* § 242; and *El-Masri* § 212; (decision to remove, and removal itself may give rise to an Art. 3 violation "where substantial grounds have been shown for believing that the person in question would, if removed, face a real risk of being subjected to treatment contrary to that provision in the destination country") More generally, the ECtHR has determined that removal generally requires an individualized assessment of the transferee before removal. See, e.g. *N.D. and N.T. v. Spain*, Apps. No. 8675/

Peoples' Rights against Djibouti for its role in the Extraordinary Rendition Program.[40] Two cases are pending before the Inter-American Commission on Human Rights against the United States for its actions regarding the US Extraordinary Rendition Program as well.[41]

The rules pertaining to transfers to a risk of grave abuse, as in extraordinary rendition, have been consistent and increasingly protective.[42] The minimum standard articulated below is based on jurisprudence, commentary, and doctrine in the fields of international human rights law, humanitarian law, and refugee law, and draws on the norms set out in international human rights conventions, especially the International Covenant on Civil and Political Rights (ICCPR) and the Convention Against Torture and All Forms of Cruel, Inhuman or Degrading Treatment (CAT). The framework set out below consists first of threshold requirements regarding informal transfer—requirements that must be met before an informal transfer may happen. Working within those threshold obligations, the framework then consists of a number of substantive and procedural rights that must also be guaranteed whenever a transfer is carried out.

Thresholds regarding informal transfer: formal processes should not be bypassed; apprehension must be legally valid

International legal norms require that two threshold conditions be met for informal transfer. The first is that, where they exist, formal procedures may not be intentionally bypassed.[43] UN bodies have repeatedly highlighted this requirement,

15 and 8697/15 (Eur. Ct. H.R., Oct. 3, 2017) (finding that Spain had violated its obligations under Article 4 of Protocol No. 4 and Article 13 when it forcibly returned two migrants without any prior individualized judicial or administrative decisions).

40 See *Mohammed Abdullah Saleh Al-Asad v. the Republic of Djibouti*, Comm. 383/10, African Comm'n on Human and Peoples' Rights (Oct. 14, 2014).

41 See Report No. 21/16, Petition 419–08, Khaled El-Masri, Inter-Am. Comm'n H.R. (Apr. 15, 2016) (admissibility). *See also* Mohamed et al. Petition to the Inter-American Commission on Human Rights, submitted Nov. 14, 2011, www.aclu.org/other/mohamed-et-al-petition-inter-american-commission-human-rights?redirect=human-rights-national-security/mohamed-et-al-petition-inter-american-commission-human-rights (there has as of yet been no admissibility decision in this case). For more information about this case, see Frencesca Corbacho, *Rendition Victims Seek Justice Before International Tribunal*, ACLU Blog: Speak Freely, Nov. 15, 2011, www.aclu.org/blog/national-security/rendition-victims-seek-justice-international-tribunal.

42 See S. Borelli, The Rendition of Terrorist Suspects to the United States, at 342, in Bianchi (ed.) Enforcing International Law Norms Against Terrorism (2004).

43 In its *Legal Opinion on the Decision of the Supreme Court of the United States of America* critiquing the US Supreme Court's decision in *United States v. Alvarez-Machain* (in which the US abducted an individual in Mexico despite the existence of an extradition treaty), the Inter-American Juridical Committee underscored the requirement that states uphold extradition treaties in good faith. See Organization of American States Permanent Council, *Legal Opinion on the Decision of the Supreme Court of the United States of America*, 4 Crim. L.F. 119, 131 (1993). Similarly, Bassiouni explains that when a state uses informal transfer in a case where formal methods exist, the transfer "circumvents the intent of states who enter into extradition treaties

especially in cases relating to torture through General Assembly Resolutions, reports from the Human Rights Council, and reports from the UN Special Rapporteur on Torture.[44] Where formal procedures are unavailable or have become impossible, to ensure that the rights of the individual are respected, notice must be given to the host state and cooperation—or at a minimum, consent—must be sought before apprehending the individual.[45] To ensure that interstate cooperation does not amount to collusion in the violation of the individual's rights, the host state and transferring state should ensure that the minimum procedural and substantive standards applicable to transfer are guaranteed and that the transferring state is not, by consenting to such a transfer, otherwise infringing the individual's human rights.[46] The consent of a host state to an informal transfer in the context of rendition, where there are no due process safeguards, will therefore need to be carefully scrutinized, since the state conducting the transfer may have derivative liability under the rules of state responsibility if its actions amount to assistance in the host state's violation of the rights of the transferee. This consent and cooperation may be more difficult if the individual in question is either a national of the host state or an alien lawfully within the territory of the host state,[47] or when states involved have ratified human rights conventions that

for the specific purpose of avoiding disguised extradition" and as a result, "detrimentally affects the international rule of law." M.C. Bassiouni, *International Extradition: United States Law & Practice* Vol. IV, at 29 (2002).

44 G.A. Res. 66/150, U.N. Doc. A/Res/66/150, at 1 (Mar. 27, 2012) "… the absolute prohibition of torture and other cruel, inhuman or degrading treatment or punishment is affirmed in relevant international instruments, and that legal and procedural safeguards against such acts must not be subject to measures that would circumvent this right", similar language is found in G.A. Res. 67/161, U.N. Doc. A/Res/67/161 (Mar. 7, 2013), Human Rights Council, *Draft Resolution*, U.N. Doc. A/HRC/22/L.11 (Mar. 19, 2013), G.A. Res. 68/156, U.N. Doc. A/Res/68/156 (Feb. 14, 2014), U.N. Doc. A/HRC/25/L.32 (Mar. 24, 2014).

45 See *Öcalan v. Turkey*, 41 Eur. H.R. Rep. 985 (2005) (noting that "An arrest made by the authorities of one State on the territory of another State, without the consent of the latter, affects the person concerned's individual rights to security under Article 5 § 1 [of the European Convention]."); *Sánchez Ramirez v. France*, Eur. Comm'n on H. R., No. 28780/95 at 162 (1996) (noting the importance of cooperation among states in terrorism cases).

46 The Inter-American Commission has explained, in the context of counter-terrorism, that "As with all acts and omissions attributable [to] a state and its agents, these human rights protections oblige states to refrain from supporting or tolerating methods of inter-state cooperation that fail to conform with their international human rights commitments." The Commission cites as an example of such cooperation "extraterritorial abduction or kidnapping of a subject present in one state for prosecution in another state." Inter-American Commission on Human Rights, *Report on Terrorism and Human Rights*, OEA/Ser.L/V/II.116 (2002) at 159. Depending on the circumstances, the individual may have rights under domestic law or additional rights under international human rights law (such as rights accruing to aliens lawfully in the territory of the state).

47 Since such individuals have heightened protections against expulsion under human rights law. Note, however, that with respect to aliens, such protections have national security exceptions. See, e.g., International Covenant on Civil and Political Rights, art.

would make apprehension, detention, and transfer outside of formal procedures unlawful.[48]

Additionally, human rights law—through the right to be free from arbitrary detention—requires that states have a valid basis for apprehending an individual in contemplation of transfer. Such bases must be set out in existing law and must be valid under international norms concerning arrest and detention.[49] Detaining individuals for the purpose of interrogation without another basis for detention amounts to arbitrary detention and thus is unlawful under human rights law.[50] The substance of the norms governing the legality of the detention will depend on whether the transfer occurs within or outside the context of armed conflict.[51]

In practice, then, states with functioning legal systems must—before consenting to a transfer—at a minimum ensure that the transferring state has a valid basis for apprehension and detention, and that the procedural rights due to the individual

13, Dec. 16, 1966, 999 U.N.T.S. 171 (hereinafter "ICCPR") (guaranteeing aliens lawfully within the territory of a state the ability to challenge the decision to expel them "except where compelling reasons of national security otherwise require").

48 This may be the case for all European states. The Venice Commission stated that "There are only four legal ways for Council of Europe member States to transfer a prisoner to foreign authorities: deportation, extradition, transit and transfer of convicts for the purpose of their serving the sentence in another country. Extradition and deportation proceedings must be defined by the applicable law, and the prisoners must be given access to the competent authorities." European Commission for Democracy Through Law (Venice Commission), *Draft Opinion on the International Legal Obligations of Council of Europe Member States in Respect of Secret Detention Facilities and Inter-State Transport of Detainees*, Opinion No. 363/2005 (March 8, 2006), Doc. No. CDL-DI(2006)001rev, at para. 160(f). See also *Abu Zubaydah v. Poland* § 452; *El-Masri* § 239.

49 Under human rights law, no one may be deprived of their liberty "except on such grounds and in accordance with such procedure as are established by law." ICCPR, art. 9(1). The Human Rights Committee has made clear that the substantive and procedural aspects of article 9(1) apply to all deprivations of liberty by the state. See U.N. Human Rights Committee, *General Comment No. 8: Right to Liberty and Security of Persons*, U.N. Doc. CCPR/30/06/82, para. 1 (1982) (referring to "all deprivations of liberty," including those for "immigration control."). States may not detain individuals "to repress the exercise of fundamental freedoms, such as freedom of religion, freedom of opinion, freedom of association." See U.N. Working Group on Arbitrary Detention, *Report of the Working Group on Arbitrary Detention*, U.N. Doc. A/HRC/4/40 (Jan. 9, 2007). Counter-terrorism laws that criminalize such freedoms may not be relied upon as a valid basis for apprehension in contemplation of transfer.

50 The goal of intelligence-gathering rather than prosecution has been one of the hallmarks of recent rendition operations in the context of counter-terrorism. See *Assessing Damage, Urging Action: Report of the Eminent Jurists Panel on Terrorism, Counter-Terrorism and Human Rights*, International Commission of Jurists, 78–90 (2009). Improper detention for the purpose of intelligence gathering is also a concern with proxy-detention, where individuals have been detained by foreign governments on behalf of the United States, without warrants or charges, and interrogated.

51 For further discussion on these requirements and differences, see Satterthwaite *supra* note 1, at 611–15.

will be respected.[52] In countries without an effective government or functioning judicial system, it may be lawful to conduct a transfer without the consent of the state without such action amounting to the deprivation of rights vis-à-vis that state so long as the human rights of the individual are otherwise protected by the transferring authority.[53]

Substantive guarantees of non-refoulement

Taken together, international humanitarian law, international refugee law, and human rights law require states to refrain from transferring any individual to the custody of a state where he is at a real risk[54] of: torture or ill-treatment; persecution; enforced disappearance; and arbitrary deprivation of life.[55] This is the principle of *non-refoulement.*

No transfers to a risk of torture or cruel, inhuman or degrading treatment

The CAT (explicitly, in Article 3) and the ICCPR (implicitly, through Article 7) require that states refrain from transferring persons under their effective control to the custody of another state if the transfer would put the individual at a real

52 Another way of viewing the host state's human rights obligations would be to conclude that only individuals who have been found by a local court to be deportable or excludable are eligible for informal transfer, since informal apprehension would not thereby deprive the individual of the opportunity to avail himself of the protection of local law.

53 See, e.g., D. C. Findlay, Abducting Terrorists Overseas for Trial in the United States: Issues of International and Domestic Law, 23 *Tex. Int'l L.J.* 1, 16–17 (1988). In addition to the potential acceptability of transfers from failed states, some authors and policy-makers argue that the consent of the host state is not required in two other circumstances: (a) when the host state has failed to either prosecute or extradite an individual suspected of committing a grave international crime, see, e.g., B. Izes, Drawing Lines in The Sand: When State-Sanctioned Abductions of War Criminals Should Be Permitted, 31 *Colum. J.L. & Soc. Probs.* 1, 18 (1991); and (b) where the host state is knowingly harboring international terrorists, see, e.g., Rendition to Torture: The Case of Maher Arar: Joint Hearing before the US House of Representatives Committee on Foreign Affairs and Committee on the Judiciary, 110th Cong. 82 (2007), (statement of Daniel Benjamin, Director, Center on the United States and Europe, Senior Fellow, Foreign Policy Studies, the Brookings Institution) https://fas.org/irp/congress/2007_hr/arar.pdf.

54 For sake of brevity, the term "real risk" is used in this chapter to encompass these varying thresholds. For a discussion of the differing standards, see E. Gillard, There's No Place Like Home: States' Obligations in Relation to Transfers of Persons, 90 *Int'l Rev. Red Cross* 703, 725 (2008).

55 In addition to these guarantees, emerging principles suggest that states should not transfer persons to countries where they will face arbitrary detention or an unfair trial. International humanitarian law provides additional guarantees to protected persons with specific statuses in times of international armed conflict, but those will not be explored in-depth here, as the focus is on the minimum standards required for informal transfer. See Satterthwaite, *supra* note 1.

risk of torture or cruel, inhuman or degrading treatment or punishment.[56] Indeed, the protection against transfer to a risk of torture or cruel treatment is understood to be so essential to the norm against such treatment that it is not considered to be a separate rule at all.[57] Human rights bodies have repeatedly underscored the importance of upholding the prohibition on transfers to a risk of torture with respect to individuals suspected of crimes of terrorism as an independent, non-derogable obligation, even in the face of security risks.[58] In the context of armed conflict—both international and non-international—these human rights protections continue to apply and are found in Article 3 common to the four Geneva Conventions of 1948 ("Common Article 3"), which forbids "cruel treatment and torture" of anyone in the custody of a party to the conflict.[59] In light of the humanitarian nature of the norm and the interpretations of similar provisions under human rights law, Common Article 3 should be

56 See United Nations Convention Against Torture and Other Cruel, Inhuman or Degrading Treatment or Punishment, *opened for signature* Dec. 10, 1984, S. TREATY DOC. NO. 100–20 (1988), 1465 U.N.T.S. 85 (entered into force June 26, 1987), art. 3; ICCPR, art. 7, as interpreted in General Comment No. 20. See U.N. Human Rights Comm., *General Comment No. 20: Prohibition of Torture, Cruel, Inhuman or Degrading Treatment or Punishment*, para. 9 (1992). See also UN HRC, *Byahuranga v. Denmark*, U.N. Doc. CCPR/C/82/D/1222/2003 (Aug. 15, 2003) (finding that the transfer of an individual to a risk of treatment contrary to Article 7 was a violation of the ICCPR).

57 See Special Rapporteur on torture and other cruel, inhuman or degrading treatment or punishment, *Report of the Special Rapporteur on torture and other cruel, inhuman or degrading treatment or punishment*, ¶ 28, U.N. Doc. A/59/324 (Sept. 1 2004). See also *Soering v. United Kingdom*, App. no. 14038/88, 161 (ser. A) para. 91 (Eur. Ct. H.R., 1989) (finding that protection against transfer to a real risk of torture or cruel treatment was inherent in Article 3 of the European Convention on Human Rights). All of the recently decided ECtHR cases on rendition determined that the states in question had violated their Convention obligations both in light of the treatment the complainants suffered on their territory, as well as for the treatment they suffered after they were transferred outside of the territory, explaining that a transfer to such risk is a violation of article 3 (*Abu Zubaydah v. Poland* § 213, *Al Nashiri v. Poland* § 518, *Nasr and Ghali* § 288, and *El-Masri* §§ 218–220)

58 See, e.g., U.N. Committee Against Torture, *Communication No. 39/1996: Paez v. Sweden*, ¶ 14.5, U.N. Doc. CAT/C/18/D/39/1996 ("the text of article 3 is absolute ... The nature of the activities in which the person concerned engaged cannot be a material consideration when making a determination under article 3 of the Convention."); *Saadi v. Italy*, App. No. 37201/06, para. 137 (Eur. Ct. H. R., Feb. 28, 2008). The European Court of Human Rights has also emphasized that the determination of a *non-refoulement* claim must be decided independently of consideration of national security concerns. See *Chahal v. United Kingdom*, 23 Eur. Ct. H.R. (ser. A) 413, 457, ¶ 80 (1996). However, it is important to note that it has been challenged that this is not a "limitless" obligation, and a number of states include a more holistic analysis of the context, balancing against the rights of the society in which the individual currently finds himself.

59 Common Article 3 has been found to "constitute a minimum yardstick" applicable to both international and non-international armed conflict. *Nicaragua v. United States of America*, 1986 I.C.J. 14, para. 218 (Jun. 27, 1986).

understood to include protection against *refoulement* through transfers to such treatment.[60]

Torture and the transfer to torture were integral parts of the US Extraordinary Rendition Program. At the time of writing, it was unclear whether President Trump would officially embrace the use of torture and informal transfer to countries that use torture as he had previously said he intended to do.[61] However, a draft executive order that was leaked to the press in early 2017 regarding anti-terrorism measures included provisions to re-open CIA detention centers, and to allow for interrogation tactics that were recognized as illegal during the Obama administration.[62] Although President Trump had not, at the time of writing, issued an order granting the CIA new detention authorities, he issued an executive order on January 30, 2018 revoking Obama's order to close the Guantánamo Bay detention facility, as well as ordering the Secretary of Defense to recommend policies "regarding the disposition of individuals captured in connection with armed conflict, *including policies governing transfer of individuals to U.S. Naval Station Guantánamo Bay*."[63] The Executive Order also stated that "the detention operations at the US Naval Station Guantánamo Bay are legal, safe, humane, and conducted consistent with United States and international law,"[64] despite the manifest inaccuracy of the international law claim.[65] While President Trump has

60 This is consistent with the way that authoritative bodies have interpreted the prohibition on torture and cruel treatment set out in human rights instruments. See, e.g., U.N. Human Rights Comm., *General Comment No. 31: Nature of the General Legal Obligation Imposed on State Parties to the Covenant*, U.N. Doc. CCPR/C/21/Rev.1/Add. 1326, para. 12 (May 2004) (interpreting Article 7 of the ICCPR) and *Soering v. United Kingdom*, para. 86–91 (interpreting Article 3 of the European Convention for the Protection of Human Rights and Fundamental Freedoms). Droege, *supra* note 34 at 675, also makes this argument concerning Common Article 3.

61 M. Sidahmed, Trump: "Torture Works," *Guardian* (Jan. 26, 2017), www.theguardian.com/us-news/2017/jan/26/donald-trump-torture-works (discussing President Trump's statements that he believes that torture works and that he would ask to determine what would be legally permissible); D. Welna, Plenty of Room at Guantanamo Bay of Trump's "Bad Dudes," *NPR* (Feb. 8, 2017), www.npr.org/sections/parallels/2017/02/08/513979856/plenty-of-room-at-guantanamo-bay-for-trumps-bad-dudes.

62 The White House, Executive Order – Detention and Interrogation of Enemy Combatants (undated, leaked January 2017), https://assets.documentcloud.org/documents/3412672/Trump-draft-executive-order-on-detention-and.pdf

63 The White House, Executive Order – Presidential Executive Order on Protecting America Through Lawful Detention of Terrorists, Jan. 30, 2018, www.whitehouse.gov/presidential-actions/presidential-executive-order-protecting-america-lawful-detention-terrorists/ (emphasis added). Secretary of Defense Mattis submitted the requested policy update to President Trump on May 2, 2018, though the content of the policy has not been made public. See R. Kheel, Mattis Offers New Criteria for Sending Inmates to Guantanamo, *The Hill*, May 2, 2018, http://thehill.com/policy/defense/385868-mattis-delivers-guantanamo-guidance-to-white-house.

64 The White House, Executive Order – Presidential Executive Order on Protecting America Through Lawful Detention of Terrorists, Jan. 30, 2018, at §1(c).

65 A wide range of international human rights mechanisms have found the indefinite detention, inhumane treatment, and isolation of detainees at Guantánamo to amount

not yet begun to transfer detainees to Guantánamo, this executive order was a preparatory step in that direction, meaning that US detention and mistreatment of ISIS detainees may be around the corner, in addition to being a current possibility in US proxy detention contexts.[66] These developments have placed states on notice of the risk of torture that individuals transferred to US terrorism-related detention may face, especially if the handover is effected through informal mechanisms.

No transfers to a risk of persecution

The 1951 Convention Relating to the Status of Refugees ("Refugee Convention"), the 1967 Protocol Relating to the Status of Refugees, and the Geneva Conventions of 1948 additionally prohibit states from transferring individuals to countries where they face a risk of persecution. Article 33(1) of the Refugee Convention prohibits states from transferring an individual to a country where his or her "life or freedom would be threatened on account of his race, religion, nationality, membership of a particular social group or political opinion." While the Convention contains exclusion criteria, these clauses must be construed narrowly, and even when those criteria are met, individuals retain the protection against *refoulement* to a risk of persecution.[67]

In the context of international armed conflict, Article 45 of Geneva Convention IV specifies that no protected person may be transferred "to a country where he or she may have reason to fear persecution for his or her political opinions or religious beliefs."[68] With respect to persons detained in connection with non-international armed conflict, the International Committee of the Red Cross ("ICRC") has found that practice establishes that all individuals subject to repatriation or release have protection from such repatriation or release if they

to torture and/or cruel, inhuman, and degrading treatment, even following the discontinuance of so-called "enhanced interrogation techniques." See, e.g., Inter-American Commission on Human Rights, *Towards the Closure of Guantánamo*, at para. 120 (2015) ("the IACHR is especially concerned with the suffering, fear and anguish caused by the situation of ongoing indefinite detention"), www.oas.org/en/iachr/reports/pdfs/Towards-Closure-Guantanamo.pdf#page=51.

66 M. Michael, In Yemen's Secret Prisons, UAE Tortures and US Interrogates, AP News, Jun. 22, 2017, https://apnews.com/4925f7f0fa654853bd6f2f57174179fe

67 For more information in exclusion criteria under international refugee law, and the protections that are retained even in the case of exclusion, see Satterthwaite, *supra* note 1, at 618, n. 112. See also A. Farmer, Non-refoulement and Jus Cogens: Limiting Anti-Terror Measures that Threaten Refugee Protection, 23 *Geo. Immig. L. J.* at 1 (2008); see also U.N. Committee Against Torture, *Communication No. 39/1996: Paez v. Sweden*, ¶ 14.5, U.N. Doc. CAT/C/18/D/39/1996 (Apr. 28, 1997). The Committee's finding echoed the holding of the European Court of Human Rights, which has found that "the activities of the individual in question, however undesirable or dangerous, cannot be a material consideration" in determining whether an expulsion would be legal under article 3 of the ECHR (*Chahal v. United Kingdom*, para. 80).

68 Geneva Convention IV, Article 45. This is also emerging as a customary norm.

fear persecution.[69] Additionally, the UN High Commissioner for Refugees (UNHCR) has become more involved in protecting former detainees when they are repatriated or released in situations of armed conflict, including working with states to assist individuals who fear persecution should they be returned to their country of nationality to find alternative settlement options.[70] Therefore, even absent protections against *refoulement* under humanitarian law, international refugee law continues to apply in the context of armed conflict to prevent transfers to a risk of persecution.[71]

Religious persecution and discrimination were key components of the US Extraordinary Rendition Program. During transfer and in CIA prisons, detainees were routinely subjected to treatment specifically tailored to deny or interfere with their religious practices as observant Muslims (such as not allowing them to pray in the appropriate manner or at the appointed times, withholding or disrespecting the Quran, etc.), as well as torture techniques intended to abrogate US understandings of Muslim traditions (such as forced nudity and invasive touching). The Trump administration has already targeted Muslims as a group (for example, through various forms of travel restrictions put into effect in 2017, as well as through fiery anti-Muslim discourse). States cooperating with the United States must therefore weigh the risk of persecution involved in the transfer of Muslim detainees to US custody, especially in the counter-terrorism context.

No transfers to a risk of enforced disappearance

Enforced disappearances are grave rights violations in themselves,[72] as well as amounting to cruel, inhuman and degrading treatment and—depending on the circumstances—torture and a deprivation of the right to life under international

69 See *Customary International Humanitarian Law, IHL Database*, Rule 125, ICRC, https://ihl-databases.icrc.org/customary-ihl/eng/docs/v1_rul_rule125 (hereinafter "*Customary International Humanitarian Law*") see also H. Gasser, Protection of the Civilian Population, in *The Handbook of International Humanitarian Law* 232, 237 (Dieter Fleck, ed., 2008) (explaining that the refusal of transfer by a former internee to a country where he or she faces persecution "must at all times be respected"); H. Fisher, *Protection of Prisoners of War*, in *ibid.* 367, 416–417 (concluding that although practice is mixed, the duty to repatriate prisoners of war (POWs) has in recent practice been modified by need to assess, on an individual basis, whether former POWs fear persecution upon repatriation). With regard specifically to the "war on terror" see ICRC, *Guantanamo Bay: Overview of the ICRC's Work for Internees* (Jan. 30, 2004), www.icrc.org/eng/resources/documents/update/5qrc5v.htm.

70 For example, the UNHCR has worked with the United States to find settlement options for individuals set for release from detention at Guantánamo Bay.

71 See, e.g., Executive Committee, U.N. High Commissioner for Refugees, *Conclusion No. 94* (2002) ("Respect for the right to seek asylum, and for the fundamental principle of *non-refoulement*, should be maintained at all times.")

72 Human rights bodies have found disappearances to be composite violations (citing to, among others, the rights to be free from arbitrary detention, the right to security of the person, the right to be free from torture or ill-treatment, the right to due process, and the right to life). See Satterthwaite, *supra* note 1, at 620, n. 119.

human rights law.[73] As such, transfers to a risk of enforced disappearance—like transfers to a risk of other forms of cruel treatment—are prohibited under human rights law.[74]

In the context of international armed conflict, prisoners of war and aliens in the territory of a state party may not be transferred to a country that is unwilling or unable to ensure that all the protections owed to such persons under the Geneva Conventions are upheld.[75] Enforced disappearance is forbidden by the Geneva Conventions[76] and by customary international humanitarian law,[77] meaning that prisoners of war and other protected persons may not be transferred to a risk of secret detention during international armed conflict. With respect to non-international armed conflict both non-derogable international human rights norms, which continue to apply, and customary international humanitarian law applicable to such conflicts prohibit enforced disappearance.[78] Insofar as disappearance amounts to torture or cruel treatment, transfers to a risk of such treatment should be understood to be prohibited by customary international humanitarian law.

73 The Human Rights Committee has determined that being disappeared amounts to cruel and inhuman treatment, and may also amount to torture, depending on the duration and circumstances. See Satterthwaite, *supra* note 1, at 620, n. 120.

74 Article 16 of the International Convention for the Protection of All Persons from Enforced Disappearance includes an explicit prohibition of transfers to a risk of enforced disappearance.

75 Article 12 of Geneva Convention III provides that prisoners of war may "only be transferred by the Detaining Power to a Power which is a party to the Convention and after the Detaining Power has satisfied itself of the willingness and ability of such transferee Power to apply the Convention." Article 45 of Geneva Convention IV includes an almost identical provision concerning aliens in the territory of a party to an international armed conflict. These provisions mean that a state may not transfer prisoners of war or aliens to states that will not, in practice, apply all of the provisions of the Geneva Conventions relevant to those persons. Such provisions include a wide variety of requirements concerning, *inter alia*, humane and fair treatment. Individuals who are not covered by these protections set out in Geneva Conventions III and IV must nonetheless be protected against transfer to a situation in which the fundamental guarantees set out in Article 75 of Additional Protocol I to the Geneva Conventions, which reflects customary international law, would be violated.

76 See articles 122, 123, 125, and 126 of Geneva Convention III (concerning prisoners of war), and articles 136, 140, 142, and 143 of Geneva Convention IV (concerning enemy aliens and civilian internees). See also *Report submitted by Mr. Manfred Nowak, independent expert charged with examining the existing international criminal and human rights framework for the protection of persons from enforced or involuntary disappearances, pursuant to paragraph 11 of Commission resolution 2001/46*, U.N. Doc. E/CN.4/2002/71, para. 56 (Jan. 8, 2002) (explaining that "While international humanitarian law does not utilize the term 'enforced disappearances' as such, there is no doubt that many of its provisions are aimed at preventing enforced disappearances in the context of armed conflict").

77 See *Customary International Humanitarian Law*, at Rule 98.

78 *Id.*

Enforced disappearance was an inherent feature of the US Extraordinary Rendition Program. US officials refused to acknowledge the detention of individuals in the program, and families of detainees were denied information about the fate or whereabouts of their loved ones who were placed outside the protection of the law. In at least one case the family of an individual who died in US custody was not notified of his detention or death, and the family still does not know where his body is.[79] In other cases, individuals were held by allied governments while their families searched for them in vain.[80] A proxy form of this practice appears to continue: a number of individuals are rumored to be held incommunicado at the behest of the United States outside the protection of the law.[81] For example, Sharif Mobley was believed to be held in Yemen at the time of writing with the connivance of the US government.[82] States that cooperate with the United States on informal transfers as part of US counter-terrorism initiatives must recognize that there is a risk that those who they transfer will be subjected to enforced disappearance.

No transfers to a risk of arbitrary deprivation of life

Article 6 of the ICCPR prohibits the arbitrary deprivation of life. This provision, along with the general obligations set out in Article 2 to respect and ensure the rights set out in the Covenant, imposes an obligation on states to not transfer individuals to a risk of arbitrary deprivation of life.[83] Article 6 includes obligations of non-transfer to

79 L. Siems, Creators of the CIA's 'Enhanced Interrogation' Program to Face Trial, *Guardian* (Aug. 8, 2017), www.theguardian.com/law/2017/aug/08/cia-torture-program-lawsuit-trial-enhanced-interrogation?CMP=share_btn_tw.

80 For example, Mohammed Al-Asad, a victim of CIA rendition program, was not able to communicate with his family, nor was his family made aware of his detention or location for the sixteen months he was held. See *Mohammed Abdullah Saleh Al-Asad v. the Republic of Djibouti*, Comm. 383/10, African Comm'n on Human and Peoples' Rights (2014). For more detail on Mr. Al-Asad's family's lack of knowledge about his detention, ***see*** Al-Asad Declaration, at paras. 49, 53, http://chrgj.org/wp-content/uploads/2013/01/Al-Asad-Signed-Declaration.pdf, and the declaration of his wife, Zahra Al-Asad, at paras. 10–20. http://chrgj.org/wp-content/uploads/2013/01/Zahra-Mohamed-Signed-Declaration.pdf.

81 N. Shabibi, *Disappeared, Tortured, and Bombed: This American's Story Is a Microcosm of US Policy in Yemen*, VICE News (Jan. 6, 2016), https://news.vice.com/article/disappeared-tortured-and-bombed-this-americans-story-is-a-microcosm-of-us-policy-in-yemen.

82 American Dad Missing in Yemen Due in Court on Death Penalty Case, *Reprieve*, Dec. 23, 2016, www.reprieve.org.uk/press/american-dad-missing-yemen-due-court-death-penalty-case/ (as of December 2016, Mobley had not been heard from for a year). For further information on Sharif Mobley's case, see N. Shabibi, *Disappeared, Tortured, and Bombed: This American's Story is a Microcosm of US Policy in Yemen, VICE News* (Jan. 6, 2016), https://news.vice.com/article/disappeared-tortured-and-bombed-this-americans-story-is-a-microcosm-of-us-policy-in-yemen.

83 See U.N. Human Rights Comm., *General Comment No. 31: Nature of the General Legal Obligation Imposed on State Parties to the Covenant,* U.N. Doc. CCPR/C/21/Rev.1/Add. 1326, para. 12 (May 2004).

extrajudicial executions, the imposition of the death penalty in circumstances where basic procedural guarantees have not been observed,[84] and targeted killings.[85]

While the right to life is non-derogable under human rights law,[86] in the context of armed conflict, the *lex specialis* of international humanitarian law modifies the right to life by allowing limited targeting of persons in specific categories.[87] In both international and non-international armed conflict, persons deprived of their liberty, civilians taking no active part in the hostilities, and those otherwise *hors de combat* are protected against "violence to life and person, in particular murder of all kinds."[88] Applying human rights law concurrently with the *lex specialis* of targeting rules, states are prohibited from transferring any person to a risk of acts that would constitute arbitrary deprivation of life in the context of armed conflict.[89]

There is arguably a real risk of violations of *non-refoulement* to the arbitrary deprivation of life in the context of US counter-terrorism operations. States

84 See U.N. Human Rights Comm., *General Comment No. 6: The Right to Life*, para. 7 (Apr. 30, 1982). The Human Rights Committee has held, in *Kindler v. Canada*, that a state would violate the right to life as protected by the ICCPR if it transferred an individual within its jurisdiction to the custody of a state where the individual faced a real risk of having his or her right to life violated. See *Kindler v. Canada*, U.N. Doc. CCPR/C/48/D/470/1991, para. 14.3 (1993). This includes transfer to a real risk of the imposition of the death penalty in circumstances where procedural guarantees are not upheld and no appeal is possible, or where the method of execution itself amounts to torture or cruel, inhuman or degrading treatment. See *Wright v. Jamaica*, U.N. Doc. CCPR/C/55/D/459/1991, para. 0.6 (1995); and *Ng v. Canada*, U.N. Doc. CCPR/C/49/D/469/1991, para. 16.4 (1994). While the European Court of Human Rights has determined that capital punishment carried out following unfair trial amounts to a violation of the right to life, it has not had the opportunity to rule on the issue of protections against transfer to a risk of such treatment. See Droege, *supra* note 34 at 673.

85 See Human Rights Committee, *General comment No. 36 on article 6 of the International Covenant on Civil and Political Rights, on the right to life* [Advance unedited version], paras. 32, 67, July 2017, www.ohchr.org/Documents/HRBodies/CCPR/GCArticle6/GCArticle6_EN.pdf.

86 See, e.g., ICCPR, art. 4.

87 See article 3 common to the Geneva Conventions of 1949; article 46, Geneva Convention I; article 47, Geneva Convention II; article 13, Geneva Convention III; article 33, Geneva Convention IV. For a discussion of the distinction between permissible targeting and unlawful killings in the context of counter-terrorism, see N. Melzer, Targeted Killing in International Law, 396 (2008), and H. Duffy, *The Interplay of Legal Regimes Governing International Peace and Security and the Protection of Persons Under International Law*, at 340–44 in Larissa van den Herik and Nico Schrijver (eds.), *Counter-Terrorism Strategies in a Fragmented International Legal Order: Meeting the Challenges* (Cambridge: Cambridge University Press, 2013).

88 See article 3 common to the Geneva Conventions of 1949; see also Human Rights Committee, *General comment No. 36 on article 6 of the International Covenant on Civil and Political Rights, on the right to life* [Advance unedited version], paras. 32, 67, July 2017.

89 Applying human rights law concurrently with the *lex specialis* of targeting rules, states should be understood to be prohibited from transferring any person to a risk of arbitrary deprivation of life in the context of armed conflict—i.e., to a country where they may be at a risk of unlawful targeted killing.

cooperating with the United States by transferring an individual to a state where the United States is actively engaged in killings via armed drones puts those individuals at risk of arbitrary deprivation of life. There are at least a few confirmed incidents of the United Kingdom revoking UK citizenship from individuals who then became drone targets for the United States in third countries, suggesting some possible level of cooperation between the two governments.[90] In settings such as these, the difficult question is when such a killing is permissible or whether it is an unlawful targeted assassination. The legal debate is intense, hinging on whether individuals who are not members of enemy forces have nonetheless taken on "continuous combat functions" and are therefore arguably no longer civilians and may be targeted.[91]

There is also the risk of the arbitrary deprivation of life within US custody, as at least one individual was confirmed to have died in a CIA "black site" as a result of torture.[92] President Trump has continued the US drone program and has openly praised the techniques used by the CIA during the Extraordinary Rendition Program. Any state considering the transfer of an individual that the United States may consider to be within the scope of permissible targeting to a state where drone strikes have been carried out by the United States is on notice that individuals so transferred may face a risk of arbitrary deprivation of life.

Procedural guarantee: the right to challenge transfer in advance before an independent decision-maker

The right to challenge one's transfer has been understood to be a procedural aspect of the guarantee of *non-refoulement*, has been considered as part of the right to an effective remedy, and as inherent in the right to due process of

90 See, e.g. C. Woods, A.K. Ross, and O. Wright, *British Terror Suspects Quietly Stripped of Citizenship … Then Killed by Drones, Independent* (Feb. 28, 2013), www.independent.co.uk/news/uk/crime/british-terror-suspects-quietly-stripped-of-citizenship-then-killed-by-drones-8513858.html.

91 See R. Goodman, *Why the Laws of War Apply to Drone Strikes Outside "Areas of Active Hostilities" (A Memo to the Human Rights Community)*, Just Security (Oct. 4, 2017), www.justsecurity.org/45613/laws-war-apply-drone-strikes-areas-active-hostilities-a-memo human rights community/; G. Rona, Responding to Goodman's Memo to the Human Rights Community: Context Is Critical, *Just Security* (Oct. 10, 2017), www.justsecurity.org/45775/responding-goodmans-memo-human-rights-community-context-critical/.

92 Gul Rahman, a detainee at one of the secret CIA detention centers, died during his detention following torture. Reports indicate that he likely froze to death in his cell. See Senate Select Committee on Intelligence, *Committee Study of the Central Intelligence Agency's Detention and Interrogation Program*, 54 (Dec. 3, 2014), https://fas.org/irp/congress/2014_rpt/ssci-rdi.pdf; see also J. Leopold, After a Detainee Died at a Black Site, the CIA Blamed Training From the Federal Bureau of Prisons, *VICE News* (Jun. 3, 2016), https://news.vice.com/article/gul-rahman-death-at-cia-black-site-prison-cobalt. For the CIA's report in response to a FOIA request on the matter of Gul Rahman's death, see CIA Memorandum: Death Investigation – Gul Rahman (Jan. 28, 2003), www.cia.gov/library/readingroom/docs/0006555318.pdf.

law.[93] Informal transfers, including rendition, generally lack these important procedural safeguards.[94] Although some procedural rights guaranteed under human rights law may be subject to derogation, certain essential procedural guarantees, such as the right to challenge transfer, may not be restricted even in times of great strife.[95]

The most commonly—and clearly—set out procedural obligation in the context of transfer is the requirement that states provide individuals being transferred with the opportunity to challenge the transfer on the basis that they fear mistreatment in the receiving country. This procedural requirement is inherent in the various norms of *non-refoulement* since *non-refoulement* standards include a subjective and an objective element: the individual must demonstrate his or her fear of mistreatment, and an official of the state considering transfer must objectively weigh this fear in light of relevant evidence.[96] This requires a process that allows the individual the opportunity to make out his or her claim, and to challenge the evidence

93 See, e.g., *Chahal v. The United Kingdom*, para. 80 (holding that independent review of a decision to transfer in the face of a claim of *refoulement* must be independently scrutinized); UN Committee Against Torture, *Ahmed Hussein Mustafa Kamil Agiza v. Sweden*, U.N. Doc. CAT/C/34/D/233/2003, para. 13.5 (May 24, 2005) (finding that "the right to an effective remedy contained in article 3 requires, in this context, an opportunity for effective, independent and impartial review of the decision to expel or remove, once that decision is made, when there is a plausible allegation that article 3 issues arise"); U.N. Human Rights Comm., *Mansour Ahani v. Canada,* U.N. Doc. CCPR/C/80/D/1051/2002, paras. 106.-10.8 (2006) ("the closest scrutiny should be applied to the fairness of the procedure applied to determine whether an individual is at substantial risk of torture").

94 As the Inter-American Juridical Committee has stated, there is an inherent "incompatibility of the practice of extraterritorial abduction with the rights of due process to which every person is entitled, no matter how serious the crime they are accused of, a right protected by international law" (Inter-American Juridical Committee, *Legal Opinion Regarding the Decision of the Supreme Court of the United States of America* C.J.I./RES/II/15/91). There are some contexts in which pro-forma assessments are made, such as in the case interdiction on the high seas. For further discussion on the nature of these varied forms of informal and formal transfer, and the risks they each present, see Satterthwaite, *supra* note 1, at 624.

95 The Human Rights Committee has made clear that states may not derogate from the right to challenge the basis of detention—even in the context of administrative detention imposed as a counter-terrorism measure. See UN Human Rights Committee, *General Comment No. 29: States of Emergency*, UN doc. CCPR/C/21/Rev.1/Add.11, para. 16 and n. 9 (citing concluding comments concerning Israel's administrative detention scheme). Further, the *non-refoulement* obligation is non-derogable and has been found to include the right to challenge transfer on a basis of a fear of *refoulement*. See discussion *infra*.

96 See, e.g., Convention Relating to the Status of Refugees, art. 1, Jul. 28, 1951, 189 U.N.T.S. 150. See S.E. Lauterpacht and D. Bethlehem, *The Scope and Content of the Principle of Non-Refoulement*, at 128, in Refugee Protection in International Law (Feller, Türk, & Nicholson eds., 2003). See also U.N. Committee Against Torture, *Conclusions and Recommendations of the Committee Against Torture: United States of America*, para. 20, U.N. Doc. CAT/C/USA/CO/2 (Jul. 25, 2006) (finding that "The State party should always ensure that suspects have the possibility to challenge decisions of *refoulement*").

brought forward by the state proposing transfer. Any process whereby the transferring state purports to make the *non-refoulement* assessment on its own and without the participation of the individual facing transfer is therefore impermissible under international law.[97]

Individuals facing transfer must therefore have the opportunity to mount a pre-transfer challenge on the basis of any fear of *refoulement*. Although human rights bodies have not held unequivocally that such a challenge must be heard by a court,[98] the review must be by an independent decision maker[99] with the power to suspend the transfer during the pendency of review.[100] Extraordinary rendition

97 For example, the Inter-American Commission on Human Rights found that the United States violated the rights of individuals it interdicted at sea when it transferred them to their country of origin without a hearing concerning their fear of *refoulement*. See *The Haitian Centre for Human Rights et al. v. United States (U.S. Interdiction of Haitians on the High Seas)*, Case 10.675, Inter-Am. C.H.R., Report No. 51/96, OEA/ser. L/V.II. 95 doc. 7 rev. at paras. 167–171 (1997). A recent articulation of this requirement arose out of the Trump administration's travel ban in early 2017. In response to the ban, the international community highlighted that the ban inherently violated procedural guarantees; see UN Office of the High Commission for Human Rights, *US travel ban: "New policy breaches Washington's human rights obligations" – UN Experts* (Feb. 1, 2017), www.ohchr.org/EN/NewsEvents/Pages/DisplayNews.aspx?NewsID=21136&LangID=E. Similar issues have also arisen recently before the ECtHR regarding the return of asylum seekers under the European Union's "Dublin Process." For a brief overview of these cases, see ECtHR Press Unit, *Fact Sheet – "Dublin" cases*, June 2016, www.echr.coe.int/Documents/FS_Dublin_ENG.pdf. In a recent decision, the ECtHR also found that Spain had violated its obligations under article 4 of Protocol No. 4 and Article 13 when it forcibly returned two migrants without any prior judicial or administrative decisions. See *N.D. and N.T. v. Spain* (Eur. Ct. H.R., 2017).

98 See Droege, *supra* note 34 at 680. The issue of whether a court is required or not depends in part on whether human rights bodies construe a pre-transfer process as more akin to a deportation hearing, a criminal proceeding, or an extradition hearing. Different standards have been applied to these different procedures by various human rights bodies. For example, the Human Rights Committee has held that all detainees challenging the legality of their detention should have access to a court for such determination. See OSCE Office for Democratic Institutions and Human Rights, *Protecting the Rights of Victim of Terrorist Attacks*, in Countering Terrorism, Protecting Human Rights: A Manual, at 160–161 (2007). The current Special Rapporteur on Torture has said that review may be conducted by either a judicial or an administrative body. See N. Melzer, Special Rapporteur of the Commission on Human Rights on Torture and Other Cruel, Inhuman or Degrading Treatment or Punishment, Report of the Special Rapporteur on Torture and Other Cruel, Inhuman or Degrading Treatment or Punishment, U.N. Doc. A/HRC/#&/50 (Feb. 26, 2018) (hereinafter "Report of the Special Rapporteur on Torture and Other Cruel, Inhuman or Degrading Treatment or Punishment").

99 See *Agiza* (2005). See also *Jabari v. Turkey*, App. no. 40035/98, para. 50 (Eur. Ct. H. R., 2000) (stressing that the prohibition on *refoulement*, combined with the right to a remedy requires "independent and rigorous scrutiny of a claim that there exist substantial grounds for fearing a real risk of treatment contrary to Article 3").

100 See *Abu Qatada* (2012); *Gebremedhin v. France*, App. no. 25389/05, para. 66 (Eur. Ct. Hum. Rts., 2007) ("In view of the importance which the Court attaches to Article 3 of the Convention and the irreversible nature of the damage which may result if the

has historically provided no due process for those rendered, either before or after their transfer.[101] Individuals subjected to transfers outside formal procedures must be afforded the opportunity to challenge their detention and potential transfer.[102]

Actions of the Trump administration, including the promulgation of a series of executive orders barring travel to the United States by citizens of majority-Muslim countries, demonstrate the president's anti-Muslim animus and contempt for

risk of torture or ill-treatment materializes … [the right to a remedy] requires that the person concerned should have access to a remedy with automatic suspensive effect"); *Chahal v. United Kingdom*, para. 80; *Conka v. Belgium*, App. no. 51564/99 (Eur. Ct. Hum. Rts., 2002); *Agiza* (2005) at para. 13.5; Inter-Am. Comm. Hum. Rts., Extension of Precautionary Measures (N. 259) regarding Detainees in Guantánamo Bay, Cuba (Oct. 28, 2005), www.oas.org/en/iachr/pdl/decisions/GuantanamoMC.asp#28oct. See also *Report of the Special Rapporteur on torture and other cruel, inhuman or degrading treatment or punishment*, para. 29, U.N. Doc. A/59/324 (2004) ("… in cases where the risk of torture and ill-treatment is elevated, it is particularly important that proceedings leading to expulsion respect appropriate legal safeguards, at the very least a hearing before a judicial instance and the right to appeal"). The High Commissioner for Human Rights has stressed that "judicial oversight and review must be available prior to any transfer" of a terrorism suspect. See UN High Commissioner for Human Rights, *Report of the United Nations High Commissioner for Human Rights on the Protection of Human Rights and Fundamental Freedoms While Countering Terrorism*, U.N. Doc. A/HRC/4/88 (2007). On the requirement that transfer be suspended during review of the decision to transfer, see *Jabari v. Turkey* (2000), para. 50 (holding that the right to a remedy in the context of *non-refoulement* requires the suspension of transfer during review of a claim of *refoulement*), U.N. Human Rights Comm., *Concluding Observations of the Committee Against Torture: Australia*, para. 17, UN Doc. CAT/C/AUS/CO/3 (2008), (expressing concern that transfer was not automatically stayed pending review of a claim of *refoulement*). See also N. Melzer, Report of the Special Rapporteur on Torture and Other Cruel, Inhuman or Degrading Treatment or Punishment, para. 40, U.N. Doc. A/HRC/#&/50 (Feb. 26, 2018).

101 Inter-American Juridical Committee, *Legal Opinion Regarding the Decision of the Supreme Court of the United States of America*, C.J.I./RES/II/15/91.

102 See Inter-Am. Comm. Hum. Rts., *Extension of Precautionary Measures (N. 259) regarding Detainees in Guantánamo Bay, Cuba* (2005) (finding that the right to determination of protection from *refoulement* applies to individuals held by the United States at Guantánamo and requesting that the United States provide to detainees facing transfer "an adequate, individualized examination of their circumstances through a fair and transparent process before a competent, independent and impartial decision-maker"). The UN Committee Against Torture has found that the *non-refoulement* provision of the Convention was violated when an individual was transferred informally by French authorities to Spanish police officers. The Committee stressed "its concern at the practice whereby the police hand over individuals to their counterparts in another country … without the intervention of a judicial authority … That meant that a detainee's rights had not been respected and had placed the author in a situation where he was particularly vulnerable to possible abuse." Committee Against Torture, *Arana v. France*, Communication No. 63/1997, U.N. Doc. CAT/C/23/D/63/1997 (2000), at 11.5 & n. 12. For a discussion of how rendition violates procedural guarantees, see OSCE Office for Democratic Institutions and Human Rights, Protecting the Rights of Victims of Terrorist Attacks, in *Countering Terrorism, Protecting Human Rights: A Manual* at 143–145 (2007).

individual procedural guarantees, including those against *refoulement*. The US track record on due process in terrorism-related immigration procedures is similarly troubling.[103] Taken together, these developments paint a bleak picture for the transfer of suspected terrorists, especially those that take place outside of the already-inadequate formal procedures.[104]

Specific procedural rights regarding the use of diplomatic assurances

Diplomatic assurances, once most commonly used to protect against the risk of a transferee being subjected to the death penalty, have now become a common tool for states wishing to engage in terrorism-related transfers. A number of countries, including the United States, have developed a practice of seeking diplomatic assurances—promises by states receiving the individual that they will not subject the transferee to torture or cruel treatment—when they transfer an individual to a country where the individual may be at risk of torture or other ill-treatment.[105] The human rights community decries the use of diplomatic assurances in this context, and legal challenges concerning the permissibility, form, and procedure for using such assurances have been mounted in many countries with differing results.[106] Despite the human rights community's strong objections to the use of diplomatic assurances, many states continue to engage in the practice.[107]

103 See M. Nezer and A. Hughes, Inadmissibility Grounds: A Practitioner's Guide, in *Immigration & Nationality Law Handbook*, 577–587 (2009–10 Edition).

104 This picture is made all the darker in light of the recent case of the US government's detention of a US citizen alleged ISIS fighter, where the state spent months denying the citizen detainee access to counsel, despite his requests.

105 This practice has long been used for transfers from a state that does not use the death penalty where there is a concern that the receiving state may impose the death penalty on the detainee, and is now used frequently for transfers relating to terrorism, both for transfers to third states where there is a concern of systematic torture, and specifically regarding transfers to Guantánamo Bay. States that accept diplomatic assurances as third party states (i.e., those seeking to ensure that their territory or facilities are not used to facilitate informal transfers that breach international law) present different issues. For a brief discussion of those concerns, see Satterthwaite, *supra* note 1, at 627–630.

106 See *Diplomatic Assurances Against Torture – Inherently Wrong, Inherently Unreliable*, Amnesty International, April 2017; see also *Transnational Injustices, supra* note 24, at 64–69; see also *Still at Risk: Diplomatic Assurances No Safeguard Against Torture*, Human Rights Watch, Apr. 2005, at 47–57 (Canada); 57–66 (Sweden); 67–72 (United Kingdom); 72–76 (The Netherlands); 75–79 (Austria); and 79 (Turkey). For an outstanding review of US practice, see also *Promises to Keep: Diplomatic Assurances Against Torture in US Terrorism Transfers*, Columbia Law School Human Rights Institute, 2010.

107 See, e.g. *Transnational Injustices* at 64–68 (discussing the use of diplomatic assurances by Central Asian States). The Obama White House Framework articulated the US policy on diplomatic assurances at the time, indicating that it would continue to rely on them in a case-by-case basis, and reserved the right to not transfer an individual if the assurances it receives are not sufficient. See The White House, *Report on the Legal and Policy Frameworks Guiding the United States' Use of Military Force and Related*

The international standard for when, how, and if at all diplomatic assurances may be used to satisfy a state's obligations concerning *non-refoulement* is somewhat ambiguous. International human rights mechanisms and human rights organizations have repeatedly spoken out against the use of diplomatic assurances in the context of torture, and various courts and states have articulated different substantive and procedural rules governing the practice.[108] The CAT Committee has determined that diplomatic assurances cannot be considered as a safeguard against torture or other ill-treatment where there are substantial grounds for believing such a risk exists,[109] and that states should refrain from seeking or relying upon them in such circumstances.[110] In early 2017 the CAT Committee

National Security Operations, 42–43 (Dec. 2016), www.justsecurity.org/wp-content/uploads/2016/12/framework.Report_Final.pdf. Many other states have, and continue to engage in this practice as well.

108 For a brief overview of the various approaches to diplomatic assurances, see P. Alston and R. Goodman, International Human Rights, 445–456 (Oxford: Oxford University Press, 2013).

109 UN Committee against Torture, *Concluding observations on the third periodic report of Slovakia*, CAT/C/SVK/CO/3, para. 17 (Sept. 8, 2015) ("The Committee recommends that the State party: (c) Refuse to accept diplomatic assurances in relation to the extradition of persons from its territory, since those assurances cannot be considered as a safeguard against torture or ill-treatment in States in which there are substantial grounds for believing that such persons would be in danger of being subjected to torture upon their return."); UN Committee against Torture, *Concluding observations on the seventh periodic report of Switzerland*, CAT/C/CHE/CO/7, para. 13 (Sept. 7, 2015) ("The Committee recalls that it has adopted the position that under no circumstances should a State party regard diplomatic assurances as being a safeguard against torture or ill-treatment where there are substantial grounds for believing that a person would be in danger of being subjected to torture upon his or her return").

110 UN Committee against Torture, *Concluding observations on the sixth periodic report of Spain*, U.N. Doc. CAT/C/ESP/CO/6, para. 12 (May 29, 2015) ("the State party should refrain from seeking or accepting diplomatic assurances as a safeguard against torture or ill treatment in such cases."); UN Committee against Torture, *Concluding observations on the combined third to fifth periodic reports of the United States of America*, U.N. Doc. CAT/C/USA/CO/3–5, para. 16 (Dec. 19, 2014) (The Committee "urges the State party to refrain from seeking and relying on diplomatic assurances 'where there are substantial grounds for believing that [a person] would be in danger of being subjected to torture'"); UN Committee against Torture, *Concluding observations on the third periodic report of Kazakhstan*, U.N. Doc. CAT/C/KAZ/CO/3, para. 16 (12 Dec., 2014) ("The State party should: (f) Refrain from the use of an reliance on diplomatic assurances, which should not be used to alter the absolute prohibition of non-refoulement"); UN Committee against Torture, *Concluding observations on the sixth and seventh periodic reports of Sweden*, U.N. Doc. CAT/C/SWE/CO/6–7, para. 11 (Dec. 12, 2014) (the State should respect its non-refoulement obligations by "(d) Refraining from the use of diplomatic assurances as a means of returning a person to another country where the person would face a risk of torture"); UN Committee against Torture, *Concluding observations on the third periodic report of Belgium*, CAT/C/BEL/CO/3, para. 22 (Jan. 3, 2014) ("States parties may in no circumstances rely on diplomatic assurances rather than observing the principle of non-refoulement, which may alone service as a guarantee of adequate protection

proposed a draft General Comment on article 3 of CAT that considered diplomatic assurances "contrary to the principle of 'non-refoulement,'" and that "they should not be used as a loophole to undermine that principle, where there are substantial grounds for believing that [a transferee] would be in danger of being subjected to torture in that State."[111] Many member states challenged the CAT Committee's position. At the time of writing, the final version of the General Comment had not yet been published, though an advance unedited draft was adopted on 6 December 2017 that did not include language indicating that diplomatic assurances are "contrary to the principle of 'non-refoulement.'"[112] The Human Rights Committee has found that diplomatic assurances should be evaluated with the "utmost care" and that states should "refrain from relying on such assurances where [they are] not in a position to effectively monitor the treatment of such persons" after their transfer.[113]

against the risk of torture or ill-treatment when there are substantial grounds for believing that a person would be in danger of being subjected to torture"); UN Committee against Torture, *Concluding observations on the fifth periodic report of the United Kingdom of Great Britain and Northern Ireland*, CAT/C/GBR/CO/5, para. 18 (Jun. 24, 2013) ("[the Committee] urges the State party to refrain from seeking and relying on diplomatic assurances 'where there are substantial grounds for believing that [the person] would be in danger of being subjected to torture' (art 3). The more widespread the practice of torture or other cruel, inhuman or degrading treatment, the less likely the possibility of the real risk of such treatment being avoided by diplomatic assurances, however stringent any agreed follow-up procedure may be. Therefore, the Committee considers that diplomatic assurances are unreliable and ineffective and should not be used as an instrument to modify the determination of the Convention").

111 CAT Committee, *General Comment No. 1 (2017) on the implementation of article 3 of the Convention in the context of article 22*, U.N. Doc. CAT/C/60/R.2, para. 20 (2017). See also UN Human Rights Committee, *Concluding Observations of the Human Rights Committee: United States of America*, U.N. Doc. CCPR/C/USA/CO/3/Rev.1, 21 (2006) ("the more systematic the practice of torture or cruel, inhuman or degrading treatment, the less likely it will be that a real risk of such treatment can be avoided by diplomatic assurances, however stringent any agreed follow-up procedure may be"). However, the ECtHR has recently accepted assurances given by a state where torture was "widespread and routine" *Abu Qatada* (2012), para. 191; *Saadi v. Italy*, para. 237.

112 On February 9, 2018, the CAT Committee made public an Advance Unedited Version of the renamed General Comment, *see General Comment No. 4 (2017) on the implementation of article 3 of the Convention in the context of article 22*, www.ohchr.org/Documents/HRBodies/CAT/CAT-C-GC-4_EN.pdf. Paragraph 20 reads, in its entirety: "The Committee considers that diplomatic assurances from a State party to the Convention to which a person is to be deported should not be used as a loophole to undermine the principle of non-refoulement as set out in Article 3 of the Convention, where there are substantial grounds for believing that he/she would be in danger of being subjected to torture in that State."

113 See U.N. Hum. Rts. Comm., *Concluding observations on the second periodic report of Tajikistan*, CCPR/C/TJK/CO/2, para. 12 (Aug. 22, 2013); U.N. Hum. Rts. Comm., *Concluding observations on the fourth periodic report of the United States of America*, CCPR/C/USA/CO/4, para. 13 (Apr. 23, 2014); U.N. Hum. Rts. Comm., *Concluding observations on the seventh periodic report of the United Kingdom of Great Britain and Northern Ireland*, CCPR/C/GBR/CO/7, para. 19 (Aug. 17, 2015).

A series of experts who held the position of Special Rapporteur on Torture have set out a more stringent rule, suggesting that *any* use of diplomatic assurances to protect against torture and ill-treatment is impermissible.[114]

International and regional human rights courts have, however, conceded that diplomatic assurances can, if they fulfill certain conditions, theoretically be sufficient to obviate the risk of *refoulement*, though the bar is very high.[115] For example, in *Othman (Abu Qatada) v. the United Kingdom* the ECtHR identified some key problems with diplomatic assurances in general, but decided that it would, on a case-by-case basis, assess the quality of the assurances given, and determine whether in light of the receiving state's practices those assurances could be relied upon, and that only in rare cases would the general situation within a country preclude considering assurances in a specific case.[116] Specifically, the Court said

114 This position was first espoused by Special Rapporteur Manfred Nowak, was taken up by his successor, Special Rapporteur Juan Mendez, and then by his successor, Special Rapporteur Nils Melzer. *See* M. Nowak, Special Rapporteur of the Commission on Human Rights on Torture and Other Cruel, Inhuman or Degrading Treatment or Punishment, *Report of the Special Rapporteur on Torture and Other Cruel, Inhuman or Degrading Treatment or Punishment*, para. 51, U.N. Doc. A/60/316 (Aug. 30, 2005); J. Mendez, Special Rapporteur on Torture and Other Cruel Inhuman or Degrading Treatment or Punishment, *Report of the Special Rapporteur on torture and other cruel, inhuman or degrading treatment or punishment*, para. 79, U.N. Doc. A/HRC/25/60 (Apr. 10, 2014) and N. Melzer, Special Rapporteur of the Commission on Human Rights on Torture and Other Cruel, Inhuman or Degrading Treatment or Punishment, *Report of the Special Rapporteur on Torture and Other Cruel, Inhuman or Degrading Treatment or Punishment*, para. 50, U.N. Doc. A/HRC/#&/50 (Feb. 26, 2018) (use of diplomatic assurances is impermissible in the face of a substantial risk of torture or cruel, inhuman or degrading treatment because they are "inherently incapable of providing sufficient protection against such abuse").

115 See *Abu Qatada* (2012). This was the first case to challenge the UK's recent practice of engaging in a Memorandum of Understanding (MOU) with a state seeking assurances in the face of an established history of torture. While the ECtHR ruled that Qatada could not be deported to Jordan, the court did indicate that diplomatic assurances could be relied upon in some circumstances to obviate the otherwise manifest risk of *refoulement*. For analysis of the Abu Qatada case, and its implications for diplomatic assurances more broadly, see M. Giuffre, An Appraisal of Diplomatic Assurances One Year after Othman *(Abu Qatada) v. United Kingdom (2012)*, 2 *Int'l Human Rights L. Rev.* 266 (2013), see also A. Jillions, Torture, Diplomatic Assurances, and the Politics of Trust, 91 *International Affairs* 489, 495 (2015) ("The impact of [Abu Qatada] has essentially been to establish that where [diplomatic assurances] incorporate sufficiently robust monitoring provisions they are capable of protecting the integrity of *non-refoulement* or other human rights obligations. It also established that the practical sufficiency of [diplomatic assurances] in safeguarding the individual will depend on a range of criteria … In other words, this judgment is evidence that the scope of a state's liability for or complicity with torture can be limited by taking reasonable measures to ensure an individual's safety. By the same token it also sends the signal that there are now few countries … which are so bad that assurances cannot be sought to enable deportation, subject to sufficiently rigorous safeguards being put in place to prevent ill-treatment") (internal citations omitted).

116 *Abu Qatada* (2012), paras. 186–188.

> it is not for this Court to rule upon the propriety of seeking assurances, or to assess the long term consequences of doing so; its only task is to examine whether the assurances obtained in a particular case are sufficient to remove any real risk of ill-treatment.[117]

Importantly, the fact that the ECtHR, a human rights court, examined the issue suggests that those subjected to transfer with the use of such assurances can seek their review as a human rights matter.

In *Abu Qatada*, the Court set out stringent criteria to evaluate whether the diplomatic assurances in question provide "a sufficient guarantee that the applicant will be protected against the risk of ill-treatment."[118] Those criteria are: transparency of the terms of the assurances; specificity of the assurances; authority of the individual/entity providing the assurances; whether the assurances are legally binding and enforceable; whether the treatment feared is legal or illegal in the receiving state; the quality of interstate relations; whether the assurances can be objectively verified; whether there is an effective system of protection against torture, including the acceptance of international monitoring; any history of ill-treatment of the individual; and whether reliability of the assurances has been examined by domestic courts in the sending state.[119] The ECtHR reaffirmed this list of criteria for evaluating diplomatic assurances in *Azimov v. Russia* a year later.[120] The ECtHR has repeatedly held that diplomatic assurances are "highly unlikely" to provide sufficient guarantees that the transferees "will be protected against the risk of prohibited treatment sufficient to allow a transfer to countries where there are reliable reports that the authorities resort to or tolerate torture or other ill-treatment."[121]

Although European human rights jurisprudence is not binding on states outside the Council of Europe such as the United States, it provides authoritative guidance on how diplomatic assurances should be assessed, and has been relied upon by many states in interpreting their obligations under CAT. Indeed, in their Joint Observations on the CAT Committee's Draft General Comment in early 2017, Canada, Denmark, the United Kingdom, and the United States relied on *Abu Qatada* and other regional case law to support their argument that diplomatic assurances are a valid tool to protect against *refoulement*, as long as they meet certain requirements.[122]

117 *Id.* at para. 186.
118 *Id.* at para. 187.
119 *Id.* at para. 189.
120 *Azimov v. Russia*, App No. 67474/11, paras. 135, 143 (Eur. Ct. H.R., 9 Sept. 2013).
121 See *Transnational Injustices* at 65 (referencing ECtHR jurisprudence) (internal citations omitted).
122 The Permanent Mission of the United States of America to the United Nations and Other International Organizations in Geneva, *Diplomatic Note No. 008-17: Joint Observations of Canada, Denmark, the United Kingdom, and the United States of America on Paragraphs 19–20 of the Committee Against Torture's Draft General Comment No. 1 (2017) on Implementation of Article 3 in the Context of Article 22,*

The United States has relied on, and continues to rely on, diplomatic assurances, even in circumstances where international law suggests it may not. The continuing lack of transparency related to the US use of diplomatic assurances is extremely concerning, and places third party states that engage in transfers to US custody on notice of potential rights violations in circumstances where a detainee may be transferred on to another state.

Conclusion: rendition in these extraordinary times

The Obama administration's efforts to halt blatantly abusive detainee transfers in the context of counter-terrorism may soon be a faint memory. As Human Rights Watch Executive Director Kenneth Roth said toward the end of Obama's second term in office, "Obama is essentially leaving the door open for some future, unscrupulous president to re-embark on the torture policies of the Bush administration."[123] This risk is now manifest, and informal transfers may once again become a key tool in US counter-terrorism practice. Some cross-border transfers and proxy detentions are already taking place; the question is how much the practice will increase under the Trump administration and whether critical safeguards will remain absent.[124] States that would cooperate with the United States on counter-terrorism measures—including informal transfers—are on notice concerning these risks and must ensure that they actively protect the range of procedural and substantive rights for any detainee facing transfer by the United States or to US custody, whether physical or by proxy.

March 31, 2017, www.ohchr.org/Documents/HRBodies/CAT/GCArticle3/JointSubmission.pdf.

123 Human Rights Watch, *US: Still Time to Investigate Bush Era Torture* (video), Dec. 1, 2015, www.hrw.org/report/2015/12/01/no-more-excuses/roadmap-justice-cia-torture.

124 B. Woodruff & S. Ackerman, U.S. Military: American Fighting for ISIS "Surrenders," *The Daily Beast* (Sept. 14, 2017), www.thedailybeast.com/us-military-american-isis-fighter-reportedly-surrenders?source=twitter&via=mobile; M. Michael, In Yemen's Secret Prisons, UAE Tortures and US Interrogates, AP News (Jun. 22, 2017), https://apnews.com/4925f7f0fa654853bd6f2f57174179fe.

7 US torture on "black sites"

A lesson from Great Britain?

Satvinder S. Juss[1]

Introduction

The grandiloquence of the ill-phrased "war on terror", with its invasions of Afghanistan and Iraq, and the state abnegation of cherished fundamental rights and freedoms that had been painstakingly cultivated through centuries of procedural and substantive legal protections, is by now well recognized.[2] Equally well recognized by now is the use of Military Orders to place suspected al-Qaeda members as "enemy combatants" in extra-judicial detention at Guantánamo Bay,[3] who had not just been apprehended in conflict zones, but elsewhere also.[4] Military commissions were then used to try them for terrorist offences, and this too is well documented. The Bush government justified this on the basis "that it should have the power to detain U.S. citizens on U.S. territory and hold them indefinitely without charge".[5] What was not made explicit at the time was how detention occurred also in territories other than those owned by the USA, in foreign lands and with the complicity of foreign sovereign states. This raises far broader questions of legality that have not yet been fully addressed. Fortunately, a UK Supreme

1 I am indebted to the valuable research assistance provided by Emily Campbell in the preparation of this chapter.

2 See Rosa Brooks, "War Everywhere: Rights, National Security Law, and the Law of Armed Conflict in the Age of Terror", 153 *U. Pa. L. Rev.* 675, 745 (2004).

3 Military Order No. 1 of November 13, 2001: Detention, Treatment, and Trial of Certain Non-Citizens in the War Against Terrorism, 66 Federal Register 57,831 (Nov. 16, 2001).

4 Perhaps the most notorious case here is that of the British citizen Moazzam Begg, who was seized by Pakistani intelligence at his home in Pakistan in February 2002. He was then transferred to the custody of US Army officers. They held him in the detention centre at Bagram Air base in Afghanistan. From there he was transferred onwards to Guantanamo Bay. He was held there until January 2005, a total of three years in detention without being charged: see Moazzam Begg, *Enemy Combatant: The Terrifying True Story of a Briton in Guantánamo* (Simon & Schuster UK; new edition, 5 Feb. 2007)

5 Military Order No. 1 of November 13, 2001: Detention, Treatment, and Trial of Certain Non-Citizens in the War Against Terrorism, 66 Federal Register 57,831 (Nov. 16, 2001) at p. 719.

Court decision has now made a start in the case of *Belhaj*.[6] In so far as this has been done, there are lessons here for the USA to learn, as well from its approach in upholding the rule of law and protecting fundamental human rights.[7] The UK Supreme Court decision is bold and on the whole it is welcome but it is also tendentious, which strays into the area of foreign policy and international relations, in circumstances where the detentions and transfers involved were undertaken at the behest of foreign states and their agents. Courts traditionally have steered clear of involvement in the actions of foreign states, treating them as "non-justiciable" on grounds that they fall within the sole preserve of sovereign states, but the UK decision now makes such actions justiciable where fundamental human rights are violated. This means that courts are now prepared to engage with "political" questions. This can be a major problem in the unresolved fight against terror because governments often have to switch sides, and erstwhile foes may have to become friends in the fight against terror. The *Belhaj* decision may therefore be difficult to apply. If so, is it a one-off? And, if not, does it prioritize human rights protections over national security in a way that is unrealistic? This chapter sets out to consider some of these questions.

The case of Abdel Hakim Belhaj

Abdul Hakim Belhaj was a Libyan national, and a member of the Libyan Islamic Fighting Group (LIFG), set up two decades ago to fight Colonel Gaddafi. The LIFG was at one time supported both the USA and the UK. This is because Colonel Gaddafi had been a long-time scourge of their security and intelligence community. In 2004, however, the USA and its ally, the UK, switched sides and began to support Colonel Gaddafi, in the hope that he would eliminate his store of weapons of mass destruction (WMDs) because unlike Saddam Hussain in Iraq, who did not at the relevant time have any WMDs, the Libyan leader was known to have them. Belhaj found himself caught in the midst of these machinations because in return for Libyan help to the USA and UK, Colonel Gaddafi wanted to have members of the LIFG targeted by them. The story is well recounted in the UK Supreme Court when it gave judgment in favour of Belhaj in January 2017. In the words of Lord Sumption, "[i]n February 2004 Mr Belhaj and Mrs

6 *Belhaj & Anor v Straw & Ors* (Rev 1) [2017] UKSC 3

7 In fact, recently Mr Tobias Ellwood, a UK defence minister and a former soldier, has echoed such sentiments, observing that, "The horror of 9/11 meant that we briefly lost the sight of the standards and rule of law that took centuries to develop and fundamentally distinguish us from the terrorist. Guantanamo Bay created a new combatant status that bypassed the Geneva Convention, used torture and failed to address (indeed fuelled) a wider global jihadist insurgency that continues today. Give the scale of foreign fighters attracted to ISIS we should consider an agreed international process involving The Hague, which ensures terrorists from any origin are transparently and fairly held to account for their actions": see G. Rayner, J. Ensor & S. Swinford, "'Beatles' Jihadis Captured in Syria Must Be Tried in the Hague Not Sent to Guantanamo, Says Minister" (*Telegraph*, 9 Feb. 2018) (available at www.telegraph.co.uk/politics/2018/02/09/exclusive-britain-washes-hands-two-beatles-jihadis-captured/).

Boudchar were living in China but wished to come to the United Kingdom to claim asylum", but instead of being able to do so, "[t]hey allege that Chinese officials detained them at Beijing airport as they were about to board a flight to London, and later put them on a flight to Kuala Lumpur in Malaysia", where "they were held for two weeks by the Malaysian authorities". They were "then allowed to leave for the United Kingdom but were required to go via Bangkok" and "[o]n 7 March 2004 they were put on a commercial flight to London via Bangkok" but then in Bangkok "they were taken off the aircraft by Thai officials and delivered to agents of the United States". Plainly, sending these prospective asylum seekers via Bangkok on a London flight, where they planned to apply for refugee status under the *Geneva Convention 1951 on the Status of Refugees*,[8] was nothing short of a ruse, to abduct them, and Lord Sumption describes their plight further by explaining how "[a]t some time in the next two days they were flown to Libya in a US-registered aircraft said to have been owned by a CIA front company". It is not clear how the Libyan authorities got wind of their whereabouts. If they were being put on a flight to London from Bangkok it is conceivable that the British authorities would have known of them. What is without doubt is that having arrived in Libya, both husband and wife "were taken to Tajoura prison" from which "Mrs Boudchar was released in June 2004 after being held there for rather more than three months" but Mr Belhaj was held successively at Tajoura and Abu Salim prisons for six years before being released in March 2010".

Lord Sumption explains how, during their rendition in this way, "they were tortured and subjected to other serious mistreatment by US officials in Bangkok and in the aircraft carrying them to Libya, and by Libyan officials in Libya". The claim against the *British* government was that its officers "are said to have been complicit in what happened to them", and in this the defendants included "the intelligence services, the departments of state responsible for them", which included the then Foreign Secretary and the senior official of the Secret Intelligence Service (SIS). It was that "the SIS, having learned that Mr Belhaj and Mrs Boudchar were being detained in Malaysia, passed the information to the Libyan intelligence services and assisted the rendition flight with transit facilities at the British-owned but American operated base at Diego Garcia in the Indian Ocean." What made the claim for damages against the British authorities legally difficult to prosecute was that,

8 It remained to be seen if Mr Belhaj would have been successful in his asylum claim in the UK and, of course, if he had committed atrocities he stood to be excluded from the Refugee Convention under Article 1F which states that:

"The provisions of this Convention shall not apply to any person with respect to whom there are serious reasons for considering that:

(a) he has committed a crime against peace, a war crime, or a crime against humanity, as defined in the international instruments drawn up to make provision in respect of such crimes;

(b) he has committed a serious non-political crime outside the country of refuge prior to his admission to that country as a refugee;

(c) he has been guilty of acts contrary to the purposes and principles of the United Nations."

> [i]t is not alleged that British officials were directly involved in the rendition, torture or mistreatment of the claimants. But it is said that they enabled it to happen, knowing of the risk that the defendants would be unlawfully detained, tortured and otherwise mistreated by the Americans and the Libyans. (Emphasis added)

The actual torture and mistreatment was allegedly against third parties. The claim against the British government was that they facilitated it and were ultimately complicit in it. Moreover, the "British officials took advantage of Mr Belhaj's detention in Libya by interrogating him there at least twice" and so British officials "thereby incurred liability in tort".[9] When after his release, in 2013, Belhaj and his Libyan wife, Mrs Boudchar, decided to sue, they also did so on the basis that their rendition flight assistance with transit facilities was provided by the British-owned, but American-operated base at Diego Garcia, in the Indian Ocean.

The American base at Diego Garcia

The American base at Diego Garcia was not entirely unknown for nefarious activities. Allegations that it had a dark side had been circulating before the Belhaj action was initiated in 2013. Two years earlier, in 2011, David Vine's *Island of Shame: The Secret History of the U.S. Military Base on Diego Garcia*,[10] in tracing US foreign policy from the Cold War to the war on terror, had showed how the United States had forged a new and pervasive kind of empire that was quietly dominating the planet with hundreds of overseas military bases. Vine had adverted to the possibility of how the atoll of Diego Garcia in the Chagos Islands may house a top-secret CIA prison where terror suspects are interrogated and tortured. In fact, a barely known story by seasoned Pakistani journalist Masood Anwar[11] in

9 *Belhaj & Anor v Straw & Ors* (Rev 1) [2017] UKSC 3 at para. 177.

10 David Vine, *Island of Shame: The Secret History of the U.S. Military Base on Diego Garcia* (Princeton, NJ: Princeton University Press, 2011).

11 See Saad Hussain, "How a Pakistani Journalist Exposed the CIA's Most Secretive Operation", *TRT World*, 18 May 2017 (available at www.trtworld.com/magazine/how-a-pakistani-journalist-exposed-the-cia-s-most-secretive-operation-7126), who writes how, ""My initial source didn't have the exact details," he [Pakistan's veteran journalist Masood Anwar] told *TRT World* in a recent interview. "I knew there had to be someone among the ground handling staff who could have more information … Known as "extraordinary renditions", the transfers were a way for US agents to detain and interrogate prisoners without trial. Using private jets registered to shell companies, the CIA flew shackled and blindfolded men mainly to Egypt, Syria and Jordan. These countries were infamous for extreme interrogation methods, and later testimonies showed that suspects were subjected to brutal torture. "If you want a serious interrogation, you send a prisoner to Jordan. If you want them to be tortured, you send them to Syria. If you want someone to disappear – never to see them again – you send them to Egypt," Robert Baer, a former CIA agent, famously said: "For the White House – most notoriously then-vice president Dick Cheney – the renditions helped the US avoid the Geneva Convention and US laws that prohibit use of torture to extract information. The Bush administration, which authorized the extraordinary renditions, believed it

October 2001 had a decade previously drawn attention to how "the CIA was illegally moving suspects to be tortured in a network of secret prisons around the world".

When many years later, and with the "war on terror" in full swing, there was the publication in December 2014 of the long-awaited US Senate Intelligence Report into renditions, Jamie Doward[12] was able to remark how it was that "fresh questions were raised about what the UK knew about the CIA's – torture programme – and in particular the role played by an obscure overseas British territory." These questions arose because "Al-Jazeera reported earlier in the year that the committee had seen evidence that Diego Garcia … had been used for extraordinary rendition 'with the full cooperation' of the UK." The difficulty in resolving these questions, however, lay in the fact that, "when the heavily redacted report was published, it made no mention of Diego Garcia, raising questions about whether references to it had been removed at the request of the UK". This led Sir Malcolm Rifkind,[13] a former British Foreign Secretary, and chair of the parliamentary inquiry into the complicity of British intelligence agencies in the US programme, to express concern. He suggested that British MPs would seek the intelligence relating to Britain's role in CIA's abduction and torture programme, and demand the unredacted Senate report. This had concluded that the CIA repeatedly lied over its brutal but ineffective interrogation techniques. Andrew Tyrie, chair of the all-party parliamentary group on rendition, said any negotiations on the island of Diego Garcia's future "should address allegations that it was used by the CIA to render terror suspects around the world, possibly with British involvement".

By the end of the year in 2014, there was mounting international concern. Professor Manfred Nowak,[14] who between 2004 and 2010 had served as the UN special rapporteur on torture, expressed the opinion that the publication in December 2014 of a 500-page US Senate report into the CIA's torture programme would eventually mean that even the role played by European Union (EU) member states in extraordinary rendition would also finally come out. Nowak was of no doubt that "[t]he UK must launch an independent investigation into its alleged role in the CIA torture programme, in the light of new evidence "that the British territory of Diego Garcia was used as a 'black site' to hold

could not be held responsible for the mistreatment of prisoners – so long as the torture happened in another country."

12 Jamie Doward, "Diego Garcia Guards Its Secrets Even as the Truth on CIA Torture Emerges", *Observer*, 13 December 2014 (available at www.theguardian.com/world/2014/dec/13/diego-garcia-cia-us-torture-rendition).

13 Mark Townsend and Jamie Doward, "Come Clean on British Links to Torture, MPs Tell US Senate", Observer, 13 December 2014 (available at www.theguardian.com/world/2014/dec/13/britain-link-cia-torture-us-senate-unredacted-report).

14 Jamie Doward, "UK Must Probe Its Role in CIA Torture, Says UN Legal Expert: UN's Former Special Rapporteur on Torture Says Claims Such as Sanctioned Use of Diego Garcia as 'Black Site' to Render Libyans Must Be Examined", *Observer*, 20 December 2014 (available at www.theguardian.com/us-news/2014/dec/20/uk-cia-torture-links-report-probe-un).

detainees". So far that has been a forlorn hope. Neither the role of the EU member states nor that of the UK has thus far been clarified in the extraordinary rendition of detainees. This is why a judicial reckoning of this episode is so much to be welcomed when eventually it came in *Belhaj*.

On the other hand, on the other side of the Atlantic, the fog over the US role did show some signs of lifting. By January 2015, as the pressure began to mount, a senior Bush administration official appears to have confirmed that "Interrogations of US prisoners took place at a CIA black site on the British overseas territory of Diego Garcia". It was said that "[t]he island was used as a 'transit location' for the US government's 'nefarious activities' post-9/11 when other places were too full, dangerous, insecure, or unavailable, according to Lawrence Wilkerson, Colin Powell's former chief of staff". This was significant as it "was the first time a senior Bush administration official has stated on the record that the remote British territory was a part of the CIA's global network of black sites". At the time, it was being suggested that "[t]he question of British cooperation is an extremely sensitive one for the British government, which has sought to distance itself from any suggestion of complicity in the US's post-9/11 rendition and torture program". The British government itself had said that "only two rendition flights stopped over at Diego Garcia to refuel, both in 2002" but "Manfred Nowak, the United Nations' former special rapporteur on torture," had indicated in 2008 "that sources had told him detainees were held on Diego Garcia between 2002–3". Moreover, "[a] former US general, Barry McCaffrey, also said Diego Garcia held detainees—but later retracted the claim". Notwithstanding such obfuscation, the man who was then suing the UK government over his kidnap, namely Abdel Hakim Belhaj, had no doubt that he was rendered through Diego Garcia when he was abducted in a joint MI6–CIA operation.[15]

Judicial authorities in the UK continued to give guarded support to the emerging exceptions to "sovereign immunity principle" during the time that the *Belhaj* case was subject to ongoing litigation. Blake J in *Ponnusamy*[16] stated that, "I accept that an investigation into allegations of gross violations of human rights on the territory of another sovereign state may be required in the course of civil litigation and this is an emerging exception to the sovereign immunity principles …"[17] In *Al Attiya*,[18] a year later, while the *Belhaj* case was still not before the Supreme Court, Blake J felt able to say that, "the act of state doctrine was subject to an exception in the case of

15 Ben Bryant and Rupert Stone, "Exclusive: CIA Interrogations Took Place on British Territory of Diego Garcia, Senior Bush Administration Official Says", *Vice News*, 30 January 2015 (available at https://news.vice.com/article/exclusive-cia-interrogations-took-place-on-british-territory-of-diego-garcia-senior-bush-administration-official-says).

16 *Ponnusamy & Ors v Secretary of State for Foreign and Commonwealth Affairs* [2015] EWHC 1760 (QB) (30 March 2015), URL: www.bailii.org/ew/cases/EWHC/QB/2015/1760.html. Blake J. went on to refer to the judgment of Lloyd-Jones LJ in *Belhaj v Straw [2014] EWCA Civ 1394* at 114–121

17 Blake J. at para. 44.

18 Blake J. in *Al Attiya v Bin-Jassim Bin-Jaber Al Thani* [2016] EWHC 212 (QB) (15 February 2016) (available at www.bailii.org/ew/cases/EWHC/QB/2016/212.html).

serious abuse of core human rights including peremptory norms of international law such as the use of torture".[19] He went on to explain how although the act of state doctrine was engaged here, this did not bar the claim from proceeding because by contrast with state immunity, the act of state principle "is a common law doctrine that is subject to some exemptions such as where fundamental human rights were said to be breached".[20]

The fall of Colonel Gaddafi

Following the so-called "Arab Spring", protests broke out in February 2011 in Libya against Colonel Gaddafi, spreading from Tunisia and Egypt. When Gaddafi came down hard on them the revolt against his rule turned into a military conflict. Initially the Western nations were not supportive of the rebels. The United Nations declared sanctions against Libya. There was even call by them for his trial in the international court. The US and the UK switched sides and turned against him. After he was shot on 20 October 2011[21] secret papers surfaced consisting of "several extraordinary caches of secret British, American and Libyan intelligence documents that were discovered amid the chaos of the Libyan revolution in 2011, scattered around abandoned government offices, prisons and officials' private residences".[22] These not only confirmed covert CIA operations, but British complicity in them. Information gleaned from them enabled writers on the *Belhaj* case, such as Ian Cobain, to subsequently explain how, after "the pair were taken to Tripoli on a flight that took 17 hours" and after being "driven separately to Tajoura prison, east of the city", Mr Belhaj was chained to a wall and beaten and

> [a]lmost immediately, MI5 and MI6 began sending questions that they wanted the Libyans to put to him. Many concerned the lives of other Libyan dissidents around the world. And the questions would keep coming. They are all there, in the secret papers discovered in Tripoli: more than 1,600 questions …[23]

The secret papers were explosive in another respect. By May 2016 it began to be reported that these "controversial and clandestine rendition operations provoked an unprecedented row between the UK's domestic and foreign intelligence services, MI5 and MI6, at the height of the 'war on terror'", and yet, what was really

19 Blake J. at para. 18(iv) of *Al Attiya* was referring to *Belhaj v Straw* [2014] EWCA Civ 1394; [2015] 2 WLR 1105 at [81] to [102] and [114] to [126].
20 Ibid, at para, 20.
21 For a brief account, see Satvinder Juss, "Complicity, Exclusion, and the 'Unworthy' in Refugee Law", *Refugee Survey Quarterly* (2012, Vol. 31, November 3 Issue, pp. 1–39) at pp. 10–11
22 Ian Cobain, "How Britain Did Gaddafi's Dirty Work", *Guardian*, 9 November 2017 (available at www.theguardian.com/news/2017/nov/09/how-britain-did-gaddafis-dirty-work-libyaF).
23 Ian Cobain, "Torture a Shared Value," Salaam Blogs, 7 November 2017 (available at www.salaam.co.uk/blogs-new/?p=82).

significant was how "[t]he secret role played by MI6 was revealed after the fall of Gaddafi, when documents were found in ransacked offices of his intelligence chief, Moussa Koussa". In fact, it has transpired also that Mr Belhaj and his wife were not alone in being mistreated in this way. With them was a man known as "Sami al-Saadi and his family [who] were abducted from the Far East to Gaddafi's interrogation and torture cells in Tripoli in 2004". In his case, however, "[t]he British government paid £2.2m to settle a damages claim brought by al-Saadi and his family" but "Belhaj has refused to settle unless he receives an apology".[24] The British mainstream press refused to let the story die. So much so that even a year after the UK Supreme Court judgment in *Belhaj* was handed down in January 2017, it still continued to report that "secret papers show how far MI6 went to please Libya's ruthless intelligence agents – including helping to kidnap the dictator's enemies", in what was now directly being castigated as a sordid story of "How Britain did Gaddafi's dirty work".[25] There appear to be two reasons for why this was allegedly being done.

The first reason that was given was to do with MI6 spy chief Mark Allen's pursuit of Mr Belhaj for British security reasons. This arose because,

> [a]lthough some LIFG members had joined al-Qaida in Afghanistan, its leadership had for years rejected the overtures of Osama bin Laden, and remained focused on the overthrow of Gaddafi. Despite this, Allen clearly believed LIFG members could provide information about the threat from al-Qaida. *In particular, he expressed interest in one of the LIFG's military leaders, a 35-year-old veteran of the Soviet-Afghan war by the name Abdel Hakim Belhaj.* (Emphasis added)

The second quite contradictory reason, given that Gaddafi had posed a threat to UK security interests for years, was "the post-9/11 rapprochement between the Gaddafi regime and the west – and Tony Blair's government in particular" which, it was suggested, "went far deeper than was previously known". With the war in Iraq going badly, and WMDs not being found on Saddam Hussain, it was thought that if Gaddafi could be "persuaded to abandon his own nuclear plans, those who had pressed for war against Iraq could claim the invasion had been vindicated" and so "the CIA and MI6 built relationships with Libya" and "the two agencies assisted Libyan spies in the kidnapping of Gaddafi's enemies".[26] Therefore, once Mr Belhaj had been handed over to the Libyans, it is alleged that on 18 March 2004 Sir Mark Allen sent a letter to his Libyan counterpart, Moussa

24 Nick Hopkins and Richard Norton Taylor, "Blair Government's Rendition Policy Led to Rift Between UK Spy Agencies", *Guardian*, 31 May 2016 (available at www.theguardian.com/uk-news/2016/may/31/revealed-britain-rendition-policy-rift-between-spy-agencies-mi6-mi5).

25 Ian Cobain, "How Britain Did Gaddafi's Dirty Work", *Guardian*, 9 November 2017 (available at www.theguardian.com/news/2017/nov/09/how-britain-did-gaddafis-dirty-work-libyaF).

26 Ibid.

Koussa, congratulating him on the successful rendition of Belhaj. A week later Prime Minister Tony Blair famously met Gaddafi in his tent in Libya, a meeting at which Allen was present. It has been reported that in his letter to Koussa, Allen said: "I congratulate you on the safe arrival of [Belhaj]. This was the least we could do for you and for Libya to demonstrate the remarkable relationship we have built over recent years ..."[27]

In fact, "[t]wo leading figures in the Libyan opposition who had fled the country were kidnapped, one from Hong Kong, one from Thailand, and flown back to Tripoli along with their wives and children. Both men were tortured." It did not end there. Libyans in the UK too began to fear for their safety as "[o]pponents of the Gaddafi regime who had been living legally in the UK for years were detained by British police, and the British government made a determined attempt to have them deported to Tripoli." So much so British state sovereignty itself was happily compromised as "[a]sylum seekers and British-Libyan nationals in Manchester and London were menaced by Gaddafi's agents, who were invited into the UK and permitted to operate on the streets of Britain alongside MI5". It was only after the gruesome killing of Gaddafi[28] in October 2011 that it transpired that he had fooled both the UK and the USA in that at a remote depot in the south east of Libya, the National Transitional Council established after his death "discovered that the dictator had concealed large stocks of chemical weapons" when they "found mustard-gas artillery shells and precursors for the creation of other chemical weapons" so that he had never actually shut down his WMDs programme at all. Unsurprisingly, Dame Eliza Manningham-Buller, who for five years served as director general of MI5 (2002–2007), frustratingly in 2011 inquired "whether the UK supped with a sufficiently long spoon" in dealing with the Libyan dictator". Ian Cobain ruefully observed that, "[i]ndeed, the story of Britain's attempt to make an ally of Libya has an uncomfortable postscript".[29]

All of this only serves, however, to underline the fact that the Supreme Court may have gone too far in emphasizing individual rights over state interests, which involved matters of political judgment. It is one thing to say that this is not an area for judicial restraint. It is another thing to ensure that it is free from judicial restraint. Yet, the *Belhaj* case has succeeded in becoming a landmark case[30] of how

27 Jamie Doward, "MI6 Chief's Role in Abduction of Gaddafi Foe Belhaj Set to Be Revealed High Court to Consider Review of Decision Not to Prosecute Former MI6 Director Over Abdel Hakim Belhaj Case", *Guardian*, 19 February 2017 (available at www.theguardian.com/world/2017/feb/19/mi6-mark-allen-review-role-gaddafi-libya-abdel-hakim-behaj?CMP=Share_iOSApp_Other).

28 See Satvinder Singh Juss, "Complicity, Exclusion, and the 'Unworthy' in Refugee Law", *Refugee Survey Quarterly* (2012, Vol. 31, November 3 Issue, pp. 1–39) at pp. 10–11.

29 Ian Cobain, "How Britain Did Gaddafi's Dirty Work", *Guardian*, 9 November 2017 (available at www.theguardian.com/news/2017/nov/09/how-britain-did-gaddafis-dirty-work-libyaF).

30 Landmark cases "mark a turning point in judicial approach, indicating a break with the past: see Satvinder S. Juss and Maurice Sunkin, *Landmark Cases in Public Law* (London: Bloomsbury, 2017) at p. viii.

state investigation may be required into allegations of gross violations of human rights on the territory of another sovereign state in the course of civil litigation. It established that there is an emerging exception to sovereign immunity.[31] The process by which this result was arrived at was not straightforward. It bears consideration, and not least given how difficult the questions of 'justiciability' were for a court of law in deciding an issue which was intensely political and had enormous consequences for the UK's international relations and security. Let us then now consider the Supreme Court decision in *Belhaj.*

"Non-justiciability" and the "act of state" doctrine

The UK Supreme Court handed down its decision in January 2017.[32] Lord Mance explained that "[w]hether an issue is non-justiciable falls to be considered on a case-by-case basis. Considerations both of separation of powers and of the sovereign nature of foreign state or inter-state activities may lead to a conclusion that an issue is non-justiciable in a domestic court ..." In fact, he added that, "... in deciding whether an issue is non-justiciable, English law will have regard to the extent to which the fundamental rights of liberty, access to justice and freedom from torture are engaged by the issues raised ..."[33] There remained limitations, however. As Lord Neuberger explained,[34] the issues that are inappropriate for the courts of the United Kingdom to resolve would be "a challenge to the lawfulness of the act of a foreign state which is of such a nature that a municipal judge cannot or ought not rule on it" so that "the courts of this country will not interpret or question dealings between sovereign states". The "[o]bvious examples are making war and peace, making treaties with foreign sovereigns, and annexations and cessions of territory" has already been recognized in long-established case law.[35] The courts of this country also "will not, as a matter of judicial policy, determine the legality of acts of a foreign government in the conduct of foreign affairs". In the same way, "international treaties and conventions, which have not become incorporated into domestic law by the legislature, cannot be the source of domestic rights or duties and will not be interpreted by our courts". The rationale for this is "that domestic courts should not normally determine issues which are only really appropriate for diplomatic or similar channels".[36] Such a rule

31 See the judgment of the Supreme Court in *Belhaj & Anor v Straw & Ors* (Rev 1) [2017] UKSC 3 and also Lloyd-Jones LJ in *Belhaj v Straw* [2014] EWCA Civ 1394 at 114–121.

32 *Belhaj & Anor v Straw & Ors* (Rev 1) [2017] UKSC 3 (17 January 2017), URL: www.bailii.org/uk/cases/UKSC/2017/3.html.

33 Ibid., at para. 11(iv)(c)

34 Ibid., at para. 123.

35 Here Lord Neuberger referred to Lord Pearson's judgment in *Nissan v Attorney General* [1970] 237, which, however, concerned a Crown act of state, but where the remark was none the less equally apposite to the foreign act of state doctrine.

36 Lord Neuberger here referred to *Shergill v Khaira* [2015] AC 359 paras 40 and 42.

> is based on judicial self-restraint, in that it applies to issues which judges decide that they should abstain from resolving .... It is purely based on common law, and therefore has no international law basis, although ... its application (unsurprisingly) can be heavily influenced by international law.[37]

A seminal case in Australia may well have guided the UK Supreme Court in coming to the decision that it did contrary to what had been determined in the Court of Appeal below. This concerned a claim by Mr Habib, an Australian citizen, that Australian officials had committed various torts – including misfeasance in public office and indirect infliction of harm by aiding and abetting, and counselling – in his torture and ill-treatment by agents of a foreign government while he was in Pakistan, Egypt, Afghanistan and Guantanamo Bay. The issue before the Court was whether Mr Habib's case should be dismissed on the grounds that his claims were not justiciable, since their resolution would require a determination of whether agents of foreign states had acted unlawfully within the territories of those foreign states. The issue was decided within the framework of the Australian Constitution, and what is interesting is how Jagot J., in delivering the leading judgment in the Federal Court of Australia, held[38] that the modern cases on the foreign act of state doctrine "do not support a conclusion that the act of state doctrine prevents an Australian court from scrutinising the alleged acts of Australian officials overseas in breach of peremptory norms of international law to which effect has been given by Australian laws having extra-territorial application". The decision was cited with approval by the Supreme Court in Belhaj.[39] This is just as well because in his critique of the first-instance judgment of Simon J. in the High Court, Samuel Shepson had pointedly remarked that "[i]t is open to question ... why the Australian court found the act of state doctrine to be no barrier to jurisdiction and the British court found otherwise, given that both courts cited the other's jurisprudence, and both came from the same legal tradition".[40]

In the Supreme Court, Lord Sumption[41] explained Mr Belhaj's background pointing out how, as a Libyan national, "[i]n 2004 he was the leader of the Libyan Islamic Fighting Group, an organisation opposed to the government of Colonel Gaddafi" .This organization "is alleged to have been a terrorist organisation at the relevant time" but with the US and UK switching sides to topple Gaddafi, the reference to this as a "terrorist" organization may well have been

37 Ibid., at para. 151.

38 Ibid., at para. 114.

39 See Lord Sumption in *Belhaj & Anor v Straw & Ors (Rev 1)* [2017] UKSC 3. at para. 265.

40 Samuel Shepson, "Jurisdiction in Complicity Cases: Rendition and Refoulement in Domestic and International Courts", *Columbia Journal of International Law* (2015, vol. 53, pp. 701–751) at p. 737.

41 *Belhaj & Anor v Straw & Ors (Rev 1)* [2017] UKSC 3. Lord Sumption's detailed and comprehensive judgment appears at paras 175–285, with whom Lord Hughes agreed. What follows below is drawn from para. 177 of Lord Sumption's judgment.

overlooked a decade later when the US sought his abduction and rendition. In fact, "[h]e led an attempted uprising against the Gaddafi regime in 1998, and fled the country when it was suppressed". His wife, Mrs Boudchar, however, was a Moroccan national.

For, the UK Supreme Court, the question was whether the "act of state" doctrine would stand in the way of holding the perpetrators of human rights violations to account simply because foreign states were principally involved. Lord Sumption explained that "[t]he English decisions have rarely tried to articulate the policy on which the foreign act of state doctrine is based and have never done so comprehensively" but that there is "what is commonly called 'comity'" which is "an awareness that the courts of the United Kingdom are an organ of the United Kingdom" and as "Like any other organ of the United Kingdom, the courts must respect the sovereignty and autonomy of other states".[42]

However, it is as well to notes that critics of the foreign act of state doctrine have long found fault with it. In the UK Supreme Court, Lord Mance recounted how Dr Francis Mann had in his 1986 book *Foreign Affairs in English Courts*[43] written that,

> Public policy dominates one of the most difficult and most perplexing topics which, in the field of foreign affairs, may face the municipal judge in England: the doctrine of the foreign act of State displays in every respect such uncertainty and confusion and rests on so slippery a basis that its application becomes a matter of speculation.[44]

Lord Neuberger for his part observed of the doctrine that it "has all the advantages and disadvantages of a principle that has been developed on a case by case basis by judges over the centuries".[45] However, as Matthew Nicholson has pointed out, "[v]ague and undefined legal doctrines that are nevertheless determinative present a paradox; how can doctrines whose content, scope and application are uncertain lead to a legal judgment?"[46] The doctrine is almost universally regarded as uncertain in nature, scope and application, and Matthew Alderton summed it up well when he noted how,

> Common law judges have historically taken an indifferent, and at times outwardly hostile, view to the examination of issues with "international significance" in

42 At para 225

43 F. A. Mann, Foreign Affairs in English Courts (Oxford: Oxford University Press, 1986) where he uses this description in the introduction to the chapter entitled "The Foreign Act of State". This has since been published in the Oxford Scholarship Online in March 2012 and is available at www.oxfordscholarship.com/view/10.1093/acprof:oso/9780198255642.001.0001/acprof-9780198255642.

44 Lord Mance in *Belhaj & Anor v Straw & Ors (Rev 1) [2017] UKSC 3* at para. 33.

45 Ibid., at para. 118.

46 Matthew Nicholson, "The Political Unconscious of the English Foreign Act of State and Non-Justiciability Doctrine(s)" *Int'L & Comp. Law Quarterly* (Volume 64, Issue 4, pp. 743–781) at p. 744.

> domestic courts. The reluctance of the judiciary to adjudicate upon such issues is founded on what are considered the axiomatic principles of state sovereignty, the separation of powers and the comity of nations. In sum, it has been the case that the judiciary has traditionally abstained from adjudicating upon issues which may impact upon the relations between states—that being the duty and province of the executive arm of government. Although the foundations of this practice are ostensibly sound, the judicial application of these principles to cases that contain complex factual and legal questions of a transnational nature often creates confusion and leads to inconsistent decision-making.[47]

Perram J., for example, in the seminal Australian decision on the subject, neatly describes how "beyond the certainty that the (doctrine) exists there is little clarity as to what constitutes it".[48]

In *Rahmatullah (No 2)*, decided at the same time as *Belhaj*, Lord Sumption had explained that, "'[n]on-justiciability' is a treacherous word, partly because of its lack of definition, and partly because it is commonly used as a portmanteau term encompassing a number of different legal principles with different incidents".[49] He went onto say how "[s]trictly speaking, … it should be reserved[50] for cases where an issue is said to be inherently unsuitable for judicial determination by reason only of its subject matter".[51] The results of this innovative way of

47 Matthew Alderton, Matthew, "The Act of State Doctrine: Questions of Validity and Abstention from Underhill to Habib", *Melbourne Journal of International Law* (2011, Vol. 12, Issue 1); see Introduction online at www5.austlii.edu.au/au/journals/MelbJIL/2011/1.html.

48 Perram J. in *Habib v Commonwealth* [2010] FCAFC 12 at para. 38.

49 *Rahmatullah (No 2) v Ministry of Defence & Anor (Rev 1)* [2017] UKSC 1 (17 January 2017).

50 In this, Lord Sumption drew upon recent jurisprudence in *Shergill v Khaira* [2015] AC 359 (at para. 41).

51 The examples that Lord Sumption then gave were where there are no juridical standards by which to determine it, as in *Buttes Gas and Oil Co v Hammer (No 3)* [1982] AC 888; or because its determination is not within the constitutional competence of the courts, for example because it would trespass on Parliamentary privilege, as in *Prebble v Television New Zealand Ltd* [1995] 1 AC 321 (Lord Sumption at para. 79 of *Belhaj*). All of these, as he explained, "are mandatory rules of public policy, originating in the law's recognition of the separation of powers between different organs of the state. They define the limits of the court's jurisdiction or juridical competence." However, there was also in Lord Sumption view a second category of cases where "there are other principles, also originating in the separation of powers and described as principles of non-justiciability, which do not go to the court's jurisdiction or competence but to the existence or scope of legal rights". An example here was *R (Campaign for Nuclear Disarmament) v Prime Minister* [2002] EWHC 2777 (Admin), where "the court proceeded on the footing that it had both jurisdiction and competence to determine whether a resolution of the United Nations Security Council authorised military operations against Iraq, but declined to do so because, among other reasons, there were no relevant 'rights, interests under domestic law': paras 14–15, 36". Lord Sumption in this regard was clear, however, in stating that, "I venture

thinking about where the courts should exercise judicial restraint and where they should be judicially active are already plain to see. It means that rigid doctrinal interpretation of an act of state will not be allowed to impede state accountability for human rights violations.[52] In a recent case requiring the interpretation of international law, but which involved also the exercise of individual contractual rights, Blair J. held that "[t]he principle of deference has no application where the English court is required to determine the contents of international law as part of a determination of English law rights, here whether an English law contract is voidable".[53] In fact, as he explained, "[n]on-justiciability may be dis-applied on grounds of public policy where there is a violation of peremptory public international law, permitting no derogation (i.e. *jus cogens*). This was applied in *Belhaj* to the case of unlawful rendition".

So much so that the distinction between "justiciable" and "non-justiciable" is now to all intents and purposes collapsed where the state acts unlawfully and where fundamental rights are infringed. This is clear from Blair J. in *The Law Debenture Trust Corporation* case which concerned "the relevant rule of international law" in that case, namely "the prohibition on the threat or use of force: see Art. 2(4) of the UN Charter which prohibits the threat and use of force", leading Blair J. to declare that "[t]hreats of the unlawful use of force by Russia against Ukraine during 2013 are just as clearly proscribed as the unlawful use of force subsequently".[54]

Whether the foreign act of state doctrine is a result of what Paul Daly has described as the "so-called 'political question' doctrines" such that "[n]o definition has common currency, which makes discussion difficult and increases the risk of attacking a straw man",[55] or whether, as has been suggested by Collins, it is to do with "what may be described as sensitivity to foreign policy interests, and certainly not deference to the views or objectives of the executive",[56] the reality is that learned opinion has up to now been divided as to its proper foundation. This is perhaps unsurprising given that the doctrine's shortcomings date back to its

to suggest that if domestic law rights, interests or duties had been engaged, the court would not have regarded the issues as non-justiciable" (Lord Sumption at para. 79 of *Belhaj*).

52 See Samuel Shepson, "Jurisdiction in Complicity Cases: Rendition and Refoulement in Domestic and International Courts", Law (2015) 53 (3) *Columbia Journal of Transnational Law*.

53 *The Law Debenture Trust Corporation PLC v Ukraine, Represented By the Minister of Finance of Ukraine Acting Upon the Instructions* (Blair J. at para. 242, where he drew upon *Shergill v Khaira* [2015] AC 359 at para 43.

54 Mr. Justice Blair in *The Law Debenture Trust Corporation PLC v Ukraine, Represented By the Minister of Finance of Ukraine Acting Upon the Instructions of the Cabinet of Ministers of Ukraine (Rev 1)* [2017] EWHC 655 (Comm) (29 March 2017) at para. 245.

55 Paul Daly, "Justiciability and the 'Political Question' Doctrine", *Public Law* (2010, January, pp. 160–178) at p. 160.

56 Lawrence Collins, "Foreign Relations and the Judiciary", *Int'l & Comp. Law Quarterly* (Vol. 51, July 2002, pp. 485–510) at p. 510.

inception in *Buttes Gas*,[57] a case that raised a whole series of boundary and other international and inter-state law issues arising from a dispute about the extent of the territorial waters of the emirate of Sharjah around the island of Abu Musa in the Persian Gulf. Lord Wilberforce in enunciating the principle that "the courts will not adjudicate upon acts done abroad by virtue of sovereign authority"[58] drew upon the US Supreme Court's decisions in *Underhill v Hernandez*[59] and *Oetjen v Central Leather Co*,[60] which provided the foundation for the act of state doctrine in the United States and which he had cited with approval at".[61] Such a statement was at the expense of principles of judicial competency and the doctrine of separation of powers. In *Buttes Gas*, Lord Wilberforce had "quoted i*n extenso* from a letter written by the Legal Adviser to the US Department of State" that

> issues relating to disputed territorial jurisdiction should be analysed by reference to "the so-called Act of State doctrine which is traditionally limited to governmental action within the territory of the respective state", and arguing that judicial self-restraint "rather follows from the general notion that national courts should not assume the functions of arbiters of territorial conflicts between third powers even in the context of a dispute between private parties" (p 936B-C). In essence, this was the argument that Lord Wilberforce accepted.[62]

Writing in 2002, Lawrence Collins observed summed up the position thus:

> The idea that some matters are simply not justiciable is not one which comes easily to lawyers and judges. But in the field of foreign affairs it is an idea which has gained much currency as a result of constitutional doctrine in the United States, and as a result of its adoption by the House of Lords in the *Buttes Gas* case.[63]

The question in *Belhaj*, however, was whether the "act of state" doctrine could be applied to the violation of fundamental human rights, such as acts of torture.

Belhaj in January 2017 in the UK Supreme Court did not overlook the constitutional limits on the court's competence where foreign states are involved. Indeed, Lord Sumption took great care to explain how even a private law cause of action would fail if it engaged the dealings between foreign states. In his words,[64] "English courts will not adjudicate on the lawfulness of the extraterritorial acts of

57 *Buttes Gas and Oil Co v Hammer (No 3)* [1982] AC 888.
58 Ibid., at pp. 933–934.
59 *Underhill v Hernandez* 168 US 250 (1897).
60 *Oetjen v Central Leather Co* 246 US 297 (1918).
61 Per Lord Sumption at para. 219 of Belhaj
62 Per Lord Mance in *Belhaj* at para. 57.
63 Lawrence Collins, "Foreign Relations and the Judiciary", *Int'l & Comp. Law Quarterly* (Vol. 51, July 2002, pp. 485–510) at p. 497.
64 Ibid., at para. 234.

foreign states in their dealings with other states or the subjects of other states". This is because "once such acts are classified as acts of state, an English court regards them as being done on the plane of international law, and their lawfulness can be judged only by that law". Lord Sumption emphasized that "[i]t is not for an English domestic court to apply international law to the relations between states, since it cannot give rise to private rights or obligations". Moreover, it cannot be the case that the "sovereign acts of a foreign state" can be subjected "to its own rules of municipal law or (by the same token) to the municipal law of a third country". In fact, even if there was "a recognised a private law cause of action", and it "disclosed a justiciable claim of right" it would still fail in a municipal court if "the cause of action was seen to depend on the dealings between sovereign states", because "the court would decline to treat it as being governed by private law at all". What this meant for present purposes was that,

> [i]f a foreign state deploys force in international space or on the territory of another state, it would be extraordinary for an English court to treat these operations as mere private law torts giving rise to civil liabilities for personal injury, trespass, conversion, and the like.

He explained that "[t]his is not for reasons peculiar to armed conflict, which is no more than an ill-defined extreme of inter-state relations" because "[t]he rule is altogether more general ..."[65] This means that "once the acts alleged are such as to bring the issues into the 'area of international dispute' the act of state doctrine is engaged".[66] The upshot of this, as subsequently explained by Blair J. in *The Law Debenture Trust Case* in 2017, is "that there is no single criterion for non-justiciability, which falls to be considered on a case-by-case basis, where the issue concerns dealings between sovereign states".[67]

This, however, is a far cry from a domestic court tolerating torture by its own state officials. As Lord Sumption explained,[68] "[t]he purpose of the foreign act of state doctrine is to preclude challenges to the legality or validity of the sovereign acts of foreign states". But, "[i]t is not to protect English parties from liability for their role in it". Although, this "[i]n itself, ... would not prevent them from taking incidental advantage of the foreign act of state doctrine" and indeed this was known to have happened in a case where British officials took advantage of the doctrine when they assisted in military action overseas by a foreign sovereign,[69] the stark reality was that "torture is different". Torture was "by definition an act of

65 Here Lord Sumption referred to Lord Wilberforce in *Buttes Gas* (p 931D-E).

66 Ibid., at para. 234.

67 Mr Justice Blair in *The Law Debenture Trust Corporation PLC v Ukraine, Represented By the Minister of Finance of Ukraine Acting Upon the Instructions of the Cabinet of Ministers of Ukraine (Rev 1)* [2017] EWHC 655 (Comm) (29 March 2017) at para. 282.

68 Lord Sumption, at para. 266.

69 Lord Sumption gave the example of *R (Noor Khan) v Secretary of State for Foreign Affairs* [2012] EWHC 3728 (Admin).

a public official or a person acting in an official capacity".[70] Moreover, the United Kingdom was required under the Torture Convention "to criminalise not only torture (as defined) but acts constituting complicity in torture".[71]

Against this background, Lord Sumption was able to rule[72] how "it would be contrary to the fundamental requirements of justice administered by an English court to apply the foreign act of state doctrine to an allegation of civil liability for complicity in acts of torture by foreign states". This is because

> [r]espect for the autonomy of foreign sovereign states, which is the chief rationale of the foreign act of state doctrine, cannot extend to their involvement in torture, because each of them is bound *erga omnes* and along with the United Kingdom to renounce it as an instrument of national or international policy and to participate in its suppression.

Otherwise, one would have the paradoxical result whereby "the only point of treating torture by foreign states as an act of state would be to exonerate the defendants from liability for complicity". But the fact was that

> [t]he defendants are not foreign states. Nor are they the agents of foreign states. They are or were at the relevant time officials and departments of the British government. They would have no right of their own to claim immunity in English legal proceedings, whether *ratione personae* or *ratione materiae*.[73]

70 Lord Sumption here drew attention to the *Convention against Torture and Other Cruel, Inhuman or Degrading Treatment or Punishment 1984* (hereafter the 'Torture Convention"), Article 1 of which states: "For the purposes of this Convention, the term "torture" means any act by which severe pain or suffering, whether physical or mental, is intentionally inflicted on a person for such purposes as obtaining from him or a third person information or a confession, punishing him for an act he or a third person has committed or is suspected of having committed, or intimidating or coercing him or a third person, or for any reason based on discrimination of any kind, when such pain or suffering is inflicted by or at the instigation of or with the consent or acquiescence of a public official or other person acting in an official capacity. It does not include pain or suffering arising only from, inherent in or incidental to lawful sanctions."

71 Lord Sumption here referred to Article 4 of the Torture Convention which states that: "1. Each State Party shall ensure that all acts of torture are offences under its criminal law. The same shall apply to an attempt to commit torture and to an act by any person which constitutes complicity or participation in torture. 2. Each State Party shall make these offences punishable by appropriate penalties which take into account their grave nature."

72 Lord Sumption at para. 262.

73 Lord Sumption does go onto say that (at para. 262) that, "On the other hand, they would be protected by state immunity in any other jurisdiction, with the result that unless answerable here they would be in the unique position of being immune everywhere in the world. Their exoneration under the foreign act of state doctrine would serve no interest which it is the purpose of the doctrine to protect."

The judgment of the UK Supreme Court in *Belhaj* is consistent with modern judicial trends with respect to what a domestic court can and cannot determine in disputes brought before it. In 2014 the UK Supreme Court had already considered the lawful parameters of a court of law in an entirely different matter in *Shergill.*[74] It explained how under the doctrine of the Separation of Powers an issue is treated beyond the constitutional competence of the courts if, for example, it involves certain transactions of foreign states, "although the boundaries of the category of 'transactions' of states which will engage the doctrine now are a good deal less clear today than they seemed to be forty years ago". The constitutional limits of the court's competence are "as against that of the executive in matters directly affecting the United Kingdom's relations with foreign states".[75]

Conclusion

Belhaj brings to its logical conclusion the shift that has been taking place, as observed by Aileen Kavanagh, from strict non-justiciability to "variable intensity of review in light of the overall context of the case, where the courts will strive to the constitutionally appropriate degree of restraint in that context".[76] This is best epitomized by the decision in *Belmarsh,*[77] which as she explained represented an emphatic rejection of "a completely hands-off approach"[78] to judicial review. *Belhaj,* decided thirteen years later, has helped confirm Kavanagh's early observations of a new judicial approach that limits the remit of judicial no-go areas and heightens executive accountability where substantive constitutional values are at stake. *Belhaj* goes further still because it subjects the relevant foreign "act of state" to close scrutiny from the outset and avoids the courts having to overlook the judicial determination of individual rights violations arising from international state transactions, which an absolute doctrinal reading of an "act of state" would otherwise produce. As McGoldrick explains, what the courts have done is to signal their intent to invoke domestic standards of public policy to uphold fundamental domestic legal values, even where the area of action is abroad, so that "[t]he Courts are exercising a more intense review over international law issues if they can find a domestic foothold for doing so".[79] McGoldrick puts it well that the

74 *Shergill & Ors v Khaira & Ors* [2014] UKSC 33 (11 June 2014) (available at www.bailii.org/uk/cases/UKSC/2014/33.html). For a discussion, see Satvinder Juss, "Back to the Future: Justiciability, Religion, and the Figment of 'Judicial No-Man's Land'" [2016] *Public Law*, April, pp. 198–206..

75 Ibid., at para. 42.

76 Aileen Kavanagh, "Constitutionalism, Counterterrorism, and the Courts: Changes in the British Constitutional Landscape", *International Journal of Constitutional Law* (2011, Vol. 9, No. 1, pp. 172–199) at pp. 183–184.

77 *A and Others v. Secretary of State for the Home Department* [2004] UKHL 56.

78 Aileen Kavanagh, "Constitutionalism, Counterterrorism, and the Courts: Changes in the British Constitutional Landscape", *International Journal of Constitutional Law* (2011, Vol. 9, No. 1, pp. 172–199) at p. 183.

79 Dominic McGoldrick observes a judicial trend in favour of justiciability and a shift in focus to the degree and intensity of the review exercised. On this view, that trend is

elimination of judicial "no-go areas" is in this way consonant with the rule of law, and what should be the proper judicial function of a court of law, in a contemporary constitutional democracy, so that "[t]he modern jurisprudential trend in relation to acts and decisions of the UK executive is to prefer an analysis of issues by reference to relative institutional competence or variable degrees of deference or weight rather than to non-justiciability".[80] The doctrine of state immunity, as Ernest Banks has shown in his book, often led to an ill-informed reliance upon it by claimants, and this has been accompanied by an unpredictability about the doctrine's judicial invocation.[81] This is what makes the decision in *Belhaj* so significant because it is to be best viewed within an evolving progressive constitutional framework in which the judiciary has been increasingly emboldened, as Daly has observed, to find matters justiciable.[82] In *Shergill*,[83] the Supreme Court justices held that religious matters are justiciable, despite the long-held view that they are incapable of being subject to objective assessment by the courts. As I have elsewhere commented, the court in *Shergill* finds theology to be a legitimate matter of discussion, provided that what the court is deciding are not questions of theology, but issues of individual rights and interests.[84] Displacing the view that inherently religious matters fall outside the proper judicial function, the court held instead that they may be justiciable where subjecting them to review will answer "a matter of disputed legal right".[85]

In fact, the decision in *Belhaj* follows logically and inexorably from *A(FC)*, which concerned the issue of whether the court could receive evidence which has or may have been procured by torture inflicted, in order to obtain evidence, by officials of a foreign state *without* the complicity of the British authorities.[86] In that case Lord Hoffman was clear that "[t]he use of torture is dishonourable. It corrupts and degrades the state which uses it and the legal system which accepts it"[87] and that "the rejection of torture by the common law has a special iconic

shaped and supported by respect for human rights and the rule of law; see Dominic McGoldrick, "The Boundaries of Justiciability", *The International and Comparative Law Quarterly* (October 2010, Vol. 59, pp. 981–1019) at p.1016

80 Ibid., 1018.

81 Ernest Banks, *The State Immunity Controversy in International Law: Private Suits Against Sovereign States in Domestic Courts* (Heidelberg: Springer, 2005).

82 P. Daly, "Justiciability and the 'Political Question' Doctrine£ (2010) *Public Law*, 160.

83 *Shergill v Khaira* [2014] UKSC 33, per Lord Neuberger, "the court may have to adjudicate upon matters of religious doctrine and practice" (at para. 59).

84 Satvinder S. Juss, "Case Comment, Back to the Future: Justiciability, Religion, and the Figment of 'Judicial No-Man's Land'" (2016) *Public Law* 198.

85 *Shergill & Ors v Khaira & Ors [2014] UKSC 33*, per Lord Neuberger: "This clear line of authority contradicts the idea that a court can treat a religious dispute as non-justiciable where the determination of the dispute is necessary in order to decide a matter of disputed legal right" (at para. 53).

86 *A & Ors v. Secretary of State for the Home Department* [2005] *UKHL* 71 (8 December 2005).

87 Ibid., at para. 82.

importance as the touchstone of a humane and civilised legal system".[88] Curiously, the Secretary of State at that time, as Lord Hoffman noted,

> does not contend … that evidence obtained from third parties by torture in the United Kingdom would also be admissible. He accepts that it would not. But he submits that the exclusionary rule is confined to cases in which the torture has been used by or with the connivance of agents of the United Kingdom …[89]

Belhaj was the case, of course, where torture was undertaken allegedly with the "connivance of agents". The whole point there was that there was an allegation of the complicity of UK officials in foreign torture. Where *Belhaj* goes further than the *A(FC)* case is in rejecting unequivocally Lord Hoffman's *obiter* statement that

> there may be cases in which he [i.e. the Home Secretary] is required to act urgently and cannot afford to be too nice in judging the methods by which the information has been obtained, although I suspect that such cases are less common in practice than in seminars on moral philosophy.[90]

Yet, it is precisely in the area where the Home Secretary "cannot afford to be too nice in judging the methods by which the information has been obtained", to use Lord Hoffman's phrase, that the difficulty lies. In fact, it is questionable whether the principle in *Belhaj* can be applied as a consistent rule of law in all cases of shifting allegiances of Western governments engaged in protecting national security. One need only look at the recognition of this difficulty in *Kamoka*,[91] a case of five other Libyans that arose in late 2017. They claimed damages for detention by the Home Secretary pending their appeals against the decision to deport them. The judge, Flaux LJ, noted how they "have been at all material times members or associates of the Libyan Islamic Fighting Group ('LIFG') formed in the 1990s in opposition to the regime of Colonel Qadhafi" and how subsequently "[t]hey had all sought asylum in the United Kingdom".[92] Flaux LJ referred to the shifting allegiances of the UK government, making friends out of sworn enemies in the Middle East, so that

> [f]ollowing the 9/11 terrorist attacks, the UK government formed an increasingly close relationship with the Qadhafi regime. It was only in

88 Ibid., at para. 83.
89 Ibid., at para. 89.
90 Ibid., at para. 93.
91 *Kamoka & Ors v Security Service & Ors* [2017] EWCA Civ 1665 (25 October 2017), URL: www.bailii.org/ew/cases/EWCA/Civ/2017/1665.html.
92 Ibid. at para. 3. They had brought a claim damages against the various defendants "for the torts of false imprisonment, trespass (to person and property) and misfeasance in public office" (para. 1).

> October 2005, during that period of rapprochement with the regime, that the LIFG was proscribed as a terrorist organisation in the United Kingdom.[93]

As he explained,

> [t]he genesis of the present claims was documentation obtained from the archives of the Libyan intelligence service after the fall of the Qadhafi regime during the uprising in the autumn of 2011. Those documents ... are relied upon as showing the extent to which the UK Security Services had knowledge of and complicity in the unlawful conduct (including torture and extraordinary rendition) of the Libyan Security Services and other foreign state agencies.[94]

His Lordship went on to say that

> [a]n important aspect of their case against the various respondents is that the UK Security Services actively assisted the United States intelligence agencies in the unlawful rendition to Libya of a number of detainees alleged to be members of the LIFG, in particular, Messrs Belhaj and Al Saadi.[95]

Given this judicial recognition of the "political" question involved, with the involvement of another sovereign country, it is remarkable that the UK Supreme Court eventually reached the decision that they did.

In this, *Belhaj* clearly demonstrates a decisive shift to a muscular approach to overseeing national security, at precisely the time when terrorism concerns are most heightened, such as to imply a judicial obligation to uphold fundamental freedoms rooted in the Magna Carta. It makes clear that national security considerations by and in themselves do not suggest a policy of judicial deference to the executive. The invocation of the foreign act of state doctrine, where torture is exercised, does not trump judicial redress in the regular courts. *Belhaj* is a reminder to all those officials wishing to operate "on the dark side" that the absolute prohibition on torture is a *jus cogens* of international law, so that any evidence obtained by torture will be treated as offensive to the common law.[96] This is so even where the subject matter is politically sensitive and the accompanying notions

93 Ibid., at para. 4.
94 Ibid, at para. 6.
95 Ibid., at para. 7.
96 See, generally, *A v Secretary of State for the Home Department* [2004] UKHL 56. As Lady Hale said (at para. 237): "Democracy values each person equally. In most respects, this means that the will of the majority must prevail. But valuing each person equally also means that the will of the majority cannot prevail if it is inconsistent with the equal rights of minorities." As Her Ladyship (at para. 238) continued: "No one has the right to be an international terrorist. But substitute 'black', 'disabled, 'female', 'gay', or any other similar adjective for 'foreign' before 'suspected international terrorist' and ask whether it would be justifiable to take power to lock up that group but not the 'white', 'able-bodied', 'male or "straight" suspected international terrorists. The answer is clear."

of sovereign respect and international comity are implicated. The decision in *Belhaj* will no doubt force counter-terrorist officials to comply with UK obligations to respect human rights now more than ever, given the additional layer of judicial reviewability to which the decision in *Belhaj* confirms they will be subject. How far this will be the case remains to be seen.

Yet, for what it's worth, there may be a lesson here for America. Whether it heeds it or not is another matter.

8 Litigation across borders

Enforcing human rights in transnational counterterrorism operations

Jonathan Hafetz

Introduction

The United States' widespread and systematic use of torture after 9/11 is among the most glaring human rights violations by a liberal democratic state in recent history. Responsibility reached the highest levels of the US government. The abuses have been extensively documented, most notably by the Senate Select Committee on Intelligence, which released a 525-page executive summary (Senate Summary) of its report on Central Intelligence Agency (CIA) torture in December 2014. (The full 6,700-page report has yet to be released.) Torture violates clear prohibitions under domestic and international law, triggering duties to prosecute those responsible and provide redress to victims.[1] The US torture program was also closely connected to other grave human rights violations, including enforced disappearance and arbitrary detention.

Yet, those most responsible for designing and implementing the torture program have avoided accountability. Only a handful of low-level officials have faced prosecution, while Congress and the judiciary have failed to provide compensation or other forms of redress to victims. The United States has largely insulated itself from accountability before its regional human rights tribunal (the Inter-American Court of Human Rights), international human rights bodies (the United Nations (UN) Committee against Torture and Human Rights Committee), and the International Criminal Court. While supranational and international institutions may exert pressure on the United States, they have not held US officials to account. Actions brought to prosecute US officials in foreign courts under universal jurisdiction statutes have been dismissed, although some are still pending.

1 See, e.g., Convention against Torture and Other Cruel, Inhuman or Degrading Treatment or Punishment, art. 14, G.A. Res. 39/46, U.N. GAOR, 39th Sess., Supp. No. 51, U.N. Doc. A/39/51 (Dec. 10, 1984) (duty to prosecute and provide effective remedy); International Covenant on Civil and Political Rights, art. 2, Dec. 16, 1966, S. Treaty Doc. No. 95–20 (1978), 999 U.N.T.S. 171 (ICCPR) (obligation to provide effective remedy); Michael P. Scharf, "The Amnesty Exception to the Jurisdiction of the International Criminal Court," 32 *Cornell Int'l L.J.* 507, 515–16 (1999) (duty to prosecute or expedite for torture and other war crimes under the 1949 Geneva Conventions).

The continued impunity for torture and related human rights violations arising out of the extrajudicial detention of terrorism suspects after 9/11 has created an accountability gap. The absence of criminal or civil liability not only contradicts international human rights law's requirement of effective investigation and redress, but also has broader ramifications. It reinforces the perception that international human rights law and international criminal law are enforced in an uneven manner that protects the interests of the most powerful states.

Other nations participated in the US torture program and engaged in abuses on their own. But the United States remains exceptional in the chasm between the evidence of systematic torture and near complete absence of accountability. Moreover, several countries, including the United Kingdom, Sweden, Canada, and Australia, have provided compensation to former detainees held by the CIA or US military in cases where their own public officials engaged in wrongdoing.[2]

Thus far, the greatest success in closing the accountability gap has been achieved through litigation in supranational human tribunals against other states for their complicity in US torture. In 2012, the European Court of Human Rights (ECtHR, or "Strasbourg Court") issued a judgment against Macedonia, finding it in violation of the European Convention on Human Rights (ECHR) for its role in the torture and enforced disappearance of Khalid El-Masri.[3] In 2014, the ECtHR issued judgments against Poland for similar abuses against two other detainees, Abd al-Rahim al-Nashiri and Abu Zubaydah at secret CIA prisons (also known as black sites).[4] Most recently, in 2016, the ECtHR issued a judgment against Italy for its role in the abduction and rendition of a terrorism suspect from Milan, and its subsequent failure to conduct an effective investigation. All three cases resulted in awards of monetary compensation to the victims. The cases have helped spur litigation against other countries for their participation in US torture and against states for participation in other US-led counterterrorism operations, such as recent actions filed in Germany for Germany's allowing the US to use its military base at Ramstein for targeted killings conducted around the world.

This chapter examines accountability for US torture after 9/11. As the chapter explains, the recent ECtHR rulings illustrate both the opportunities and challenges associated with holding states responsible for human rights violations in a pluralistic system with multiple centers of enforcement. The first part summarizes attempts to hold the United States accountable through criminal prosecutions and civil actions in the United States and internationally. The second part describes the

2 Human Rights Watch, *No More Excuses: A Roadmap to Justice for CIA Torture* 107–08 (2015), www.hrw.org/report/2015/12/01/no-more-excuses/roadmap-justice-cia-torture.

3 *El-Masri v. Former Yugoslav Republic of Macedonia*, 57 Eur. H.R. Rep. 25, (2012).

4 *Al-Nashiri v. Poland* (Judgment), App. No. 2876/11, Eur. Ct. H.R. (2014), http://hudoc.echr.coe.int/sites/eng/pages/search.aspx?i=001-146044; *Husayn (Abu Zubaydah) v. Poland* (Judgment), App. No. 7511/13, Eur. Ct. H.R. (2014), http://hudoc.echr.coe.int/sites/eng/pages/search.aspx?i=001-146047.

recent litigation in the ECtHR that resulted in judgments against Macedonia and Poland for their respective participation in CIA torture. The third part discusses the implications of these cases for future enforcement of human rights in the counterterrorism context.

Accountability for US torture

Accountability in the United States

Domestic criminal prosecution

US law contains multiple criminal prohibitions against torture, including the federal anti-torture statute, enacted to implement US obligations under the Convention Against Torture (CAT), which bars torture committed outside the United States;[5] the Uniform Code of Military Justice (UCMJ), which prohibits torture and other abuse by US military personnel and others to whom the UCMJ applies;[6] and the War Crimes Act of 1996, which prohibits the commission of torture or other war crimes by or against US personnel.[7] Shortly before taking office, however, President Barack Obama famously remarked that the United States must "look forward, as opposed to looking backwards," indicating he would not aggressively pursue criminal liability for torture committed during the Bush administration.[8] When Obama released redacted versions of the Office of Legal Counsel (OLC) torture memos to the public a few months after taking office, he called for "reflection, not retribution," insisting that "nothing will be gained by spending our time and energy laying blame for the past."[9]

Domestic criminal investigations into US torture have accordingly been narrow in scope. In 2009, Attorney General Eric Holder opened a preliminary inquiry into the United States' interrogation of detainees at several unspecified overseas locations.[10] But Holder apparently confined the investigation to cases where officials failed to act "in good-faith and within the scope of the legal guidance" provided by the OLC memoranda.[11] This constraint effectively cordoned off the torture program—and its architects—from potential liability. In June 2011,

5 18 U.S.C. §§ 2340 & 2340A.
6 M. Cherif Bassiouni, "The Institutionalization of Torture under the Bush Administration," 37 *Case W. Res. J. Int'l L.* 389, 393–94 (2006).
7 18 U.S.C. § 2441.
8 George Stephanopoulos, "Obama Leaves Door Open (a Bit) on Prosecuting Bush Officials," *ABC News*, Jan. 11, 2009.
9 Statement by President Obama on Release of OLC Memos, Apr. 16, 2009.
10 Press Release, US Dep't of Justice, "Attorney General Eric Holder Regarding a Preliminary Review into Interrogation of Certain Detainees," Aug. 24, 2009, www.justice.gov/ag/speeches/2009/ag-speech-0908241.html.
11 *Id.*

Holder announced that of the more than 100 prisoners whose treatment had been reviewed in connection with the Justice Department inquiry, only two cases—one involving a prisoner's death in Afghanistan, the other a prisoner's death in Iraq—remained under investigation.[12] The following year, Holder announced the closure of the investigation, stating that no prosecutions would be brought.[13] The release of the Senate Summary on CIA torture prompted calls for a full investigation based on new evidence, including evidence that CIA officials did not rely in "good faith" on advice from the OLC, thus eliminating a potential barrier to prosecution.[14] The Obama administration nonetheless refused to appoint a special prosecutor or conduct a full investigation.[15]

The upshot is that the only person prosecuted in connection with the CIA torture program is former CIA agent John Kiriakou, who was convicted for disclosing the identity of other agents who participated in abusive interrogations, including waterboarding, which Kiriakou had labeled torture during an ABC News interview.[16] Beyond that, only twelve low-level soldiers were court-martialed and convicted of crimes stemming from the mistreatment of detainees at Abu Ghraib in Iraq, and only nonjudicial action was taken against the officers who managed the prison and oversaw interrogations there.[17] No high-ranking military or civilian leader has been prosecuted despite the potential for liability under established doctrines, such as command responsibility, designed to hold superiors responsible for crimes committed by their subordinates that they knew or should have known were being committed, but failed to take reasonable steps to prevent.[18]

12 Scott Shane, "No Charges Filed on Harsh Tactics Used by the C.I.A.," *New York Times*, Aug. 30, 2012.

13 Press Release, Department of Justice, "Statement of Attorney General Holder on Closure of Investigation into the Interrogation of Certain Detainees," Aug. 30, 2012, www.justice.gov/opa/pr/2012/August/12-ag-1067.html.

14 Letter from Amnesty International et al. to Honorable Loretta Lynch, Attorney General, Re: Request for Appointment of a Special Prosecutor for Torture, June 23, 2015, www.hrw.org/news/2015/06/23/human-rights-watch-aclu-amnesty-call-special-prosecutor-torture.

15 Kevin Johnson, "Justice Department Will Not Reopen Torture Inquiry," *USA Today*, Dec. 10, 2014, www.usatoday.com/story/news/politics/2014/12/09/justice-cia-torture/20138065/. See also Statement by the President on the Report of the Senate Select Committee on Intelligence, Dec. 9, 2014, www.whitehouse.gov/the-press-office/2014/12/09/statement-president-report-senate-select-committee-intelligence.

16 Michael S. Schmidt, "Ex-C.I.A. Officer Sentenced to 30 Months in Leak," *New York Times*, Jan. 25, 2013.

17 Robert Bejesky, "The Abu Ghraib Convictions: A Miscarriage of Justice," 32 *Buff. Pub. Int. L.J.* 103, 105 (2014). Of the twelve soldiers, only three served sentences of longer than ten months. Samuel Brenner, "'I am a Bit Sickened': Examining Archetypes of Congressional War Crimes Oversight after My Lai and Abu Ghraib," 205 *Mil. L. Rev.* 1, 68–69 (2010).

18 "Getting Away with Torture? Command Responsibility for the U.S. Abuse of Detainees," 17 *Human Rights Watch* No. 1(G) 1, 2–3 (Apr. 2005), www.hrw.org/reports/2005/us0405/us0405.pdf.

Civil liability and reparations

Numerous civil suits have been filed in US courts seeking compensation for the most controversial policies and practices of the global war on terrorism, including secret detention, torture, and extraordinary rendition (the extrajudicial transfer of an individual to another country for purposes of abusive interrogation). The suits have challenged the treatment of prisoners at the US naval base at Guantanamo, at US-operated detention facilities in Iraq and Afghanistan, and at CIA black sites. Suits against US officials have all been dismissed. The only suits to survive thus far have been those brought against civilian contractors, for their role in abuse of detainees by the military[19] or the CIA.[20] Courts, moreover, have dismissed suits against US officials on justiciability grounds, thus avoiding a determination on the merits of the plaintiffs' torture claims. The dismissals highlight the significant obstacles victims face in obtaining redress for torture and other grave human rights violations committed by US officials in the area of national security and counterterrorism.

The United States has repeatedly invoked the state secrets privilege to bar suits challenging CIA torture. In 2005, Khaled El-Masri, a German citizen seized while traveling in Macedonia and rendered by the CIA to Afghanistan, sued former CIA director George Tenet and other high-ranking US officials. Two years later, five individuals brought suit against Jeppesen Dataplan, Inc., a US corporation, for its role in transporting them among various locations where they were secretly detained and tortured by the CIA. Both suits invoked the Alien Tort Statute, which provides a federal civil remedy to foreign nationals for torture and other well-established violations of international law.[21] Both cases were dismissed under the state secrets privilege based on the risk that information harmful to national security might be disclosed.[22] While the privilege could have been applied more narrowly to specific items of evidence, courts refused to allow the suits to proceed.[23] As the US Court of Appeals for the Ninth Circuit explained in *Jeppesen*,

19 *Al Shimari v. CACI Premier Technology, Inc.*, No. 15–1831 (4th Cir. Oct. 21, 2016) (rejecting the conclusion that allegations of torture and other abuse by civilian contractors necessarily present a nonjusticiable political question to be left to the discretion of the political branches); *Al Shimari v. CACI Premier Technology, Inc.*, 758 F.3d 516 (4th Cir. 2014) (holding that federal courts can consider the claims of foreign nationals under the Alien Tort Statute against a US corporation for its role in torture and other mistreatment of detainees at Abu Ghraib prison in Iraq). *But see Saleh v. Titan Corp.*, 580 F.3d 1, 7 (D.C. Cir. 2009) (dismissing suit against civilian contractors based on doctrine of "battlefield preemption," which bars plaintiffs' claims under state tort law by precluding any civil liability arising out of combat operations).

20 *Salim v. Mitchell*, Civ. No. 15–0286 (E.D. Wash. Apr. 28, 2016) (refusing to dismiss suit against James Mitchell and John ("Bruce") Jessen for their role in designing and implementing the Enhanced Interrogation Program at CIA detention sites after 9/11; rejecting the argument that plaintiffs' claims of torture and other prisoner abuse present a nonjusticiable political question).

21 28 U.S.C. § 1350; *Sosa v. Alvarez-Machain*, 542 U.S. 692 (2004).

22 *Mohammed v. Jeppesen Dataplan, Inc.*, 614 F.3d 1070, 1077 (9th Cir. 2010) (en banc); *El-Masri v. United States*, 479 F.3d 296 (4th Cir. 2007).

23 *Jeppesen Dataplan*, 614 F.3d at 1099 n. 13 (Hawkins, J., dissenting).

the plaintiffs' claims were "so infused with [state] secrets, *any* plausible effort by Jeppesen to defend against them would create an unjustifiable risk of revealing [those] secrets."[24] Both suits were dismissed despite voluminous evidence in the public domain documenting CIA torture and rendition, the capacity of federal courts to address sensitive evidentiary issues, and the absence of any other remedy.[25]

Courts have invoked other doctrines to bar suits for torture against US officials. In *Arar v. Ashcroft*, plaintiff Maher Arar sued multiple government agents, including high-level Justice Department officials, for conspiring to render him from the United States to Syria, where he was detained incommunicado and tortured for nearly a year. Arar sought relief under *Bivens v. Five Unnamed Federal Agents*, a US Supreme Court decision empowering individuals to sue federal officials for violations of their constitutional rights.[26] In a divided opinion, the US Court of Appeals for the Second Circuit rejected Arar's claims based on an exception to *Bivens* where special factors counsel hesitation.[27] Specifically, the court cited the risk of interfering with sensitive matters of foreign relations and national security.[28] It distinguished more routine examples of abuse—such as a prison guard beating an inmate—from those that occur in a context like extraordinary rendition, which "involve[es] ... a complex and rapidly changing legal framework beset with critical legal judgments that have not yet been made, as well as policy choices that are by no means easily reached."[29] Judges have invoked similar rationales in dismissing other *Bivens* suits seeking compensation for US torture, including suits by former enemy combatants held in the United States[30] and at Guantánamo,[31] prisoners held in Afghanistan and Iraq,[32] and two civilian whistleblowers in Iraq.[33] As the US Court of Appeals for the Seventh Circuit explained, courts should not provide a remedy for constitutional violations during counterterrorism operations or armed conflict absent clear instruction from Congress.[34] Immunity doctrines have provided another basis for dismissing suits against US government officials.[35]

US courts have, to be sure, considered claims by detainees challenging their ongoing detention and treatment and afforded some protection in that context. At Guantánamo, for example, the Supreme Court has recognized a constitutional

24 *Id.* at 1088.
25 In *Jeppesen*, the court, apparently pained by its decision in light of the gravity of the violations, pointed to possible remedies that could be created by the executive or legislative branches. *Id.* at 1091–92.
26 *Bivens v. Six Unknown Named Agents*, 403 U.S. 388 (1971).
27 *Arar v. Ashcroft*, 585 F.3d 559 (2d Cir. 2009) (en banc).
28 *Id.* at 575–78.
29 *Id.* at 580.
30 *Lebron v. Rumsfeld*, 670 F.3d 540 (4th Cir. 2012).
31 *Rasul v. Myers*, 563 F.3d 527, 532 n.5 (D.C. Cir. 2009).
32 *Ali v. Rumsfeld*, 649 F.3d 762, 774 (D.C. Cir. 2011)
33 *Vance v. Rumsfeld*, 701 F.3d 193 (7th Cir. 2012) (en banc).
34 *Id.* at 199–200.
35 *Rasul*, 563 F.3d at 529–32; *Ali v. Rumsfeld*, 649 F.3d at 771.

right to habeas corpus[36] and required minimum standards of treatment of all detainees under Common Article 3 of the Geneva Conventions.[37] But courts have denied habeas jurisdiction over other offshore US detention centers, such as the Bagram Airfield Base in Afghanistan, by adopting limits on the extraterritorial application of constitutional rights.[38] Those limits are in tension with the effective control test for jurisdiction widely accepted by human rights tribunals and expert bodies, including the ECtHR,[39] the Human Rights Committee,[40] and the Committee against Torture.[41] More importantly, these habeas challenges address only ongoing violations and can offer only injunctive relief. They do not provide reparations to torture victims and, therefore, cannot fully satisfy the United States' obligations under human rights law.

Further, the United States has failed to provide other forms of reparation beyond compensation. International law generally recognizes that redress for serious violations of international human rights and humanitarian law includes not only compensation, but also restitution, rehabilitation, satisfaction, and guarantees of non-repetition.[42] Reparations should, to the extent possible, wipe out the consequences of the illegal act and reestablish the situation that would likely have existed had the violations not been committed.[43] The United States has failed to provide for rehabilitation for former detainees subjected to torture, focusing instead on future security concerns when detainees are transferred.[44]

For years, the United States denied that it engaged in torture. While President Obama acknowledged the use of torture, he never offered a formal apology to the victims, but instead tempered his criticism of prior abuses with an appeal for

36 *Boumediene v. Bush*, 553 U.S. 723 (2008).

37 *Hamdan v. Rumsfeld*, 548 U.S. 557 (2006).

38 *Al-Maqaleh v. Gates*, 605 F.3d 84 (D.C. Cir. 2010).

39 *Al-Skeini v. United Kingdom*, App. No. 55721/07, Eur. Ct. H.R. ¶ 80 (2011) (discussing the holding of the UK Court of Appeal).

40 U.N. Human Rights Comm., *General Comment No. 31, Nature of the General Legal Obligation Imposed on States Parties to the Covenant*, U.N. Doc. CCPR/C/21/Rev.1/Add.13, P 10 (May 26, 2004).

41 U.N. Committee Against Torture, *Considerations of Reports Submitted by States Parties Under Article 19 of the Convention: Conclusions and Recommendations of the Committee Against Torture: United States*, P 15, U.N. Doc. CAT/C/USA/CO/2 (July 25, 2006).

42 Basic Principles and Guidelines on the Right to a Remedy and Reparation for Victims of Gross Violations of International Human Rights Law and Serious Violations of International Humanitarian Law, U.N. G.A. Res. 60/147, U.N. Doc A/60/147, at Annex P 18. (Dec. 16, 2005).

43 Lisa Magarrell & Lorna Peterson, International Center for Transitional Justice, *After Torture: U.S. Accountability and the Right to Redress* 9 (2010), www.ictj.org/sites/default/files/ICTJ-USA-Right-Redress-2010-English.pdf.

44 See, e.g., Periodic Review of Individuals Detained at Guantánamo Bay Naval Station Pursuant to the Authorization for Use of Military Force, Exec. Order No. 13,567, 76 Fed. Reg. 13,277 (Mar. 10, 2011) (focusing exclusively on future threat posed by Guantanamo detainees—including those subject to torture and other abuse—in determining whether, and under what conditions (if any), a detainee should be transferred).

understanding the pressures US officials faced after the 9/11 attacks.[45] President Obama did issue an executive order in January 2009 designed to prevent the future use of torture,[46] which Congress largely codified in recent legislation.[47] Since torture was already illegal before 9/11, however, some question whether these prophylactic measures will be effective without criminal prosecutions, particularly where individuals who authorized the conduct documented in the Senate Summary and other reports continue defending torture's necessity, effectiveness, and legality.[48] The election of President Donald J. Trump has sharpened these concerns with his continued defense of torture, calls for increasing the number of prisoners at Guantanamo,[49] and support for reviving CIA detentions.[50] While several key members of Trump's cabinet have indicated they do not share all of these views, including on the effectiveness and desirability of torture, Trump's comments cannot be discounted given as presidents typically seek to fulfill their campaign promises.[51]

Regional and international human rights bodies

The United States has largely insulated itself from regional and international human rights bodies as well. The United States has not ratified the American Convention on Human Rights and thus does not recognize the jurisdiction of the Inter-American Court. While the Inter-American Commission on Human Rights (IACHR) may hear cases against the United States, it has no enforcement powers.[52] In 2002, the IACHR imposed precautionary measures (injunctive relief intended to avoid irreparable harm and protect fundamental rights) regarding

45 Josh Gerstein, "Obama: 'We tortured some folks,'" *Politico*, Aug. 2, 2014, www.politico.com/story/2014/08/john-brennan-torture-cia-109654.

46 Executive Order No. 13,491, "Ensuring Lawful Interrogations," 74 Fed. Reg. 4893 (Jan. 27, 2009) (banning the CIA from operating detention facilities or holding detainees, except on transitory basis; mandating that US personnel adhere to the US Army Field Manual on Interrogations; and guaranteeing prompt access by the International Committee of the Red Cross to detainees held under the law of armed conflict).

47 Doug Cassel, "The United States and Human Rights Treaties: Can We Meet Our Commitments," 41 *DEC Hum. Rts.* 5 (Dec. 2015).

48 Letter from Amnesty International et al., *supra* note 14.

49 Carol Rosenberg, "Trump's Guantánamo: Standing by for New 'Bad Dudes,'" *Miami Herald* (Feb. 6, 2017), www.miamiherald.com/news/nation-world/world/americas/guantanamo/article131064654.html.

50 Mark Mazzetti & Charlie Savage, "Leaked Draft of Executive Order Could Revive C.I.A. Prisons," *N.Y. Times* (Jan. 25, 2017), www.nytimes.com/2017/01/25/us/politics/executive-order-leaked-draft-national-security-trump-administration.html; Adam Serwer, "Can Trump Bring Back Torture?" *The Atlantic* (Jan. 26, 2017), www.theatlantic.com/politics/archive/2017/01/trump-torture/514463/.

51 Brian Chang, "How the European Convention on Human Rights Limits Cooperation with the Trump Administration," *Just Security* (Jan. 25, 2017), www.justsecurity.org/36751/european-convention-human-rights-limit-cooperation-trumps-administration/.

52 Kathryn Sikkink, *Reconceptualizing Sovereignty in the Americas: Historical Precursors and Current Practices*, 19 *Hous. J. Int'l L.* 705, 710 n. 22 (1997).

Guantanamo detainees, rejecting US arguments designed to deny the IACHR's jurisdiction and its own legal responsibility.[53] Although the measures were twice extended, they had little impact on US policy.[54]

US treaty obligations do require it to undertake periodic reporting and to defend its policies and actions before human rights expert bodies, such as the Human Rights Committee under the International Covenant on Civil and Political Rights (ICCPR) and the Committee against Torture under the Convention against Torture and Other Cruel, Inhuman or Degrading Treatment or Punishment (CAT).[55] But the US does not accept the competence of these bodies to hear individual claims under the respective treaties. In the past, the United States has defended its refusal to submit to the jurisdiction of human rights bodies by arguing that its domestic legal system effectively implemented the same guarantees.[56] The United States also takes the position that its obligations under article 14 of CAT to provide victims of torture an enforceable right to compensation does not extend to situations of armed conflict. In such situations, the United States maintains, international humanitarian law (IHL) contemplates resolving claims for compensation relating to the treatment of detainees on a state-to-state level.[57] This position provides a further justification for denying reparations for abuses arising out of the global war on terrorism. Additionally, the United States has terminated its acceptance of the jurisdiction of the International Court of Justice (ICJ), where states rather than individuals may bring claims.[58]

International Criminal Court

The United States has sought to immunize its officials from liability before the International Criminal Court (ICC). It has refused to ratify the Rome Statute, effectively foreclosing ICC jurisdiction over US personnel except potentially where a crime occurs on the territory of a member state and that state refers those crimes to the Court.[59] To help foreclose this possibility, the United States has negotiated

53 Organization of American States, Inter-American Commission on Human Rights, Pertinent Parts of Decision on Request for Precautionary Measures, 41 I.L.M. 532 (Inter-Am. C.H.R. 2002).

54 Beth Van Schaack, *The United States Position on the Extraterritorial Application of Human Rights Obligations*, 90 *Int'l L. Stud.* 20, 55–56 (2014).

55 *Id.* at 53.

56 Denise Gilman, "Calling the United States' Bluff: How Sovereign Immunity Undermines the United States' Claim to an Effective Domestic Human Rights System," 95 *Geo. L.J.* 591, 600–03 (2007).

57 Nathalie Weizmann, "State Responsibility and Reparation for Torture as a Violation of IHL," *Just Security* (quoting US position before the UN Committee against Torture in 2014), available at www.justsecurity.org/18232/state-responsibility-reparation-torture-violation-ihl/.

58 Peter Jan Honigsberg, "In Search of a Forum for Families of the Guantánamo Disappeared," 90 *Denv. Univ. L. Rev.* 433, 453–54 (2012).

59 A non-State Party on whose territory a crime has been committed, such as Iraq, could also accept the ICC's jurisdiction on an *ad hoc* basis by lodging a declaration with the Court's Registrar. Rome Statute of the International Criminal Court, July 17, 1998,

a series of bilateral immunity agreements that seek to prevent the ICC from exercising jurisdiction over US nationals by prohibiting another state from sending US nationals to the Court without its consent. The agreements—also called "Article 98" agreements—rely on a provision of the Rome Statute that prevents the ICC from requesting that a State Party surrender an individual to the Court if it would require that Party to act inconsistently with its obligations under an international agreement.[60] In 2002, Congress enacted the American Servicemembers' Protection Act (ASPA), which authorizes the United States to withhold military assistance from States Parties to the ICC that fail to enter into these agreements with the United States that bar those States Parties from surrendering US nationals to the United States.[61] While the Dodd Amendment to the ASPA permits the United States to provide assistance to international efforts to bring to justice high-level foreign officials accused of genocide, war crimes, or crimes against humanity, this exception remains narrow.[62]

The United States has, to be sure, ceased its initial active opposition to the ICC and become more constructively engaged with the Court, including by supporting UN Security Council referrals to the Court (the situations in Darfur and Libya), urging other states to cooperate with the Court in apprehending suspects, and amending the US War Crimes Reward program to include ICC indictees.[63] But this support remains selective and narrowly cabined, and the United States has consistently sought to ensure the Court's accommodation of its interests and preferences.[64]

In late 2014, the ICC Prosecutor indicated that her office is considering whether to pursue an investigation into torture and other serious abuses allegedly committed in Afghanistan between 2003 and 2008, including by US armed forces and intelligence officials. (Afghanistan acceded to the Rome Statute in 2003.) An annual report on the ICC's preliminary examination issued just before the release of the summary of the Senate Summary in December 2014 identified US officials

U.N. Doc. A/Conf. 183/9 (1998), 37 I.L.M. 999, art 12(3). Additionally, the UN Security Council could refer a situation to the ICC, thus creating the possibility for jurisdiction over US personnel. But it is virtually certain that the United States would exercise its veto power to block to allow any such referral.

60 See Lilian V. Faulhaber, Recent Development, *American Servicemembers' Protection Act* of 2002, 40 *Harv. J. on Legis.* 537, 537 (2003). Rome Statute, *supra* note 59, art. 98.

61 22 U.S.C. 7421–7433 (2006) (ASPA).

62 Alex Whiting, "The U.S. Should Not Disengage from the International Criminal Court Following Palestine's Ascension," *Just Security*, Jan. 7, 2015, www.justsecurity.org/18937/u-s-disengage-international-criminal-court-palestine-joins/.

63 Harold Hongju Koh, Legal Advisor, U.S. Dep't of State "International Criminal Justice 5.0," Nov. 8. 2012, www.state.gov/s/l/releases/remarks/200957.htm.

64 See generally David Bosco, *Rough Justice: The International Criminal Court in a World of Power Politics* 173 (2014) (describing how the ICC has constrained itself to operating mainly within "a major-power comfort zone"); Chris Mahony, "The Justice Pivot: U.S. International Criminal Law Influence from Outside the Rome Statute," 46 *Geo. J. Int'l L* 1071 (2015).

as potential targets based on abusive interrogations.[65] In late 2016, the ICC prosecutor announced that there was a reasonable basis to conclude that US soldiers and CIA agents had committed war crimes in Afghanistan, including torture.[66] Yet, despite these developments, the strength of US influence and the relative weakness of the ICC suggests the continued obstacles to the Prosecutor's opening a full investigation or charging US officials with international crimes.

International Court of Justice

The ICJ does not provide a viable avenue for accountability for US torture. The ICJ is the preeminent international court and exercises broad subject-matter jurisdiction.[67] However, only states, and not individuals, can bring claims before the ICJ.[68] Even if another state were to bring suit before the ICJ against the United States for breach of its international legal obligations in the global war on terror, that suit would fail. The United States appended a reservation to its accession to the ICJ statute stating that it would decide what questions of national security the ICJ is competent to decide.[69] The United States also bars other states from bringing a complaint concerning the interpretation or application of the Convention against Torture before the ICJ.[70] Most importantly, the United States withdrew its consent from the compulsory jurisdiction of the ICJ following an adverse ICJ judgment in the case brought by Nicaragua for US support of the contras in their rebellion against the Nicaraguan government during the 1980s.[71]

Universal jurisdiction and prosecutions of US officials in foreign jurisdictions

Given the failure of the United States to investigate or prosecute torture and other war crimes, and the steep obstacles to any international criminal prosecution,

65 Office of the Prosecutor, International Criminal Court, "Report on Preliminary Examination Activities 2014," para. 94, Dec. 2, 2014, www.icc-cpi.int/iccdocs/otp/OTP-Pre-Exam-2014.pdf.

66 Office of the Prosecutor, *Report on Preliminary Examination Activities* 47, Nov. 16, 2016, www.icc-cpi.int/iccdocs/otp/161114-otp-rep-PE_ENG.pdf; Somini Sengupta & Marlise Simons, "U.S. Forces May Have Committed War Crimes in Afghanistan, Prosecutor Says," *N.Y. Times*, Nov. 14, 2016.

67 Alex Glashausser, "What We Must Never Forget When It Is a Treaty We Are Expounding," 73 *U. Cin. L. Rev.* 1243, 1263 (2005).

68 Statute of the International Court of Justice, June 26, 1945, at art 34, para. 1, 59 Stat. 1055, T.S. 993, 3 Bevans 1179.

69 Reservation to the Optional Clause of the ICJ by the United States, 61 Stat. 1218, 1947 WL 25470; Ingrid Detter Frankopan "Extraordinary Rendition and the Law of War," 33 *N.C. J. Int'l L. & Com. Reg.* 657, 683 (2008).

70 Reservations of the US upon accession to the UN Convention Against Torture, http:// untreaty.un.org/ENGLISH/bible/englishinternetbible/partI/chapterIV/treaty14.asp; Craig Forcese, "The Capacity to Protect: Diplomatic Protection of Dual Nationals in the 'War on Terror,'" 17 *Eur. J. Int'l. L.* 369, 392 (2006).

71 United States: Department of State Letter and Statement Concerning Termination of Acceptance of I.C.J. Compulsory Jurisdiction, 24 I.L.M. 1742 (1985).

victims and human rights organizations have pursued criminal actions in several European countries. These cases rely on principles of universal jurisdiction that authorize states to bring perpetrators to justice for the most serious international crimes, including war crimes, torture, and crimes against humanity, regardless of where the crime occurred or the nationality of the perpetrator or victim.[72] Multiple jurisdictions in Europe permit victims and civil society groups to file criminal complaints based on allegations of universal crimes.[73] Since the arrest of former Chilean President Augusto Pinochet in 1998 based on accusations of torture committed in Chile, an increasing number of states, especially in Europe, have enacted some form of universal jurisdiction legislation.[74] Universal jurisdiction nonetheless remains controversial,[75] and several states have narrowed formerly expansive universal jurisdiction statutes.[76] As a result, actions commonly assert a connection to the forum state, such as the nationality of the victims, to satisfy restrictions on the prosecution of universal crimes under that state's domestic law, such as in Spain. The use of universal jurisdiction to pursue claims against US officials for torture in the global war on terror has prompted intense opposition by the United States government and led to the dismissal of most cases brought thus far. While these cases have increased public attention on the US torture program in Europe and potentially discouraged travel in Europe by some US officials for fear of being arrested, they have thus far failed to generate formal legal accountability for post-9/11 abuses.

Actions for US torture have been brought in several countries, including France, Germany, and Spain. In Germany, complaints filed by the Center for Constitutional Rights and other human rights groups in 2004 and 2006 against former Defense Secretary Donald Rumsfeld and other senior US officials for their role in the torture at Abu Ghraib have been dismissed.[77] A third complaint against senior US officials filed by the European Center for Constitutional and Human

72 *Restatement (Third) Foreign Relations Law of the United States*, § 404 (1987); *Princeton Principles on Universal Jurisdiction* 29 (Stephen Macedo ed., 2001).

73 Máximo Langer, "The Diplomacy of Universal Jurisdiction: The Political Branches and the Transnational Prosecution of International Crimes," 105 *Am. J. Int'l L.* 1, 2 (2011). Countries vary on whether victims can initiate proceedings as *partie civile* (as in France and Spain), thus triggering the opening of a criminal investigation, or merely can file the complaint with the prosecutor (as in Germany, Belgium, the Netherlands, and other countries), who then has discretion to initiate an investigation. International Federation for Human Rights, *A Step by Step Approach to the Use of Universal (Criminal) Jurisdiction in Western European States* 13 (2009), www.refworld.org/pdfid/4a2637292.pdf.

74 Human Rights Watch, *No More Excuses, supra* note 2, at 113.

75 Anthony J. Colangelo, "The Legal Limits of Universal Jurisdiction," 47 *U. Va. L. Rev.* 149, 151–52 (2006)

76 Stephen Ratner, Editorial Comment, "Belgium's War Crimes Statute: A Post-Mortem," 97 *Am. J. Int'l L.* 888, 891 (2003) (describing the narrowing of Belgium's universal jurisdiction statute in response to controversy over its use).

77 Center for Constitutional Rights, "Accountability for US Torture: Germany," *CCRJustice.org*, https://ccrjustice.org/home/what-we-do/our-cases/accountability-us-torture-germany (last visited Feb. 23, 2017).

Rights in December 2014 after release of the Senate Summary on CIA torture has yet to be acted on by federal prosecutors.[78] Munich state prosecutors opened a criminal investigation into the rendition and torture of German national Khaled el-Masri by CIA agents, but the German government, which had been warned by the United States about the potential impact on US–German relations, never sought the suspects' arrest or extradition.[79]

Spanish judicial authorities have opened cases into torture and other abuses by US officials. Cases include allegations of abuse of Spanish nationals and residents at Guantanamo and the use of Spanish territory by CIA rendition flights. The cases have all been stayed or dismissed (although appeals are still pending).[80] In France, a Paris district prosecutor dismissed on immunity grounds a criminal complaint filed by civil society groups in anticipation of a visit to Paris by Rumsfeld.[81] An earlier criminal complaint filed on behalf of three French citizens formerly detained at Guantanamo remains under investigation, and a French appeals court recently ordered the lower court in that case to summon former Guantanamo commander US Army General Geoffrey Miller to address allegations of his role in abuses of French citizens at the US detention center.[82] Miller, however, disregarded the subpoena and failed to appear before the court.[83] Plaintiffs are urging the court to issue subpoenas for other US officials.[84]

A number of factors have been cited to justify the state's refusal to proceed in these cases, including: the exercise of prosecutorial discretion; subsidiarity (based on US representations that it was investigating or had investigated the claimed war crimes); the absence of links to the prosecuting country; the lack of cooperation by the United States in gaining access to witnesses and evidence; and the obstacles to obtaining personal jurisdiction over the defendants. In each case, the United States has asserted substantial pressure on the particular European state and warned that exercising universal jurisdiction would harm its relations with the country in question.

78 *Id.*

79 Human Rights Watch, *No More Excuses, supra* note 2, at 120–26.

80 *Id.* at 130–36. An appeal of the dismissal of the criminal complaint filed against several US officials known as the "Bush Six" for aiding and abetting torture is now before the Spanish Constitutional Court. See Center for Constitutional Rights, "Accountability for US Torture: Spain," *CCRJustice.org*, https://ccrjustice.org/home/what-we-do/our-cases/accountability-us-torture-spain (last visited Feb. 23, 2017).

81 "French Prosecutors Throw Out Rumsfeld Torture Case," Reuters (Nov. 23. 2007), www.reuters.com/article/us-france-rights-rumsfeld-idUSL238169520071123.

82 Human Rights Watch, *No More Excuses, supra* note 2, at 126–29.

83 Alex Emmons, "Former Guantánamo Commander Ignores Summons from French Court Probing Torture," *The Intercept* (Mar. 1, 2006), https://theintercept.com/2016/03/01/former-guantanamo-commander-ignores-summons-from-french-court-probing-torture/.

84 Center for Constitutional Rights, "Accountability for U.S. Torture: France," *CCRJustice.org*, https://ccrjustice.org/home/what-we-do/our-cases/accountabili ty-us-torture-france (last visited Feb. 23, 2017).

Only one criminal case has proceeded to trial and judgment: the conviction of twenty-five CIA agents in Italy for their role in the abduction of Egyptian cleric Mustafa Osama Nasr (known as Abu Omar), who was kidnapped in Italy and rendered to Egypt, where he was repeatedly tortured. The case's significance is qualified by the fact that the crimes took place within the European country asserting jurisdiction, the convictions were obtained *in absentia*, and the CIA agents have not been extradited (although European Arrest Warrants, valid only in Europe, appear to have been issued).[85]

It is possible that other cases will go forward. The US failure to take action following the release of the Senate Summary weakens arguments for not proceeding based on subsidiarity. Barriers have been reduced in Germany, which has established a specialized war crimes tribunal empowered to open broad preliminary investigations with little direct link to Germany and limited exercise of prosecutorial discretion.[86] Moreover, even where cases do not go forward, but where arrest warrants are issued, as in Germany, US suspects can be arrested if they travel within Europe.[87] Universal jurisdiction cases will, however, continue to face significant challenges given the strength and determination of US opposition.

The European Court of Human Rights and liability for participation in US torture

The ECtHR has now held three European states (Poland, Macedonia, and Italy) responsible for their respective participation in US torture. The actions—*El-Masri v. Macedonia* (decided in 2012), *Al-Nashiri v. Poland* and *Husayn (Abu Zubaydah) v. Poland* (decided together in 2014), and *Nasr v. Italy* (decided in 2016)—demonstrate the relative strength of human rights protections in the ECtHR system. They also reflect the degree of involvement of European countries in the CIA torture program, which included both hosting CIA-operated black sites and assisting the United States in rendering detainees to countries in secret. Of the fifty-four foreign governments that provided some form of support to the CIA program, twenty-one were located in Europe.[88] These rulings do not adjudicate or establish the state responsibility of the United States. They therefore, cannot hold directly accountability the government most responsible for the illegal conduct. But the decisions nonetheless strengthen accountability in important ways.

85 Human Rights Watch, *No More Excuses, supra* note 2, at 118–20.

86 The prosecutor may exercise discretion now only when a suspect is never likely to come to Germany and where no potential victims and witnesses can be identified in the country. *Id.* at 124.

87 Andreas Schüller & Morenike Fajana, European Center for Constitutional and Human Rights, "Piecing Together the Puzzle: Making US Torturers in Europe Accountable," at 4, Sept. 2014, www.statewatch.org/analyses/no-256-torture-schuller-fajana.pdf.

88 Open Society Justice Initiative, *Globalizing Torture: CIA Secret Detention and Extraordinary Rendition* 6 (2013), www.opensocietyfoundations.org/sites/default/files/globalizing-torture-20120205.pdf.

El-Masri v. Macedonia

The Strasbourg Court's first ruling on the legality of the US torture program involved Khaled El-Masri, the German citizen seized in December 2003 while traveling on vacation in Macedonia. After stopping him at the Macedonia–Serbia border, Macedonian agents took El-Masri to a hotel in Skopje, Macedonia where he was detained, continually interrogated and threatened with death, and prohibited from contacting the German embassy, a lawyer, or his wife.[89] After twenty-three days of captivity, El-Masri was taken blinded and handcuffed to the Skopje airport, where he was beaten, grossly abused (including by being stripped and sodomized with an object), and handed over to the CIA.[90] The CIA rendered El-Masri to Afghanistan, where he was held in a secret prison later identified as the Salt Pit. During four months of captivity, El-Masri was beaten by guards, forced to endure violent and prolonged interrogations, force-fed following a hunger strike, and denied medical treatment.[91] After realizing it had mistaken him for someone else, the United States released El-Masri by leaving him blindfolded on a road near the Macedonia–Serbia border.[92]

In 2009, El-Masri brought suit against Macedonia in the ECtHR for its role in his torture, mistreatment, and arbitrary detention. Prior attempts at accountability had failed or stalled: US courts had dismissed El-Masri's civil suit against CIA officials based on the state secrets privilege;[93] the CIA agents indicted by a German prosecutor had not been arrested;[94] the Inter-American Commission for Human Rights had failed to act in a case filed by El-Masri after communicating the case to the US government for a response; and actions filed in Macedonia had either been dismissed or had failed to advance.[95] Investigations had, however, helped lay the basis for El-Masri's action. A Council of Europe report by Swiss Senator Dick Marty, for example, not only detailed the participation by Council of Europe member states in US secret detentions and renditions, but also declared that such participation was illegal.[96]

In 2012, the Grand Chamber issued a judgment against Macedonia, finding multiple violations of the ECHR: torture and other inhuman and degrading treatment (article 3);[97] arbitrary and unlawful detention (article 5);[98] failure to

89 *El-Masri*, 2012 Eur. Ct. H.R. paras. 17–18.
90 *Id.* paras. 20–22.
91 *Id.* paras. 24–30.
92 *Id.* paras. 31–32.
93 *El-Masri v. United States*, 479 F.3d 296 (4th Cir. 2007).
94 See *supra* text accompanying note 79.
95 *El-Masri*, 2012 Eur. Ct. H.R. at para. 70 (criminal complaint dismissed as unsubstantiated); *id.*at paras. 72–73 (lack of hearings in civil proceedings for damages).
96 Dick Marty, Alleged Secret Detentions in Council of Europe Member States, Parliamentary Assembly Council of Europe (Jan. 22, 2006), http://assembly.coe.int/CommitteeDocs/2006/20060124_Jdoc032006_E.pdf.
97 *El-Masri*, 2012 Eur. Ct. H.R. at para. 223.
98 *Id.* para. 240.

investigate (articles 2, 3, and 5);[99] and the denial of an effective remedy (article 13).[100] It found Macedonia liable both for its complicity in El-Masri's torture and abuse in Macedonia and for exposing El-Masri to the foreseeable risk of additional mistreatment by transferring him to US custody given the United States' known use of enhanced interrogation techniques. The ECtHR ordered Macedonia to pay El-Masri damages of 60,000 euros due to the severity of the violations.[101]

The ECtHR's decision marked the first ruling by a court on the legality of the US torture program.[102] With respect to El-Masri's torture and other abuse, the ECtHR found Macedonia liable for: the cruel and inhuman treatment of El-Masri by Macedonia agents in the Skopje hotel;[103] El-Masri's gross mistreatment at the airport, which the ECtHR said constituted torture and which it attributed to Macedonia because the acts were carried out on its territory and in the presence of its agents who failed to take measures to avoid it;[104] and El-Masri's subsequent torture in Afghanistan because Macedonia transferred El-Masri to CIA custody despite the serious risk he would be tortured and failed to take any steps to prevent it.[105] The ECtHR also found that Macedonia had not investigated adequately credible allegations of torture, resulting in impunity for serious human rights violations.[106] It further ruled that Macedonia had denied El-Masri an effective remedy by failing to conduct an effective criminal investigation or provide for civil remedies.[107]

Al-Nashiri v. Poland *and* Husayn (Abu Zubaydah) v. Poland

In two follow-on cases, *Al-Nashiri v. Poland* and *Husayn (Abu Zubaydah) v. Poland*, the ECtHR ruled in 2014 that Poland had violated multiple provisions of the ECHR for its role in the CIA torture program, principally for helping render the applicants to Poland and then hosting a secret CIA detention center at a military training base on its territory.[108] While in Poland, the men were brutally mistreated. In Poland, US interrogators subjected al-Nashiri to mock executions with a power drill as he stood naked and hooded; threatened to shoot him in the head as he sat shackled; and threatened to bring in his mother and sexually abuse

99 *Id.* paras. 263–65.
100 *Id.* para. 262.
101 *Id.* para. 270.
102 Marta A. Orpiszewska, "*El-Masri v. Former Yugoslav Republic of Macedonia*: Implications for the CIA Extraordinary Rendition Program," *N.C. J. Int'l L. & Comm. Reg.* 1165, 1186 (2014).
103 *El-Masri*, 2012 Eur. Ct. H.R. at paras. 200–04.
104 *Id.* paras. 205–211.
105 *Id.* paras. 212–22.
106 *Id.* paras. 186–94.
107 *Id.* paras. 258–62.
108 *Al-Nashiri v. Poland* (Judgment), App. No. 2876/11, Eur. Ct. H.R. (2014), http://hudoc.echr.coe.int/sites/eng/pages/search.aspx?i=001-146044; *Husayn (Abu Zubaydah) v. Poland* (Judgment), App. No. 7511/13, Eur. Ct. H.R. (2014), http://hudoc.echr.coe.int/sites/eng/pages/search.aspx?i=001-146047.

her in front of him.[109] Interrogators subjected Abu Zubaydah to waterboarding, sleep deprivation, forced nudity, and painful stress positions.[110]

Al-Nashiri and *Husayn* solidify the grounds for detainees to seek redress in the ECtHR against European countries that participated in US torture. (The Grand Chamber's refusal to hear Poland's appeal suggests that the Court believes the central legal questions surrounding member state liability for participation in US torture have been resolved.) The cases also establish state responsibility for hosting a CIA detention site on a state's territory. Further, the Court found an additional violation of the ECHR for transferring the applicants to Guantanamo given the risk the United States would torture them and subject them to unfair trials and the death penalty there.[111] The Court ordered Poland to pay 130,000 euros to Abu Zubaydah and 100,000 euros to Al-Nashiri.

Nasr v. Italy

In a third decision on European participation in the US global war on terrorism, the ECtHR issued a judgment in *Nasr v. Italy* in February 2016 against Italy for its role in the extraordinary rendition of Egyptian cleric Osama Mustafa Hassan Nasr (also known as Abu Omar).[112] The ruling represents a further contribution to the Strasbourg Court's accountability jurisprudence.

Nasr v. Italy concerns one of the most notorious instances of extraordinary rendition. In 2003, Nasr, who had been granted political asylum in Italy, was abducted in broad daylight from a street in Milan and taken to Aviano air base, which is operated by the US Air Force. Nasr was subsequently taken, by way of the United States' Ramstein air base in Germany, to Cairo where he was interrogated by Egyptian intelligence services. Egyptian authorities held Nasr in secret for more than a year and subjected him to repeated torture before releasing him in April 2004. Approximately twenty days after his release—and after submitting a statement to Milan's public prosecutor describing his abuse—Nasr was rearrested and detained without charges. He was released in 2007, but prohibited from leaving Egypt.

The ECtHR ruling centers on Italy's role in Nasr's abduction in Milan, his rendition to Egypt where he faced a real risk of abuse, and its subsequent failure to conduct an effective domestic investigation or to provide any redress. The ECtHR found Italy liable for multiple violations of the ECHR, including article 3 (the

109 *Al-Nashiri*, 2014 Eur. Ct. H.R. paras. 98–102.

110 *Husayn* 2014 Eur. Ct. H.R. paras. 100–07

111 *Al-Nashiri*, 2014 Eur. Ct. H.R. at para. 390. Both men remain imprisoned at Guantanamo. Al-Nashiri is currently facing charges before a military commission for his role in the 2000 bombings of the USS *Cole*, and faces the death penalty in those proceedings. Zubaydah remains in law-of-war detention as an alleged member of al Qaeda, although he too could potentially be charged before a military commission.

112 *Nasr v. Italy*, ECtHR, Feb. 23, 2016. An English-language summary of ruling is available at www.justsecurity.org/wp content/uploads/2016/03/Nasr-Ghali-v.-Italy-Summary-Feb2016-Abu-Omar.pdf.

prohibition on inhuman or degrading treatment); article 5 (the right to liberty and security); and article 13 (the right to an adequate remedy). It ordered Italy to pay 70,000 euros to Nasr and 15,000 euros to his wife, Nabila Ghali, for the suffering and anguish caused by her husband's enforced disappearance.[113]

The Milan public prosecutor had previously investigated and prosecuted twenty-five CIA officers, including the agency's Milan station chief, Robert Seldon Lady, and seven Italian military intelligence officers, for aiding and abetting in Nasr's abduction and rendition.[114] The US government strenuously opposed the prosecution, warning that it would harm US–Italian relations, and the Italian government successfully challenged much of the evidence on the grounds it could jeopardize national security.[115] The trial court convicted twenty-two CIA agents *in absentia* and gave them prison sentences of between six to nine years; a Milan appeals court upheld the convictions and overturned the acquittals of the other three US defendants.[116] Italy's highest court, however, overturned the conviction of five of the Italian military intelligence agents based on state secrecy grounds.[117] The Italian government has refused to seek the extradition of the convicted US nationals.[118]

Significance of the ECtHR rulings

The ECtHR rulings in *El-Masri, Al-Nashiri/Husayn*, and *Nasr* are important for several reasons. The ruling advance accountability norms; deter participation by states in human rights violations in transnational counterterrorism operations; serve as a potential catalyst for other accountability efforts; and reinforce the cosmopolitan foundation of international human rights law. The rulings also suggest, however, the limitations of establishing liability for participation in torture and other abuses without holding the primary perpetrators responsible.

Norm development

The ECtHR's rulings in *El-Masri, Al-Nashiri/Husayn*, and *Nasr* advance accountability norms in several ways. In *El-Masri*, the Court strengthened the principle of state responsibility for human right violations. The Court found Macedonia responsible for El-Masri's mistreatment for cooperating with the CIA on Macedonia's territory and under *non-refoulement* principles for his rendition to Afghanistan where it knew or should have known of the risk of torture.[119]

113 *Id.*
114 Rachel Donadio, "Italy Convicts 23 Americans for C.I.A. Renditions," *New York Times*, Nov. 4, 2009.
115 Human Rights Watch, *No More Excuses, supra* note 2, at 118.
116 *Id.* at 119.
117 *Id.*
118 *Id.* at 118.
119 *El-Masri*, 2012 Eur. Ct. H.R. at para. 176.

In connection with the state's failure to investigate, the Court emphasized in *El-Masri* "the great importance of the present case not only for [El-Masri] and his family, but also for other victims of similar crimes and the general public, who had the right to know what had happened."[120] It thus tied a state's duty to investigate to a right to truth and to a broader norm of anti-impunity.[121] Once the state had been made aware of the allegations, the Court said, it "should have endeavored to undertake an adequate investigation in order to prevent any appearance of impunity in respect of certain acts." Such an investigation was "essential in maintaining public confidence in [a state's] adherence to the rule of law and in preventing any appearance of collusion in or tolerance of unlawful acts."[122] While other tribunals had previously articulated this basic principle,[123] *El-Masri* demonstrated the principle's applicability to transnational counterterrorism operations involving multiple states.

Additionally, *El-Masri* addressed challenges of enforcing these protections given the level of state secrecy. It ruled that "where events at issue lie within the exclusive knowledge of [state] authorities," a showing of government custody by the applicant shifts the burden to the state to provide a "plausible and satisfactory explanation as to what happened" and that "strong presumptions of fact" will arise where injury and death occur during detention.[124] The decision thus establishes procedures to secure the protection of fundamental rights under the ECHR. More broadly, it signals a decreased tolerance by international courts for excessive deference to state secrecy.[125]

The ECtHR's rulings in *Al-Nashiri/Husayn* and *Nasr* reinforce state responsibility for participation in abuses committed during the global war on terrorism. In particular, *Nasr* advances the jurisprudence surrounding a state's duty to conduct an effective domestic investigation into torture. The Strasbourg Court noted that Italian courts had conducted a detailed investigation and that the evidence disregarded by Italy's highest court on grounds of state secrecy had been sufficient to convict the five Italian military intelligence defendants.[126] It further observed that because the evidence inculpating those defendants had been widely available in the press and on the Internet, the court's invocation of state secrecy doctrine was not only unpersuasive, but also calculated to secure impunity for the defendants.[127] Further, the Strasbourg Court noted that the Italian government had never sought the extradition of the convicted CIA agents. As result, the court ruled that

120 *Id.* para. 190.

121 Ruti Teitel, "Transitional Justice and Judicial Activism," 48 *Cornell Int'l L.J.* 385, 409–10 (2015).

122 *El-Masri*, 2012 Eur. Ct. H.R. at para. 192.

123 See, e.g., *Velásquez-Rodríguez v. Honduras*, Judgment of July 29, 1988, Inter-Am. Ct. H.R. (ser. C) No. 4, para. 166 (1988). See also Teitel, *supra* note 121, at 409–10.

124 *Velásquez-Rodríguez v. Honduras*, para. 152–53.

125 Alexandra H. Perina, "Black Holes and Secrets: The Impact of Covert Action on International Law," 53 *Columbia J. Transnat'l L.* 507, 554 (2015).

126 *Nasr, supra* note 112 (Summary at 4).

127 *Id.*

despite the efforts of Italian investigators and judges, who had identified the responsible individuals and secured their convictions, the domestic proceedings failed to satisfy article 3 of the European Convention, due to the failure of the executive. *Nasr* thus imposes liability not only where a state takes *no* steps towards a genuine domestic investigation and prosecution (as in *El-Masri* and *Al-Nashiri/Husayn*), but also where efforts by a state's judges and prosecutors are thwarted by government agencies' sweeping assertions of state secrecy.

Deterring state participation by raising the cost of human rights violations

A growing body of literature examines how international human rights law affects (or fails to affect) the behavior of repressive states.[128] Less attention has been paid to how human rights law affects the conduct of liberal democracies that are more commonly associated with promoting human rights obligations than breaching them but who also can seek to circumvent those obligations in the area of national security. The ECtHR rulings provide a window into assessing the costs states faces in participating in human rights violations in this context.

The deterrent effect of judgments of international tribunals is a matter of debate even in the area of criminal prosecutions, where that effect is typically greater than in civil cases.[129] The ECtHR decisions should nevertheless discourage future cooperation by Council of Europe member states in transnational terrorism operations that flout human rights protections in the manner that the CIA torture program did. The Obama administration halted secret detention and took steps to bring US interrogation methods in compliance with international law.[130] The ECtHR judgments—and associated stigma—will make it more difficult to obtain assistance from European partners should the Trump administration (or a future administration) seek to revive prior practices or otherwise attempt to skirt existing prohibitions. The rulings, in short, impose financial and reputational costs on states that allows their territory to be used by another government seeking to avoid responsibility for human rights violations, as European states allowed their territory to be used by the United States after 9/11.

The decisions also discourage the type of interstate cooperation often necessary to conduct illegal cross-border counterterrorism operations by increasing the stigma and public relations costs associated of breaching legal commitments.[131] The negative public reaction to lawbreaking tends to be higher in democratic

128 See, e.g., Beth A. Simmons, "Reflections on Mobilizing for Human Rights," 44 *N.Y. U. J. Int'l L. & Pol.* 729, 732–35 (2012).

129 Anita Ramasastry, "Corporate Complicity: From Nuremberg to Rangoon; An Examination of Forced Labor Cases and their Impact on the Liability of Multinational Corporations," 20 *Berkeley J. Int'l L.* 91, 153 (2002).

130 See *supra* note 46 and accompanying text.

131 ***See generally*** James D. Fearon, "Signaling Foreign Policy Interests: Tying Hands Versus Sinking Costs," 41 J. *Conflict Resolution* 68 (1997); Kenneth A Schultz, "Looking for Audience Costs," 45 *J. Conflict Resolution* 32 (2001).

societies with strong rule-of-law traditions.[132] The ECtHR rulings, as formal and binding judgments, heighten the audience costs associated with torture, even if they do not impose direct legal consequences on the United States. The rulings thus increase the media and political pressures on Council of Europe member states— particularly on those states that value their respect for human rights—not to submit to requests by another administration to assist in the torture and extra-judicial detention of terrorism suspects.[133]

Potential catalyst for further accountability

The Strasbourg Court rulings serve as a possible catalyst for other accountability efforts. The rulings support attempts by civil society groups to force the United States to reopen a criminal investigation into CIA torture by providing judicial findings and determinations of illegality. They also provide additional legal and political cover for the ICC to open a criminal investigation within an available jurisdictional opening, such as Afghanistan. By reinforcing the perception of the United States as an outlier for its failure to offer any form of accountability, the rulings strengthen demands for reparations. The rulings will make it more difficult for the United States to maintain its present stance and will diminish its credibility if it persists in blocking all accountability.

In addition, the rulings pave the way for victims to hold other countries responsible for their roles in the CIA torture program. Similar cases have been brought against Romania and Lithuania in the ECtHR and against Djibouti in the African Commission on Human and Peoples' Rights.[134] Such suits not only provide a potential remedy to victims, but also help diffuse anti-impunity norms to other countries and jurisdictions.

The United States, moreover, continues to rely on the assistance of European partners for other counterterrorism operations, from electronic surveillance to armed drone strikes. In 2015, family members of individuals killed in drone strikes in Yemen filed suit in administrative court in Cologne, Germany, claiming that Germany violated the right to life under its constitution by allowing the United States access to its air base at Ramstein to facilitate drone strikes in Yemen. The court dismissed the suit, ruling that Germany could not cancel agreements with foreign troops stationed on its territory where it would jeopardize vital and authorized geopolitical and defense-related interests.[135] The court also, however,

132 Tim Wood, "Reinforcing Participatory Governance through International Human Rights Obligations of Political Parties," 28 *Harv. Hum. Rts. J.* 147, 202 (2015).

133 Chang, *supra* note 51.

134 Meg Satterthwaite, "European Court Urged to 'Break Conspiracy of Silence' on CIA Black Sites in Europe," *Just Security*, Dec. 4, 2013, www.justsecurity.org/4095/eal-nashiri-zubaydah-poland-echr-cia/.

135 Ryan Devereux, "German Court Turns Down Lawsuit But Leaves Door Open to Others," *The Intercept*, May 30, 2015, https://theintercept.com/2015/05/30/german-court-turns-drone-lawsuit-leaves-door-open-others/.

granted plaintiffs permission to seek an immediate appeal.[136] A separate administrative action and criminal complaint were subsequently filed in Germany raising similar legal challenges to a drone strike that killed a Somali herdsman who was not the intended target of the attack.[137]

Other actions in the ECtHR and in the Court of Justice of the European Union (CJEU) challenge the adequacy of intelligence sharing arrangements between Europe and the United States. While they vary in respects, these actions primarily assert that intelligence-sharing arrangements between European countries and the United States do not adequately protect the privacy and data protection rights of Europeans.[138] Evidence that this intelligence is being used to facilitate torture, extrajudicial detention, and other severe human rights abuses by the United States will likely strengthen challenges to data sharing arrangements and further deter European cooperation with US counterterrorism efforts.[139]

The ECtHR's rulings in *El-Masri, Al-Nashiri/Husayn*, and *Nasr* thus suggest the potential for developing principles of state responsibility in the context of targeted killing and data-sharing agreements. They strengthen arguments for holding countries in Europe responsible for cooperating in counterterrorism operations that violate human rights protections. The decisions also suggest how such cooperation can lead to the imposition of new legal and policy constraints on European states.

Cosmopolitanism and human rights

In addition to strengthening the accountability norms surrounding torture, the ECtHR decisions reinforce the cosmopolitan foundations of international human rights law. Cosmopolitanism posits that all individuals, despite their differences, belong to a single community based on a shared morality.[140] The central premise of moral cosmopolitanism—cosmopolitanism's most common strand—"is that every human being has a global stature as an ultimate unit of moral concern."[141]

136 Kate Connolly, "Court Dismisses the Claim of German Complicity in Yemini Drone Killing," *Guardian*, May 27, 2015, www.theguardian.com/world/2015/may/27/court-dismisses-yemeni-claim-german-complicity-drone-killings.

137 Open Society Justice Initiative, "New Legal Action Targets Germany's Support for U. S. Drone Strikes," Sept. 21, 2015, www.opensocietyfoundations.org/press-releases/new-legal-action-targets-germanys-support-us-drone-strikes.

138 *Digital Rights Ireland v. Commission*, Case T-670/16 (CJEU) (challenge to EU–US Privacy Shield data transfer agreement, which permits transfer of EU citizens' data to the United States); *La Quadrature du Net and Others v. Commission*, Case T-738/16 (same); *10 Human Rights Organizations v. United Kingdom*, (Eur. Ct. Hum. Rts.) (challenge by human rights organizations to surveillance activities of the British government in connection with the US bulk data collection programs).

139 Chang, *supra* note 51.

140 Solon Solomon, "Judicial Regionalism's Thwarting of UN Security Council Chapter VII Punitive Cosmopolitanism: Measuring the Effects on International Jurisdictional Constitutionalism," 16 *German L.J.* 261, 261 (2015).

141 Thomas W. Pogge, "Cosmopolitanism and Sovereignty," 103 *Ethics* 48, 49 (1992)

The notion of a universal citizenship based on shared values underpins the duties owed to individuals under human rights law.[142]

The CIA torture program—a transnational operation conducted in secret and outside legal constraints—constituted a direct assault on the cosmopolitan ideal of human rights. Multiple states assisted in the enforced disappearance and abuse of individuals through their respective security apparatus. As suspected terrorists—and, more concretely, suspected sources of actionable intelligence—a group of "high value detainees" were effectively denied status as individual moral units and, consequently, stripped of all legal protections, including the categorical prohibition against torture. The collective nature of the CIA torture program—in which multiple states participated even if one state was primarily responsible—exposed the fragility of a shared conception of the universality of rights.

Revelations about the nature and scope of CIA torture have placed pressure on accountability mechanisms to demonstrate the continued vitality of moral cosmopolitanism and the human rights protections that underlie it. Legal judgments, even if only civil in nature, help counter the notion that states can exclude certain individuals from universal protections based on security considerations. By preventing complete impunity and holding states responsible for their participation in grave violations of international law, the ECtHR rulings reinforce the cosmopolitan underpinnings of human rights. Even if the accountability they provide remains partial, the rulings help prevent the creation of security-based exceptions to principles of moral cosmopolitanism.

The limitations of a pluralistic system of strong versus weak human rights enforcement

The Strasbourg Court rulings in *El-Masri, Al-Nashiri/Husayn*, and *Nasr* supply a remedy to victims of torture and other grave human rights violations who would otherwise lack one. They also illustrate the opportunities of pluralistic international system in which multiple fora exist to enforce rights that are universal in nature but applied unevenly and selectively.

Yet, the opportunities provided by this model of rights enforcement can also produce gaps of its own. An individual's ability to recover depends on establishing a jurisdictional hook in a country or regional human rights system with a strong accountability backbone. The victims in *El-Masri, Al-Nashiri/Husayn*, and *Nasr* ultimately obtained redress because a state subject to ECtHR jurisdiction had participated in the CIA torture program. Victims unable to establish the needed nexus to Europe's human rights system—including those held in CIA detention centers in Africa, Asia, and the Middle East or rendered by the United States to locally operated detention sites in those regions—remain outside the orbit of the

142 Andrew M. Bell, "Using Force against the 'Weapons of the Weak': Examining a Chemical-Biological Weapons Usage Criterion for Unilateral Humanitarian Intervention under the Responsibility to Protect," 22 *Cardozo J. Int'l & Comp. L.* 261, 299 (2014).

ECtHR rulings, absent some basis to attribute responsibility to a Council of Europe member state. Restrictions placed on universal jurisdiction statutes by European countries that require a nexus to the forum state, such as the nationality (or physical residence) of the perpetrator or victim, impose similar requirements.[143] The pragmatic search for remedies where and when they are available strengthens the overall fabric of accountability by developing norms and increasing financial and reputational costs for violators. But channeling litigation towards strong accountability fora also highlights the uneven enforcement of universal norms across borders.

Another consequence of strengthening principles of state responsibility in one system, such as the ECtHR, is to skew the search for partners in transnational counterterrorism operations towards states without strong domestic or regional human rights enforcement systems. A government looking beyond its borders for assistance in detention or interrogations will seek to identify states where extralegal actions will remain immune from accountability mechanisms. Even if the dominant state (the United States in the CIA torture program) cannot be held liable, it will face scrutiny and endure negative attention when its operations are subjected to review by another jurisdiction (ECtHR review of Macedonia, Poland, and Italy's participation in CIA torture). Powerful countries, such as the United States, will have greater incentives to seek partners that offer greater security from exposure. To that extent, realizing the full impact of rulings by strong accountability bodies such as the ECtHR depends on their extension to weaker accountability jurisdictions.

Conclusion

One of the main contributions of the ECtHR's rulings in *El-Masri*, *Al-Nashiri/Husayn*, and *Nasr* is to apply principles of state responsibility to cross-border counterterrorism operations. The decisions chip away at the wall of impunity erected by the primary rights violator by targeting those countries that assisted it and holding them responsible in a system of relatively strong human rights enforcement. The rulings also maintain human rights protections in the face of claims of state secrecy, stimulate other efforts to achieve accountability, and help deter states from facilitating or allowing human rights violations on their territory in the future. They support a political climate in which, as German Chancellor Angela Merkel warned President Trump, continued cooperation in counterterrorism operations between the two countries depends on US respect for shared values, including the rule of law and human dignity.[144]

143 Máximo Langer, "The Diplomacy of Universal Jurisdiction: The Political Branches and the Transnational Prosecution of International Crimes," 105 *Am. J. Int'l L.* 1, 31 (2011) (amendments to Belgium's universal jurisdiction statute); *id.* at 41 (amendments to Spain's universal jurisdiction statute).

144 Anthony Faiola, "Angela Merkel Congratulates Donald Trump—Kind Of," *Washington Post* (Nov. 9, 2016).

This model of rights enforcement nonetheless has limitations. It provides remedies only to those victims who can establish a foothold in a strong human rights jurisdiction. It does not, moreover, provide full redress even to the victims who receive compensation. Reparation includes not only damages but also satisfaction, and there has been only limited acknowledgment by the primary violator of its responsibility. Holding accountable only those states complicit in torture or other grave rights violations, but not the primary violator, deviates from international criminal justice's emphasis on pursuing those most responsible for atrocities.[145] Additionally, it weakens the expressive value of judgments that otherwise advance the norm of anti-impunity by reinforcing the perception—long expressed by realist critiques in international relations theory—that the most powerful states remain capable of shielding themselves from the consequences of violating norms designed to apply to all.

In sum, while the Strasbourg Court rulings on the US torture program advance important human rights objectives, they highlight the continued potential for accountability gaps in a system predicated on universal norms but weakened by limited and selective enforcement.

145 Margaret M. de Guzman, "Choosing to Prosecute: Expressive Selection at the International Criminal Court," 33 *Mich. J. Int'l L.* 265, 285 (2012) (citing ICC OTP, Criteria for Selection of Situations and Cases 1–7 (2006))

9 Groups and the war on terror

Steven R. Morrison and Annique M. Lockard

Introduction

In this chapter, we offer the following thesis: large-scale threats, whether they are real or perceived, generate greater law-enforcement attention to groups, whether the groups are real or perceived, and less attention to the actual culpability of individuals, which results in increased error rates in the connected fields of criminal law and human rights.

We establish this thesis in four steps. First, we set forth a meaning of the term "human rights." Second, we provide a normative theory of groups in American criminal law, specifically counterterrorism. Third, we provide a short history of group-theoretic criminal law in the United States, from the war against the labor movement in the nineteenth century, to the suppression of anti-war speech in World War I and World War II, and finally to the post-9/11 war on terror. Finally, we look ahead optimistically by summarizing the advent of membership crime concepts, their connection to and conflict with the substantive First Amendment, and recent philosophical inquiry into collective action and responsibility. Our final contention is that American criminal law and, by extension, much of worldwide human rights, is on the cusp of a revolution away from individualistic norms of accountability and toward a more nuanced understanding of collectives. This revolution will produce systems of criminal law and of human rights that are more responsive to collective realities. Responsibility for crimes and atrocities will be more accurately assigned, and governmental responses more measured, producing fewer human rights violations.

Defining human rights

While declarations and conventions of human rights and much of Western political philosophy share substantial overlap in their often-voluminous definitions of human rights, a universal definition has not been agreed upon.[1] For clarification,

1 Brian M. Awe, Religion in the EU: Using Modified Public Reason to Define European Human Rights, 10 *German L.J.* 1439, 1457–58 (2009); Erin E. Douglas, The Struggle for Human Rights Versus Stability: The Chinese Communist Party and Western Values Clash, 29 *Denv. J. Int'l L. & Pol'y* 151, 151–60 (2001).

then, this chapter adopts a dual definition of human rights. First, it adopts a "First Amendment" set of rights, which includes the freedom of speech/expression, association, assembly, and religion. Second, it adopts a "criminal due process" set, which includes a number of premises necessary for a fair criminal process, and a general mandate to ensure fair process on case-by-case bases. Both the First Amendment and criminal due process sets are generally accepted and understood worldwide.[2]

A normative theory of groups in American criminal law

In times of low threat perception, states attend to individuals' rights on a relatively equal basis with law enforcement's mandate to protect the public safety. In turn, large-scale threats result in discounting the importance of individuals' rights and elevating public safety to a priority. The primary way that these entities do so is to rely increasingly on proxy indicators of intent to commit some future crime.

The use of proxies effectively expands the perceived size and population of suspected groups as well as criminal liability based on association with those groups. Efforts to protect public safety result in targeting not only dangerous criminals and their associates, but their associates' associates and beyond, sweeping up people who may have some affinity with criminal groups but who do not share the criminal intent normally necessary to investigate, charge, convict, or, in some cases, kill.

This occurs in two ways. First, the government defines the scope of terrorist group membership broadly, sweeping within its ambit a normatively troubling number of people. This is an evident result of the United States material support statute.[3] While it prohibits providing obvious forms of material support to terrorists, courts have interpreted it to prohibit providing medical support,[4] training groups to pursue their goals peacefully,[5] funding the social welfare aims of terrorist groups,[6] speaking in favor of groups as a member,[7] and independently translating religious documents that might help a group.[8] The tension between the freedom to associate and the imputation of group criminality persists[9] as the government

2 For First Amendment set rights, see *The Universal Declaration of Human Rights*, Preamble; Art. 18; Art. 20, sec. 1; *European Convention on Human Rights*, Art. 9; Art. 10; Art. 11; *International Covenant on Civil and Political Rights*, Art. 18, sec. 1; Art. 19, sec. 2; Art. 21; Art. 22, sec. 1; for criminal due process set rights, see *The Universal Declaration of Human Rights*, Art. 3; Art. 5; Art. 9–11; *European Convention on Human Rights*, Art. 3; Art. 5–7; *International Covenant on Civil and Political Rights*, Part III, Art. 6, sec. 1; Part III, Art. 7; Part III, Art. 9.

3 18 U.S.C.A. §§ 2339A, 2239B (West 2013).

4 *United States v. Shah*, 474 F. Supp. 2d 492 (S.D.N.Y 2007).

5 *Holder v. Humanitarian Law Project*, 130 S. Ct. 2705 (2010).

6 *United States v. El-Mezain*, 664 F.3d 467 (5th Cir. 2011).

7 *United States v. Taleb-Jedi*, 566 F. Supp. 2d 157 (E.D.N.Y. 2008).

8 Second Superseding Indictment, *United States v. Mehanna*, No. 1:09-cr-10017-GAO, 2010 WL 2516469 (D. Mass. June 17, 2010).

9 Liat Levanon, Criminal Prohibitions on Membership in Terrorist Organizations, 15 *New Crim. L. Rev.* 224, 274 (2012).

imputes criminal intent to law-abiding people who may, for some reason, associate with terrorists.[10]

Second, the government becomes more imaginative in its law-enforcement efforts, engaging in pseudo-entrapment,[11] charging people with sometimes tenuous conspiracy crimes,[12] charging people with pretextual crimes such as false statements[13] and immigration crimes,[14] and arresting people as material witnesses.[15]

This behavior generates three outcomes that expand the scope of the perceived threat and confirm and reinforce the threat's supposed reality. First, the group at issue assumes evidentiary value independent of its individual actors.[16] This means

10 National Commission on Terrorist Attacks upon the United States, Monograph on Terrorist Financing: Staff Report to the Commission 9 (2004), available at http://govinfo.library.unt.edu/911/staff_statements/911_TerrFin_ Monograph.pdf.

11 See Superseding Indictment, *United States v. Aref*, No. 1:04-cr-402-TJM, 2005 WL 5785418 (N.D.N.Y. Sept. 29, 2005); *United States v. Cromitie*, 727 F.3d 194, 199 (2d. Cir. 2013); *United States v. El-Hindi*, 2009 WL 1373268, at *1 (N.D. Ohio May 15, 2009); see also Stephen Downs, From Sting to Frame-Up: The Case of Yassin Aref, *Washington Report on Middle East Affairs*, Sept./Oct. 2007, at 19–20, 23; Rick Perlstein, How FBI Entrapment is Inventing 'Terrorists'—and Letting Bad Guys Off the Hook, *Rolling Stone*, May 15, 2012, www.rollingstone.com/politics/blogs/national-affairs/how-fbi-entrapment-is-inventing-terrorists-and-letting-bad-guy s-off-the-hook-20120515; Eric Schmitt & Charlie Savage, In U.S. Sting Operations, Questions of Entrapment, *New York. Times*, Nov. 29, 2010, www.nytimes.com/2010/11/30/us/politics/30fbi.html? pagewanted=all; Mary Beth Sheridan, Hardball Tactics in an Era of Threats, *Washington Post*, Sept. 3, 2006, www.washingtonpost.com/wp-dyn/content/article/2006/09/02/AR2006090201096.html; Carl Strock, Verdict Is In, but Who Is Really Guilty?, *Daily Gazette*, Oct. 12, 2006, www.nepajac.org/Strock.htm.

12 See *United States v. Al-Arian*, 514 F.3d 1184 (11th Cir. 2008); *United States v. Kassir*, 2009 WL 2913651, *3 (S.D.N.Y.); *United States v. Amawi*, 552 F. Supp. 2d 669, 671 (N.D. Ohio 2008); *United States v. Al-Arian*, 280 F. Supp. 2d 1345 (M.D. Fla. 2003); Indictment, *United States v. Shah*, 474 F. Supp. 2d 492 (S.D.N.Y 2007); Hiroshi Fukurai & Richard Krooth, The Establishment of All-Citizen Juries as a Key Component of Mexico's Judicial Reform: Cross-National Analyses of Lay Judge Participation and the Search for Mexico's Judicial Sovereignty, 16 *Tex. Hisp. J. L. & Pol'y* 37, 43 (2010).

13 See *Indictment, United States v. Mehanna* at 1, 1:09-cr-10017-GAO, 2009 WL 3400492 (D. Mass. Jan. 15, 2009) (in material support case, original charge was for making a false statement).

14 See *Turkmen v. Ashcroft*, 915 F. Supp. 2d 314, 325 (E.D.N.Y. 2013).

15 *Ashcroft v. Al-Kidd*, 131 S. Ct. 2074 (2011); *United States v. Awadallah*, 349 F.3d 42, 44 (2d Cir. 2003); *United States v. Warsame*, 488 F. Supp. 2d 846, 861 (D. Minn. 2007); *United States v. Padilla*, 2006 WL 3678567, *11 (S.D. Fla. 2006); *Mayfield v. Gonzales*, 2005 WL 1801679, *7 (D. Or. 2005); *Higazy v. Millennium Hotel and Resorts*, 346 F. Supp. 2d 430, 439 (S.D.N.Y. 2004); Sahar F. Aziz, Caught in a Preventive Dragnet: Selective Counterterrorism in a Post-9/11 America, 47 *Gonz. L. Rev.* 429, 439 (2012).

16 See In re Terrorist Attacks on September 11, 2001, 714 F.3d 659, 667 (2d Cir. 2013); *Am. Freedom Def. Initiative v. Suburban Mobility Auth. for Reg'l Transp.*, 698 F.3d 885, 889 (6th Cir. 2012); *United States v. Elmardoudi*, 611 F. Supp. 2d 864, 866 (N.D. Iowa 2007).

that evidence of the group's dangerous nature is often admissible against an individual.[17] There is little that defendants can do to rebut this evidence; in the face of a suspicious connection to a dangerous group, it is difficult for a defendant to argue the absence of criminal intent. When the charge is conspiracy, evidentiary rules disadvantage the defendant,[18] and where pseudo-entrapment or pretextual charges are in play, there may be factual guilt, but not the level of culpability that the charge's connotations imply.

Second, the expansion of the perceived threat encourages law enforcement to engage in intense data mining and group targeting.[19] This re-maps, or re-imagines, the linked world, which discerns people and conduct not along traditional evidentiary lines (can a crime be proven?), constitutional lines (is conduct protected?), or normative lines (should a person be prosecuted?), but pursuant to an expansive public safety imperative.

Third, based on this re-mapping, law enforcement increasingly focuses on the groups and communities from which prior suspects have come.[20] Because the 9/11 attackers were defined along religious-political lines, subsequent suspects overwhelmingly are Muslims who express discontent with American policies (but probably at a rate no higher than the American population at large).[21]

Group-theoretic criminal law in United States history

This theory of groups in times of high threat perception is not unique to the post-9/11 war on terror. Early nineteenth-century labor combinations were treated under a pro-business theory that "viewed any combination of workingmen to improve their wages or conditions as a criminal conspiracy."[22] Courts used conspiracy law to regulate labor.[23] They were hostile to the labor

17 *Yates v. United States*, 354 U.S. 298, 339 (1957); Second Superseding Indictment at 17, *United States v. Mehanna*, No. 1:09-cr-10017-GAO, 2010 WL 2516469 (D. Mass. June 17, 2010).

18 *Krulewitch v. United States*, 336 U.S. 440, 446 (1949) (Jackson, J., concurring); *United States v. Dellosantos*, 649 F.3d 109, 125 (1st Cir. 2011); Note, The Objects of Criminal Conspiracy Inadequacies of State Law, 68 *Harv. L. Rev.* 1056, 1056 (1955).

19 Lucas McMillen, Eye on Islam: Judicial Scrutiny Along the Religious Profiling/Suspect Description Reliance Spectrum, 4 U. *St. Thomas L.J.* 114, 116 (2006); see Margaret B. Hoppin, Overly Intimate Surveillance: Why Emergent Public Health Surveillance Programs Deserve Strict Scrutiny Under the Fourteenth Amendment, 87 *N.Y.U. L. Rev.* 1950, 1970 (2012).

20 See Andrew Guthrie Ferguson, Crime Mapping and the Fourth Amendment: Redrawing "High-Crime Areas," 63 *Hastings L.J.* 179, 229 (2011).

21 Charles Kurzman, *Muslim-American Terrorism in the Decade Since 9/11 2* (2012); Richard Cohen, Rep. Peter King's Hearings on Islamic Radicalization: Fuel for the Bigots, *Washington Post*, Mar. 8, 2011, www.washingtonpost.com/wpdyn/content/article/2011/03/07/AR2011030703896.html.

22 See *Anthony Woodiwiss, Rights v. Conspiracy* 21 (1990).

23 Victoria C. Hattam, Labor Visions and State Power 30 (1993); John T. Nockleby, Two Theories of Competition in the Early 19th Century Labor Cases, 38 *Am. J. Legal Hist.* 452, 471 (1994).

movement[24] and interested in preventing the restraint of trade, not ensuring unions' right to organize.[25] It took until 1842 for the Massachusetts Supreme Judicial Court to become the first court to declare that labor unions were not per se criminal conspiracies.[26] However, the possibility of "riotous" and therefore illegal and dangerous combinations occupied judges' minds, both before and after the rise of labor unions.[27] Indeed, it came to be accepted that labor unions were "always dangerous to the public peace and to private security."[28]

In 1887, for example, the Connecticut Supreme Court in *State v. Glidden* reflected the national fear of labor groups considering the legality of a conspiracy of workmen to boycott their company and distribute flyers.[29] Affirming the conviction, the court wrote that if boycotts and the distribution of flyers were deemed legal, "[t]he end would be anarchy, pure and simple."[30] An Ohio Superior Court seconded this, writing that union boycott activities amount to conspiracy, and "[would] be restrained and punished by the criminal law as oppressive to the individual, injurious to the prosperity of the community, and subversive of the peace and good order of society."[31]

The nineteenth-century labor movement evolved into the anti-war movement during World War I, led primarily by the Socialist Party.[32] With the country's entry into the war, a regime of censorship, investigation of dissident groups, and the use of conspiracy law followed. Within one year of its passage, 250 people had been convicted under the Espionage Act.[33]

While the Espionage Act, Sedition Act, and a collection of other war enabling acts were being used to charge dissidents with conspiracy at the federal level, a concomitant system of membership crime was emerging state by state. Criminal syndicalism statutes began to be passed around 1917, and by 1921 the majority of the states had nearly identical laws.[34] The Oregon Supreme Court likened these laws to conspiracy and criticized both.[35]

24 See Deborah A. Ballam, Commentary: The Law as a Constitutive Force for Change: The Impact of the Judiciary on Labor Law History, 32 *Am. Bus. L.J.* 125, 126–27 (1994).
25 Woodiwiss, *supra* note 22, at 42–43.
26 Commonwealth v. Hunt, 45 Mass. 111, 134 (Mass. 1842); Woodiwiss, *supra* note 22, at 23.
27 See Hattam, *supra* note 23, at 49; see also Woodiwiss, *supra* note 22, at 87.
28 *Commonwealth v. Judd*, 2 Mass. 329, 337 (Mass. 1807).
29 *State v. Glidden*, 8 A. 890, 891–92 (Conn. 1887).
30 *Id.* at 895. According to the court, "[t]he exercise of irresponsible power by men, like the taste of human blood by tigers, creates an unappeasable appetite for more." *Id.* at 894.
31 *Id.* at 674 (quoting *Crump v. Commonwealth*, 6 S.E. 620, 628 (Va. 1888)).
32 James Weinstein, Anti-War Sentiment and the Socialist Party, 1917–1918, 74 *Pol. Sci. Quarterly* 215, 216 (1959).
33 Stephen M. Feldman, *Free Expression and Democracy in America: A History* 246, 248 (2008), Chicago: University of Chicago Press.
34 *People v. Lloyd*, 304 Ill. 23, 106 (1922) (Carter, J., dissenting).
35 *State v. Boloff*, 138 Or. 568, 646–47 (1932) (describing both as "the quicksands of the law … subject to the shifting public sentiment which always affects matters pertaining to government").

The California syndicalism act, passed in 1919 and applied more than any other state's syndicalism law, was representative. It prohibited advocating or teaching any doctrine of industrial or political change based on sabotage or other criminal acts,[36] as well as membership in organizations that advocated or taught such doctrines.[37]

Syndicalism statutes therefore criminalized mere membership in any group that advocated—but did not necessarily commit or plan to commit—unlawful acts as a means of accomplishing industrial or political change. These membership crime statutes went further than conspiracy because their proof was membership only, and required no agreement or overt act.[38]

Most of the syndicalism defendants were Industrial Workers of the World (IWW) members and were charged not for any violent actions they took, but for being members of a group presumed to be criminal, single-minded, and cohesive.[39] This meant that only a defendant's membership in the IWW needed to be proven at trial. The mens rea required of the defendant varied from case to case, but was always set at a low bar.[40] Courts took judicial notice of the IWW's criminal nature, relieving the prosecution of having to prove an element of the crime. They also seated jurors who were prejudiced against the IWW.[41] Membership crime was useful against the IWW because, like the presumption of the IWW's criminality, conspiracy and syndicalism laws were vague,[42] applicable to any unpopular group. The primary goal of a prosecution was to prove the criminal nature of a group, not the actual crimes of either the group or an individual defendant.[43]

Two World War II cases illustrated the use of group tropes in that era. *Dennis v. United States* was striking by the extent to which the Court approved of the government reaching far into a crime's inchoateness to prosecute mere ideas.[44] In that case, the defendants were found guilty of conspiring to advocate the overthrow of the government.[45] The Court had no difficulty affirming the conviction for violating the Smith Act, rejecting "the contention that a conspiracy to advocate, as distinguished from the advocacy itself, cannot be constitutionally restrained, because it comprises only the preparation." According to the *Dennis* Court, "It is the existence of the conspiracy which creates the danger."[46]

36 *People v. McClennegen*, 195 Cal. 445, 450 (1925).
37 *Id.* at 451.
38 See *Windsor v. United States*, 286 F. 51, 54–55 (6th Cir. 1923).
39 *People v. Lesse*, 52 Cal. App. 280, 282 (1921).
40 *State v. Boloff*, 138 Or. 568, 615 (1932) (syndicalism, including membership, was a strict liability crime); *State v. Steelik*, 187 Cal. 361, 376 (1921) (required that a defendant knowingly belong to a conspiratorial organization).
41 *People v. Thompson*, 68 Cal. App. 487, 490 (1924).
42 *Krulewitch v. United States*, 336 U.S. 440, 446–47 (1949); Francis B. Sayre, Criminal Conspiracy, 35 *Harv. L. Rev.* 393, 393 (1922).
43 See *Burns v. United States*, 274 U.S. 328, 340 (1927).
44 341 U.S. 494, 499–500 (1951).
45 *Id.* at 497–98, 516–17.
46 *Id.* at 511.

In *Yates v. United States*, Justice Black highlighted the First Amendment problems with conspiracy law, and suggested that the underlying problem with the system of modern conspiracy is that it has subjected unpopular ideas and the speech that expresses them to prosecution.[47] He observed that when speech was at issue in a criminal trial, the prosecution was likely to focus not on criminality, but on the unpopularity of the speech.[48]

Post 9/11 war on terror

Just as in earlier periods of high threat perception, in the post-9/11 war on terror a complex of First Amendment-inspired and criminal due process human rights are threatened. While apparently disparate, they all share a basic assumption: that groups are particularly dangerous and when faced with large-scale threats, the public safety imperative overrides individual rights norms and permits governments to pursue individuals for their connections with certain groups, whether those connections are real or perceived, and whether or not those connections reliably suggest criminal intent.

The Right of free speech/expression

Two cases, *United States v. Mehanna* and *United States v. Al-Hussayen*, illustrate how membership crime tropes in the war on terror generate infringements on the rights of free speech and expression.

Sami Omar Al-Hussayen was a doctoral student in computer science at the University of Idaho[49] when, in 2004, he was charged with providing and conspiring to provide material support to a designated foreign terrorist organization.[50] His indictment indicated that between 1994 and 2003, Al-Hussayen provided "expert advice and assistance, communications equipment, currency, monetary instruments, financial services and personnel."[51] He did so "by, among other things, creating and maintaining internet websites and other internet media designed to recruit mujahideen and raise funds for violent jihad in Israel, Chechnya, and other places."[52]

At trial, the government argued that Al-Hussayen had a "dual persona. One face to the public and a private face of extreme jihad."[53] It defined "violent jihad" as the taking of action against persons or governments that are deemed to be

47 See *Yates v. United States*, 354 U.S. 298, 339 (1957), overruled on other grounds by *Burks v. United States*, 437 U.S. 1, 8–12 (1978).

48 *Id.*

49 Maureen O'Hagan, A Terrorism Case That Went Awry, *Seattle Times*, Nov. 22, 2004, seattletimes.com/html/localnews/2002097570_ sami22m.html.

50 Second Superseding Indictment at 2, *United States v. Al-Hussayen*, CR 03–048-C-EJL, 2004 U.S. Dist. LEXIS 29793 (D. Id. Mar. 4, 2004).

51 *Id.*

52 *Id.*

53 *Id.*

enemies of a fundamentalist version of Islam. The government also argued that Al-Hussayen's "'fingerprints were intricately involved in the building of Web sites that called on young people to go and kill themselves' and to make donations for attacks." No evidence, however, emerged that the websites actually recruited people, or that Al-Hussayen believed their jihadi message.

The websites that Al-Hussayen volunteered for were those of Muslim charities. The government alleged that buried deep within them were a handful of violent messages—written by people other than Al-Hussayen—that encouraged attacks on the United States and donations to terrorist organizations. The defense argued that the hyperlinks from Al-Hussayen's website to the website that facilitated donations to Hamas were removed before Al-Hussayen became involved.

The indictment and the government's opening statement led one juror to believe that Al-Hussayen was "going to be in jail for life."[54] By the end of the trial, the juror had changed his mind. Over the course of the trial, he had heard no evidence that Al-Hussayen supported terrorism. The government's case, he said, "was a real stretch."[55] The entire jury agreed, acquitting Al-Hussayen of all the terrorism charges after only a few hours of deliberation.[56]

In *Mehanna*, Tarek Mehanna was found guilty in December 2011 of providing and conspiring to provide material support to al-Qaeda, and conspiracy to kill in a foreign country.[57] These charges were based on two factual allegations. First, Mehanna was charged with conspiracy based on a 2004 trip he took to Yemen, the purpose of which the government alleged was to find and train at a terrorist training camp so that he could proceed to Iraq to fight against United States forces.[58] Second, Mehanna was charged with conspiracy to provide and actually providing material support based on his translation of a publicly available document[59] called *39 Ways to Serve and Participate in Jihad*[60] and a "jihadi video" called *The Expedition of Umar Hadid*,[61] also publicly available.[62] There was no evidence that Mehanna performed these translations at al-Qaeda's behest, or that he had any contact at all with al-Qaeda.[63]

54 *Id*

55 *Id.*

56 *Id.*

57 Jury Verdict Form, *United States v. Mehanna*, No. 09-10017-GAO, 2011 WL 6813890 (D. Mass. Dec. 20, 2011).

58 Second Superseding Indictment at 5, 13, *United States v. Mehanna*, No. 09-CR 10017-GAO, 2010 WL 2516469 (D. Mass. June 17, 2010).

59 See Muhammad bin Ahmad as-Salim, *39 Ways to Serve and Participate* (2003), available at www.archive.org/stream/39WaysToServeAndParticipate/39WaysToServeAndParticipateInJihad_ djvu.txt.

60 Second Superseding Indictment at 17, *United States v. Mehanna*, No. 09-CR-10017-GAO, 2010 WL 2516469 (D. Mass. June 17, 2010).

61 *Id.* at 15–16.

62 *The Expedition of Shaykh 'Umar Hadid*, Live Leak, available at http://www.liveleak.com/view?i=5e5_1182736217.

63 Rick Holmes, Tarek Mehanna, political prisoner, Holmes & Company: A blog for independent minds (Dec. 20, 2011), http:// blogs.wickedlocal.com/holmesandco/2011/12/20/tarek-mehanna-political-prisoner/ #axzz1jMHdJpOD; Adam Serwer, I

The government argued that Mehanna's translation work was itself material support, because it encouraged others to fight jihad and otherwise support al-Qaeda.[64] This translation work, as well as instant messages between Mehanna and others,[65] jihadi videos,[66] and images of 9/11 and Osama bin Laden,[67] were all "bad" speech that was introduced to show Mehanna's state of mind[68] as well as infer the alleged conspiracy's agreement and overt act. The First Circuit affirmed Mehanna's conviction,[69] and the Supreme Court, although presented with an important First Amendment question,[70] denied certiorari in October 2014.[71]

The rights of assembly and association

There are three ways that the rights of assembly and association have been undermined in the post-9/11 war on terror. First, conspiracy charges continue to be normatively questionable, involving prosecutorial overreach[72] and

Guess Posting Videos Online Can Make You a Terrorist, Mother Jones, Dec. 20, 2011, http://motherjones.com/mojo/2011/12/i-guess-posting-videos-online-can-make-you-terrorist;*39 Ways to Serve and Participate in Jihad*, Daily Coverage of Tarek Mehanna's Trial, http://freetarek.wordpress.com/the-defendant/discussion-of-the-governments-proffer/39-ways-to-serve-and-participate-in-jihad/.

64 Second Superseding Indictment at 6, 8, 17, *United States v. Mehanna*, No. 09-CR-10017-GAO, 2010 WL 2516469 (D. Mass. June 17, 2010).

65 Julia Spitz, Mehanna trial closings raise a familiar question, *MetroWest Daily News*, Dec. 17, 2011, www.metrowestdailynews.com/features/x2140450734/Spitz-Mehanna-trial-closings-raise-a-familiar-question.

66 Patrick Tracey, Convicted for Words, Not Deeds, *Salon*, Dec. 21, 2011, www.salon.com/topic/tarek_mehanna/.

67 Laurel J. Sweet, Jury Convicts Sudbury Man of Terror Plot, *Boston Herald*, Dec. 20, 2011, www.bostonherald.com/news_opinion/local_coverage/2011/12/jury_convicts_sudbury_man_terror_plot.

68 See Milton J. Valencia, Tarek Mehanna Guilty of Terror Charges, *Boston Globe*, Dec. 20, 2011, www.bostonglobe.com/metro/2011/12/20/tarek-mehanna-found-guilty-all-terror-charges/chpbwimRMbvdNMOladJ08J/story.html?camp=pm.

69 *United States v. Mehanna*, 735 F.3d 32 (1st Cir. 2013).

70 Amna Akbar, How Tarek Mehanna Went to Prison for a Thought Crime, *The Nation*, www.thenation.com/article/177750/how-tarek-mehanna-went-prison-thought-crime;*Mehanna v. United States*, SCOTUSBlog (Oct. 6 2014), www.scotusblog.com/case-files/cases/mehanna-v-united-states/.

71 *Mehanna v. United States*, No. 13–1125, 2014 U.S. LEXIS 5478, at *1 (Oct. 6, 2014).

72 A number of cases demonstrate potential overreach: *United States v. Goba*, 240 F. Supp.2d 242, 244–45 (W.D.N.Y. 2003); Third Superseding Indictment, *United States v. Sadequee* at 1–3, 5, 12–14, No. 1:06-cr-147-WSD-GGB, Dec. 9, 2008; Judgment in a Criminal Case at 1, *United States v. Sadequee*, No. 1:06-cr-147-WSD-GGB (Dec. 14, 2009); *United States v. Lindauer*, 2004 WL 2813168, *1 (S.D.N.Y.); Indictment, *United States v. Shah*, 1:05-cr-00673-LAP (S.D.N.Y. Dec. 6, 2006); Plea Agreement, *United States v. Shah*, 1:05-cr-00673-LAP (S.D.N.Y. Apr. 2, 2007); Phil Hirschkorn, Al Qaeda Trainee Gets 10-Year Sentence, CNN (Dec. 3, 2003), www.cnn.com/2003/LAW/12/03/buffalo.six/; Associated Press, American is Convicted of Aiding Terrorists, *New York Times* (Aug. 12, 2009), www.nytimes.com/2009/08/13/us/13convict.html?_r=0.

misconduct,[73] and evidentiarily questionable government stings[74] may create criminals out of law-abiding people,[75] through the use of career government witnesses,[76] with an admitted discriminatory focus on Muslims.[77]

Second, Muslim charities have been subjected to a "complete taint" theory,[78] which imposes liability for any involvement at all with a terrorist group. The Seventh Circuit rejected this theory in *Boim v. Quranic Literary Institute and Holy Land Foundation for Relief and Development*,[79] holding that to be liable, a donor had to have the intent to further the donee's violent crimes.[80] This meant that a donor could give money to Hamas if it was intended to fund a hospital or school.

A later US Supreme Court case, *Holder v. Humanitarian Law Project*,[81] effectively overruled *Boim* in favor of the complete taint theory, based arguments that

73 Rabea Chaudhry, Effective Advocacy in a Time of Terror: Redefining the Legal Representation of a Suspected Terrorist Facing Secret Evidence, 8 *UCLA J. Islamic & Near E. L.* 101, 124–25 (2008–2009); Barry Tarlow, Terrorism Prosecution Implodes, The Detroit 'Sleeper Cell' Case, *Champion* 61, 63–64, 66 (Jan–Feb 2005).

74 *United States v. Aref*, 285 Fed. App'x. 784, 789 (2d Cir. 2008); Superseding Indictment, *United States v. Aref*, No. 1:04-cr-402-TJM, 2005 WL 5785418 (N.D.N.Y. Sept. 29, 2005); Criminal Complaint, *United States v. Aref*, No. 1:04-cr-402-TJM (Aug. 5, 2005); Stephen Downs, From Sting to Frame-Up: The Case of Yassin Aref, *Washington Report on Middle East Affairs* (Sept./Oct. 2007), www.wrmea.org/wrmea-archives/313-washington-report-archives-2006-2010/september-october-2007/9409-from-sting-to-frame-up-the-case-of-yassin-aref.html; Fred LeBrun, History Will Remember Albany Terrorism Sting as a Witch Hunt, *Albany Times Union* (Feb. 12, 2007), www.nepajac.org/FredLeBrun.htm; Carl Strock, Verdict is in, but Who is Really Guilty?, *Daily Gazette* (Oct. 12, 2006), www.nepajac.org/Strock.htm.

75 *United State v. Cromitie*, 727 F.3d 194, 199 (2d Cir. 2013) ("Only the government could have made a terrorist out of Mr. Cromitie, a man whose buffoonery was positively Shakespearean in its scope … . I believe beyond a shadow of a doubt that there would have been no crime here except the government instigated it, planned it and brought it to fruition"); Kendall Coffey, The Lone Wolf—Solo Terrorism and the Challenge of Preventative Prosecution, 7 *FIU L. Rev.* 1, 17 (2011); T. Ward Frampton, Predisposition and Positivism: The Forgotten Foundations of the Entrapment Doctrine, 103 J. *Crim. L. & Criminology* 111, 142 (2013).

76 Sahar F. Aziz, Caught in a Preventive Dragnet: Selective Counterterrorism in a Post-9/11 America, 47 *Gonz. L. Rev.* 429, 440 (2011–2012); David S. Kris, Law Enforcement as a Counterterrorism Tool, 5 *J. Nat'l Security L. & Pol'y* 80, 92 (2011).

77 American Civil Liberties Union, Blocking Faith, Freezing Charities: Chilling Muslim Charitable Giving in the "War on Terrorism Financing" 60 (2009). (A former Treasury Department official stated, "We are not going into Irish bars looking for people who support the IRA right now. There is a reason that we are focusing on the Muslim community. There is a greater proportion of Muslims engaged in ethnic terror than other groups. Everybody knows [targeting Muslim charities is] not baseless." A second official observed, "I think the attack on the Muslim charities was just easy, it was an easy, soft target.")

78 Malick W. Ghachem, Of "Scalpels" and "Sledgehammers": Religious Liberty and the Policing of Muslim Charities in Britain and America Since 9/11, 9 *UCLA J. Islamic & Near E. L.* 25, 32 (2009–2010).

79 *Boim v. Quranic Literary Institute and Holy Land Foundation for Relief and Development*, 291 F.3d 1000 (7th Cir. 2002).

80 *Id.*

81 *Holder v. Humanitarian Law Project*, 130 S. Ct. 2705 (2010).

money is fungible and a criminal group's legal conduct gives it legitimacy. Now, Muslim charities and donors that intend only to support Hamas's hospital or school construction projects will be frozen as well as civilly and criminally liable.[82] This is controversial; a 2009 ACLU report claimed that the move amounted to an a priori condemnation of virtually all Muslim charities,[83] and the 9/11 Commission recognized the overreach.[84]

Third, the government uses immigration violations as proxy terrorism investigations where evidence of actual terroristic intent is lacking. In *Turkmen v. Ashcroft*, for example, Arab and Muslim detainees filed a *Bivens* action for being detained after 9/11 on pretextual immigration charges.[85] They were held from three to eight months after receiving final orders for deportation or grants of voluntary departure. This was done so that the government could "round[] up" Arabs and Muslims to be questioned in connection with the 9/11 investigation. The detainees were treated as "of interest"[86] despite a lack of evidence of connections to terrorism, and the harsh conditions of their confinement were meant to get them to talk.[87] The court found that these measures were unnecessary because detainees were always fully compliant with orders.[88]

The right to religious exercise/expression

In addition to the *Mehanna* case, in which the defendant was convicted in part based on his translation of publicly available religious texts, Dawinder Sidhu has statistically analyzed how the war on terror has chilled Muslims' exercise of First Amendment rights.[89] The perception that the government monitors the digital communications in the Muslim community has led members to modify aspects of their daily lives and avoid using the Internet and even telephones.[90] Edward Snowden's revelations remove that perception from the realm of paranoia and suggest that it is real. Furthermore, the New York City Police Department's policy of secretly classifying some mosques as terrorist organizations[91] and engaging in covert surveillance of numerous mosques, as far as an hour outside its jurisdiction

82 *United States v. El-Mezain*, 664 F.3d 467, 483–85 (5th Cir. 2011).
83 ACLU, *supra* note 77.
84 National Commission on Terrorist Attacks Upon the United States, Monograph on Terrorist Financing: Staff Report to the Commission 9 (2004), available at http://govinfo.library.unt.edu/911/staff_statements/911_TerrFin_Monograph.pdf.
85 *Turkmen v. Ashcroft*, 915 F. Supp. 2d 314, 325 (E.D.N.Y. 2013).
86 *Id.*
87 *Id.* at 326–28.
88 *Id.* at 328.
89 Dawinder S. Sidhu, The Chilling Effect of Government Surveillance Programs on The Use of the Internet by Muslim-Americans, 7 *Md. L.J. Race, Religion, Gender & Class* 375 (2007).
90 *Id.* at 375.
91 Adam Goldman & Matt Apuzzo, NYPD Secretly Designated Entire Mosques as Terrorism Organizations, *Huffington Post* (Aug. 28, 2013), www.huffingtonpost.com/2013/08/28/nypd-spying-mosques_n_3827567.html.

and with Central Intelligence Agency (CIA) assistance,[92] instantiate this form of religious group surveillance. Although it appears that such religious profiling is ineffective,[93] government officials have openly admitted to religious profiling,[94] which has been documented as pervasive.[95] As a result, Attorney General Eric Holder has announced that he plans to expand the Justice Department's ban on ethnic and religious profiling. The Department of Homeland Security, however, has refused to adopt the new rules for its agencies.[96]

The right to due process

In July 2011, the United States designated Anwar al-Awlaki a Specially Designated Global Terrorist because he was acting on behalf of al-Qaeda in the Arabian Peninsula and providing support to that group.[97] He was a radical cleric who communicated with Umar Farouk Abdulmutallab and Nidal Hasan, both of whom engaged or attempted to engage in actual acts of terrorist violence. He also called for jihad against the West, and encouraged attacks against the United States, but had not been charged with any crime. He was a US citizen.

The United States had placed Al-Awlaki on a kill list,[98] which Al-Awlaki's father challenged in court. The challenge was unsuccessful because the father did not have third party or next friend standing, the court observing that Al-Awlaki could present himself to the US Embassy in Yemen, where he was living, to vindicate his own rights. Would he have done so, the court noted that the

92 Matt Apuzzo & Adam Goldman, With CIA Help, NYPD Moves Covertly in Muslim Areas, Associated Press (Aug. 23, 2011), www.ap.org/Content/AP-in-the-News/2011/With-CIA-help-NYPD-moves-covertly-in-Muslim-areas.

93 Adam Goldman & Matt Apuzzo, *NYPD: Muslim Spying Led to No Leads, Terror Cases*, Associated Press (Aug. 21, 2012), www.ap.org/Content/AP-In-The-News/2012/NYPD-Muslim-spying-led-to-no-leads-terror-cases; Aziz Z. Huq, The Signaling Function of Religious Speech in Domestic Counterterrorism, 89 *Tex. L. Rev.* 833, 900 (2011).

94 Timothy Phelps, Justice Department to ban profiling by federal law enforcement, *L.A. Times* (Sept. 26, 2014), www.latimes.com/nation/la-na-0927-holder-profiling-20140927-story.html.

95 American Civil Liberties Union, Protecting the Religious Freedom of Muslims, available at www.aclu.org/protecting-religious-freedom-muslims; Amnesty International, Surveillance of American Muslims Underscores Lack of Safeguards (July 9, 2014), available at www.amnestyusa.org/news/press-releases/surveillance-of-american-muslims-underscores-lack-of-safeguards-0; Religious Profiling of Muslim-Americans in U.S., *Wall Street Journal* (Mar. 25, 2011), www.wsj.com/video/religious-profiling-of-muslim-americans-in-us/5C9C645A-6E57-427B-9E43-D94AABB28326.html; Conor Friedersdorf, The Horrifying Effects of NYPD Ethnic Profiling on Innocent Muslim Americans, *The Atlantic* (Mar. 28, 2013), www.theatlantic.com/politics/archive/2013/03/the-horrifying-effects-of-nypd-ethnic-profiling-on-innocent-muslim-americans/274434/.

96 Evan Perez, Justice Department to Expand Ban on Profiling, CNN (Sept. 29, 2014), www.cnn.com/2014/09/29/politics/justice-racial-ethnic-profiling-ban/.

97 *Al-Aulaqi v. Obama*, 727 F. Supp. 2d 1, 10 (2010).

98 *Id.*

government would have been prohibited from using lethal force or other violence against Al-Awlaki.[99]

A US drone strike in September 2011 killed Al-Awlaki. While Al-Awlaki was the target, along with him were also killed his son and Samir Khan, both US citizens.[100] During proceedings in district court involving an ultimately unsuccessful *New York Times* Freedom of Information Act request regarding the targeted killing, the government claimed that it could target a US citizen as it did and still ensure that citizen's due process rights.[101]

In June 2014, the Second Circuit released a government memo, purporting to justify Al-Awlaki's killing.[102] The memo contained two arguments. First, it argued that the killing was justified under the Authorized Use of Military Force against al-Qaeda, which Congress passed in the wake of 9/11. It claimed that because Al-Awlaki defected to the enemy's side, the laws of war justified the killing.[103] Second, the memo argued that Al-Awlaki had been given due process. Because of substantial redactions, that due process, as published, appears to be based on four factors: Al-Awlaki's activities posed a "continued" and "imminent" threat; the government's intent was to capture, not kill, Al-Awlaki if possible; the "highest officers of the intelligence community … reviewed the factual basis" for the targeting; and the government continually evaluated the feasibility of capture as opposed to killing.[104]

This explanation of Al-Awlaki's due process is facially deficient because it does not explain why Al-Awlaki posed such a threat; why the government was unable to capture him; or who these "highest officers" were, why they were equipped to sign off on Al-Awlaki's targeting, or what checks were in place to ensure accurate inclusion on the kill list.

Al-Awlaki's case presents only the starkest of the due process questions arising in the war on terror. There are more mundane instances that call into question the adequacy of process. These include secretive inclusion on no-fly or enhanced screening lists;[105] freezing of assets;[106] use of material witness statutes solely to imprison people;[107] and the presumption of pre-trial detention when a terrorism charge is filed.[108]

99 *Id.* at 17.
100 *N.Y. Times Co. v. U.S. Dept. of Justice*, 915 F. Supp. 2d 508, 520, 530 (2013).
101 *Id.* at 521.
102 Matt Sledge, Drone Memo Justifying Anwar al-Awlaki's Killing Released, *Huffington Post* (June 23, 2014), www.huffingtonpost.com/2014/06/23/anwar-al-awlaki-drone-memo_n_5522067.html.
103 Memorandum for the Attorney General at 14–23, *Al-Aulaqi v. Obama*, 727 F. Supp. 2d 1, 10 (2010) (June 23, 2014).
104 *Id.* at 29–30.
105 *Latif v. Holder*, No. 3:10-cv-00750-BR, 2014 U.S. Dist. LEXIS 85450 (D. Or. June 24, 2014).
106 Cian Murphy, UN Asset-Freezing Scheme Represents an 'Atrocious Lack' of Due Process, *Guardian* (Aug. 25, 2010), www.theguardian.com/law/2010/aug/25/un-security-council-asset-freezing.
107 *Ashcroft v. Al-Kidd*, 131 S. Ct. 2074 (2011).
108 18 U.S.C. §3142 (e)(3)(C).

Looking ahead: first amendment, membership crime, and the philosophy of collective action

Although this chapter's thesis may seem persistent and intractable, there is reason to believe otherwise. This is so due to the confluence of three relatively recent developments: the substantive advent of the First Amendment in 1919, the advent of membership crime tropes in the nineteenth century and their maturity in the twentieth century, and the advent of philosophical inquiries into collective action and responsibility. Membership crime tropes created a normative problem, the advent of the First Amendment introduced a constitutional conflict with these tropes and the emergence of collective action philosophy implies an important attention to the undertheorized and overly problematic concept of membership crime.

Before 1919, the First Amendment had a very small jurisprudential footprint.[109] In that year, the Supreme Court began to shape the First Amendment into the highly speech-protective form existing today.[110] It introduced the "clear and present danger" test in *Abrams v. United States*,[111] *Schenck v. United States*,[112] *Frohwerk v. United States*.[113] This test permitted the restriction of speech only if "the words used are used in such circumstances and are of such a nature as to create a clear and present danger that they will bring about the substantive evils that Congress has a right to prevent."[114] The "clear and present danger" test gradually evolved into the *Brandenburg* test, which the Court set forth in the 1969 case of the same name.[115]

Under *Brandenburg*, advocacy of the use of force or violating the law could be restricted only if it was "directed to inciting or producing imminent lawless action and is likely to incite or produce such action."[116] The *Brandenburg* test highlights a First Amendment-related conceptual problem with the system of membership crime. If the government suspects that someone is preparing, or has agreed with another, to commit a crime, speech that is purely advocacy will normally be admissible and may be enough to convict.[117] On one hand, the *Brandenburg* test should protect the speaker because protected speech is being used as the basis for punishment.[118] On the other hand, if the advocacy is part of the crime of

109 See David M. Rabban, *Free Speech in Its Forgotten Years 1870-1920* 1–2 (1st ed. 1997), Cambridge: Cambridge University Press.
110 Thomas I. Emerson, Freedom of Expression in Wartime, 116 U. *Pa. L. Rev.* 975, 975 (1968); Mathieu J. Shapiro, Note, When is a Conflict Really a Conflict? Outing and the Law, 36 *B.C. L. Rev.* 587, 589 (1995).
111 250 U.S. 616 (1919).
112 249 U.S. 47 (1919).
113 249 U.S. 204 (1919).
114 *Schenck*, 249 U.S. at 52.
115 *Brandenburg v. Ohio*, 395 U.S. 444, 447 (1969) (per curiam).
116 *Id.*
117 See *Fed. R. Evid.* 801(d)(2)(E).
118 See Steven R. Morrison, Conspiracy Law's Threat to Free Speech, 15 *U. Pa. J. Const. L.* 865, 920 (2013).

conspiracy, then it may, in fact, be directed to producing the lawless action of criminal conspiracy.[119] In the war on terror the government has obtained convictions for material support against people who have merely advanced viewpoints sympathetic to foreign terrorist organizations.[120] Thus far, *Brandenburg* has not convinced courts to dismiss the charges.[121]

There are two problems with First Amendment law in the membership crime context. First, although the *Brandenburg* test appears to protect unpopular speakers, it does not in fact protect them against conspiracy charges. The speech that provides the building blocks of a conspiracy charge may not be intended to lead to substantive and imminent lawless action, but it may appear to be probative of the lawless action of conspiracy.[122] Such speech may, in fact, constitute the crime itself.[123] Second, protected speech may be used as evidence of a crime. Thus, speech can simultaneously be the evidence of conspiracy and the conspiracy itself,[124] even though this may chill speech.[125] Enter the philosophy of collective conduct and responsibility.

Western theories of accountability have tended to focus on the individual.[126] It was only in the late 1980s and early 1990s that philosophers began to turn their attention to collectives.[127] Thus, however important philosophical models of collective conduct may be to the law,[128] the field is still in its infancy.[129]

Many contemporary philosophers present more or less detailed accounts of the creation of collectives from individuals and the assignment of

119 See *id.* at 918.

120 See Sahar Aziz, Tarek Mehanna: Punishing Muslims for free speech only helps Al Qaeda, *Christian Science Monitor* (April 19, 2012), www.csmonitor.com/Commentary/Opinion/2012/0419/Tarek-Mehanna-Punishing-Muslims-for-free-speech-only-helps-Al-Qaeda; Va. Man Pleads Guilty to Helping Terror Group, NBC4 Washington (Dec. 2, 2011), www.nbcwashington.com/news/local/Va-man-expected-to-plead-to-helping-terror-group-134894608.html.

121 See Transcript of Record, Day Thirty-Five at 24–25, *United States v. Mehanna*, (No. 09–10017–6A0 2011) WL 3511226 (Dec. 16, 2011); Jerry Markon, Va. Muslim Lecturer Sentenced to Life, *Washington Post*, July 14, 2005, at B1, B9.

122 See Morrison, *supra* note 118, at 889–90.

123 *Id.*

124 *Id.* at 892–95, 900.

125 See Susan Gellman, Sticks and Stones Can Put You in Jail, but Can Words Increase Your Sentence? Constitutional and Policy Dilemmas of Ethnic Intimidation Laws, 39 *UCLA L. Rev.* 333, 360–61 (1991); Tobias Barrington Wolff, Political Representation and Accountability Under Don't Ask, Don't Tell, 89 *Iowa L. Rev.* 1633, 1696 (2004).

126 Margaret P. Gilbert, *Joint Commitment: How We Make the Social World* 94 (2013), New York: Oxford University Press; Christopher Kutz, *Complicity: Ethics and Law for a Collective Age* 3–5 (2007), Cambridge: Cambridge University Press.

127 *Id.* at 166; Christian List & Philip Pettit, *Group Agency: The Possibility, Design, and Status of Corporate Agents* 1 (2011), Oxford: Oxford University Press; John R. Searle, *Making the Social World: The Structure of Human Civilization* 45 (1st ed. 2010), Oxford: Oxford University Press [hereinafter *Making*].

128 Gilbert, *supra* note 126, at 167; List & Pettit, *supra* note 127, at 11.

129 Gilbert, *supra* note 126, at 180.

accountability.[130] Taken together, they present three problems of translation into pragmatic legal practice: they are probably too detailed and nuanced to satisfy the law's efficiency imperative, too positivist to satisfy the law's normative imperative,[131] and too truth-seeking to meet the limitations of evidence law.[132] Nevertheless, they make two points about how the law ought to go about determining whether an individual defendant committed a crime in a group context. First, individuals are never wholly autonomous or subsumed in a group, but remain both in degrees. Second, an understanding of group dynamics need not—and should not—relieve individuals of responsibility.

John Searle observes that collective behavior is "a biologically primitive phenomenon"[133] that is a basis of human society.[134] Put another way, individuals always already exist in multiple collectives, sometimes through conscious intentional agency, sometimes through awareness or acceptance, and sometimes unconsciously,[135] as individual actors living mundane, inevitably collective lives.

Not only is the Searlean model important for understanding a subject's guilt for a crime, but it is also important for understanding the extent of the subject's

130 Most individualistically, Bratman finds agency solely in individuals, who begin with individual desires that evolve into individual planning. This "individual planning agency" can then feed into shared intention with others and a conservative theory of collective conduct that Bratman calls "modest sociality." Michael E. Bratman, *Shared Agency: A Planning Theory of Acting Together* 4, 31 (2014), New York: Oxford University Press. Kutz focuses on collective agency while ultimately concluding that the agency is reducible to individuals. This permits him to posit collective ends alongside individual contributions and yet ultimately locate accountability in individuals. Kutz, *supra* note 126, at 3. Gilbert posits collective intentionality that is irreducible to individuals but remains tied strongly to individual agency through her concept of "joint commitment." According to Gilbert, groups are created by the intentionality of individuals. Gilbert, *supra* note 126, at 4, 6. Searle argues that groups emerge organically from "institutional," and ultimately "brute" facts. John R. Searle, *The Construction of Social Reality*, 24, 37 (1997), New York: Free Press [hereinafter *Construction*]. While he attempts to connect natural individual drives seamlessly to collectives, he rejects the notion that individuals are subsumed into these groups. *Id.* at 38. Tuomela argues that collective intentionality is the "cement" of society. Raimo Tuomela, *Social Ontology: Collective Intentionality and Group Agents* (2013), New York: Oxford University Press; while he does not explicitly reject the possibility of individual agency, he focuses on collective agency as a discrete entity that is in fact an intentional agent. *Id.* at 2; put another way, he argues that the individualism of rational choice theory is a "conceptually impoverished framework," but that individualism and collectivism are needed to express "the whole truth." *Id.* at 4.

131 Gilbert, for example, posits a theory of "joint commitment" that she explicitly divorces from theories of moral requirements. Gilbert, *supra* note 126, at 5.

132 *Id.* at 235; Kutz, *supra* note 126, at 206.

133 Searle, *Construction, supra* note 130, at 24.

134 Searle, *Making, supra* note 127, at 26 ("to understand society, you have to understand collective human behavior. Collective human behavior is a manifestation of collective intentionality").

135 *Id.* at 60.

culpability.[136] This model helps to accurately answer questions of culpability based on causation, culpability based on resulting harm, determination of one's mens rea, and the assignment of responsibility for group action. If an individual is part of a criminal collective, she shares a certain collective intentionality with others in the group, but Searle's approach would accept the individual's membership in the collective as more neutral than the law currently views such membership. The questions, then, would not center on *whether* the individual is a member, but on the *nature* of that membership.

Other philosophers' location of accountability in the individual support the Searlean mandate to shift the question of group membership from *whether* to *nature*. To find modest sociality and shared intention—or, more colloquially, group conduct—Michael Bratman provides a multi-part test that persistently locates ultimate intentionality in the individual.[137] Margaret Gilbert's view is more collectivist, but she still locates what she calls "joint commitment" in individual commitments to work toward a joint end.[138] More to the point, for Gilbert blameworthiness, while it must be informed by the group context, remains individual.[139] Christopher Kutz, for his part, is concerned with "collective wrongdoing"[140] and allows for individual accountability for group conduct under some circumstances,[141] but also argues that moral responsibility ultimately rests in the individual. Put another way, to vindicate a theory of collective wrongdoing, accountability for collective harms must reside in the individual.[142]

Conclusion: toward a better criminal law

These recent philosophical inquiries into collective action bode well for criminal law as well as human rights. While the violations associated with these areas of law are indeed systemic, a major reason for this is that the law lacks a principled theory of group action. In the best of times, the law's all-in/all-out approach to group membership promotes efficiency and public safety, but gives short shrift to individual rights. When large-scale threats are perceived, this approach is enhanced, more people at the margins of dangerous groups are drawn into their ambit and the number of human rights violations increases.

The response cannot be to eliminate the use of membership crime models. Such a move would be politically and systemically impossible, and unwise from a public safety standpoint; sometimes groups and individuals in groups are indeed

136 Kutz, for example, differentiates between the "Complicity Principle," which "answers the threshold question of individual moral accountability," and "complicitous accountability," which is a positional theory that judges the individual vis-à-vis his relationship with the group. Kutz, *supra* note 126, at 165.

137 Bratman, *supra* note 130, at 40–84, 103.

138 Gilbert, *supra* note 126, at 82–85.

139 *Id.* at 78.

140 Kutz, *supra* note 126, at 2.

141 *Id.* at 108, 122.

142 *Id.* at 137.

dangerous and ought to be stopped as early as possible. The better response is to understand how individuals interact with groups. This understanding can, in turn, result in staking out the border between criminal conduct and protected activity in the group context and generating an evidentiary regime capable of locating individuals on either side of that border.

This will take time to achieve. First Amendment-inspired human rights, modern criminal due process norms, and membership crime models are relatively new constructs. Philosophical inquires into collective action are newer yet, and have not had the time adequately to influence criminal law. When that time comes, however, we may see a criminal law that is more oriented toward the collective rather than the individual. This could bode well for public safety *and* individual rights. As to public safety, a nuanced understanding of collective action could result in greater accountability for individuals acting vis-à-vis groups who would normally escape liability. As to individual rights, a collective action understanding could increase the space in which individuals can express unpopular opinions and even associate with unpopular or criminal groups without fear of liability. If we take First Amendment-inspired and criminal due process human rights seriously, this is a salutary outcome.

Index

Note: italic page numbers indicate figures; numbers preceded by *n* indicate footnotes.

www.ingramcontent.com/pod-product-compliance
Ingram Content Group UK Ltd.
Pitfield, Milton Keynes, MK11 3LW, UK
UKHW010959180926
475701UK00004B/469

* 9 7 8 0 3 6 7 4 9 9 0 3 7 *